MALT WHISKY YEARBOOK 2007

www.maltwhiskyyearbook.com

First published in Great Britain in 2006 by
MagDig Media Limited

ISBN 0-9552607-1-X

Translations by Hirschfeld Media.
www.hirschfeld.se

MagDig Media Limited
1 Brassey Road
Old Potts Way, Shrewsbury
Shropshire SY3 7FA
ENGLAND

E-mail: info@maltwhiskyyearbook.com
www.maltwhiskyyearbook.com

Contents

Introduction

The first edition of **Malt Whisky Yearbook** was published in autumn 2005. As malt whisky fans, we had a notion that there was a niche in whisky literature waiting to be occupied and **Malt Whisky Yearbook 2006** was our contribution to it.
We had not fully anticipated how great the interest and need for such a book covering this wide and changeable field was. In fact, the thirst for the latest facts within the malt whisky business turned out to be comparable to that of the favourite dram!

So, we are back with a new, revised and fully up-dated edition
- the **Malt Whisky Yearbook 2007**. Some of the world's most distinguished whisky writers also join us this year:

Charles MacLean tells us about ten, 'earth-shattering' days that shaped the whisky we drink today and he assists with the sorting out of the complicated terminology involved with casks and maturation. The world map of whisky consumption will have to be completely redrawn in a few years and *Gavin D. Smith* explains why. Climb into a still with *Ian Wisniewski* and let him explain what happens during the first, crucial hours of a whisky-to-be. When the professional elite meet for the first World Whiskies Conference, *Ian Buxton* is there to report on the current trends. Volume-wise, malt whisky is overshadowed by grain whisky. *David Stirk* takes a stand for the poor sibling. The marketing people in the whisky business are facing more crossroads than ever before. *Dominic Roskrow* sorts out the options they face.

The unique, detailed and much appreciated *160-page section on malt whisky distilleries* is thoroughly revised and up-dated and with most of the pictures new since the last edition.

Many readers have contacted us since publication of the first edition and we appreciate this very much, so please keep doing so. We have listened, and in this edition you will find a list of *120 of the best whisky shops* in Europe with full details. A comprehensive list of more than *450 new bottlings* during the year and a *summary of the most important happenings* are also new for this edition. We also present *the best whisky web sites, the best whisky books* and, of course, include *the latest available statistics* for those of you who cannot live without tables and graphs.

Thank you for buying **Malt Whisky Yearbook 2007**. We hope that you will experience many enjoyable moments reading it and we can assure you that we will be back with a new edition in 2008.

Great care has been taken to ensure the accuracy of the information presented in this book. We can, however, not be held liable for inaccuracies. To ensure reliable and correct facts in the next edition of Malt Whisky Yearbook, we would appreciate your emails at info@maltwhiskyyearbook.com. Please state the source of the information.

Acknowledgments

First of all I wish to thank the writers who have shared their great specialist knowledge on the subject in a brilliant and entertaining way
– Ian Buxton, Charles MacLean, Dominic Roskrow, Taylor Smisson, Gavin D. Smith, David Stirk, Ian Wisniewski and Hideo Yamaoka.

The following persons have also made important photographic or editorial contributions:

Emily Ambrose, Paul Aston, Sarah Bailey, David Baker, Nicola Ball, Ian Bankier, Lynn Bauer, Alex Bruce, Ian Chapman, Michael Cockram, Frank Coleman, Jason Craig, Katherine Crisp, Andrew Currie, Peter Currie, Alex Delaloye, Gary Donaldson, Graeme Dunnet, Frances Dupuy, Matt Edwards, Campbell Evans, Robert Fleischmann, Robert Fleming, Iain Gardiner, Jess Graber, Alan Gray, Jay Harman, Johannes van den Heuvel, David Hume, Emrys Inker, Anne Jack, Ben Jenkins, Christine Jones, Tommy Leigh, Mark Littler, Iain Lochhead, Jim Long, Horst Lüning, Grant MacPherson, Stephen McCarthy, Barbara McEwan, Sharon McGuire, Frank McHardy, Carol McLaren, Gill MacLeod, Dennis Malcolm, Brian Megson, Marcin Miller, Stephanie Mingam, Glen Moore, Jemma Morris, Karen Murray, Louise Nicoll, B A Nimmo, Rupert Patrick, Lucy Pritchard, Robert Ransom, Walter Schobert, Jacqui Seargeant, Rory Steel, Richard Sutton, Jack Teeling, Alistair Walker, Iain Weir, Susan Webster, Cristina Wilkie, David Williamson, Neil Wilson, Allan Winchester

Thank you!

Ingvar Ronde
Editor

Ten Days that shook the Whisky World

Several events throughout history have shaped the whisky that we see – and taste – today. Charles MacLean has selected the ten most significant days in whisky history and describes their influence on the end product.

DAY 1: Easter 1300
The arrival of Fergus MacBeatha in Scotland

The first date in the history of Scotch is usually that of the first written reference to distilled spirits – the famous order of King James IV to Friar John Cor in 1494. I prefer to look beyond this...

Fergus MacBeatha (or Beaton) came from a family of scholars and doctors in Ulster. By the time he left northern Ireland in the spring of 1300, in the marriage train of Lady Margaret O'Kane betrothed to Angus Og Macdonald of the Isles, he was already described as an 'ollamh' a physician, renowned for his medical knowledge.

He immediately became physician to Angus Og, who leant his brother, Patrick MacBeatha, to his friend Robert I (the Bruce), when the king was sick with an ailment that all his other 'leeches' had failed to cure. Patrick succeeded and was appointed 'principal physician to the king', a position which seems to have remained in his family, for in 1386, another MacBeatha, Ferchard, was granted the island of Jura by the Robert II.

What has this to do with whisky?

Over many generations, the Beatons were assiduous translators of classical medical texts from Greek and Latin into Gaelic – texts by the 'fathers' of medicine: the Greek masters Hippocrates, Galen and Aristotle, and their early medieval Islamic successors, Geber, Avicenna and Averroes. There is an outstanding collection of such translations in the National Library of Scotland, most known to have been penned by Beatons. When that redoubtable traveller, Martin Martin, visited Dr. Fergus Beaton in South Uist about 1695, he reported that the latter posessed "the following ancient Irish manuscripts in the Irish character; to wit, Avicenna, Averroes, Johannes de Vigo, Bernardus Gordonus, and several volumes of Hippocrates".

Bear in mind that Geber (8th century) gave a detailed description of distilling to extract aromas from plants; Avicenna, 'the Prince of Physicians' (980-1037), is reputed to have invented the condensing 'worm'; Arnoldus Villanova (c1235-1313), described as 'the Father of Distilling', first applied the word 'alcohol' to the product of distilled wine, and made spirits which he described as *potabile* (drinkable) as well as perfumes and medicines. It seems certain that the Beatons knew the secrets of distilling.

Photo: © VisitScotland

Kildalton Cross on Islay

Their base was on Islay, where they were granted lands at Kilchoman (a fine Celtic cross stands to commemorate them there). Where did King James IV first encounter distilled spirits? Why on Islay, where he was campaigning against the Lord of the Isles in 1493 and 1494...

DAY 2: January 1644

The First Introduction of Excise Duty

The word 'excise' comes from the Middle Dutch excijs or exziis, meaning a duty charged on domestically produced goods, especially alcohol, and the Dutch are credited with first introducing this cunning way of combining the puritan purpose of controlling excessive drinking with raising revenue.

The idea for such an impost was first proposed by Charles I's treasurer, and when Parliament got wind of it they protested vigorously in the Grand Remonstrance of 1641, about the "unjust and pernicious attempt to extort great payments from the subject by way of excise". The following year, when it was rumoured that parliament itself intended to introduce the tax, there was a furore and the House of Commons declared "that these rumours were false and scandalous; and that their authors should be apprehended and brought to condign punishment".

Less than a year later, in September 1643, the English politicians did what they denied intending to do, and the scheme was eagerly taken up the following year by their Scottish counterparts, to raise money for the army warring against the King.

Originally the tax was imposed for one year only, at 8d per English gallon (1 euro per litre), but it has remained ever since, at higher and higher levels. Henceforward, much of the history of Scotch whisky was determined by raising duty and avoiding it.

It is important to remember that tax was due only on spirits that were sold. 'Home brewing' was perfectly legal, so long as the whisky was made from home-grown grains, in small stills for home consumption...This brings me to my third significant date:

Photo: © SWA

Sir Edwin Henry Landseers's 'The Highland Whisky Still', painted in the 1820s

DAY 3: February 1781

The Banning of Domestic Distilling

As excise duty became more onerous, increasing amounts of illicit whisky came onto the Lowland market, mainly from the Highlands. To meet this competition, many legal distilleries had to resort to fraud in their tax declarations, and in the attempt to prevent this, the government passed a series of increasingly complex and draconian measures. Their effect was simply to stimulate smuggling and discourage producers from taking out licenses.

One such measure was the banning of domestic distilling, in 1781. The Scots were outraged – making whisky was part of their way of life – and many simply ignored the unjust law. By the 1790s smuggling was out of control. Further ill-conceived legislation reduced the quality of legal whisky, increasing the demand for 'moonshine'. An official Report commented in1790: "Travelling in bands of 50, 80 or 100 or 150 horses remarkably stout and fleet (having) the audacity to go in this formidable manner in the open day upon the public high roads and through the streets of such towns and villages as they have occasion to pass".

The government was bereft of ideas about how to cope with the situation. Duty was tripled in 1793, doubled again in 1795 and again in 1800; further increases took place in 1804, 1811 and 1814. Penalties for breaking the law were increased. There was a riot in England and Scotland, brutally crushed.

By 1815 there was growing concern among landowners in the Highlands about the growth of violent crime. This was mostly due to food shortages, evictions and land clearances for sheep parks, but it was blamed on the "lawless smugglers".

The 4th Duke of Gordon, one of the most powerful landowners in the north-east, addressed the House of Lords on the subject in 1820, urging a reduction of duty and a more moderate attitude towards legal distillers. In return, he pledged the landowners´ co-operation in putting down smuggling.
A Commission of Inquiry into the Revenue was set up in 1822, and following its Report, the law was completely overhauled by my fourth key date...

DAY 4: May 1823

The Excise Act

The Excise Act of 1823 redressed many of the distillers´ key grievances, and made it more attractive for farmers to 'go legal'. It was combined with the Illicit Distillation (Scotland) Act 1822, which greatly increased penalties for illicit distilling, and provided that landowners who sanctioned the practice could also be fined. These were 'carrot and stick measures', but they laid the foundations of the modern whisky industry.

As Michael Moss writes: "The small distilleries in the Highlands and Lowlands could now make whiskies that tasted as good as those supplied formerly by the smugglers and sell it at a lower price...The only restraint on the industry was now the market".

Scotch whisky was still an acquired taste. Malt was drunk in the Highlands, and grain in the Lowlands – and much grain spirit was sent to England for rectification into gin – but the former was heavy and smoky, while the latter was hot and fiery.
The next major breakthrough was the invention of a form of whisky which was more generally palatable, and more consistent: blended whisky...

DAY 5: 14th June 1844

The First Blend

"The Real Glenlivet Whisky. Matured in bonded warehouses in Scotland. This whisky... pronounced by all connoisseurs to be far the purest and finest spirit made in any part of these dominions, is now, for the first time, introduced to London...Andrew Usher & Co, sole consignees..." [*The Morning Post, 14th June 1844*]

I am cheating a bit with the date here, since we do not know for certain whether this was a blended malt or a single malt. What we do know is that by 1853, Usher was vatting different casks of Glenlivet at different ages to create a drink which was more consistent, 'Old Vatted Glenlivet' – not only was this the first blend; it was the first brand of Scotch.

Then the Spirit Act of 1860 allowed the mixing of grain whisky with malt whisky before duty had to be paid; Andrew Usher's

Labels of Old Vatted Glenlivet

Andrew Usher

Photo: © Diageo

son, Andrew II, soon turned OVG into a blend of grains and malts – and others followed suit, notably Charles Mackinlay of Leith, William Lowrie of Glasgow and John E. Macpherson of Newcastle.

Licensed grocers like Matthew Gloag of Perth, John Dewar (Perth), Chivas Bros (Aberdeen), Arthur Bell (Perth), John Walker (Kilmarnock), George Ballantine (Edinburgh, then Glasgow) and William Teacher (Glasgow) soon joined the bandwagon.

The importance of this cannot be over-emphasised. I have said how variable Scotch was, and how it did not have general appeal. Now it became possible a) to produce a drink with broad appeal, and b) to brand and market it – only with consistency of product can you brand it.

But Scotch was still to find a market wider than Scotland. Several factors contributed to this, the oddest of which was…

DAY 6: Summer 1863

The Arrival of Phylloxera vastatrix

In the summer of 1863 traces of the vine-louse *Phylloxera vastatrix* were discovered in England. The aphids had come from America, and by the late 1860s were found in the Midi, the Gironde and the Duoro; by the late 1870s the vineyards of the Grande Champagne region of Cognac had been almost completely destroyed.

Ordinary brandy became unobtainable in England, and at that time, 'ordinary' brandy and soda was *the* drink of the English middle classes. Blended whisky (and soda) was there to replace it, and there followed a period known to history as 'The Whisky Boom'.

It lasted until 1899, and then the bubble dramatically burst. That year the quantity of whisky in bond topped 100 million gallons for the first time (4.5 m LPA); production that distilling season was over twice what it had been two years before. This was far in excess of what the market could accommodate.

Hard on the heels of this crisis came another…

DAY 7: 6th November 1905
The 'What is Whisky?' Case

Some retailers in London were sued for selling whisky 'not of the nature, substance and quality demanded'. One of the individuals accused had been asked for 'a bottle of Scotch' and had been sold a bottle containing 90% grain spirit, less than a year old, although labelled 'Fine Old Scotch Whisky'. They were all found guilty, and the judge directed that "Whisky, whether malt, grain or blended must be made in a pot still".

The case went to appeal, but the judges were equally divided and no decision was reached. In February 1908 a Royal Commission was set up, reporting in July 1909 that to restrict the definition to pot still make, would "destroy a flourishing industry".

It was acknowledged, even by the malt distillers, that the blenders were now their key customers, and that "the majority of Englishmen who drink whisky seldom drink anything other than a blend".

What if the decision had gone the other way? Romantically, we might think that the world would embrace malt whisky. More likely, the whisky industry would have collapsed, and most of the 161 operating malt distilleries have been closed.

There was no time for celebration, for the same year duty was increased by the highest amount since 1860. Domestic consumption dropped by nearly half. Then came the First World War, when efforts were made by the government to ban alcohol altogether.

Such measures failed in the U.K., but succeeded in the U.S.A...

DAY 8 : 1st January 1920
The Introduction of Prohibition in the U.S.A.

On New Years Day 1920 the manufacture, sale, transportation, import and export of intoxicating liquors was banned in the United States. The Scotch whisky industry's reaction was one of dismay, but it was quickly realised that demand for Scotch was undiminished, indeed increased, and by making use of ports in adjacent territories like the West Indies, Mexico and Canada, cargoes could be brought within striking distance of the USA. A blind eye was cast upon how the goods reached the prohibited country.

Exports climbed dramatically, but the industry was very aware that they were sowing the seeds for the future. The U.S. must not be sold short: quality must be kept up. Brands were graded and priced accordingly and bulk shipments were discouraged (they facilitated adulterating the goods). A secret body named the Scheduled Area Organisation controlled all this, as well as regulating prices and credit. It had to be secret, since the British government was obliged to be seen to support the law of another country, and was continually pressed by Congress to stop the trade.

By the time Prohibition was repealed in 1933, Scotch had won a huge reputation in the States, and had established all the required distribution networks. By 1938 America was the biggest export market for Scotch.

Then came World War II, and this lucrative export market was more or less closed by the activity of German U-Boats. Duty was immediately increased (doubling the price of a bottle by 1943). Shortage of grains led to the closure of all distilleries by October 1943, and by the end of the war stocks of whisky were at an all-time low: the output of the previous six years had been equivalent to one year pre-war.

DAY 9: June 1946
The Scotch Whisky Order

One of the measures taken to stimulate whisky production was an Order in Council instigated by H.M. Customs & Excise (against the wishes of most of the industry) to allow simultaneous mashing and distilling, and working at weekends. This had been prohibited since 1823.

It was only in 1953 that home-grown cereals were finally taken off ration, and the benefit of the new law appreciated: it immediately became possible to produce twice as much whisky.

The Order made it possible to meet the huge international demand for Scotch that followed: the period1953-1974 was the second great 'Whisky boom'. Worldwide sales grew at a compound rate of 9% per annum, but, like

Photo: © DISCUS

the boom of the 1890s, it did not last. Global recession in the mid-1970s encouraged many American consumers to trade down, or move to beer; in Europe, supermarkets began to drive the price down. By 1980, Scotch was no longer 'cool' in the U.S.; younger drinkers switched to white spirits, and, increasingly, to wine. In the UK Scotch was punitively taxed, while wine was favoured (in terms of EC regulations).

And there was a huge 'Whisky Loch' surplus. Between 1960 and 1980 production more than doubled (to over 100 million proof gallons a year), and the amount of whisky being held in bond more than quadrupled (to well in excess of a billion gallons).

One way of using up this surplus, when blending orders were reducing, was for distillers to offer their product as single malt. This had been done in a small way by The Glenlivet in the U.S. (from the 1930s) and by Glen Grant in Italy (from the 1960s), but the real impetus came from Glenfiddich…

DAY 10: 23rd October 1964
Glenfiddich Goes For It

At a board meeting of William Grant's descendants, held at Glenfiddich Distillery on 23rd October 1964, it was decided to rebottle Glenfiddich Pure Malt as an 8YO, present it in a dark green version of the characteristic triangular bottle used for *Standfast*, the company's blend, and market it vigorously. It took some years for stocks to mature, but by 1970 the brand was selling 24 000 cases in the UK and even more in Europe. Grants took full advantage of the newly enfranchised duty free shops, to bring it to the attention of holiday-makers. Their efforts were rewarded by a Queen's Award for Export Achievement in 1974.

Photo: © William Grant & Sons

Other independent distillers looked on with interest, notably Macallan-Glenlivet and Glenmorangie. The former had taken note of the interest in single malt whiskies about the same time as Glenfiddich, but was not ready to go to market until 1978. The latter was ready by 1981, in which year £200 000 was allocated to an advertising campaign for the single malt.

Cardhu was promoted by the Distillers Company, but otherwise the giant held aloof from promoting single malts until 1988. Justerini & Brooks launched Knockando in 1978; Highland Park, Bunnahabhain and Tamdhu were repackaged in 1979; The Balvenie in 1982; Aberlour began to sell well in France around 1980. Bell's made Blair Athol, Inchgower, Bladnoch and Dufftown available for the first time in 1983.

Today, the massive markets of India and China beckon, but how can Scotch satisfy them? No individual distillery can produce enough to meet the demand with a single. Maybe our next 'earth-shattering day' will be the arrival of a globally respected blended malt?

Photo of Mr MacLean, Dmitry Plisov.

Charles MacLean has spent the past twenty-five years researching and writing about Scotch whisky and is one of the leading authorities.
*He spends his time sharing his knowledge around the world, in articles and publications, lectures and tastings, and on TV and radio. His first book (*Scotch Whisky*) was published in 1993 and since then he has published nine books on the subject, his most recent being* Charles MacLean's Whisky Tales, *published in 2006. He was elected a Keeper of the Quaich in 1992, in 1997* Malt Whisky *won the Glenfiddich Award and in 2003* A Liquid History *was short-listed for the André Simon Drinks Book of the Year prize.*

Scotch Whisky conquers new markets

Scotch whisky has been sold overseas for more than 100 years but new markets are emerging. Gavin D. Smith takes us on a tour to three countries, which will play a significant role in the years to come and explains the differences in their relation to Scotch.

"We should not say 'how's business?' but we should say 'where's business?'" -Tommy Dewar

Scotch whisky distillers have been targeting overseas markets in a major way since the heady days of the late 19th century, when buccaneering entrepreneurs like Tommy Dewar, James Buchanan and Peter Mackie set out to make blended Scotch whisky a true drink for the world.

In 2005 overall Scotch whisky exports increased by four per cent to a grand total of £2.36 billion, with almost 990 million bottles being sold worldwide. Consequently, this was the third best year for exports in the history of Scotch, and sales of malt whisky rose by eight per cent to their highest ever level.

However, exporting any commodity is a business based on shifting sands. Old, established markets decline while new ones develop and flourish. It is all about fashions and finance. In recent years many countries in Asia, such as South Korea and Taiwan, have become major Scotch whisky consumers as their economies have boomed. In 2005 Asia recorded an overall growth figure of 24 per cent, yet at the same time some traditional markets, particularly in Europe, have shrunk.

Generally, though, the message is a positive one. According to Richard Burrows, Chairman of the Scotch Whisky Association, "All the signs are that we are seeing a renaissance for Scotch whisky in its international markets. The industry is rising to the challenge of broadening the appeal of Scotch whisky to new consumers in new markets".

"The geographic diversity of growth is notable. We believe Asia, Eastern Europe and the Americas all offer further strong opportunities for the Scotch whisky industry to build on the worldwide growth in bottled in Scotland malt and blended Scotch whisky brands."

By common consent there are currently three major 'emerging markets', namely Russia, China and India, but the Scotch Whisky Association (SWA) suggests that the names of Brazil and Turkey should also be added to the list. All these countries have a number of factors in common: comparative economic stability, a growing aspirational middle class

Photo: © Glenmorangie Co.

Photo: © Edrington Group

with significant disposable income and an established taste for spirits of one kind or another.

In terms of single malts, Glenfiddich is the leader in each of the key emerging export markets, with Glenmorangie, Diageo's Classic Malts and Johnnie Walker Green Label blended malt, plus The Glenlivet among the other bestsellers.

In the UK, Scotch whisky sales fell by six per cent in 2005, and one factor in this decline is that younger consumers almost invariably rebel against whatever their parents drink. Hence the popularity of vodka and flavoured spirits among young Britains. In countries such as Russia, China and India, however, Scotch whisky has either not been available or affordable, and it is seen as a sophisticated alternative to established domestic drinks.

Scotch whisky takes a punch at Russian vodka

Vodka firmly remains Russia's staple national tipple, but it is perceived in some quarters as the drink of the Communist old guard. It has much the same status among young drinkers as Scotch has in the UK. During 2004 sales of Scotch whisky in Russia rose by 35 per cent, while vodka sales went up by just 4.4 per cent! In fact, Scotch whisky is really in competition with upmarket Champagne rather than with vodka.

The equivalent of 7.5 million bottles of Scotch whisky were shipped to Russia in 2004, and percentage increases in volume and value continued during the early months of the following year. Indeed, in 2005 the Russian Federation enjoyed its seventh successive year of GDP growth, with an increasing number of self-made millionaires keen to sample the once forbidden delights of western luxury goods.

However, the Scotch Whisky Association's David Williamson strikes a warning note by saying "There were difficulties entering the market in 2005, particularly during the latter part of the year, due to changes to the local tax stamp system and a subsequent shortage of stamps for imported products. It also remains a difficult market in which to operate due to, for example, problematic import licensing requirements".

"In the whole of 2005, exports to Russia were down 12 per cent in volume (to 0.5 million nine-litre cases) and 28 per cent in value (to £20 million). That said, despite these reductions, there was encouraging growth among bottled in Scotland malt whiskies, with export value up 47 per cent to £2 million. Bottled in Scotland malt whisky accounts for eleven per cent of the market."

Unsurprisingly, the Scotch whisky industry's major players are targeting Russia with a great deal of energy and money. Muscovites, in particular, tend to drink single malts straight, sometimes with ice. One of the distillers at the forefront of a drive to woo the discriminating drinkers of Moscow and other Russian cities is The Macallan, though Glenfiddich has a significantly larger share of the malt market than its rivals, being followed in popularity by Johnnie Walker malt, Glenmorangie and The Macallan.

In April 2006 The Macallan revealed that it had doubled sales in the previous 12 months alone, making it the fastest growing malt in the country, and Stewart MacRae was appointed Area Director for Eastern Europe. He says "The Scotch whisky market in Russia is growing at 30 per cent per annum, so this is a very exciting territory for The Macallan. The premium nature of this brand is well suited to the increasingly refined and affluent Russian consumer. The on-trade sector is extremely dynamic and consumption is growing, particularly in upmarket outlets, such as Café Pushkin and Karo Casino in Moscow."

Luxury bottles generate interest

The Macallan's performance in Russia has been bolstered by the success of two of the brand's most exclusive expressions, a luxury partner initiative with Lalique and the unveiling of a Fine & Rare Collection.

In November 2005, The Macallan and Lalique launched an exclusive limited edition crystal decanter holding rare 50-year-old single malt, priced at US$6 000. The 20 decanters allocated to the Russian market sold out in just 24 hours and the brand was left with orders for a further 13.

The Macallan Fine & Rare collection - the world's most expensive whisky collection, worth £14.5 million – has been well received since its launch in Moscow late in 2004. One full collection, costing a six-figure sum, has already been sold in Russia, as have 50 individual bottles with an average price tag of US$2 000. Interestingly, over 50 per cent of these bottles have been bought for personal consumption, as Muscovites want to be seen to be enjoying their wealth rather than keeping whisky as an investment.

"Russian consumers of single malt are also bucking the global trend in terms of the age at which they start drinking premium spirits like The Macallan," reckons Stewart MacRae. "In Russia the target market is aged between 25 and 45, whereas US and UK drinkers of single malts would generally be 45 plus. Younger consumers in many Eastern European countries are often far more affluent than their parents and have the disposable income to satisfy their exquisite taste".

"There is also a growing number of younger females in and around Moscow becoming single malt connoisseurs, and growth in this sector of the drinks industry is predicted to increase at a greater rate than any other category."

Macallan 50 years old Lalique

Photo: © Edrington Group

Meanwhile, deluxe blends are also extremely popular with Russian drinkers, and Chivas opened a cocktail bar and gentlemen's lounge in Moscow in April 2006. This new venture is jointly owned by Pernod Ricard Rouss, who markets and sells all of the Chivas Brothers brands in Russia, and prominent Russian gastronomic entrepreneur Stepan Mikhalkov.

Located within the fashionable new Indus Restaurant in the heart of Moscow, The Chivas Bar and Lounge features the full range of premium Chivas Brothers' Scotch whiskies including Chivas Regal, which is the base for a menu of over 30 premium cocktails. The bar also boasts a variety of memorable features such as Asprey gilded siphons and other crystal bar accessories, while whisky is served in antique quaichs.

According to Stepan Mikhalkov, "Chivas is one of the most fashionable and status-affirming brands in Russia so the opening of the Chivas Bar and Lounge provides an elite and elegant venue that brings the sophistication of international bar culture to the centre of Moscow."

Scotch with green tea and ice

Sophisticated bar culture is very much the fashion in China too, these days, though deluxe Scotch whisky blends still dominate at the expense of malts, with bottled-in-Scotland blends accounting for 93 per cent of the market in 2005. During that year China rose to become the 13th largest export market by volume, and the industry's 15th largest market by value. Export volume grew by 115 per cent (to 1.6 million nine-litre cases) and value grew no less than 86 per cent (to £46 million).

Johnnie Walker Black Label and Chivas Regal dominate the Asian market in general and China in particular, and Scotch is often consumed as a long drink with green tea and ice. Chivas' chairman and chief executive Christian Porta says "Our main thrust is with Chivas Regal 12-year-old. China is our fastest growing market for Chivas – there is spectacular growth, and in a comparatively short time we have more than doubled our sales in the market.

"One reason for this is growth of the Chinese

Photo: © Chivas Brothers

The Chivas Bar and Lounge in Moscow

economy itself. More and more Chinese people are affluent enough to afford it, so there are more consumers and potential consumers. Secondly, there is the quality of the product and the quality of the marketing done there by our team.

"It's a very promising market. Traditionally, Chinese people drank Cognac if they were drinking imported spirits, but younger adults - in the 24-35 age group – are now drinking Chivas and other brands of Scotch. They will go out after a hard day at work to a club, bar or restaurant, and share a bottle of Chivas."

In China, volumes of all Johnnie Walker expressions grew 54 per cent from a relatively low base in 2005, while volumes of Black Label soared by 75 per cent. Paul Walsh, Diageo's chief executive, says "Scotch in emerging markets is very important for us and very important for Britain." He noted that promotional expenditure during 2005 grew by 24 per cent in emerging markets, with significant increases in China.

With a population of some 1.3 billion people, China is obviously a potentially huge market for Scotch whisky. Just six years ago exports of Scotch whisky to China languished around the £1million mark, so progress has been rapid.

David Williamson of the SWA says "The industry was quick to identify China as a top priority emerging market and worked hard to both seek the removal of barriers to trade and establish a presence in the market. A key development was China's accession to the WTO [World Trade Organisation]. As part of its accession, China agreed to gradually liberalise both its tariff on spirits and distribution rules."

As a result of this, since liberalisation began in January 2000, when the import tariff stood at 65 per cent, the level has gradually been lowered, leading to its final 'binding' of 10 per cent on 1st January 2005.

Not only has Scotch whisky become more affordable, but it has also become more readily available. Initially, from 2000, foreign companies were permitted to enter into joint ventures with Chinese partners, and from the end of 2004 they have enjoyed full importation and distribution rights.

Despite tariff concessions, however, Scotch whisky faces strong competition from the locally-produced white spirit bai jiu, which, while it lacks the sophistication of Scotch, has been selling for around one-fifteenth of the price of a bottle of imported Scotch whisky. Rice wine, with the addition of medicinal herbs, is also a popular drink.

Malt whisky is becoming increasingly popular in China

Although Johnnie Walker and Chivas Regal dominate the market for Scotch whisky in China at present, it seems highly likely that as Scotch whisky drinking becomes more widespread and tastes mature, there will be an increased demand for single malts in the future.

The value of bottled in Scotland malt whisky was £2 million in 2005, and The Macallan is already very active in China, selling 3,000 cases in 2004. Market leader William Grant & Sons Ltd, which formed a new company – William Grant & Sons Shanghai – earlier this year, sold 4 500 cases during the same period, according to The International Wine & Spirit Record figures. Third in the Chinese malt 'league table' was The Famous Grouse Malt.

According to Kevin Fong of William Grant & Sons, "One group of people who drink single malt whisky in China is visitors from outside the country. They are mostly Taiwanese businessmen who have previous exposure to Glenfiddich or The Macallan in Taiwan or elsewhere in the world. They are an influential group with local drinkers given the similarity in culture, language and their relative wealth".

"Our growth in the future will be directed. We do not believe that everyone can appreciate a single malt product at this time. A lot of our marketing efforts are focused on training, education and public relations to spread the single malt gospel. Like The Macallan, we are working aggressively to convert discriminating blended malt drinkers to the single malt world."

However, not everyone is entirely positive about the allure and potential of the Chinese market for Scotch whisky. Iain Bankier, boss of the Whisky Shop chain and former chief executive of Burn Stewart Distillers, offers a voice of dissent.

Bankier says that "China has been the market of many false dawns and this could be another. When it comes to China, people see an enormous population and don't appreciate that 99.9 per cent of that population don't have two pennies to rub together."

"Everybody is rushing at it and therefore not everybody is going to win. As a result there will be disappointment because people overestimate what China can deliver."

MACALLAN
12

Photo: © Edrington Group

Tough competition in India

The same may, of course, be true of other key emerging markets, and certainly one of the hardest to crack at the present time is India, where Scotch whisky faces an incredibly uphill task in competing with domestic Indian spirits. Although India consumes 90 million cases of spirits a year, imported Scotch is estimated to represent just one per cent of that total, and nothing seems likely to change in the immediate future.

As the SWA's David Williamson explains "Overall Scotch whisky exports to India rose by 89 per cent in value in 2005, reaching £26 million. The total volume of Scotch whisky exported to India was 1.2 million nine-litre cases, an increase of 26 per cent on 2004. The market is split at around 80 per cent blended Scotch whisky and 20 per cent malt. The bottled in Scotland malt whisky category grew by 96 per cent in value last year, and bottled in Scotland blended Scotch grew by 52 per cent.

William Grant's Kevin Fong says "Sales of single malt whisky in India have been increasing in recent years. Basically, consumers have become wealthier and there is an increase in the number of foreign tourists to India."

The International Wine & Spirit Record figures show that during 2004 8 500 nine litre cases of Glenfiddich were sold in India, as opposed to 3 000 cases of "other premium malts."

According to David Williamson, "India is now the industry's 16th largest export market by volume and is the 20th largest export market by value. However, Scotch whisky is unable to take advantage of the opportunities offered because access is unfairly restricted by the discriminatory fiscal regime for imported spirits, which is contrary to WTO rules. The overall duty burden is currently between 225 and 550 per cent."

Whatever difficulties India currently holds for Scotch, there can be no doubt of its massive overall potential for whisky. The country has a population of more than one billion people, an estimated 70 million of whom now have annual disposable income in excess of US$10 000. During the last ten years what may be termed the urban-based middle class has doubled in size.

Mohan Krishna of Cheers Spirits India Ltd declares "The one market that can change the character of the whisky industry overnight will not be China, will not be Russia or Eastern Europe or Brazil, but India. Despite all the hype

Photo: © Teachers

Photo: © Teachers

Teachers Achievement Awards

surrounding potentially enormous emerging markets in South America and the Far East, they still all pale into insignificance compared with that of India."

Largest whisky market in the world

India is already the largest whisky market in the world, with an annual consumption of between 65 and 70 million cases, and Indian distillers and legislators argue that the country's high tariffs are justified because many of its domestically-produced whiskies cannot legally be sold in Europe or the USA because they do not meet their definitions of 'whisky', often being distilled using molasses.

Counterfeiting is a major problem with Scotch whisky in India, but a landmark ruling in April 2006 saw the high court in Delhi rule that an Indian-distilled whisky called Red Scot could no longer be sold under that name on the grounds that it led consumers to believe what they were buying was genuine Scotch whisky.

The SWA had filed a lawsuit against the whisky's producers, Golden Bottling Limited, and David Williamson says "In this case, use of the word 'Scot' on the bottle label was an attempt to mislead consumers into thinking they were buying Scotch whisky rather than locally-produced spirit."

When it comes to legitimate Scotch whisky, Teachers is a key brand in the Indian market, as Michael Cockram, Scotch Category Director for Beam Global Spirits & Wine Inc explains.

"Teacher's is the number one bottled in India Scotch whisky," he says. "We have the biggest volume share and we're the biggest in value now, too. We sell 120 000 cases of Teachers a year in India."

"Historically, India has been a good market for Teachers for a long time, and one of the ways in which we promote the brand now is with Teachers Achievement Awards, which honour the highest achievers in Indian culture, arts and sport each year."

"Teachers drinkers in India are corporate achievers, usually 30 plus, and they usually work for large Indian companies or multi-nationals. They tend to be comparatively well educated males, and they have to have a certain level of income to be able to afford Teachers with the trade barriers that are in place."

To get a sense of just how expensive genuine Scotch whisky is in India it is worth noting that the most modest locally-produced 'whisky' sells for around 75 rupees per bottle, while Famous Grouse costs some 1 400 rupees – not far off a month's salary for the average Indian worker. Johnnie Walker Black Label weighs in at around 2 500 rupees.

Exporting Scotch whisky remains a fascinating and unpredictable business, especially in the principal emerging markets. Were he alive today, Tommy Dewar would still find many challenges and rewards to satisfy his evangelical thirst.

Gavin D Smith is one of Scotland's leading whisky writers and Contributing Editor to www.whisky-pages.com. He hosts whisky talks and tastings and produces feature material for a wide range of specialist and general interest publications. He is the author of 17 books, eight on the subject of whisky. These include Whisky, Wit & Wisdom, The A-Z of Whisky, Worts, Worms & Washbacks, The Secret Still *and, most recently,* The Whisky Men. *He lives on the Fife coast in Scotland.*

The first hours in the life of a whisky

Whisky drinkers can spend hours discussing how their favourite tipple has fared in the cask in which it has matured. But what happens during distillation and which conditions affect the flavour of the new make spirit? Ian Wisniewski takes a closer look at the still inside out.

There are essentially three ways of enjoying a malt whisky. Simply indulging in the experience is one, while thinking about the flavours, or talking about them are two others. And with up to 70% of the flavour of a malt whisky developing during maturation, the influence of oak aging provides a natural focal point when analysing the character of a malt whisky.

A vast increase in the understanding of maturation over the past 15-20 years also means that the influence of different cask types, as well as evaporation, oxidation, and conditions in different types of aging warehouses, has become a far more detailed and fulfilling discussion.

However, without the appropriate quality and character of new make spirit, maturation would be a redundant process. Similarly, without the preceding stages being successfully completed, including low wines, fermentation, mashing and milling, the new make spirit wouldn´t reach the required parameters either.

The quality and character of the low wines and new make spirit rests on a combination of factors during each distillation. This includes the size and shape of the stills, the still charge, the degree of interaction between the vapours and copper surface of the still, the heating method, the rate of reflux and distillation, the spirit cut and type of condensers used.

As though that wasn´t enough to think about, additional details such as seasonal fluctuations in the ambient temperature, and in the temperature of the water which cools the condensers, are even more factors to incorporate into an already complex equation.

Moreover, quantifying how influential any of these aspects are individually is hardly straight-forward. But it´s also clear that changes to any part of the process can have a significant influence, and compromise consistency.

There is of course another vital factor to consider, which is the skill of the master distiller. Although the entire distillation process is computerised, with various screens providing detailed information, this essentially serves as a back up, enabling the distiller to monitor each stage. But that still means having to make numerous decisions, and remain in control of the process.

Photo: © William Grant & Sons Ltd.

Fill the still with moderation

An initial aspect to consider is the still charge (ie. the volume of liquid within the still). A traditional approach is to fill around two-thirds of the boil pot (base of the still). This also reflects a practical consideration, to ensure that the heating elements within the still are covered, and to maximise on energy efficiency in heating the still (and avoiding the risk of caramelising the wash or low wines, which would compromise consistency).

Maintaining the same still charge is actually a vital factor, as the level of liquid within the still also determines the surface area of copper available to the vapours. A still charge which was higher/lower than usual would correspondingly result in a decreased/increased area of copper.

As copper interacts with the vapours during distillation, and effectively absorbs sulphurous compounds, the degree of copper contact has a significant influence on the distillate.

Sulphurous compounds include a range of rubbery, meaty, struck match notes, which means they can mask or even overwhelm other flavour compounds within the distillate. Consequently, reducing the level of sulphurous compounds in the vapours through interaction with copper can help reveal the underlying congeners, including esters. Meanwhile, depending on the house style, a certain level of sulphur compounds may be entirely appropriate.

Another consequence of changing the still charge is recounted by Chivas Bros´ Alan Winchester.

"In the 1960s things got out of kilter. To increase production, a wee drop more was put in the stills which created more low wines, but upset the usual reflux of the still. Less available head space means less reflux."

Stills come in all shapes and sizes

With more on reflux later in this article, let´s continue looking at copper, which offers other significant advantages during distillation. An ability to conduct heat at a rapid and uniform rate, for example. Being incredibly malleable is another vital asset, considering the vast range of still shapes and sizes in distilleries across Scotland.

Among distilleries with an 'ultimate' tag line, Glenmorangie has the tallest stills in

Photo: © Glenmorangie Co.

Glenmorangie - the tallest stills in the industry

the industry, extending 5.13 meters, while at the other end of the scale Edradour has the industry´s smallest. Whether taller or smaller, some distilleries have uniform shapes for the wash and spirit stills.

"We have 3 wash and 3 spirit stills basically the same shape and design, only the size varies. We started with 2 stills then went up to 4 in 1960, and then up to 6 in 1976. The extra stills were added by Forsyth's, who followed the existing shape," says Ian McWilliam of Glenfarclas.

But then it´s also possible to see a range of still shapes and sizes within the same distillery, as at Laphroaig.

"We have 7 stills, including 3 pairs of wash and spirit stills, with the wash stills different in shape from the spirit stills. Number 1 spirit still was installed by Bessie in 1967 to increase production capacity, it´s the same shape as the other spirit stills but twice the size, and produces new make spirit with a different character, a bit more sweetness at first," says Laphroaig´s John Campbell.

Meanwhile, at Mortlach, founded in 1823, an extensive repertoire means that every wash

Photo: © J.&G. Grant, Glenfarclas

Laphroaig stillhouse

and spirit still is individual.

"At Mortlach all 6 stills are different sizes and shapes, which includes 1 wash still being much bigger than the other two, and one spirit still (known as 'wee witchie') being smaller than the other two. There´s a lot of discussion as to why this should be. Some say the owner knew what he was doing and bought stills to match the spirit he wanted. Others say he bought what was available on the market," says Diageo´s Douglas Murray.

The importance of design

What ultimately matters of course is the quality and character of the new make spirit, so whether this is achieved by using stills with a uniform design, or a variety of shapes, isn´t really the issue. However, this raises the question of when distillers realised the significance of still design.

"Originally, stills were of a plain, simple style. Boil bowls evolved as people realised that the shape and size of the stills affected the flavour of the spirit they were producing. People were placing orders for specific shapes of stills quite early on, in the 1850s-1900s, I think from then people were using specific styles of stills to promote their individuality, though this is unprovable," adds Douglas Murray.

The significance of still design is the degree of reflux this promotes. Taller stills with narrower necks promote a greater degree of reflux, and consequently a lighter distillate. Correspondingly, a still with a shorter neck sees less reflux which promotes a richer, heavier character.

This is because heavier, denser, oilier flavour compounds have a higher boiling point than lighter flavour compounds, and as the vapours ascend the neck of the still the temperature becomes relatively lower, and the longer the neck the more significant the temperature differential. Consequently, this temperature differential can be sufficient to cause some vapours to condense, and start trickling back towards the boil pot (base) of the still.

Moreover, reflux is something of a continuous process as the condensate trickles down the copper surface. The condensate

Photo: © J.&G. Grant, Glenfarclas

Keeping a close watch on the spirit still at Glenfarclas

doesn´t need to reach the boil pot (base) in order to re-vapourise, as some may be re-vapourised en route by the heat of ascending vapours. As different compounds have different boiling points, re-vapourised condensate will consequently result in different flavour compounds rising back up the neck of the still.

In addition to still size and shape, the level of reflux can also be increased by adding extras such as a boil bowl (bulbous section between the boil pot and neck). As this creates a larger, relatively cooler area, vapours carrying heavier flavour compounds condense within the boil bowl, and begin the journey back to the boil pot. The dimensions of the boil bowl determine the degree of reflux, with a more convex shape promoting greater reflux.

The choice between direct and indirect heating

The rate of distillation is another factor influencing the degree of reflux, which in turn depends on the way the still is heated.

"The first thing you need to do is set the distillation rate, which is determined by the amount of energy that goes into the still. Faster or slower, each distillery has its own rate depending on the sensory quality desired. The faster you distill the less your reflux ratio. Reflux is determined by the amount of energy used, and the size and shape of the still," says Wm Grant´s John Ross.

The traditional method of direct heating, using a coal fire or gas flame, is still employed by distilleries such as Glenfiddich and Glenfarclas. A consequence of using direct-fire is the risk of solids within the wash burning onto the base of the still, which can caramelise and influence the distillate. This is prevented by installing rummagers, essentially long copper chains, that circulate around the boil pot removing any solids which may have lodged there.

Just how influential the heating method is, and how integral to the character of the distillate, is clear when considering the experience at Glenfarclas.

"We use direct heat (gas burner) which is easy to control with a series of rings that prevent hot spots from forming. In 1980, as an experiment, we installed indirect heat (steam kettle) which is more efficient to one of our spirit stills. But when we analysed the new make spirit it had totally changed the character and taken all the body out of it so the indirect heating system was promptly removed," says Ian McWilliam.

Steam coils began to replace direct-fire from the 1960s-70s, using steam conducted through pipes within the boil pot (base) of the still. However, earlier exponents of this method include Scapa, where steam heating was installed in 1885.

Steam coils are generally considered to provide the best heat control and distribution within the still. Another option are steam-heated pans, also known as kettles, which developed around the same time as coils, with each option offering the same level of control.

Installing pans (kettles) in wash stills, but coils in the spirit still reflects a practical consideration.

"We have pans in the wash stills, as there´s a lot of solids in the wash so coils would be harder to keep clean. We use steam coils in the spirit stills," says John Campbell.

Copper sets the character

While the first distillation produces low wines, the second distillation entails three separate stages, the foreshots (or heads), the spirit cut, and feints (also known as tails). As the initial and concluding stages of the distillation run, the foreshots and feints are of an inappropriate quality and alcoholic strength, and are collected separately to be redistilled with the next batch of low wines.

Photo: © J.&G. Grant, Glenfarclas

Glenfarclas still with rummagers

The spirit cut is collected as new make spirit, with the spirit showing different characteristics as the alcoholic strength diminishes. Starting to collect spirit at around 75% abv, down to around 65% abv, yields a spirit cut that focuses on lighter, fruitier flavours. Extending the spirit cut to a lower strength broadens the range of characteristics to include heavier, oilier flavour compounds.

However, the spirit cut is only one aspect of manipulating the character of the new make spirit, in conjunction with still design, the rate of distillation, and temperature of the distillate.

Vapours are conducted from the still to the condenser by the lye pipe (also known as lyne arm), with the angle of the lye pipe an important factor. Extending at an incline encourages a greater level of reflux, promoting lighter flavour compounds, while a broader range of flavour compounds make it through a descending lye pipe. The length of the lye pipe also matters, with a longer pipe extending the degree of contact with copper.

The choice of condenser is either the more traditional worm (a coiled copper pipe of decreasing diameter, set in a worm tub with cold running water, on the exterior wall of the still house), or a more modern shell and tube condenser.

The large number of copper pipes within a shell and tube condenser, cooled by flowing water, provide a greater surface area than a typical worm. This in turn promotes a greater degree of contact with copper, helping to reduce the level of sulphurous compounds.

Moreover, the temperature of the water which cools the condenser is another vital factor, the colder the water the quicker the vapours condense. As the temperature of a distillery´s water source can vary significantly between summer and winter, potentially warmer water during the summer was a traditional reason for having a silent season. Potentially less water being available during the summer may have been another practical reason.

One way of countering seasonal fluctuations in water temperature is to use a cooling tower.

"We have a cooling tower on site which helps give more control of temperature, in summer we can cool it down to 18 degrees centigrade, while in the winter it could be down to 5-8 degrees centigrade. Occasionally we need to slow down the distillation rate to get the temperature and balance the same," says John Campbell.

The shell and tube way of condensing used at Strathisla

Worm tubs, the more traditional way of cooling the spirit vapours, used at Balmenach

Temperature plays it´s role

Another aspect of the flow rate and cooling ability of the condenser is raised by Douglas Murray.

"The lyne arm and condenser provide copper contact, if you run it cold then vapours condense at the top and there is less influence from copper contact. If you run it hot vapours go further in a condenser before condensing, so there is maximum copper interaction. Liquid interaction with copper is significantly less than vapours," says Douglas Murray.

In addition to the temperature of the water within the condensers, another consideration is the ambient temperature around the exterior of the condensers, ie. within the still house.

"A warmer temperature in the still house means slightly less reflux, if we ran the stills in exactly the same way during summer and winter we´d notice a difference, normally it´s the flow rate/temperature of the water that´s adjusted," says Douglas Murray.

Depending on the location of the condensers, another variation on this theme is the ambient temperature outside the still house.

"We have shell and tube condensers which are outside the still house, so we have the added benefit of the ambient temperature, whereas most distilleries have condensers in the still house. The temperature of the condenser is controlled by an automatic valve, allowing cooling water in, so we need a faster rate of water in summer. During the summer the water temperature is around 9-12 degrees centigrade, and in winter it´s about 2 degrees centigrade, so we´re using considerably more water in the summer, which we take from an open stream called the 'Green Burn' located on Ben Rinnes," says Ian McWilliam.

And once the new make spirit has been assessed, it´s time for the next stage, filling into casks and beginning the maturation process in the aging warehouses. But that´s another, separate article.

Photo: © Finlandia Vodka

Ian Wisniewski is a food, drink and travel writer and broadcaster specialising in spirits. He contributes to various publications and has written 8 books on drinks, including Classic Malt Whisky, and is a regular visitor to distilleries in Scotland.

The outside temperature can play a significant role, especially at Dalwhinnie, the highest working distillery in Scotland

Global whisky summit

– the insiders share expectations, concerns and trends

Have you ever wondered what the people in the whisky business are talking about when you are not around? Share their expectations and concerns and learn about the trends when Ian Buxton reports direct from the inaugural World Whiskies Conference.

I suppose I should start with a confession: this isn't an entirely independent article. The World Whiskies Conference was my idea and I am the Conference Director. So think of this as an insider's view rather than a critical evaluation.

It seemed to me that there was a need for a conference that looked at the whisky business from a global standpoint and tried to cross company and national barriers. Fortunately, as I began to ask around, it seemed that others agreed: in fact, the question most often asked, once I'd explained the idea, was "why aren't we doing that already?" And so the World Whiskies Conference was born.

It took about 2½ years of planning and support from a great number of people to make it happen but, in April 2006 at the Edinburgh International Conference Centre, we were able to hold the inaugural event. And, such was its success, that on April 18th and 19th 2007, it will happen again.

So what exactly was it? Well, you can check it out yourself at *www.whiskyconference.com* and see that it aimed to attract the senior management of the global whisky business. Everyone, in fact, with an interest in selling more whisky. As you (presumably) like to drink whisky you ought to know what went on.

In 2006, over two very full days, we had 30 speakers presenting a total of 24 separate sessions to well over 100 delegates, who came from the USA, Germany, Switzerland, Canada, India, South Africa, Holland, Sweden, Japan, Italy, Ireland and, of course, Scotland. Every major whisky-producing region was represented and a wide range of companies, large and small, sent delegates.

There were formal presentations from major industry associations such as the Scotch Whisky Association (SWA) and the Distilled Spirits Council of the United States (DISCUS); break-out sessions from distillers, marketers, agencies, retailers and even a brewer; informal working sessions, a glittering Gala Dinner and much late-night delegate networking (and product sampling – purely for quality assurance reasons).

Afterwards, delegates praised the Conference. Frank Coleman, Senior Vice President, Public Affairs and Communications, for DISCUS told me:

"The World Whiskies Conference is to be commended for bringing together an interesting and diverse group of industry leaders to discuss the critical issues we are facing, including the importance of actively promoting responsible consumption and rigorous, effective self-regulation."

Delegates at World Whiskies Conference 2006

Will spirits follow tobacco?

And this is really the point. The global drinks industry is under increasing pressure some of it rationally expressed and well-argued, some little more than vindictive anti-alcohol propaganda. Indeed, many delegates compared the position of the drinks industry today to that of the tobacco industry 20 years ago whilst making the critical point that whilst even one cigarette can be proven harmful, the same cannot be said of beverage alcohol. So a mature debate leading to industry viewpoints on moderation and self-regulation is vital.

A critically-important keynote presentation on this topic opened day two of the Conference, with senior representatives of two of the most important global industry associations leading a discussion on responsibility, moderation and self-regulation – themes close to the heart of the worldwide whisky industry.

From the SWA, Campbell Evans drew attention to the diversity of drinking styles of the European consumer with a pointed contrast between sophisticated Stockholm club-goers and the binge drinking culture prevalent amongst some UK nightclub and pub users.

He also caused a sharp intake of breath from delegates by revealing the following chastening quote from Scottish Health Minister Andy Kerr,

"The way I look at the alcohol debate is that I think that we are in the foothills of the debate that we have now had on smoking".

Earlier, in a presentation entitled 'Will spirits go the way of tobacco?' delegates had seen cigarette-type health warnings applied to whisky packaging, causing a lively question and answer session with presenter Wyndham Carver who has had 25 years industry experience in both drinks and tobacco.

Smoking, of course, is now banned in all enclosed public places in Scotland and though the city authorities in Glasgow have abandoned their plan to make all licensed premises serve all alcohol in plastic containers it was an uncomfortable sign of the times.

Evans went on to describe SWA efforts to inform the political debate and outlined the five basic principles of social responsibility promoted by the World Spirits Alliance.

From the USA, Frank Coleman outlined the role of DISCUS. In a market that is still shaped by Prohibition, DISCUS has worked to educate politicians and the media about the heritage of the distilling industry, which dates back to George Washington. Coleman stressed that "cultural acceptance and responsibility were key to commercial success".

He concluded by emphasising that constant vigilance was necessary, both against pressure-group attack on the industry's freedoms and vigorous self regulation to ensure consistently high standards. If moderation and a message of 'Drink better, not more' are consistently promoted then our industry will continue to prosper.

Great potential in emerging markets

Other presentations covered a wide range of themes: developing markets such as China and India; lessons from other luxury goods categories; relationship marketing through the use of brand visitor centres; retailers' needs (a well-attended session); the value of industry competitions; the re-launch of Chivas Regal; a variety of market research reports and trends in new packaging were all discussed.

Developing markets such as India are of particular importance to the industry, though as speaker Dr Mohan Krishna reminded the conference, with a vibrant and large 'whisky' industry of its own, India was hardly 'developing'. In fact, with the bulk of Indian 'whisky' being produced from molasses, it would not meet EU quality standards but is nonetheless enjoyed by the domestic consumer, as we shall see later in this review.

As the fourth largest economy in the world, India is looking more and more like an attractive market for distillers from outside the sub-continent aiming to sell premium brands to a consumer growing in affluence. Dr Mohan Krishna, who is marketing director for Cheers Spirits India, gave delegates an overview of the market and its future, including the increased demand for better quality products.

During his seminar, Dr Krishna emphasised the complexity of the Indian market with significant entry tariffs for new entrants and severe advertising restrictions. However, as he pointed out, with 130 million cases of 'whisky' sold each year the potential for premium brands was impressive and he added that the Indian market was set to expand to 180 million cases pa by 2015.

Other speakers included Charles Allen of Diageo; Martin Riley of Chivas Brothers; Dr Hisashi Maemura of Suntory; Ian Bankier of The Whisky Shop; Thierry Benitah of La Maison du Whisky in Paris and Michael Riley of the Liquor Control Board of Ontario – all senior industry figures. Perhaps better known to the consumer are Dave Broom, the author, who presented important new research on the market for single malts, and the ebullient Richard Paterson, Master Blender at Whyte & Mackay who gave a case study on the value of competitions and awards.

One session of particular interest that was very well attended was jointly led by Sir Iain Noble of Pràban na Linne and Magnus Dandanell of new Swedish malt whisky distiller Mackmyra, who spoke on 'Opening a new distillery'.

Many who work in the whisky industry, and perhaps many who don't, have harboured the dream of opening and running their own distillery. But it's one thing to have the dream, altogether something different to go and do it. In this very popular session, two independent distilling pioneers told how they 'walked the walk'.

Sir Iain Noble's £3m project, part-funded by the local enterprise company, is due to open in late 2008.

"This is about putting Skye on the whisky trail with a new Gaelic whisky," explained Sir Iain. "Everyone is rather excited about the idea of having two distilleries in Skye and I'm sure Talisker will benefit."

Whilst the Skye project is still on the drawing board, Mackmyra Distillery is now marketing the world's first Swedish whisky.

Distillery founder Magnus Dandanell explained the genesis of the project, outlined funding sources and showed how the product was developed. Innovative marketing ideas were also shared with delegates, such as Mackmyra's 30 litre cask – which customers are able to carry away from the distillery. Such is the interest in the project that the distillery's first public release of whisky in Sweden sold out in less than 30 minutes.

You can visit the distillery, specify your own cask and, eventually, carry it away. Mackmyra are at pains to involve their customers in the whisky making process and plan to develop a range of whiskies and whisky-related products as they develop the Mackmyra brand (it's probably worth mentioning that the distillery's publicity material is beautifully produced and photographed, in keeping with their overall approach to quality).

The power of supermarkets

For whisky drinkers presentations of particular interest will be Dave Broom's Malt Report, presented in conjunction with research company just-drinks.com; Anne Nugent's session on 'Trends and Issues in World Whisky' and Rabobank's Maria Castroviejo on 'Whisky's Place in Global Drinks'.

Dave began with an analysis of the UK malt market. Though growing robustly since 2001, contrary to popular belief it actually fell in size in the last year for which figures are available. The Neilsen data for the UK in 2005 shows that malt is not on an upward curve in every market as, last year, UK sales fell by 50,000 cases, (a drop 7.5% in volume and some 6.1% in value). Though the underlying trend is still good – up by 13% in volume and 10% in value from 2001, the question has to be asked... what happened? ... why now?

And the answer in the report is 'price'. Although single malt prices have, in general, moved above the £20 mark (off promotion) the UK market is still being driven by discounted brands and no brand owner saw this cycle of discounting being broken.

The report suggests that Glenmorangie took the heaviest hit. After years of deep discounting at the Christmas period new owner LVMH held the line on pricing and appears to have paid a heavy price in the short-term at least. The fact that Glenfiddich, Glenlivet and Macallan held off from deep discounting but emerged relatively unscathed suggests that much of Glenmorangie's position of the UK's number 1 malt was built on price.

Of course, for the consumer a lower price on their favourite malt may look like good news. But for the distillers, lower prices stifle their ability to invest in brand development, reduce the incentive to bring interesting new expressions to market and devalue the category. In the long run, everyone suffers. Not surprisingly, Ian Bankier of The Whisky Shop was keen to make the point in his presentation that the industry's 'bad boys' were the large supermarkets and encourage the malt marketers to work with independent retailers (like The Whisky Shop, of course!).

Like the UK France has experienced deep discounting in supermarkets, part of an attempt by brands to claw back volume after a

Increased focus on independent retailers, like Gordon & MacPhail, could lessen the supermarkets' influence in the whisky business.

disastrous fall in 2003 which affected all spirits following a change in drink-driving laws. The report found that many distillers are worried at what they see a replication of the UK market conditions: increasing retailer power (85% of sales are through supermarkets), declining on-trade etc. Although France has the highest average prices for malt in mainland Europe its supermarkets are the cheapest.

The result, many argue is the creation of a low-margin environment within which major brands will always struggle to be profitable. In addition, France has a large, low-priced blended malt category – it remains one of the largest importers of bulk malt and delegates split on whether or not this would restrict premium growth.

However, they were heartened to see that the last of the older malt markets, Japan, is now turning in double-digit growth once more as its economy recovers. The new Japanese consumer appears to be turning towards malt. The age profile is dropping into the late 20s while more women are drinking malt. Brand owners are cautiously optimistic that this growth will continue. Importantly this is also a high value market with a brand-conscious, premium consumer.

The real story in the Far East however is Taiwan which has grown at almost 100% each year for the past four years. Should this rate of growth continue, the report predicted it will overtake Italy as the fourth largest market within two years. Whisky sales in Taiwan have, until recently, been restricted to bottles of blends drunk in the traditional on-trade (hostess bars, restaurants etc.) but the new wave of designer bars frequented by young, affluent professionals has given malt a springboard.

The pace has been set by The Macallan, but all the heavy-hitting brands are there as are blended malts. Famous Grouse Vintage Malt is currently the fastest growing brand in Taiwan while Johnnie Walker Green Label is also making significant inroads. Though brand owners are excited at the potential they are also aware that Taiwan has been a notoriously volatile market and a brand's life cycle can be heavily compressed.

Globally, malt drinkers tend to be upscale, affluent and there are, theoretically, a growing number of them. Demographics are moving in the direction of luxury. Yet the report shows that the situation is more complex than that. There is not one malt consumer type, but four.

Entry Level Consumers
— driven by price

Premium Consumers
— trading up (and into malt?)

Luxury Consumers
— show, status, knowledge

Malt Mavens
— the ones who tip?

This last group is of considerable interest. They are the ones who start a groundswell of interest in 'cool' brands, though any branded message has first to be translated from the arcane texts of the mavens before it can be comprehensible by the new premium drinkers. Dave left delegates with a challenge:

"Malt needs to resist the temptation to devalue its premium credentials for short-term volume gain. It needs also to identify not just the needs of consumers in each market, but the different needs of a range of consumer groups. There is no malt consumer, there are many – which is the greatest opportunity of all."

Future stars and fast growers

Anne Nugent of Euromonitor gave a broader-brush presentation concentrating on demographics and their long-term influence on whisk(e)y markets.

Her chart on the current top whisk(e)y markets (see Fig. 1) may contain a few surprises for readers of the Malt Whisky Yearbook – not least, India's incredible dominance, with a domestic whisky market of close to 70 m cases annually (before locally produced molasses products are added). Contrast this with the USA at 45 m cases or the UK, with less than 10 m cases sold each year.

But the chart forecasting the next five years (see Fig. 2) shows quite dramatically why the distillers' attention is drawn to the Far East, with China showing a compound growth rate of 20% per annum from 2005 to 2010 and Thailand forecast to increase its imports of whisky by a staggering 1.5 m cases. Figures like this, and the predominance of discounting in markets such as the UK and France, explain why marketing resources are being increasingly focused on the so-called 'developing' markets.

A similar story emerged from Maria Castroviejo of Dutch banking giants Rabobank

Performance of top whisk(e)y markets 2000/2005

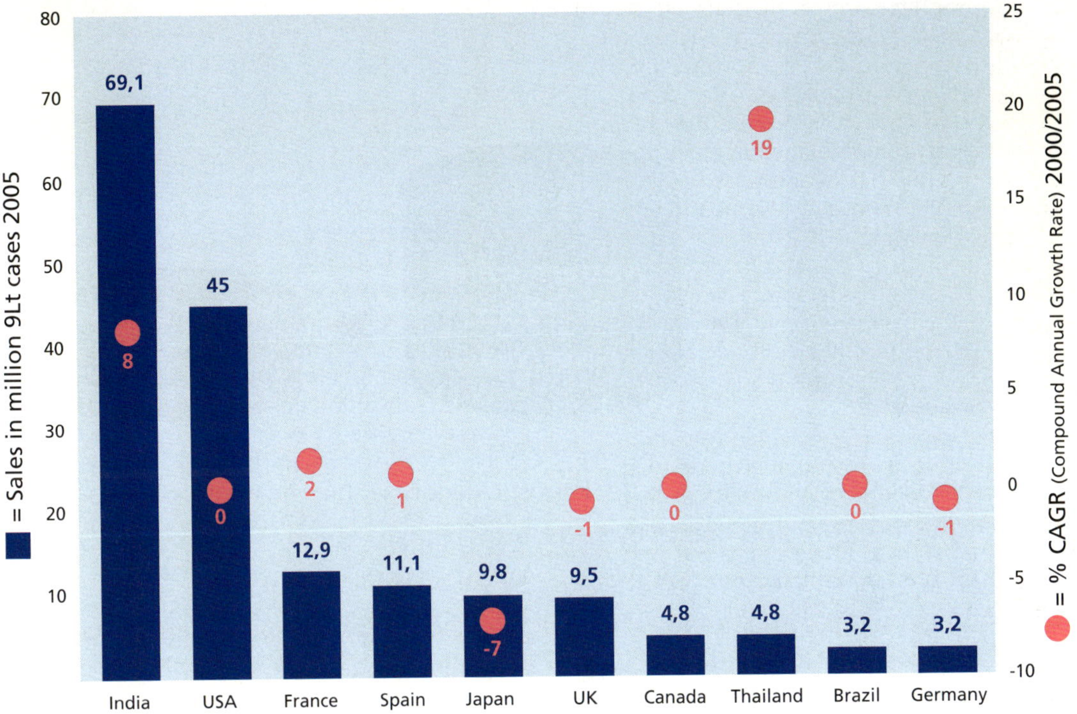

Fig 1 © Copyright 2006, Euromonitor

Whisk(e)y forecasts by top ten countries 2005/2010

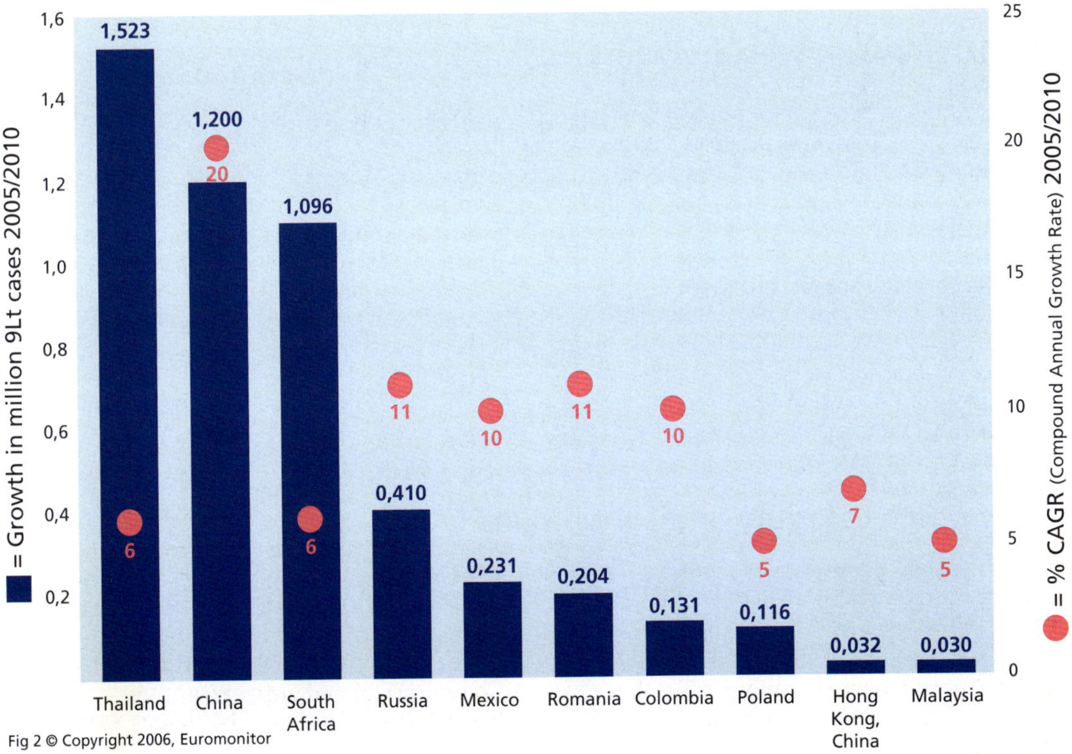

Fig 2 © Copyright 2006, Euromonitor

Whisky within the spirits industry

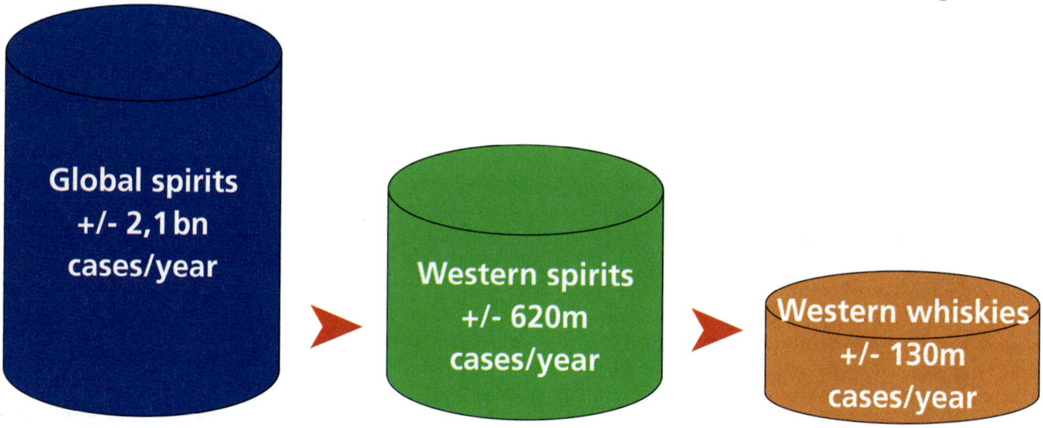

- With a 20% share, whisky is the largest category within the western spirits.
- Of the top 20 spirits brands by value, 9 are whisky.
- Of the top 20 premium spirits brands by volume, 8 are whisky.
- Global spirits consumption is flat, but demand for western, premium spirits increases. Largest markets (by volume): China, India, USA, Brazil, Japan, Russia, S. Korea, Thailand, Germany and the Philippines.

Fig 3 © Copyright 2006, Rabobank, based on Impact figures

Who is growing faster?

Top 10 growing western whiskies

	Volume (million cases)	Value (million US$)	Value per bottle (US$)	2000-2004 growth
100 Pipers	3,2	425	11,1	165,6
Jameson	1,7	320	15,7	37,3
Johnnie Walker Black	4,4	1.530	29,0	34,1
Crown Royal	4,2	1.010	20,0	29,2
Jack Daniel´s	7,6	1.605	17,6	23,4
Clan McGregor	1,6	195	10,2	23,1
Imperial	0,9	305	28,2	19,7
Teacher´s	1,8	345	16,0	16,7
Canadian Club	2,6	390	12,5	15,6
Windsor Premier	0,7	250	29,8	15,0

Must watch category: Indian whiskies

	Volume (million cases)	Value (million US$)	Value per bottle (US$)	2000-2004 growth
McDowell´s No 1	5,7	410	6,0	67,1
Bagpiper	7,3	395	4,5	35,9
Royal Stag	2,9	240	6,9	162,5
Director´s Special	3	210	5,8	34,0

Fig 4 © Copyright 2006, Rabobank, based on Impact and company figures

Of the 10 fastest growing western whisky brands...

8 belong to Diageo, Pernod Ricard or were part of Allied Domecq

3 are leading in Asian markets

2 are priced below US$11,5

5 are priced above US$17

Market polarises: US$12-17/bottle, the most vulnerable segment who presented on 'The City's view of Whisky'. Given the remarkable extent of merger and acquisition activity in the whisky industry in the recent past (think of LVMH's acquisition of Glenmorangie; Campari's purchase of Glen Grant and Diageo's absorption of the Irish whiskey portfolio of the former Allied Domecq, as a 'price' for not opposing the Pernod Ricard takeover of that company as examples) the interest of the banking community is more than understandable.

In her presentation she demonstrated the place of 'Western' whisky within the premium spirits market, against global spirits consumption of +/- 2.1 billion cases annually (that's a lot of the hard stuff we're getting through). As can be seen in Figure 3, whisky is critically important: 9 of the Top 20 brands by value are whiskies, and 8 of the Top 20 premium spirits by volume.

She also demonstrated the remarkable growth rates of some 'Growth Brands' (Fig. 4). 100 Pipers, a former Seagram brand given up for dead by its previous owners, has enjoyed an incredible renaissance under Pernod Ricard's leadership, up 165% over the period 2000 - 2004 to 3.2 million cases – large by any standards. And, be honest, had you ever even heard of 100 Pipers, let alone drunk it?

The chart also clearly shows the increasing dominance of Diageo and Pernod Ricard but, sneaking up on the outside are Indian whiskies - again exhibiting remarkable resilience. Bagpiper might seem a clichéd name for Western consumers, but it sells 7.3 m cases and grew nearly 36%, so someone clearly loves it.

McDowells No 1 showed even more remarkable growth (+67% to nearly 6 m cases) but the undoubted star of the sub-continent is Royal Stag. The name might seem old-fashioned but a growth of 162.5% from 2000 – 2004 is not to be sneezed at, and its volume grew to a very respectable 2.9 million cases.

World Whiskies Conference – to be continued

At the end of the day the 2006 World Whiskies Conference has been voted an overwhelming success. But don't just take my word for it – this isn't a 'puff' or hidden advert. Delegates were asked to complete an evaluation form and rate all aspects of the conference. They told us the following:

- 67% said it was "better value than expected"
- 82% of delegates rated the Conference "excellent" or "very good"
- 89% said "I would definitely recommend to a colleague"
- 94% said "I would attend a future event".

So, with this endorsement, the World Whiskies Conference will go into its second year in good heart. In fact, wearing my Conference Director hat (this is where I came in), I was quoted in the trade press as follows:

"We'll be back - bigger, better and bolder for 2007."

I think that says it all, really. If you are in the industry, I hope you can join us. If not, well we are thinking about you.

Find out more about the World Whiskies Conference at ***www.whiskyconference.com***

Ian Buxton is well-placed to write or talk about whisky and drinks. A former Marketing Director of Glenmorangie he lives in Perthshire on the site of a former distillery from where he conducts a love affair with Scotland's national drink!

Ian began work in the Scotch Whisky industry in 1987 and, since 1991, has run his own consultancy business. As well as giving lectures, presentations and tastings on whisky, he writes regular columns for Whisky Magazine. In 2002 his book Scotch Whisky: History, Hints and Tips *was published and he was one of the principal co-authors of* The Whisky Companion *(2005). He was elected a Keeper of the Quaich in 1991.*

In the shadow of malt whisky

Single malt is the main concern of the whisky community although more than 90% of all Scotch consumed is blended. The base of blended whisky is grain whisky and David Stirk explains the production process and why more respect should be shown for this neglected spirit.

"The patent still is a box of tricks."
James Power an Irish pot still distiller in 1908.

Tucked away like a breeze-block in a country garden is Cameronbridge Distillery; hidden behind a shopping centre like an elephant under a parasol is Loch Lomond; dominantly stealing the horizon in Girvan, like the world's largest gravestone, is Girvan Distillery. I think you get the message, Grain distilleries are not pretty or petite, but they are essential to the success and longevity of the whisky industry.

It may come as a shock to all you malt drinkers to learn that more than 90% of all Scotch consumed is blended. Grain whisky, which is the largest constituent of most blends, accounts for more than 60% of all alcohol produced in Scotland. What's more is that there are only 7 grain distilleries in Scotland (compared to around 90 malt distilleries) producing more than 200 million litres of alcohol a year. Yet while malt distilling has a history many centuries long, the history of grain whisky can be traced back to just over 170 years ago.

The birth of the column still

History shows us that there were many attempts to increase output and consistency using traditional pot still distillation methods. There were also many distillers who were using grains as part of their mash instead of 100% malted barley (as is still the case with some Irish whiskey made in traditional pot stills). Whilst distilleries and technological understanding was growing though, the ability to keep up with an ever-increasing demand was not being met.

By 1828 Robert Stein, part of the Stein distilling dynasty, had obtained permission to run trials at his brother's distillery Kirkliston, in West Lothian. This was the first attempt to rectify spirit in a columnar-shaped still. It was deemed a success by the Excise who commented: 'The spirits produced, from the absence of the essential oil, are much more pure and wholesome than those produced by common distilling... to separate this oil in the process has engrossed the attention of many distilleries, but hitherto with but little success.'

Cameronbridge Distillery
at Windygates, Fife

Photo: © Diageo

By May 1830 the first fully operational Stein Still was licensed and installed at Cameronbridge Distillery and by the end of the year it had produced nearly 150,000 gallons. Stein's still had one major drawback however - it was designed to distil the worts from 100% malted barley. Malting barley was a time-intensive and laborious operation resulting in a much heavier spirit than grain whisky. Unfortunately, continuous distillation from the Stein Still removed most of the flavour imparting congeners that were evident from a pot still distillation, thus missing the whole purpose of using 100% malted barley.

It took an Inspector General of Irish Excise, Aeneas Coffey, to further develop Stein's still utilising copper plates rather than steel plates and totally designing it with grain whisky in mind. Coffey patented his still in 1830 and the first Coffey Still was installed at Grange Distillery, Alloa, in 1834 by Andrew Philip.

This had huge implications for the industry as it greatly increased the sheer quantities of whisky that could be made. At first there was little difference in cost between malt and grain whisky. While a large pot still would cost £200, a Coffey (or Patent) Still would cost over £2 000 - and every other piece of ancillary equipment would have to be much larger in order to provide the worts required by these enormous stills.

Regardless of the costs, Coffey's still was immediately successful. By 1848 the production of grain whisky in Patent Stills had passed that of pot stills in the UK (much of this coming from England). It is no coincidence then, that this was also the first boom period for blended whisky.

Wheat, maize and barley

There are two main differences between pot still (or single malt) whisky and grain whisky: raw materials and distillation. In order to be called a 'single malt' the only grain allowed is barley which has been malted (a process whereby the grain is allowed to germinate to a point in order to release enzymes that can break down the starch molecules inside the malted barley, turning them into sugar). Grain whisky however, must have a small proportion of malted barley in the mash to break down the other grains used. Normally one of two different grains is utilised: maize (corn) or wheat.

Photo: © North British Distillery

Unloading maize at North British Distillery

Traditionally until about 1984 the main cereal used in grain production was maize (*Zea mays*), which was sourced from North America (and grain whisky made with maize often tastes very similar to Bourbon, also made with a high percentage of corn). This cereal type was attractive to the distiller as it was the cheapest cereal grain available and, importantly, has high levels of starch. There is also some evidence that grain whisky made from corn has a stronger flavour than that from other grains.

Since 1984, soft winter wheat (*Triticum aestivum*) has been the major grain used. This has been mainly due to a rise in import duty and EU measures keeping wheat prices competitive. Having said this however, only three per cent of wheat produced in the UK (approximately half a million tonnes) is used for making Scotch. Maize is still used by a few of the distilleries (notably North British Distillery) and is sourced almost exclusively from the South of France.

Barley is very rarely used as it has high levels of gums although malted barley (between 5 and 15% of the total grain input) is mandatory in the mashing process as all of the enzymes that break down the cereal's starch into fermentable sugars must come from malted barley. Grain that is not turned into malt does not carry enough of these enzymes and artificial enzymes are not allowed. When making the malted barley for grain whisky as opposed to malt whisky the barley is allowed to germinate for longer and goes through a much gentler (if at all) kilning process in order to develop and preserve the enzyme activity.

Photo: © William Grant & Sons

Bottling plant at Girvan Distillery

Photo: © North British Distillery

Column stills at North British Distillery

Photo: © Diageo

Column stills at Port Dundas Distillery

The technique behind grain whisky

The second major difference between malt and grain whisky is a difference in distillation. The Coffey Still was based on the differences in volatility of alcohol and water. Low-pressure steam is injected into the bottom half of the column-shaped still (known as the analyser), the worts are fed in and meets the steam on special plates; this results in a mixture of alcohol vapour and uncondensed steam (the equivalent of low wines in a pot still) rising up to the second half of the column, the rectifier.

In the rectifier the alcohol mixture is progressively cooled to separate the potable spirit. The hot vapours rising through the rectifier partially condenses on the long coil through which the wash is flowing. When the almost pure spirit vapour reaches the top of the column it passes over into a chamber where it is further cooled by incoming wash. Perhaps a lot more complicated than a malt still but the stillman's role is very similar in both distilleries.

Coffey's invention had one further remarkable side effect on the whisky industry. With continuous distillation comes homogeneity in whisky production - something that distillers had been trying to achieve for decades. While this meant that one batch tasted identical to the next, it also removed the regional aspect of Scotch whisky. No longer was it important to be situated near a certain peat or water source. As long as there was a steady supply of the raw materials you could, for the first time, make an exact replica almost anywhere in the world, 24 hours a day and as many weeks in the year as is possible.

Thus the Coffey Still rarely ventured outside of the central belt. Why build a distillery in Campbeltown and then have to ship all of the raw materials, when a distillery in Glasgow, the port of call for the raw materials, would have the same results?
This played a major part in the downfall of some of Scotland's more obscure distilling regions.

Photo: © Diageo

Mash tuns at Port Dundas

The English discover Scotch

Although the Coffey Still was a huge, instrumental part of the grain story, it is only really half of the story. Changing tastes and disappearing stocks of brandy meant that the UK markets (in particular England) began to open up to the distillers. The marketing at the time would have us believe that up until the invention of grain whisky, and the resulting blend of malt and grain whisky, there was no market in the South for the traditional pot still whisky. Surely the English Gentleman would find the harshness of the malt whisky made by those Northern savages too much.

There is, perhaps, a sliver of truth in this marketing strategy, but whisky was rarely marketed for its depth of taste. Rather it played upon its heritage; hailing from Scotland; the land of rugged landscape and good water. Whisky was being depicted as the drink for an old man in his armchair - an image that would last for the next 150 years.

Whatever the reason for whisky's monumental growth in the UK, grain whisky and its part was undeniable. So much so that it caused the larger of the grain distillers to band together to control what is still the most important part of the whisky industry. In May 1856, six Lowland grain distillers created the Scotch Distillers' Association. This lasted until 1876 and from it emerged the Distillers Company.

The Distillers Company (DCL) fought many grain battles in their infancy against the many burgeoning grain producers like England and Germany. The DCL was also instrumental in the development of several technological breakthroughs such as strands of distillers' yeast and non-whisky implications for the Coffey Stills.

However, it was a problem closer to home that revolutionised the face of the Distillers Company. In the latter stages of the 19th century, whisky supply and demand was at its greatest and it was felt that the growth in demand would never stop its giddy rise.

Photo: © Diageo

Wash backs at Port Dundas

Unfortunately one company, Pattison's of Leith, began to speculate and overvalued their stock. What was to be described as '...the most discreditable chapter in the history of the whisky trade', then occurred as the Pattison's crashed and the DCL were on hand to sweep up many of the numerous fallout bankruptcies that followed. The DCL remained the dominant force in grain distilling but also quickly became the largest distiller of malt whisky to boot.

The grain distillers did not get it entirely their own way of course. Malt distillers rallied around and fought their corner; after all 'grain whisky just wasn't the real thing was it!' Things came to a head when the Islington Borough Council decided that too many of their local public houses were selling whisky 'not of the nature, substance and quality demanded'.

At first the law seemed to side with the malt distillers, with magistrate E S Fordham adjudging: '...the so-called blenders have dared to concoct and place upon the market and sell to the retailers raw, new patent still spirit with a mere dash of Irish or Scotch whiskey in it.'

The Distillers Company naturally retaliated and whilst preparations were being made for the second hearing, they released (with much advertising and fanfare) Cambus Pure Patent Still Scotch Grain Whisky. The advertising slogan played upon the purity of the spirit claiming 'Not a headache in a gallon'. This tactic proved popular with the London and national press who were avidly covering the story.

The efforts of the grain distillers eventually succeeded and the Royal Commission (set up to determine 'What is Whisky?') delivered their historic verdict in June 1908. The outcome concluded:

1. *That no restrictions should be placed upon the processes of, or apparatus used in, the distillation of any spirit to which the term 'whiskey' may be applied as a trade description.*

2. *That the term 'whiskey' having been recognised in the past as applicable to a potable spirit manufactured from (1) malt, or (2) malt and unmalted barley or other cereals, the application of the term 'whiskey' should not be denied to the product manufactured from such materials.*

Grain whisky takes a place in the bar

The rest, as they say, is history. Blended whisky went on to conquer the world and is now the best selling spirit in the world. That is not quite where the story ends though. Malt whisky was to make its comeback 70 years later and with the resurgence of malt whisky came a spin-off niche market for single grain whisky. Today, although there are only seven working grain distilleries, there are more bottled expressions of grain whisky than ever before.

There are certain limitations to grain whisky especially when compared to malt whisky. Firstly, the production methods purposefully try and create as neutral a spirit as possible in order to ensure only a minimal contribution to a blended whisky (the major flavours coming from the malt whisky). But even more important than the production techniques are the maturing policies.

Oak casks contribute as much as 80% of the flavour of whisky and grain whisky, for the most part, is matured in very old, used oak casks. This means that even after 10 years of maturation, the whisky is quite colourless and lacking noticeable flavour development. This is one of the main reasons why older blended whiskies have higher malt whisky contents than younger blends. Too much old, under flavoured and light in colour grain whiskies would be noticeable in an old blend (although colour can be altered).

Grain whisky is produced and matured to be used at the first opportunity. For the majority, this means it is bottled quite soon after its third birthday. For the majority of the rest, it is destined for those blends with age statements. Some casks, though, are not used and continue to mature into their twenties and thirties, and due to the nature of the casks being used, it can often take twenty or thirty years for the cask to mature the spirit, although there have been and are noticeable exceptions.

One of the more deluxe of the grain whiskies is a 1964 bottling from Girvan Distillery. Girvan Distillery was built by William Grant & Sons as a result of supply barriers put up by the grain distillers. It is not the newest grain distillery in Scotland, the newest being Loch Lomond, but it is certainly the largest. Loch Lomond itself makes numerous different whiskies using a combination of different stills - some malt, some grain and some a mixture. When you take into consideration the number of bottlings from independent bottlers then there are plenty to choose from.

Grain whisky is often referred to as the poor sibling to malt whisky. Whilst this is for the most part an acceptable comment, there is a belief now that some grain whisky is up there with malt whisky. Certainly with bottlings of Invergordon, North British and the world's first vatted grain whisky Hedonism (made by Compass Box, London), there is a greater understanding of the taste and class that some grain whisky possesses. It will never take the place or even challenge malt whisky, but it is a delightful little extra to whisky drinkers the world over.

Current Grain Distilleries Operating

Strathclyde Distillery..Chivas Brothers
Founded 1927

Girvan Distillery..........William Grant & Sons
Founded 1963

Invergordon ....Whyte & Mackay
Founded 1959

North British...............Diageo/Edrington
Founded 1885

Port Dundas................Diageo
Founded 1811

Cameronbridge..........Diageo
Founded 1824

Loch Lomond.............Loch Lomond Distillery
Founded 1994

Total output over 200 million litres

David Stirk was born in Ripon in 1976. By his mid-twenties he had visited most of Scotland's distilleries and contributed to Whisky Magazine before writing the Malt Whisky Guide *(GW Publishing, 2002) and* The Distilleries of Campbeltown *(Neil Wilson Publishing, 2005). He is now involved in bottling small batch vatted and single malt whiskies (www.creativewhisky.com).*

Girvan 1964 single grain

Whisky marketing

getting more complicated

The days when whisky producers knew exactly what their customers looked like and what they wanted are long since gone. Competition from other drinks has stiffened and intuition, empathy and inventiveness are a must when approaching new consumers. Dominic Roskrow takes a look at what the marketing people are up to.

A tour guide is showing a group of visitors around a Scottish distillery and they have reached the end and are about to have the chance to taste some malt whisky. The guide pours the malt.

"You should drink it straight, with nothing added," he tells his guests.

"That's not the Scottish way," says one of the group. "The correct way is to add a small quantity of water to the whisky to release the aromas."

"Rubbish," says another voice. "That's not the Scottish way. Everyone knows that Scotch can only truly be appreciated over ice."

The tour guide is perplexed but spotting the distillery manager he tells his group to wait a minute while he goes and checks. So he goes over to the distillery manager.

"We're having a bit of a debate over the correct way to drink whisky in Scotland," he says. "I told them that you should drink it straight with nothing added."

"No, no, no," says the distillery manager. "That's not the Scottish way."

"Well, one of the group suggested adding a small amount of water to release the aromas," continues the guide.

"Ach, no, that's not the Scottish way," says the manager.

"Well is it to add ice like one of the others says?" asks the guide.

"No, that certainly isn't the Scottish way," says the manager.

"Well what is?" says the exasperated guide. "Hurry, I need to say something because they're all arguing among themselves back there."

"Ah," says the manager, "now THAT'S the Scottish way."

If it's a truism that Scots in general can find opposing views to any situation then it's twice as true in 2007 and in the world of whisky. Malt whisky in particular finds itself at a major crossroads and the direction it eventually goes in will dictate just how successful malt whisky producers will be in the decades to come. And key to that future is the way whisky is marketed.

The choice facing the industry is a relatively simple one: do the whisky companies stay close to a tried and tested formula and invoke the lochs and bens, the tartan and the grouse, but risk alienating a new generation of drinkers who don't like the older image of the spirit? Or do they appeal to a new generation with slick imagery and trendy names and risk reducing their whiskies to faddish products, at the whim of fashion while driving away their traditional core market?

Price and image - key factors in the US

The debate itself isn't new in itself and in some quarters has already been progressed to some fairly advanced levels. But events across the world have conspired to make the stakes higher than ever. The expansion of potentially huge markets in Russia, China, South East Asia and India, the whisky companies are playing hardball and they know it.

But it's the North American market that is making the issue of marketing malts so interesting. For not only is the demand for them rising, but the marketeers are having to deal with conflicting demands of the American consumer.

At the heart of the debate are two stark and contrasting factors; one, what price the American market is prepared to pay for premium quality Scottish malts; and two, what sort of image those malts need to have to be perceived in the market as a premium product. Both debates are linked to the same fundamental problem: that America is a patchwork quilt of small markets covering everything from the sophisticated front line players in large cities such as New York through to the much larger mass of conservative states of middle America.

An events organiser from Scotland, attempting to achieve funding from tourist authority Visit Scotland for an event during Tartan Week in America, summed up the dilemma.

"The image that Visit Scotland wanted to put across was of a modern and youthful country with great outdoors sports, particularly modern and exciting ones to appeal to the young such as mountain biking and white water rafting," he said.

"What the Scottish American associations wanted, however, was lots of kilts and tartan, and small girls doing exhibitions of Highland dancing. On the one hand was this view of Scotland as a forward-thinking playground for modern youth, and on the other, of a country with the best but most traditional branding in the world. The two don't fit."

Photo: © William Grant & Sons Ltd.

Major William Grant - a traditional whisky icon

How to attract young people

And the dilemma continues in to the world of whisky. Ken Weber, global director for Sazerac, argues that the vast majority of the many markets in America are still driven by price.

"America is a series of local markets," he says. "And in terms of pricing structure you're looking at an inverse pyramid, with the vast majority of liquor sales still coming from very cheap products. It's very hard to change that."

To a great extent Scotch whisky in general, and increasingly for malts in particular, are already well placed to take advantage of a premium positioning. Its reputation for quality coupled with strong heritage and regional identity place it in a privileged position in the style bars of New York, and the golf and sailing clubs of the west coast.

The problem facing Scotch in this scenario, however, is how to maintain its exalted position while making itself relevant to a new generation of drinkers who don't want to be associated with anything their fathers drank. Can it be done?

According to Ken Grier, director of malts for the Edrington Group, producers of The Macallan and Highland Park, the answer is an emphatic yes. It's exactly the sort of dilemma that a highly developed brand such as The Macallan has had to face up to.

"Our strategic aim is to put The Macallan in to a category so that when people think of a luxury drink they think of it automatically," he says. "But obviously not every drinker wants

Monkey Shoulder Manhattan - neither food nor drink

Photo: © William Grant & Sons Ltd.

the same thing so the task is to provide a range of whiskies that meet the demands of the consumer but are linked by the same high quality."

"Traditionally The Macallan has been a whisky with a strong sherry influence produced by using the finest sherry casks from Spain. But that taste doesn't suit everyone and might be perceived by a younger drinker as a taste associated with their fathers."

"Our response to that was to introduce the Fine Oak range. It is still very much a Macallan product but it has a different taste, is packaged in a modern and stylish packaging, and is bringing in a new generation of drinkers without sacrificing any of The Macallan's core values."

Trying to satisfy a range of different palates across the world is a delicate process. Never has the old adage 'don't throw the baby out with the bath water' been more applicable. In Taiwan, for instance, it's the demand for sherried whisky that is dominating the market, so much so that Diageo has set about challenging the dominant position of The Macallan by launching a sherried malt created specifically for that market.

Vatted malts set a new trend

This level of innovation is indicative of a general marketing move to mine new areas within the strict boundaries imposed on the production of Scotch whisky. And the area where there has been most progression is in the area of vatted malts, or as they are increasingly and controversially referred to, blended malt whiskies.

The mixing of malts from different distilleries isn't new of course, but the sector came alive a couple of years ago when Diageo mixed Cardhu single malt with malts from some of its other lesser-known distilleries and retained the Cardhu name. The ensuing row is well documented and not worth revisiting here, but the ensuing fallout resulted in a redefining of terms used to describe a mix of malts, and the introduction of the 'blended malts' tag.

And it's in this area that innovation and progressive marketing has been most advanced, with independent bottlers such as Duncan Taylor, Compass Box and Dave Mark & Robbo's Easy Drinking Whisky Company in breaking down stereotypic marketing rules and replacing them with an image makeover. Products with names such as Peat Monster, Smokehead, and the Smoky, Peaty One have become commonplace and stylish and modern labelling has replaced the traditional distillery name and age statements.

Perhaps the most successful whisky in the category is Monkey Shoulder, produced by William Grant & Sons. It is a mix of three malts, showcasing malt whisky in the best possible light, but it has won over the hearts of some of London's most stylish trend-setters.

"A drink like Monkey Shoulder allows you to break the rules to a great extent," says the company's head of public relations David Hume. "You can still focus on the fact that it is a mix of malt whiskies but we have been able to put it in to a new context and get the style bars interested."

Casino nights, retro bowling evenings and in-club tasting sessions have brought Monkey Shoulder in contact with a younger audience and proved beyond doubt that a younger audience can be turned on to malt whisky. Monkey Shoulder has been able to move in to areas such as cocktails and food pairings too, both of which hold considerable mileage for the future marketing of whisky.

Indeed the whisky has managed to combine both with the innovative creation of the Monkey Shoulder Manhattan, a cocktail that is neither food nor drink, having the constitution of an oyster. It's made by using gelatine in the cocktail mix, and it's served off a spoon, creating a talking point from the off.

Whisky caviar

Such lateral thinking may well be the future for the marketing of malts and it's a route that companies such as Diageo have already taken, not necessarily in the malt sector just yet but certainly with whisky.

Charles Allen, global director, whisky(e) portfolio brands for Diageo, argues that whisky has to rise to the challenge provided by the vodka and tequila sector.

"It is no coincidence that these are the most dynamic spirits sectors, where the products are fuelled by innovation," he says.

"It is never easy to sell consumers on a brand new idea because there is always inertia and reticence. It is even harder in whisky where consumers often buy in to the product for

Photo: © Diageo

Ad for J&B Caviar Night in Brussels

its never changing consistency, its sense of tradition. We have to overcome this but we have the weight of the whisky sector on our shoulders."

But Diageo is rising to the challenge with brands such as J&B. A clear version of the whisky, an expression known as Nox and marketed in luminous blue bottle to attract attention on the night club shelf, a version of the whisky served in a sphere and a whisky caviar which like the Monkey Shoulder Manhattan uses gelatine to create the fish roe effect, are all examples of how a whisky brand might move forward as it attempts to market itself to a new generation of drinkers.

"We have to view the situation from new angles," says Allen. "If you look at music you see how we have changed the way in which we enjoy it. That sort of approach has to be applied to sectors such as whisky."

The conflict between tradition and innovation

On a retailing front too, the next battle may well be in the High Street, as the industry tries to reach out to new drinkers.

Ian Bankier, chief executive of The Whisky Shop, a British chain that is now reaching out to city centres in England, argues that there is a great untapped market for the whisky trade.

"I'm interested in women, in people who say they don't like whisky but haven't tried it for years or have tried very little, in people who think it isn't a drink for them," he says.

"The challenge of the industry is to get to these people and offer them a choice. In that way they can be led to something they like."

One of the biggest challenges facing malt whisky is how it can continue to push at the boundaries when what constitutes what can be called Scotch whisky is so rigidly defined.

That boundary has already been called in

John Glaser and bottles from his Compass Box range of whiskies

Ian Bankier, Chief Executive of The Whisky Shop chain

to question by the likes of Bruichladdich and Compass Box, neither of which are members of the Scotch Whisky Association and who fight fiercely for their independence. It might be that both companies will be prepared just to release new drinks and not use the descriptor 'Scotch whisky', as Compass Box did with its Orangerie launch – which contained orange peel and spices and which it described as a 'whisky infusion'.

Compass Box's John Glaser is widely recognised as one of the whisky industry's true innovators and he has done a great deal to attract new drinkers, particularly women, in to the sector. He believes that as companies continue to search for new ways to market their products they will walk on the rail track parameters imposed on them by the SWA.

It has already happened to Compass Box with the launch of The Spice Tree, a truly stunning product made with the finest products including the finest French oak – and therein lies the problem. For under SWA rules, the addition of toasted staves in to a cask fall outside the definition of what can be called Scotch whisky.

"So we have a problem here," says John. "It's okay to mature malt whisky in Scotland for three years in old and shot casks and then add to a large amount of poor quality grain whisky and call it Scotch whisky but it is not permissible to make a product of the finest quality using the very best ingredients because of the definition."

"The SWA says it is not a judge of quality just of practice. But this raises a big question that needs to be addressed in the future."

With whisky companies searching out new ways to move the whisky category forward and to win back vodka and tequila drinkers to whisky, he has a point.

But no matter what direction that debate goes in, one thing is absolutely clear – there will be no one clear path to follow as whisky companies attempt to woo new markets and new drinkers while keeping the existing ones happy. The debate between old and new, modern and traditional and young and old will continue in typically Scottish fashion.

And as a marketing man might put it – watch this (ad) space.

Dominic Roskrow is consultant editor to Whisky Magazine, which he also edited for four years, and is East of England regional manager for The Whisky Shop chain, for whom he has just set up a shop in Norwich. He has been writing about drinks for 15 years and has edited a number of drinks-related magazines. His new writing, consultancy and hospitality business is called True Spirit. He lives in Norfolk, home of Whisky Magazine and England's first malt whisky distillery, and is married with three children.

Oak maturation

– required by law, essential to quality

The transformation of raw spirit into whisky can be ascribed mainly to the magic of oak. Different varieties of oak, types of casks and methods of preparation amalgamate into hundreds of possible combinations. Charles MacLean gives a clearer picture.

Once upon a time, new Scotch spirit could be filled into any kind of wood, but now only oak may be used: whisky cannot legally be called 'Scotch' unless it has been matured for a minimum of three years in 'oak casks of a capacity not exceeding 700 litres', and this in an excise warehouse in Scotland. Somewhat surprisingly, the requirement was only enshrined in law in 1988: previous definitions demanded only that the spirit be matured in 'wooden casks', and I have been told that there may still be the occasional Spanish chestnut cask lurking in the murky depths of remote warehouses...

However, for centuries oak has been the wood of choice for the whisky, wine and beer industries. It is the only wood that meets these industries' five essential requirements:

1. it does not impart an obnoxious flavour to its contents (in fact, it does the opposite)
2. it is hard-wearing
3. it is capable of being bent, when heated, without cracking
4. its grain is so tight that the liquid will not leak out (if the staves are properly cut!)
5. the pores in the wood allow the contents of the cask to 'breath'.

European Oak (*Quercus robur*)

Until 1946, most of the oak used for maturing whisky was European (*Quercus robur*). After that date an increasing amount of American oak (*Q. alba*) has been used, so that today 95% of the wood coming into the system is American.

The best oak came from Russia. It was generically called 'Memel Oak', after the port of Memel on the Baltic – named Klaipeda since 1945, when it became part of the Lithuanian Soviet Socialist Republic – and after the river of the same name, better known as the Nemen.

Memel was founded by Teutonic Knights of the Livonian Order in 1250; it became part of Prussia and remained so until after World War I, when it was made a protectorate. In 1923 it

Photo: © William Grant & Sons Ltd

was annexed by Lithuania, which surrendered to the Nazis in May 1939. The city was captured by the Red Army in January 1945. The River Nemen rises in Belarus, near Minsk, and flows for nearly 1 000 km through Lithuania, once forming the border between Poland and Russia, before debouching into the Baltic Sea near Klaipeda. British traders established sawmills in the town in the mid-1700s, and thus stimulated what became a major market in oak timber, grown in the vicinity of the river.

'Memel' oaks were tall and straight. Protected in their youth by surrounding, faster growing fir-trees, they later had to fight against the same firs for light and air, so grew tall and straight, with few branches and without any twists in the grain – ideal for coopering. Trees were felled in the winter, and either floated down to the port, or cut into staves and dried in the forest, then transported by rail. At the port they were graded by quality and length – there were seventy-two different sizes of Memel specification; top quality staves were marked with a crown.

It was reckoned that 100 cubic metres of oak yielded only 25 cubic metres of staves, so they were expensive, but it was said that "the Crown Memel Oak Stave is as near perfect as any oak". The late George Urquhart of Gordon & Macphail adds: "You could use these casks for 100 years, they were so strong, with great thick staves".

By contrast, English and Scottish oak trees (also *Q. robur*) grow in solitary splendour or in spacious woods. They tend to be twisted, with branches springing out close to the ground, giving rise to short trunks and many knots – not the kind of wood a cooper wants. They mature very slowly, which makes them at once very hard (so difficult to work) and more porous (and therefore liable to leak) than their quicker growing European cousins.

Spanish oak (also *Q. robur*) was common, on account of the popularity of sherry in the U.K. The wood itself is grown in Galicia, Northern Spain, cut into stave-lengths there and air dried for around two years before being shipped to Jerez, where drying is completed and the casks made. Sherry was shipped in bulk (i.e. in the cask) and bottled by the shipper in the U.K. The desirability of 'sherry-wood' for maturing whisky is recorded as early as the 1860s, but as sherry's popularity declined in the 1970s, fewer such casks were available to the whisky industry, and the problem was compounded in 1983 when shipping sherry in bulk was banned by the E.C.

Today, whisky companies like Macallan which want Spanish casks now have to buy their wood 'on the tree', have it staved and coopered in Spain, and make special arrangements with Spanish bodegas to have them 'seasoned' with sherry before they are shipped.

Limousin oak (also *Q. robur*) from France was more commonly used by the whisky industry when wines were shipped in bulk, although it was never as highly esteemed as 'sherry-wood'. Today, a small number of malt whiskies from The Glenlivet, Glen Moray and Glenmorangie in particular, use 'French oak' as finishing casks.

American White Oak *(Quercus alba)*

The vast increase in production of Scotch whisky since World War II has been made possible by the availability of American oak, ex-Bourbon barrels. These were almost unknown pre-1946, and their availability in large numbers since that date is simply explained: shortly before the outbreak of the war (around 1936) the American coopers' unions brokered a deal with the U.S. distillers that whiskey must be filled into new wood if it was to be described as 'Bourbon', 'Rye', etc.

The massive increase in international demand for Scotch was mirrored by a demand for American whiskey, so there were plenty of ex-Bourbon barrels available to the Scotch distillers. And they came cheap – although the price is now substantially greater, they still cost around one-fifth of the price of a European oak cask.

Bourbon is matured in 'barrels' (holding around 200 litres). Some are shipped as such, and are termed 'American Standard Barrels'. To save space on the ships transporting them, most are broken down into their staves and arrive in bundles called 'shooks'. In Scotland they are re-assembled in a slightly larger format (250 litres, by cannibalising one barrel in three) as 're-made hogsheads'. A cask of this size is easier to handle (you don't have to bend over so far to roll it around!), and it is generally believed that it matures its contents at the optimum rate. Notwithstanding this, and with the increased use of machines to move casks around, many distillers are currently filling more ASBs, which mature their contents more rapidly than hogsheads.

Photo: © Chivas Brothers

Photo: © SWA

A glossary of terms – cask types and capacities

Gorda *(600-700 litres, variable)*
Also called 'bodega butt', these large vessels are only occasionally used for maturing whisky. More commonly they are used as marrying vats. Principally American oak.

Pipe *(650 litres)*
Formerly used for maturing port, these are tall, slender, many-hooped casks, with thick walls. Invariably made from European oak, they have come to be used by the whisky industry as finishing casks over the last ten years.

Madeira Drum *(650 litres)*
Same shape as a machine puncheon (see below) but dumpier and larger. Invariable made from French oak, formerly filled with Madeira. Occasionally used by the whisky industry as finishing casks.

Butt *(500 litres)*
Formerly used for maturing sherry, or Malmsey. Also a tall, elongated cask with thick walls, but not as tall as a pipe. Almost always made from European oak, although Amontillado sherry is matured in American oak, so the shape is not an infallible guide to the wood type.

Barrique *(300-400 litres, variable)*
Another cask recently adopted by some whisky companies for 'wood-finishing'. They are made from French oak, usually bound with wood strips, and will first have held wine.

Puncheon *(500-545 litres)*
These fall into two styles: the 'machine puncheon' and the 'sherry shape puncheon'. The first and commonest is a squat, dumpy cask with thick walls, were mainly American oak. They were popular with brewers in years gone by and with the DCL and Teachers. Sherry-shape puncheons came from Spain, and are mainly Spanish oak. They look like a shortened butt but shorter, and were filled with sherry, and sometimes later with rum.

Hogshead *(225-250 litres)*
These are the commonest casks used by the whisky industry. The origin of their curious word is obscure, but it is ancient: the capacity of a 'hogges hede' was fixed at 63 'old wine gallons' in 1423. The shape was common throughout Europe, and familiar to the whisky industry, so when American barrels (see below) began to flood in post-1946, they were 're-made' into 'dump hogsheads': five ASBs make 4 hogsheads. Today they are made exclusively from American White Oak.

Barrel *(200 litres)*
'American Standard Barrel' (ASB) to give it its full name - the standard cask for maturing American whiskey. Made exclusively from American White Oak. Increasingly popular (especially with Edrington); being smaller, they mature their contents faster than traditional hogsheads.

Quarter *(50 litres, variable)*
A 'quarter' cask is a quarter of a barrel. In the language of brewers, it is known as a 'firkin'. A 'kilderkin' (not known in Scotch whisky) was half a barrel; an 'octave' was an eighth of a barrel, of half a 'firkin'. Laphroaig have recently introduced quarters as finishing casks. They are highly active.

Blood Tub *(40 litres, variable)*
This is another beer term, but the ever-inventive Bruichladdich Distillery now offers 'blood tubs' for private sale. In days gone by the capacity of the 'blood tub' was similar to that of the 'Anker', a variable capacity small cask, capable of being carried by a man, or a pony. Traditionally ankers was suspended on either side of the beast, and they were sometimes oval in shape, to make transportation easier.

Other terminology

Bourbon Casks/Sherry Casks
Commonly, American oak barrels and hogsheads are called 'Bourbon casks' or ex-Bourbon casks', while butts are called 'sherry casks/ex-sherry casks'. We also often hear about 'sherry-wood' or 'Bourbon-wood'. This simply refers to the first liquid that the cask was filled with, before Scotch.

Toasted/Charred
In order to bend the staves of the cask, they have to be heated, and this is done by rolling the 'raised up cask' (i.e. with the staves straight, and held together by the top two hoops) over a fire pit, and sloshing some water over the interior to create steam while the staves are drawn into shape by a windlass. As a result the interior surface of the cask becomes 'toasted'. In the case of Bourbon casks, a further process sets fire to the interior of the cask to create various degrees of charring, from 'light' to 'alligator'.
Toasting is essential if the cask is to mature its contents. An un-toasted cask, where the staves have been drawn in by steam alone, for example, will not mature its contents, merely imparting a 'green' woody flavour. Toasting

alters the chemical structure of the wood, caramelising hemicellulose in the wood so it adds sweetness and degrading lignin, so it contributes attractive coconut and vanilla flavours. The char itself extracts unwanted flavours, particularly sulphur notes, in exactly the same way as an extractor hood above a kitchen stove.

New Wood Casks

The casks used for maturing Scotch whisky are almost invariably 'second-hand' – they have been used to mature another liquid before being filled with Scotch spirit. The only malt I know that has been wholly matured in virgin casks is Benriach 1980 (26YO); so successful was this that the distillery had more new casks made by Speyside Cooperage, which they filled in 2006. Glenfiddich also uses a small amount of new wood as part of their 'solera' process (see below).

Plain Oak Casks

This is a confusing term, which implies that the cask is new wood, never having been filled before. More often the term is equivalent to 're-fill cask' (see below).

First-fill Casks/Re-fill Casks

The first time a cask is filled with Scotch spirit, it is a 'first-fill cask', sometimes called a 'fresh' cask. Thereafter, most companies simply call the casks 're-fills', although some (notably Glenmorangie) refer to them as 'second-fill' and 'third-fill'.

Rejuvenated Casks

The more times a cask is filled, the less 'active' it becomes, until, after four or five fills (depending on how long each fill has lasted) it becomes a mere container, unable to perform the task of maturation. However, it can be 'rejuvenated' and its activity revived by reaming it out (removing the old char and exposing new wood beneath it), then by re-toasting or charring (see above). The heat treatment is essential to degrade the structure of the wood, and thus re-activate the chemicals which give flavours and develop maturity. Ex-sherry casks will sometimes be refilled for a short period with sherry. Rejuvenated casks do not mature their contents in exactly the same way as first fill/refill casks.

Wood Finishing

Sometimes called, 'wine finishing' or 'double maturation' - is the process by which a whisky that has been matured in one kind of cask (usually a refill cask) is re-racked into another kind of cask (usually a first-fill or wine-treated cask) for the final months or years of its maturation. The second, 'finishing', cask rounds off and adds extra flavours to the mature whisky.

Solera Casks

This term, used by William Grant's for an expression of Glenfiddich, is borrowed from the sherry industry. All sherry is made by the 'solera' system, to ensure consistency of style, and on account of young sherry having the useful characteristic of quickly taking on the character of older sherry, when this is added to it.

The solera consists of a number of butts stacked on top of each other to about four high. The oldest wines are on the floor level, the youngest on the top level. As the older wines are drawn off for bottling, the butts are replenished from the level above, and so on until the top level is replenished with new wine. No more than a third of the wine will be drawn off at a time.

Correctly, an 'ex-solera sherry butt' used for maturing whisky is what it says – a cask that has held sherry for many years within a solera, and whose walls will be saturated with wine. Most 'ex-sherry butts' used for Scotch only hold sherry for about a year, to season the wood. In the case of Glenfiddich 'Solera Reserve', the whisky is matured in traditional re-fill casks, some American, some European, for around 15 years, with a small portion being drawn off and finished in fresh American oak for four months. Then the three constituents are brought together in a large tun, which they call a 'solera vat', where they are mixed. This tun is always kept at least half full. Finally, the whisky is filled into puncheons ('solera tuns') for final marrying.

Photo: Dmitry Plisov

Charles MacLean has spent the past twenty-five years researching and writing about Scotch whisky and is one of the leading authorities.
*He spends his time sharing his knowledge around the world, in articles and publications, lectures and tastings, and on TV and radio. His first book (*Scotch Whisky*) was published in 1993 and since then he has published nine books on the subject, his most recent being* Charles MacLean's Whisky Tales*, published in 2006. He was elected a Keeper of the Quaich in 1992, in 1997* Malt Whisky *won the Glenfiddich Award and in 2003* A Liquid History *was short-listed for the André Simon Drinks Book of the Year prize.*

Malt distilleries of Scotland and Ireland

126 Scottish and Irish distilleries are described in detail on the following pages. Most are active, while some are mothballed, decommissioned or demolished. Some of the latter can be considered 'active' as their whisky is still bottled and sold.

Long since closed distilleries from which whisky is very rare or practically unobtainable are described at the end together with five new and upcoming distilleries.

Japanese malt whisky distilleries and distilleries in other countries are covered on pp. 208-231.

Explanations

Owner:
Name of the owning company, sometimes with the parent company within brackets.

Region/district:
There are three formal malt whisky regions in Scotland today; the Highlands, the Lowlands, Islay and Campbeltown. Where useful we mention a location within a region e.g. Speyside, Orkney, Northern Highlands etc.

Founded:
The year in which the distillery was founded is usually considered as when construction began. The year is rarely the same year in which the distillery was licensed.

Status:
The status of the distillery's production. Active, mothballed (temporarily closed), closed (but most of the equipment still present), dismantled (the equipment is gone but part of or all of the buildings remain even if they are used for other purposes) and demolished.

Tel:
This is generally to the visitor centre, but can also be to the main office.

Visitor centre:
For distilleries having an established visitor centre, it is followed by a rating, e.g. 5/7, which means that the visitor centre has received 5 scores out of 7 possible. The ratings are courtesy of Neil Wilson Publishing and are extracted from *Visiting Distilleries* by Duncan and Wendy Graham (£10, ISBN 1-903238-64-1). Many distilleries accept visitors despite not having a visitor centre. It can be worthwhile making an enquiry.

website:
The distillery's (or in some cases the owner's) website.

Capacity:
The current production capacity expressed in litres of pure alcohol (LPA). In italics for those cases where we have been able to establish actual annual production.

% sold as malt whisky:
The share of the total production which is bottled and sold as single malt. Most owners do not publicize this. Percentages which we have not obtained directly from the owners are followed by 'unofficiall'.

Included in blended (past and/or present):
Gives examples of blended whiskies where the single malt is or has been included.

History:
The chronology focuses on the official history of the distillery and independent bottlings are only listed in exceptional cases. They can be found in the text bodies instead.

Brief distillery glossary

A number of terms occur throughout the distillery directory and are briefly explained here. We can recommend for example *A to Z of Whisky* by Gavin D Smith for more detailed explanations.

Blended malt
A type of whisky where two or more single malts are blended together. The term was introduced a few years ago by SWA to replace the previous term vatted malt. The term is controversial as those who oppose the use of it are of the opinion that it can be confused with 'blended whisky' where malt and grain is blended.

Cask strength
It has become increasingly common in recent times to bottle malt whisky straight from the cask without reducing the alcohol contents to 40, 43 or 46%. A cask strength can be anything between 40 to 65% depending on how long the cask has been matured.

Chill-filtering
A method used for removing unwanted particles and, especially used to prevent the whisky from appearing turbid when water is added. Some producers believe that flavour is affected and therefore avoid chill-filtering.

Continuous still
A type of still used when making grain whisky. The still allows for continuous distillation and re-distillation. Can also be called column still, patent still or Coffey still.

Cooling
The spirit vapours from the stills are cooled into liquids usually by a shell and tube condenser, but an older method (worm tubs) is still in use at some distilleries.

Dark grains
The draff and pot ale from the distillation process is used for making fodder pellets, so-called dark grains.

Drum maltings
The malting method used on all major malting sites today.

Dunnage warehouse
Also called traditional warehouse. The walls are made of stone and the floors of earth. The casks (up to three) are piled on top of each other.

Floor maltings
The traditional method of malting the barley on large wooden floors. This method is only used by a handful of distilleries today.

Lyne arm
The lyne arm leads the spirit vapours from the wash or spirit still to the condenser. The angle of the lyne arm has great significance for reflux and the final character of the whisky.

Mash tun
The procedure after the malt has been milled into grist is called the mashing. The mash tun is usually made of cast iron or stainless steel, but can sometimes be made of wood. The grist is mixed with hot water in order to release the sugars in the barley. The result is the wort which is drawn off through a perforated floor into the underback. The mashed grains in the mash tun are called draff and are then used for making animal feed.

Pagoda roof
A roof shaped as a pagoda which was built over the kiln to lead the smoke away from the drying peat. The pagoda roof was invented by the famous architect Charles Doig. These days pagoda roofs provide mainly aesthetical value as the majority of distilleries usually buy their malt elsewhere.

Peat
A soil layer consisting of plants which have mouldered. Used as fuel in drying the green malts when a more or less peaty whisky is to be produced. In other cases the kiln is usually heated by oil or gas.

PPM
Abbreviation for Parts Per Million. This is used to show the amount of phenols in the peated malt. Peated Islay whisky usually uses malt with 40-60 ppm, which is reduced to 10-20 ppm in the new make spirit.

Purifier
A device used in conjunction with the lyne arm which cools heavier alcohols and lead them back to the still. A handful of distilleries use this technique to make a lighter and cleaner spirit.

Racked warehouse
A modern warehouse with temperature control and built-in shelves. Casks can be stored up to a height of 12.

Reflux
When the heavier vapours in the still are cooled and fall back into the still as liquids. The amount of reflux obtained depends on the shape of the still and the angle of the lyne arm. A distillation process with high reflux gives a lighter, more delicate spirit while a small amount of reflux gives a more robust and flavour-rich whisky.

Saladin box
A method of malting barley which replaced floor maltings. It was invented by the Frenchman Charles Saladin in the late 19th century and was introduced in Scottish distilleries in the 1950s. The only distillery using the method today is Tamdhu.

Shell and tube condenser
The most common method for cooling the spirit vapours. It is a wide copper tube attached to the lyne arm of the still. Cold water is led through a number of smaller copper pipes and cools the surrounding vapours.

Spirit still
The second still, usually a little smaller that the wash still. The low wines are collected in the spirit still for redistilling. Alcohol increases to 64-68% and unwanted impurities disappear. It is only the middle fraction of the distillate (the cut) which is utilized.

Vatted malt
See blended malt.

Washback
Large tubs of stainless steel or wood in which fermentation takes place. Yeast is added to the worts and the sugars change into alcohol. The result is a wash with an alcoholic content of 6-8% which is then used for distillation.

Wash still
The first and usually largest of the stills. The wash is heated to the boiling point and the alcohol is vaporized. The spirit vapours are cooled in a condenser and the result is low wines with an alcohol content of c 21%.

Worm tub
An older method for cooling the spirit vapours in connection with distilling. This method is still used in approximately ten distilleries. The worm tub consists of a long, spiral-shaped copper pipe which is submerged in water in a large wooden tub, usually outdoors. The spirit vapours are led through the copper spiral so they can condense.

Aberfeldy

Owner:
John Dewar & Sons (Bacardi)

Region/district:
Eastern Highlands

Founded:
1896

Status:
Active

Tel:
01887 822010 (vc)

Visitor centre:
Yes (5/7)

website:
www.dewarswow.com

Capacity:
2 100 000 litres

% sold as malt whisky:
1%

Included in blended (past and/or present):
Dewar´s White Label

History:

1896 – John and Tommy Dewar embark on the construction of the distillery a stone's throw from the old Pitilie distillery which was active from 1825 to 1867. Their objective is to produce a single malt for their blended whisky - White Label.

1898 – Production starts in November.

1917-19 - The distillery closes.

1925 – Distillers Company Limited (DCL) takes over.

1930 – Operations are transferred to Scottish Malt Distillers (SMD).

1972 – Reconstruction takes place, the floor maltings is closed and the two stills are increased to four.

1991 – The first official bottling is a 15 year old in the Flora & Fauna series.

1998 – Bacardi buys John Dewar & Sons from Diageo at a price of £1 150 million. Five malt distilleries and Bombay Sapphire Gin are included in the purchase.

2000 – A lavish, ground-breaking visitor centre, Dewar´s World of Whisky, opens. It receives some 40 000 visitors annually. A 25 year old is released to commemorate.

2005 – A 21 year old is launched in October, replacing the 25 year old.

Much of the business at Aberfeldy Distillery concerns Dewar's blended whisky, the cornerstone of the group since White Label was introduced in 1899. Slightly more than 50 years later, the 12 year old Ancestor was introduced which was replaced by Special Reserve in 2000, followed by Founder's Reserve (18 years old) and Signature which was launched in 2005. White Label is the world´s fourth most sold blended whisky (number one in the USA) with sales totalling almost 50 million bottles a year. Only 50 000 of these are sold on the domestic market in the UK where a relaunch is in progress. Dewar's also introduced a 15 year old blended malt in spring 2006 aimed at the Taiwan market.

Aberfeldy itself is the staple malt in most of Dewar's blended whiskies. The distillery is situated in Perthshire at the River Tay, just southwest of Edradour and Blair Athol. The visitor centre, Dewar's World of Whisky, which opened in 2000, is very impressive, not least because of its excellent interactivity. The 'Brand Family Room' was added to it in 2006 and includes a huge 'Master Blender's nosing wheel' allowing the over 40 000 annual visitors test their nosing skills. The slightly more than 2 million litres produced at Aberfeldy is tankered away to Stirling for filling on casks and maturation.

There are currently only two official bottlings from the owners Bacardi; a *12 year old* which replaced Diageo's Flora & Fauna 15 years old, and a *21 year old* which replaced the 25 year old launched in 2000.

Independent bottlings have been very rare in recent years.

12 years old

Aberlour

Owner:
Chivas Brothers Ltd (Pernod Ricard)

Region/district:
Speyside

Founded:
1826

Status:
Active

Tel:
01340 881249

Visitor centre:
Yes (7/7)

website:
www.aberlour.com

Production/ year:
3 500 000 litres

% sold as malt whisky:
50% unofficial

Included in blended (past and/or present):
Clan Campbell

History:

1826 – James Gordon and Peter Weir found the first Aberlour Distillery.

1827 – Peter Weir withdraws and James Gordon continues alone.

1879 – A fire devastates most of the distillery. The local banker James Fleming (proprietor of Dailuaine Distillery) constructs a new distillery a few kilometres upstream the Spey river. 1879 is considered by Aberlour as the start of the distillery proper.

1892 – The distillery is sold to Robert Thorne & Sons Ltd who expands it.

1898 – Another fire rages and almost totally destroys the distillery. The legendary architect Charles Doig is called in to design the new facilities.

1921 – Robert Thorne & Sons Ltd sells Aberlour to W. H. Holt & Sons, a brewery near Manchester.

1945 – S. Campbell & Sons Ltd buys the distillery.

1962 – Aberlour terminates floor malting.

1973 – Number of stills increased from two to four.

1975 – Pernod Ricard buys Campbell Distilleries.

2000 – Aberlour a´bunadh (meaning 'of the origin' in gaelic) is marketed as a replica of malt made in James Fleming's time. A limited-edition 30 year old cask strength is released.

2001 – Pernod Ricard buys Chivas Brothers from Seagrams and merges Chivas Brothers and Campbell Distilleries under the brand Chivas Brothers.

2002 – A new, modernized visitor centre is inaugurated in August.

Aberlour distillery lies unassumingly tucked away on the outskirts of Aberlour on the A 95. Their position on the sales list can be considered anything but modest as an unusually large share of production is destined as single malt. Since more than a decade they have been among the top ten worldwide. Aberlour is a big seller in especially France and they are neck and neck with Glenfiddich as the most sold single malt in the country.

When Aberlour's visitor centre was opened in 2002, the intention was not simply to put together a 30 minute tour followed by a sampling of the standard malt. Instead Aberlour treats visitors to a tour lasting two hours. It includes sampling both wort and wash, tasting six different malts in the product range and, against an additional fee, the opportunity of filling a bottle of whisky straight from one of two available casks. Although the number of visitors per year is still not in the same league as some of the other Speyside distilleries', the quality of the tours is high.

The core range of Aberlour includes a *10 year old (sherry/bourbon)*, a *15 year old sherry finish* and *a'bunadh* of which there are 16 batches launched up to and including spring 2006. Each batch, lacking age on the label, consists of a number of ex-oloroso sherry casks (ranging from 45 to 100) of different ages. The whisky is bottled at cask strength and is non chill-filtered.

In France, a *12 year Double Cask matured*, a *15 year Cuvée Marie d'Ecosse* and a *Special Reserve* (500 bottles went to France and 500 bottles were sold through the distillery) are available. The Spanish market also has an 'exclusive'- *Distiller's Selection 1988*. Four 'exclusives' are available for the duty free market - *12 year old sherry matured, 15 year old double cask, 1990 vintage* and a *30 year old*.

Aberlour a´bunadh

Allt-a-Bhainne

Owner:
Chivas Brothers Ltd
(Pernod Ricard)

Region/district:
Speyside

Founded:
1975

Status:
Active

Tel:
01542 783200

Visitor centre:
No

website:
-

Capacity:
4 000 000 litres

% sold as malt whisky:
n/a

Included in blended (past and/or present):
Chivas Regal, 100 Pipers

History:

1975 – The distillery is founded by Chivas Brothers, a subsidiary to Seagrams, in order to secure malt whisky for their blended whiskies. The total cost amounts to £2.7 million.

1989 – Production has doubled.

2001 – Pernod Ricard takes over Chivas Brothers from Seagrams.

2002 – Mothballed in October.

2005 – Production restarts in May.

Braeval, Benriach, Allt-a-Bhainne and Caperdonich were mothballed in October 2002. By May 2005, only Benriach had been reopened by its new owners Intra Trading headed by the whisky veteran Billy Walker. Surprisingly, Allt-a-Bhainne also got a new chance around this time. Its owners Pernod Ricard decided to make Chivas Regal the number one premium blended whisky (to replace Johnnie Walker Black Label at the top). To achieve this they needed all malt output they could muster and Allt-a-Bhainne came on stream again on 27th May 2005. The distillery has operated a mix of five and seven day working weeks since re-opening and will probably operate for 46 weeks a year.

Allt-a-Bhainne lies a few miles southwest of Dufftown along the B9009 towards Glenlivet. Built by Seagrams, Allt-a-Bhainne was the third malt distillery after Braeval and Glen Keith to provide the group with malt whisky for blending. The distillery has two pairs of stills and the whole production can be managed by one person and a remote computer-assisted control unit. The whisky is not filled on casks on site but transported by lorry to a facility in Keith.

There are no official bottlings of Allt-a-Bhainne and according to Chivas Brothers there are no plans for any either.

Independent bottlings are also rare. A couple of the more recent are Gordon & MacPhail (Connoisseur's Choice) 1991 which was released in 2004, a 28 year old from 1975 released by Ian MacLeod the same year and a Signatory 1977 released in 2005.

Cadenhead's Allt-a-Bhainne 1992

Photo: Ardbeg Distillery © Glenmorangie Co

Ardbeg

Owner:
The Glenmorangie Co (Moët Hennessy)

Region/district:
Islay

Founded:
1815

Status:
Active

Tel:
01496 302244

Visitor centre:
Yes (7/7)

website:
www.ardbeg.com

Capacity:
1 000 000 litres

% sold as malt whisky:
75% unofficial

Included in blended (past and/or present):
Black Bottle, Ballantine, Teacher´s

History:
1794 – First record of a distillery at Ardbeg. It was founded by Alexander Stewart.

1798 – The MacDougalls, later to become licensees of Ardbeg, are active on the site through Duncan MacDougall.

1815 – The current distillery is founded by John MacDougall, son of Duncan MacDougall.

1853 – Alexander MacDougall, John's son, dies and sisters Margaret and Flora MacDougall, assisted by Colin Hay, continue the running of the distillery. Colin Hay takes over the licence when the sisters die.

1888 – Colin Elliot Hay and Alexander Wilson Gray Buchanan renew their license.

1900 – Colin Hay's son takes over the license.

1959 – Ardbeg Distillery Ltd is founded.

1973 – Hiram Walker and Distillers Company Ltd jointly purchase the distillery for £300 000 through Ardbeg Distillery Trust.

1974 – Widely considered as the last vintage of 'old, peaty' Ardbeg. Malt which has not been produced in the distillery´s own maltings is used in increasingly larger shares after this year.

Distillery Manager Stuart Thomson, in many ways the man behind the rebirth of Ardbeg, left the distillery during 2006.

The enthusiasm of the Ardbeg fanbase is unique for several reasons. Firstly, Ardbeg is a truly great whisky ranked highly by experts. Secondly, it is an Islay whisky with great appeal to peat enthusiasts. Finally, the founding of the Ardbeg Committee which is run by the distillery and counts some 30 000 members mainly from the UK, Sweden, Germany and the US ties the fans together. The Chairman of Ardbeg Committee and also the Distillery Manager since 1997 when Glenmorangie bought the distillery, Stuart Thomson, announced in September 2006 that he is leaving Ardbeg. When Glenmorangie entered the scene in 1997, Ardbeg had completely stopped producing malt between 1982 and 1989 and just made whisky for a few months per year during the period 1989-1996. This means that the availability of old Ardbeg has decreased radically in later years and is also the cause of the 17 year old disappearing.
Ardbeg buys ready malt, specified at 55 ppm, from Port Ellen which gives c 23 ppm in the finished spirit. There is one pair of stills with the spirit still, built as recently as in 2001, equipped with a purifier increasing the reflux. This is, according to Distillery Manager Stuart Thomson, a reason for heavily-peated Ardbeg being thought of as fruitier and lighter than for example Lagavulin and Laphroaig. Ardbeg is stored almost exclusively on bourbon casks in three dunnage and two racked warehouses with a total capacity of 24 000 casks.
Ardbeg's core range consists of *10 year old*, *Uigeadail*, *Lord of the Isles* and *Ardbeg 'Still Young'*. The last (8 years of age) replaces *'Very Young'* which was released in 2004. Next year *'Almost There'* will be released which will be followed in 2008 by the first ten year old distilled since Glenmorangie took over. There is also an abundance of limited editions and vintages. Among recent ones, the *Ardbeg 1974*, *The Oogling* (a Committee Reserve bottling, 3-4 years) and the *Ardbeg 1965* should be mentioned. There are only 261 bottles of the latter, the oldest Ardbeg ever released, and the price is just above £2 000 a bottle. Other unusual bottlings are *Kildalton*, an unpeated malt from 1980, and *Serendipity*, a vatting between Ardbeg and Glen Moray which occured by mistake!
Independent bottlers have certainly taken a liking to Ardbeg. Gordon & MacPhail have released several in their Connoisseur´s Choice series, Douglas Laing recently launched a 14 year old from 1991 and Cadenhead a 12 year old from 1993.

History (continued):

1977 – Hiram Walker assumes single control of the distillery. Ardbeg closes its maltings.

1979 – Kildalton, a less peated malt, is produced over a number of years.

1981 – The distillery closes in March.

1987 – Allied Lyons takes over Hiram Walker and thereby Ardbeg.

1989 – Production is restored with Iain Henderson as Manager. All malt is taken from Port Ellen.

1996 – The distillery closes in July and Allied Distillers decides to put it up for sale during the autumn.

1997 – Glenmorangie plc buys the distillery for £7 million (whereof £5.5 million is for whisky in storage). On stream from 25th June. Ardbeg 17 years old and Provenance are launched

1998 – A new visitor centre opens.

2000 – Ardbeg 10 years is introduced. The Ardbeg Committee (a worldwide forum for Ardbeg fans) is launched and has 30 000 members after a few years.

2001 – Lord of the Isles 25 years and Ardbeg 1977 are launched.

2002 – Ardbeg Committee Reserve and Ardbeg 1974 are launched.

2003 – Uigeadail is launched.

2004 – Very Young Ardbeg (6 years) and a limited edition of Ardbeg Kildalton (1300 bottles) are launched. The latter is a non-peated cask strength from 1980.

2005 – Serendipity is launched.

2006 – Ardbeg 1965 and Still Young are launched. Distillery Manager Stuart Thomson and his wife Jackie, responsible for the visitor centre, leave Ardbeg after nine years.

1972 Vintage

Lord of the Isles

Serendipity

10 years old

Ardbeg Still Young

Ardmore

Owner:
Beam Global Spirits & Wine

Region/district:
Speyside

Founded:
1898

Status:
Active

Tel:
01464 831213

Visitor centre:
No

website:
-

Capacity:
4 200 000 litres
2 907 000 litres

% sold as malt whisky:
0%

Included in blended (past and/or present):
Teacher´s, Ballantine´s

History:

1898 – Adam Teacher, son of William Teacher, starts the construction of Ardmore Distillery which eventually becomes William Teacher & Sons´ first distillery. Adam Teacher passes away before it is completed.

1955 – Stills are increased from two to four.

1973 – A visitor centre is constructed.

1974 – Another four stills are added, increasing the total to eight.

1976 – Allied Breweries takes over William Teacher & Sons and thereby also Ardmore. The own maltings (Saladin box) is terminated.

1999 – A 12 year old is released to commemorate the distillery's 100th anniversary. A 21 year old is launched in a limited edition.

2002 – Ardmore is one of the last distilleries to abandon direct heating (by coal) of the stills in favour of indirect heating through steam.

2005 – Fortune Brands becomes new owner.

Jim Beam Brands took over some 20 Allied spirits and wine brands in summer 2005 for five billion dollars. The emphasis on the whisky side was on Teacher's, but Laphroaig and Ardmore distilleries were also included. The change of ownership seems to have favoured Ardmore. Production increased from three to four million litres thanks to a seven-day week and four new staff. The intention is to boost Teacher's blended whisky where Ardmore plays a significant role, but a new official bottling is also rumoured to be in the pipeline.

Ardmore is one of the most heavily peated malts in Speyside and uses a malt with a phenol level of 12 ppm. The commonest barley variety among Scottish distillers since 2000 is, without comparison, Optic. Ardmore, however, uses 100% Chalice.

An important criterion when selecting barley is the yield of alcohol. Older varieties such as Golden Promise have a yield of 390 litres alcohol/ton barley while Optic and Chalice are closer to 460 litres/ton.

(The figures apply to perfect laboratory conditions, in distillery production they are reduced by 10%.)

Almost all production goes to blended whisky, especially Teacher's Highland Cream, and there are no contemporary official bottlings. The latest was a *12 year old 100th Anniversary* released in 1999.

Several independent bottlers have taken up Ardmore. Among the most recent are a 1993 12 year old from Douglas Laing (Provenance) released in 2005 and a 1992 13 year old from Signatory released in 2006.

Gordon & MacPhail Ardmore 1990

Arran

Owner:
Isle of Arran Distillers

Region/district:
Islands (Arran)

Founded:
1993

Status:
Active

Tel:
01786 431900

Visitor centre:
Yes (5/7)

website:
www.arranwhisky.com

Capacity:
750 000 litres
125 000 litres

% sold as malt whisky:
100%

Included in blended (past and/or present):
Lochranza, Glen Rosa

History:

1993 – Harold Currie founds the distillery.

1995 – Production starts in full on 17th August.

1996 – A 1 year old is released with the text '1 year old spirit' on the label as it is not, in legal terms, whisky.

1997 – A visitor centre is opened by Her Majesty the Queen.

1998 – The first release is a 3 year old (1 000 bottles).

1999 – The Arran 4 years old is released.

2002 – Single Cask 1995 is launched.

2003 – Single Cask 1997, non-chill filtered and Calvados finish is launched.

2004 – Cognac finish, Marsala finish, Port finish and Arran First Distillation 1995 are launched.

2005 – Arran 1996 is launched (6 000 bottles). Two more finishes are launched - Chateau Margaux and Grand Cru Champagne.

2006 – After an unofficial launch in 2005, Arran 10 years old is released as well as a couple of new wood finishes.

The people at Arran distillery have now produced whisky for little more than a decade and 1 200 bottles of their first ten year old was secretly released in autumn 2005, with the official release taking place in 2006. Arran was the first distillery on the island bearing the same name since Lagg distillery closed in 1837. Harold Currie certainly went against convention by opening Arran in the early nineties, a time when many other distilleries were fighting for their survival.
The capacity is 750 000 litres a year with its one pair of stills. In common with Glengyle, they installed washbacks of wood (Larch and Norwegian Spruce) instead of steel although the latter would have been much easier to keep clean and maintain. Wooden washbacks are not uncommon among established distilleries and the use of them shows how deeply valued old production methods are to new distilleries. Arran does, however, not have a mill of its own preferring to buy ready grist from the mainland.
The core range of Arran consists of *Arran Classic* (no age) and the new *Arran 10 years old* (which replaces the non-chillfiltered). Limited editions include *Arran 1996*, *Arran Single Cask* and several wood finishes (among recent are *Montepulciano D`Abruzzo*, *Cream Sherry*, *Lepanto PX Brandy* and *Bourgogne*). New bottlings for 2006 include *Sauternes Finish* and *Hardy Cognac finish*, both at cask strength and the *100% Proof Arran*.
Two different blended whiskies are in production; Glen Rosa and Lochranza. Arran also market a range of blends and malts under the name Robert Burns.

Arran 10 year old

Auchentoshan

Owner:
Morrison Bowmore (Suntory)

Region/district:
Lowlands

Founded:
1823

Status:
Active

Tel:
01389 878561

Visitor centre:
Yes

website:
www.auchentoshan.com

Capacity:
1 650 000 litres

% sold as malt whisky:
n/a

Included in blended (past and/or present):
Rob Roy

History:

1800 – First mention of the distillery Duntocher, which may be identical to Auchentoshan.

1823 – An official license is obtained by the owner Mr. Thorne.

1837-78 – Owned by James and Alexander Filshie.

1878-96 – Owned by C. H. Curtis & Co.

1903 – The distillery is purchased by John Maclachlan.

1923 – G. & J. Maclachlan goes bankrupt and a new company, Maclachlans Ltd is formed.

1941 – The distillery is severely damaged by a German bomb raid and reconstruction does not commence until 1948.

1960 – Maclachlans Ltd is purchased by the brewery J. & R. Tennant Brewers.

1969 – Auchentoshan is bought by Eadie Cairns Ltd who who starts major modernizations in 1974.

1984 – Stanley P. Morrison, eventually becoming Morrison Bowmore, becomes new owner.

1994 – The Japanese firm Suntory buys Morrison Bowmore and thus becomes new main owner of Auchentoshan.

2000 – A cask strength 31 year old is launched in a limited edition.

2002 – Auchentoshan Three Wood, with ten years of maturing in a bourbon cask, one year in an oloroso cask and six months in a Pedro Ximenez cask, is launched in May.

2004 – More than a £1 million is spent on a new, refurbished visitor centre which opens on 1st December. The oldest Auchentoshan ever, 42 years, is released.

2006 – Auchentoshan 18 year old is released.

Triple distillation is often considered as a feature of Lowland whiskies, but Auchentoshan is in fact the only Scottish single malt that is triple distilled (except for Springbank's Hazelburn which was released for the first time in September 2005). Apart from Rosebank, which closed in 1993, and Littlemill, which ceased the practice in the 1930s, one has to go back to the 19th century to find Lowland distilleries practising triple distillation. Despite being situated in the Lowlands, Auchentoshan's water is drawn from Loch Katrine in the Highlands 35 km to the north although the cooling water is taken from a pond on the premises. The pond is an ex-bomb crater, created during the Clydebank Blitz which took place between the 13th and 14th of March 1941 when German Heinkel bombers dropped between 100 000 and 200 000 bombs in the area. More than 4 000 buildings were destroyed and Auchentoshan was heavily damaged.

The core range of Auchentoshan is *Select* (no age statement), *10 years*, *21 years* and *Three Wood*. Limited editions include *17 year old Bordeaux Wine finish* and *Auchentoshan 1973*, both launched in 2005, and an *18 year old* matured in first and second fill Oloroso sherry butts, released in June 2006. There is also a *12 year old* Duty Free exclusive launched in 2005.

In connection with the 2004 Whisky Live in Glasgow, the distillery's oldest-ever malt so far, a *42 year old* bottling was released. The 104 bottles were sold for around £1 200 each.

Recent independent bottlings include a red wine finish from 1981, released by Murray McDavid in 2006, a 1991 by Dewar Rattray and a 10 year old from Douglas Laing.

10 years old *18 years old*

Auchroisk

Owner: Diageo

Region/district: Speyside

Founded: 1974

Status: Active

Tel: 01542 885000

Visitor centre: No

website: www.malts.com

Capacity: 3 100 000 litres

% sold as malt whisky: n/a

Included in blended (past and/or present): J & B Rare

History:

1972 – Building of the distillery commences by Justerini and Brooks (which, together with W. A. Gilbey, made up the group IDV) in order to produce blending whisky. In February the same year IDV is purchased by the brewery Watney Mann which, in July, merges into Grand Metropolitan.

1974 – The distillery is completed and despite the intention of producing malt for blending the first year's production is sold 12 years later as single malt thanks to the high quality.

1986 – The first whisky is marketed under the name Singleton.

1997 – Grand Metropolitan and Guinness merge into the conglomerate Diageo. Simultaneously, the subsidiaries United Distillers (to Guinness) and International Distillers & Vintners (to Grand Metropolitan) form the new company United Distillers & Vintners (UDV).

2001 – The name Singleton is abandoned and the whisky is now marketed under the name of Auchroisk in the Flora & Fauna series.

2003 – Apart from the 10 year old in the Flora & Fauna series, a 28 year old from 1974, the distillery's first year, is launched in the Rare Malt series.

International Distillers & Vintners (IDV) selected the site for this distillery with quality and availability of water in mind. They found Dorie's Well a few miles west of Keith and after analyzing the water in the Glen Spey laboratory concluded that the location was ideal. The area including its water rights was purchased for £5 million in 1970.
The objective of IDV, with big-time selling J & B Rare blended as their flagship, was to secure malt whisky for blending. Despite having expanded capacity for this purpose at Strathmill, Knockando and Glen Spey between 1968 and 1970, it was also necessary to establish Auchroisk. The quality exceeded expectations and a single malt was bottled under the name Singleton. This name was abandoned after a few years and the whisky has since been sold under the name of its distillery.
Auchroisk has four pairs of stills and, compared to a mid-sized distillery, huge storage facilities with a capacity of 265 000 casks which is enough to offer storage to other distilleries as well.
The core range consists of a *10 year old Flora & Fauna* and a *28 year old* released as a *Rare Malt* in 2003.
Independent bottlings are rare. Some of the more recent are a Port Finish 1990 and a Medoc Finish 1994 released by Ian MacLeod in 2004/2005, a 30 year old released by Douglas Laing and a Connoisseur's Choice 1993 released by Gordon & MacPhail.

Rare Malts 1974
28 years old

Flora & Fauna
10 years old

Aultmore

Owner: John Dewar & Sons (Bacardi)

Region: Speyside

Founded: 1896

Status: Active

Tel: 01542 881800

Visitor centre: No

website: -

Capacity: 2 100 000 litres

% sold as malt whisky: less than 1%

Included in blended (past and/or present):
Dewar´s, VAT 69, Johnnie Walker Black Label

History:

1896 – Alexander Edward, owner of Benrinnes and co-founder of Craigellachie Distillery builds Aultmore.

1897 – Production starts.

1898 – Production is doubled; the company Oban & Aultmore Glenlivet Distilleries Ltd manages Aultmore.

1923 – Alexander Edward sells Aultmore for £20 000 to John Dewar & Sons.

1925 – Dewar's becomes part of Distillers Company Limited (DCL).

1930 – The administration is transferred to Scottish Malt Distillers (SMD).

1971 – The stills are increased from two to four.

1991 – UDV launches a 12-year old Aultmore in the Flora & Fauna series.

1996 – A 21 year old cask strength is marketed as a Rare Malt.

1998 – Diageo sells Dewar's and Bombay Gin to Bacardi for £1 150 million.

2004 – A new official bottling is launched (12 years old).

Aultmore, lying in seclusion a few miles north of Keith on the road to Elgin, is the smallest of Dewar's five distilleries. The reconstruction embarked upon by Scottish Malt Distillers (SMD) in the early 1970s did not spare any of the old, original buildings resulting in a rather charmless exterior. In addition, all warehouses were demolished in 1996 and the spirits have been stored off-site since then. The whisky is, however, highly appreciated amongst blenders.
Aultmore has its place in history when it comes to using distillation by-products. The old practice among small, farm distillery owners was to use the draff left in the mash tun as fodder for their livestock. The draff handling became more commercialised in the mid 19th century when it was discovered that it could be dried and turned into pellets, so called 'light grains'. Another spin-off was pot ale, the high-protein residue which is the result of the first distillation in the wash still. Instead of releasing the latter into the rivers, it was used as fertilizer and this is where Aultmore stepped in. The owners embarked on a project in 1952 with the purpose of producing animal fodder instead of fertilizer from the pot ale. The project was successful and the follow-on was to combine the pot ale, concentrated into syrup, and the draff to a fodder product named dark grains. The process was conceived in the USA and introduced in Scotland by Hiram Walker in 1964. The Aultmore facility was reconstructed into a dark grains plant the following year.
Following Bacardi's take-over, small amounts of a new official bottling (*12 years*) appeared on the market in 2004. An Inverarity 10 years old, which was in fact Aultmore, was released as independently bottled by the well-known retailer Loch Fyne Whiskies in Inverarity, Argyll. Signatory and Duncan Taylor both released 15 year olds in 2004 and in late 2005 another 15 year old distilled in 1990 was released by Ian MacLeod (Dun Bheagan).

12 years old

Balblair

Owner:
Inver House Distillers (Pacific Spirit)

Region/district:
Northern Highlands

Founded:
1790

Status:
Active

Tel:
01862 821273

Visitor centre:
No

website:
www.inverhouse.com

Capacity:
1 330 000 litres

% sold as malt whisky:
8%

Included in blended (past and/or present):
Ballantine, Bell´s, Whyte & Mackay, Hankey Bannister

History:

1790 – The distillery is founded by John Ross and is one of few distilleries that can trace their origins back to the 18th century.

1824 – The son Andrew Ross starts taking over, but moves to Brora after a couple of years and John Ross takes over again.

1836 – The founder John Ross dies and Andrew Ross takes over with the help of his sons.

1872 – New buildings replace old, the latter are now used as warehouses.

1873 – Andrew Ross dies and his son James takes over.

1894 – James Ross moves to a new distillery but none of his sons take over. Balnagowan Estate signs a new lease for 60 years with Alexander Cowan. A proviso in the lease states that a new distillery must be built to replace the existing one. He builds it close to the railway, a few kilometres from the old.

1911 – Cowan is forced to cease payments and the distillery closes. The staff sell out the whole stock in the 20-year period until 1932, but no production takes place.

1941 – Balnagowan Estate goes bankrupt and the distillery is put up for sale.

1948 – The lawyer Robert Cumming from Keith buys Balblair for £48 000.

1949 – Production restarts.

1970 – Cumming sells Balblair to Hiram Walker. A third still is installed.

1988 – Allied Distillers (later to become Allied Domecq) become new owners through the merger between Hiram Walker and Allied Vintners.

1996 – Allied Domecq consider moth-balling Balblair but eventually sells to Inver House Distillers.

2000 – Balblair Elements and the first version of Balblair 33 years are launched.

2001 – Thai company Pacific Spirits (part of the Great Oriole Group) takes over Inver House.

2003 – Balblair 33 years wins Whisky Magazine's Gold Award for best mainland whisky.

2004 – Balblair 38 years is launched.

2005 – 12 year old Peaty Cask, 1979 (26 years) and 1970 (35 years) are launched.

Balblair is situated just north of Glenmorangie and is one of the oldest distilleries still in operation. Only Glenturret, Bowmore and Strathisla are older.
Balblair was the sixth Scottish distillery which the Canadian company Hiram Walker bought. It began its offensive with Glenburgie in 1936 and 40 years later they bought their final Scottish distillery, Ardbeg. Hiram Walker was acquired by Allied Distillers in 1988 but less than ten years earlier Hiram Walker had made a bid for Highland Distilleries. A merger would have made the two companies one of the absolutely largest players on the market. The risk of less competition brought with such a merger was stopped by the House of Commons in the name of public interest.
The distillery is equipped with six washbacks made of Oregon Pine and one pair of stills. The dunnage warehouse has a capacity of 28 000 casks and the majority of the production (75%) is sold on the export market.
The core range consists of *'Elements'* (no age but probably not quite as young as five years), a *10 year old* and a *16 year old*. The name Elements was chosen to highlight the fourth element, air, as Ederton, the village where Balblair is situated, is considered to have Scotland's cleanest air. Limited editions include a *26 year old* which replaced the earlier 24 year old, a *35 year old* and a *1992 Peaty Cask*.
Independent bottlings have recently become rarer. Two old ones were released by Gordon & MacPhail in 2006, 32 and 40 years respectively.

10 years old *Elements*

Balmenach

Owner:
Inver House Distillers (Pacific Spirit)

Region/district:
Speyside

Founded:
1824

Status:
Active

Tel:
01479 872569

Visitor centre:
No

website:
www.inverhouse.com

Capacity:
2 000 000 litres

% sold as malt whisky:
3%

Included in blended (past and/or present):
Ballantine, Johnnie Walker

History:

1824 – The distillery is licensed to James MacGregor who operated a small farm distillery by the name Balminoch for decades.

1897 – Balmenach Glenlivet Distillery Company is founded and the name Glenlivet is added to Balmenach.

1922 – The MacGregor family sells to a consortium consisting of MacDonald Green, Peter Dawson and James Watson.

1925 – The consortium becomes part of Distillers Company Limited (DCL).

1930 – Production is transferred to Scottish Malt Distillers (SMD).

1941 – The distillery closes.

1947 – The distillery reopens.

1962 – The number of stills is increased from four to six.

1964 – Floor maltings is replaced by a Saladin box.

1992 – The first official bottling is a 12 year old in the Flora & Fauna series.

1993 – The distillery is mothballed in May.

1997 – Inver House Distillers buys Balmenach from United Distillers.

1998 – Production recommences.

2001 – Thai company Pacific Spirits (part of Great Oriole Group) takes over Inver House at the price of £56 million. The new owners launch a 27 and a 28 year old in their Highland Selection series.

2002 – To commemorate the Queen's Golden Jubilee a limited edition of 800 bottles of 25-year old Balmenach is launched.

The old-fashioned but well-managed distillery Balmenach is situated in the south of Speyside near Grantown-on-Spey. Distillery Manager Dennis Malcolm and his team have put great effort into restoring the quite run-down distillery since Inver House took over in 1997. Malcolm has been back at Glen Grant as distillery manager since March 2006 when their mission was completed.

There is a strong belief in traditions at Balmenach. It is one of few distilleries that still use worm tubs for cooling. The mash tun is made of cast iron save for a beautiful copper lid and the six washbacks are made of Oregon Pine (or Douglas Fir, they are not quite sure themselves). The part of production destined as single malt is stored on site in three dunnage warehouses while the rest is sent away for central storage in Airdrie. Most casks are ex-bourbon although a few sherry casks are also in use.

Regular, official bottlings of Balmenach are still lacking. Virtually no casks were included when Inver House took over which means that an official bottling is not envisaged before 2008-10. Inver House's Highland Selection series included two limited releases (*27* and *28 years* respectively) in 2001 and the following year a *25 year* commemoration bottle on the occasion of the Queen's Golden Jubilee was released. All the Highland Selection stock has been depleted and Inver House has no intention in continuing that series.

There are however two other 'Balmenach' (apart from the Flora & Fauna 12 year old). One is Deerstalker, produced by an independent company called Aberko Ltd in Glasgow. There are two Deerstalker single malts on the market today; 12 and 18 years. Both are actually Balmenach. Deerstalker 10 years has also been introduced recently but is in fact a Braeval single malt.

The other 'disguised' Balmenach is named Ancestral (14 years) and can be found at Inverarity Vaults, famous importer of fine wines and producer of whisky.

Flora & Fauna 12 years old

Balvenie

Owner:
William Grant & Sons

Region/district:
Speyside

Founded:
1892

Status:
Active

Tel:
01340 820373

Visitor centre:
Yes

website:
www.thebalvenie.com

Capacity:
5 600 000 litres

% sold as single malt:
50% unofficial

Included in blended (past and/or present):
Grant´s

History:

1892 – A fire in 1891 destroyed the whole stock of Glenlivet and the blending industry was desperate for Speyside whisky. William Grant sees the opportunity and rebuilds Balvenie New House to Balvenie Distillery (Glen Gordon was the name originally intended). Part of the equipment is brought in from Lagavulin and Glen Albyn.

1893 – The first distillation is made in May.

1955 – The distillery is modernized.

1957 – The two stills are increased by another two.

1965 – Two new stills are installed.

1971 – Another two stills are installed and eight stills are now running.

1973 – The first official bottling.

1982 – Founder's Reserve, in an eye-catching Cognac-reminiscent bottle, is launched.

1990 – A new distillery, Kininvie, is opened on the premises.

1996 – Two vintage bottlings and a port wood finish are launched.

2001 – The Balvenie Islay Cask, with 17 years in bourbon casks and six months in Islay casks, is released.

2002 – Balvenie releases 83 bottles of a 50 year old that has been in sherry casks (cask 191) since January 1952. Recommended price £6 000 a bottle.

2004 – The Balvenie Thirty is released to commemorate Malt Master David Stewart's 30th anniversary at Balvenie.

2005 – The Balvenie Rum Wood Finish 14 years old is released.

2006 – The Balvenie New Wood 17 years old is released.

The premises managed by William Grant north of Dufftown housing Glenfiddich, Balvenie, Kininvie and the old warehouses of closed Convalmore within walking distance of each other, are huge. Even if overshadowed by Glenfiddich, Balvenie is one of the largest distilleries in the industry and has a reputation of its own. It is unique in having both its own floor maltings and a cooperage. The floor maltings stands for less than 10% of the malt needs and the barley comes from its own grounds, Mains of Balvenie. They employ six coopers and all casks forwarded for filling are first quality checked and, if neccesary, repaired by a cooper.

Balvenie comes at 10th place on the list of most sold single malts worldwide. No less than 1 560 000 bottles were sold in 2004 which is an increase of almost 90% the last seven years. The Balvenie *10 year old* is being phased out of the core range and replaced by more of the popular *Doublewood 12 years old*. *Portwood 21 years* is also included in the core range.

A multitude of limited editions are found in addition to these. The latest are *Rum Wood 14 years*, finished for 18 months on rum casks from Venezuela and Guyana, *New Wood*, a 17 year old that has been finished on casks of new oak and *Vintage Cask 1972*. Older limited editions include *Single Barrel 15 years*, *Portwood 1991* (13 years) and *Balvenie 30 years*.

The other distillery on the premises of Balvenie, Kininvie, is used for producing malt whisky for Grant´s blends and it also makes up the major part of Monkey Shoulder, a vatted malt that was released in 2005.

A very limited release of *Kininvie* single malt *15 years old* was launched in August 2006 to celebrate the 105th birthday of Janet Sheed Roberts, the last surviving grandchild of the founder, William Grant.

New Wood 17 years old   Double Wood 12 years old

Banff

Owner:
Diageo

Region/district:
Speyside

Founded:
1824

Status:
Demolished

Tel:
-

Visitor centre:
-

website:
www.malts.com

Capacity:
-

% sold as malt whisky:
-

Included in blended (past and/or present):
-

History:

1824 – James McKilligan & Co. builds the distillery which is known as Mill of Banff and, later on, as Inverboyndie Distillery.

1837 – Major McKilligan dies and Alex Mackay takes over.

1852 – James Simpson takes over together with his son James junior.

1863 – The distillery outgrows itself and James junior builds a new one in the village Inverboyndie which thereafter is called Banff Distillery. The managing company changes name to Simpson & Co.

1877 – On 9th May a fire devastates most of the distillery except the warehouse and the maltings. Rebuilding starts quickly and it is operational again in October.

1921 – The Simpson family sells part of the distillery to Mile End Distillery Company.

1924 – Triple distillation ceases.

1932 – Simpson & Co. files for bankruptcy and Scottish Malt Distillers (SMD) takes over at a price of £50 000.

1941 – A German warplane bombs warehouse number 12 on 16th August and thousands of litres of whisky are destroyed.

1959 – One of the stills explodes.

1983 – Banff Distillery and ten others are closed by DCL.

1985 – The distillery buildings are demolished.

1991 – The remaining buildings are destroyed in a fire.

2004 – Diageo launches a 21 year old cask strength in their Rare Malt series.

BANFF DISTILLERY.

Banff's tragic history of numerous fires, explosions and bombings have contributed to its fame. The most spectacular incident was when a lone Junkers Ju-88 bombed one of the warehouses on 16th August 1941. Hundreds of casks exploded and several thousand litres of whisky were destroyed. The Germans had a slightly different story to tell their public. Lord Haw-Haw (aka William Joyce) broadcasted in his propaganda radio bulletin from Berlin the very same night that a large ammunition depot in Scotland had been destroyed. Joyce was originally American, but he obtained British citizenship due to his Irish roots and he moved to Germany just before the outbreak of WWII where he cooperated with the Germans throughout the war. He was sentenced to death for treason on 19th September 1945 and was hanged in Wandsworth Prison on 3rd January 1946. With such a turbulent history it was no surprise that the last remaining building was destroyed in a fire in 1991 and there is nothing left to see of the distillery today.

The whisky has always been destined for blended whiskies save for a period when it was the 'House Whisky' in the House of Commons. Opinions on Banff's single malts vary, but many appreciate the whisky's ability to mature pleasantly for up to thirty years or more. Banff has only occurred once as an official bottling in the *Rare Malts* series when a *21 year old* from 1982 was released in 2004. Several casks have found their way to independent bottlers after the closure in 1983, among them Gordon & MacPhail, Douglas Laing, Signatory and Cadenhead. Two of the most recent are a Duncan Taylor from 1980 and a 29 year old from Cadenhead.

Rare Malts 1982 21 years old

Ben Nevis

Owner:
Ben Nevis Distillery Ltd (Nikka, Asahi Breweries)

Region/district:
Western Highlands

Founded:
1825

Status:
Active

Tel:
01397 702476

Visitor centre:
Yes (4/7)

website:
www.bennevisdistillery.com

Capacity:
2 000 000 litres

% sold as malt whisky:
n/a

Included in blended (past and/or present):
Dew of Ben Nevis, Glencoe (blended malt)

History:

1825 – The distillery is founded by 'Long' John McDonald.

1848 – Queen Victoria visits the distillery.

1856 – Long John dies and his son Donald P. McDonald takes over.

1878 – Demand is so great that another distillery, Nevis Distillery, is built nearby.

1908 – Both distilleries merge into one.

1941 – D. P. McDonald & Sons sells the distillery to Ben Nevis Distillery Ltd headed by the Canadian millionaire Joseph W. Hobbs. He has already bought Bruichladdich, Glenesk and Glenury Royal and he opens Lochside in 1957.

1955 – Hobbs installs a Coffey still which makes it possible to produce both grain and malt whisky.

1964 – Joseph Hobbs dies and production ceases.

1981 – Joseph Hobbs Jr sells the distillery back to Long John Distillers and Whitbread.

1984 – After restoration and reconstruction totalling £2 million, Ben Nevis opens up again.

1986 – The distillery closes again.

1989 – Whitbread sells the distillery to Nikka Whisky Distilling Company Ltd.

1990 – The distillery opens up again.

1991 – A visitor centre is inaugurated.

1996 – Ben Nevis 10 years old is launched.

2006 – A 13 year old port finish is released.

Ben Nevis, spectacularly situated at the foot of the mountain range bearing the same name, is one of two distilleries in the Western Highlands. The other is Oban. Many people also visit the village Fort William which is reflected in the number of distillery visitors (36 000 a year), which are considerably more than that of more renowned distilleries such as Macallan, Glen Grant and Glenmorangie.

Ben Nevis became the second distillery (following Tomatin) to be acquired by Japanese interests. Nikka Whisky Co. was founded by Masataka Taketsuru who spent some time in Scotland in the 1920s to learn the art of whisky distilling. However, Masataka did not live to experience the takeover of Ben Nevis in 1989. He died ten years earlier and his adopted son Takeshi managed the takeover. Nikka put great effort into refurbishing the distillery. The concrete washbacks which were installed by previous owner Joseph Hobbs were replaced by stainless steel, though the two original pairs of stills remain.

Except for a three-year period, the distillery was closed between 1979 and 1990. A strong supply of older whisky has been built up under the leadership of Distillery Manager Colin Ross, even if the 26 year old cask strength that was introduced a few years ago is now sold out. Since 1996 the core of the range has been a *10 year old*. Some one-off bottlings have appeared with regular intervals, the latest of which is a *13 year old Port finish* from 1990, bottled in 2004 but not released until spring 2006. The distillery also produces a blended malt named *Glencoe 8 years* and a range of blended whiskies called Dew of Ben Nevis. The latest Dew of Ben Nevis was a 40 year old which appeared in 2004. Recent independent bottlings include Signatory 1975 (30 years old), a 40 year old sherry finish from Douglas Laing and a 1996 released by Duncan Taylor.

10 years old

Benriach

Owner: Benriach Distillery Co

Region/district: Speyside

Founded: 1897

Status: Active

Tel: 01343 862888

Visitor centre: No

website: www.benriachdistillery.co.uk

Capacity: 2 800 000 litres
1 300 000 litres

% sold as malt whisky: 20%

Included in blended (past and/or present):
100 Pipers, Chivas Regal, Queen Anne

History:

1897 – John Duff & Company, already owner of Longmorn, founds Benriach Distillery.

1899 – John Duff gets into financial trouble and pawns his company. Finally, the bank sells Benriach to the Longmorn Distilleries Company.

1903 – The distillery is mothballed. The maltings is kept running to supply the 'sister' distillery Longmorn with malt.

1965 – The distillery is reopened by the new owners, The Glenlivet Distillers Ltd, after a major facelift.

1978 – Seagram Distillers plc takes over ownership and transfers the distillery to the subsidiary Chivas Brothers.

1983 – Seagrams starts producing a peated Benriach.

1985 – The number of stills is increased from two to four.

1994 – The first official bottling is a 10 year old.

1999 – The maltings is decommissioned.

2001 – Pernod Ricard takes over Chivas Brothers.

2002 – The distillery is mothballed in October.

2004 – A South African group, Intra Trading, buys Benriach together with the former Director at Burn Stewart, Billy Walker. The price is £5.4 million which also includes 5000 casks aged between 3-34 years.

2004 – Standard (no age), Curiositas (10 years, quite peaty), and 12, 16 and 20 year olds are released.

2005 – Four different vintages are released in limited editions - 1966, 1970, 1978 och 1984.

2006 – Sixteen new releases, among them a 25 year old, a 30 year old and 8 different vintages.

Benriach is one of the easiest distilleries to find when travelling in Speyside. Its large signs just by the A941, the main road between Rothes and Elgin, signal a perfect location for a visitor centre. Perhaps there will be one when the new owners since 2004 headed by whisky veteran Billy Walker have got everything else into place.

Despite being closed for most of the 20th century, it has always been closely associated to its closest neighbour Longmorn. Chivas Brothers and Longmorn still own 11 of the 16 warehouses on the premises. The remaining five house 20 000 casks dating back to 1966. Benriach's floor maltings was closed in 1999 but they are still in excellent condition and the current owners plan to activate them again to produce a small share of the required amounts.

The core range of Benriach is *12, 16* and *20 years old*. As an exciting sidetrack, a number of heavily peated malts are also produced. Malt with 35 ppm phenols was used for the first one, *Curiositas*, which resulted in whisky of 17 ppm. Another peated version is *Authenticus 21 years old*. A number of vintages are found among the limited editions.

The people at Benriach keep themselves pretty busy by launching new expressions.

No fewer than 16 new single malts were launched in 2006. Three were 'oldies' of *25, 30* and *40 years* age. A batch of limited-release *vintages* ranging from *1968* to *1986* with one, the *1980* matured entirely in new wood giving it a bourbon sweetness, was also launched as well as a *15 year old* with four different finishes and, finally, a *peated 12 year old* finished in port pipes.

Independent bottlings of Benriach are becoming exceedingly rare. Some of the latest include a 36 year old from Duncan Taylor, a 15 year old from Douglas Laing and an 11 year old finished in port pipes from Signatory.

12 years old

Vintage 1980

Benrinnes

Owner:
Diageo

Region/district:
Speyside

Founded:
1826

Status:
Active

Tel:
01340 872600

Visitor centre:
No

website:
www.malts.com

Capacity:
2 600 000 litres

% sold as malt whisky:
n/a

Included in blended (past and/or present):
Johnnie Walker Red Label and Black Label, J&B, Dewar´s

History:

1826 – The first Benrinnes distillery is built at Whitehouse Farm by Peter McKenzie.

1829 – A flood destroys the distillery.

1834 – A new distillery, Lyne of Ruthrie, is constructed a few kilometres from the first one. The owner John Innes files for bankruptcy and William Smith & Company takes over.

1864 – William Smith & Company goes bankrupt and David Edward becomes the new owner.

1896 – Benrinnes is ravaged by fire which prompts major refurbishment and rebuilding including electrification. David Edward dies and his son Alexander Edward takes over. Alexander Edward also founds the distilleries Dallas Dhu, Aultmore and Craigellachie and purchases Oban.

1922 – John Dewar & Sons takes over ownership.

1925 – John Dewar & Sons becomes part of Distillers Company Limited (DCL).

1930 – DCL transfers management and operations to Scottish Malt Distillers (SMD).

1955/56 – The distillery is completely rebuilt.

1964 – Floor maltings is replaced by a Saladin box.

1966 – The number of stills doubles to six.

1984 – The Saladin box is taken out of service and the malt is purchased centrally.

1991 – The first official bottling from Benrinnes is a 15 year old in the Flora & Fauna series.

1996 – United Distillers releases a 21 year old cask strength in their Rare Malts series.

Benrinnes certainly does not appear as one of the most beautiful distilleries on approaching it, but its location is stunning. A few miles southwest of Aberlour town and with Glenallachie as its closest neighbour, it is situated in the open countryside with a view stretching for miles towards the 840 metres high Ben Rinnes. The lack of Victorian charm is completely due to Benrinnes being rebuilt in the late fifties. The old worm tubs were kept despite the urge to build a modern distillery and Benrinnes is one of a select few distilleries which cool the spirit vapours this way. They chose to increase to six stills, grouped three and three, when reconstructing. One wash still and two spirit stills in each combination creates a form of partial triple distilling, similar to that of Springbank.

The only official bottling of Benrinnes is a *Flora & Fauna 15 years old*. A very special Benrinnes, was launched in 2003. Tim Morrison, fourth generation descendant of the whisky distributor Dewar Rattray in Maybole, Ayrshire managed to lay his hands on one of the few remaining bottles from the distillery Stronachie which was decommissioned in the 1920s. His objective was to resurrect the name and character of this extinct Perthshire whisky by finding a contemporary whisky with similar characteristics. It led to his bottling of a 12 year old Benrinnes without a mention of Benrinnes on the label. Apart from that, independent bottlings are pretty rare. A few of the most recent ones are Dewar Rattray 14 years old from 1990, a 21 year old from 1984 bottled by Adelphi Distillery in 2005 and a Connoisseur´s Choice 30 years old from Gordon & MacPhail.

Flora & Fauna 15 years old

Benromach

Owner: Gordon & MacPhail

Region/district: Speyside

Founded: 1898

Status: Active

Tel: 01309 675968

Visitor centre: Yes (4/7)

website: www.benromach.com

Capacity: 500 000 litres

% sold as malt whisky: 95%

Included in blended (past and/or present): The Antiquary

History:

1898 – Benromach Distillery Company starts the distillery. Duncan McCallum is one of the owners. The top distillery architect, Charles Doig, makes the drawings.

1909 – The whisky industry has been slow-moving around the turn of the century due to the Pattison crash, but production picks up this year. The distillery operates under the name Forres Distillery for a few years.

1911 – London-based Harvey McNair & Co buys the distillery.

1919 – A well-known brewer from Alloa, John Joseph Calder, buys Benromach but immediately sells it to recently founded Benromach Distillery Ltd owned by several breweries.

1931 – Benromach is mothballed.

1937 – The distillery reopens.

1938 – Joseph Hobbs buys Benromach through Associated Scottish Distillers and sells it on to National Distillers of America (NDA).

1953 – NDA sells Benromach to Distillers Company Limited (DCL). It becomes administered by Scottish Malt Distillers (SMD).

1966 – The distillery is refurbished and improved.

1968 – Floor maltings is abolished.

1983 – Benromach is mothballed in March.

1993 – Gordon & McPhail buys Benromach from United Distillers.

1998 – The distillery is once again in operation and the inauguration ceremony is attended by HRH Prince Charles as officiator. A limited edition 17 year old is released to commemorate this and the 100th anniversary of the distillery.

1999 – A visitor centre is opened.

2000 – Benromach becomes a member of the Malt Whisky Trail.

2004 – The first bottle distilled by the new owners is released under the name 'Benromach Traditional' in May. Other novelties (although distilled in UD times) include a 21 year Tokaji finish and a Vintage 1969.

2005 – A Port Wood finish (22 years old) and a Vintage 1968 are released together with the Benromach Classic 55 years.

2006 – Benromach Organic is released.

When the famous independent bottler Gordon & MacPhail bought Benromach Distillery from United Distillers in 1993, it was quite run-down after having been mothballed for ten years. The only piece of original equipment that was kept was the spirit receiver, everything else was purchased anew. The spirit safe originates from closed-down Millburn distillery and the Boby mill is almost antiquated as it was constructed in 1913. The malt comes from Bairds of Inverness and Glen Esk and is peated at 12 ppm which produces a phenol level of 4-5 ppm in the finished product. Fermentation time is unusually long, 115 hours, and in combination with a broad-necked wash still produces a robust and flavour-rich spirit which is further refined during cask maturation. The stills are indirectly heated by steam plates (rather than steam coils) and the spirit receivers are, unusually, made of wood. Two dunnage warehouses are located on site but part of the production is stored at the owners´ facilities in Elgin. The draff is given to a local farmer who uses it to sustain his cattle year round.

Benromach is the smallest working distillery in Speyside. Only two persons work in the production unit in five-day weeks allowing for a closure for a few weeks around Christmas. Around 5 000 visitors find their way to the distillery annually. The core range of Benromach consists of *Traditional, 18 years old, 21 years old, 25 years old, Cask Strength 1980, Vintage 1968* (replaced the 1969) and *Port Wood finish* (replaced the Tokaji finish). A very limited expression was launched in 2005, *Benromach Classic 55 years*. *Benromach Organic*, the first single malt to be fully certified organic by the Soil Association was launched in spring 2006. Interest was high and the 15 000 bottles sold out in record time. There are no independent bottlings of Benromach.

Benromach Organic

Bladnoch

Owner:
Co-ordinated Development Services

Region/district:
Lowlands

Founded:
1817

Status:
Active

Tel:
01988 402605

Visitor centre:
Yes (5/7)

website:
www.bladnoch.co.uk

Capacity:
100 000 litres

% sold as malt whisky:
n/a

Included in blended (past and/or present):
-

History:

1817 – Brothers Thomas and John McClelland found the distillery.

1825 – The McClelland brothers obtain a licence.

1878 – John McClelland's son Charlie reconstructs and refurbishes the distillery.

1905 – Production stops.

1911 – Dunville & Co. from Ireland buys T. & A. McClelland Ltd for £10 775. Production is intermittent until 1936.

1937 – Dunville & Co. is liquidated and Bladnoch is wound up. Ross & Coulter from Glasgow buys the distillery some time after the war. The equipment is dismantled and shipped to Sweden.

1956 – A. B. Grant (Bladnoch Distillery Ltd.) takes over and restarts production with four new stills.

1964 – McGown and Cameron becomes new owners.

1966 – The number of stills is increased from two to four.

1973 – Inver House Distillers buys Bladnoch.

1983 – Arthur Bell and Sons take over.

1985 – Guiness Group buys Arthur Bell & Sons which, from 1989, are included in United Distillers.

1988 – A visitor centre is built.

1993 – United Distillers mothballs Bladnoch in June, simultaneously with Rosebank, Pittyvaich and Balmenach.

1994 – Raymond Armstrong from Northern Ireland buys Bladnoch in October.

2000 – The agreement with United Distillers limits production to approximately 250 000 bottles a year and production commences in December.

2003 – The first bottles from Raymond Armstrong are launched, a 15 year old cask strength from UD casks.

2004 – New varieties follow suit: e. g. 13 year olds 40% and 55%.

One of the prerequisites when Irish entrepreneur Raymond Armstrong acquired Bladnoch Distillery from Diageo in October 1994 was that it would never again be used as a distillery. But in 2000, after lobbying from the local community and Armstrong, Diageo gave permission for Bladnoch to produce 100 000 litres of alcohol per year.
Bladnoch is the southernmost of the Scottish distilleries and lies almost isolated down at Wigtown Bay. Despite this 27 000 visitors a year find their way to it. It is not just the visitor centre that attracts people to Bladnoch, it has also become a place for Ceilidhs and weddings and hosts a popular whisky school too. As United Distillers had left only stills and washbacks from the original equipment when the distillery was sold, Armstrong's enthusiasm and energy was useful when re-equipping Bladnoch. The distillery now has one pair of stills and the whisky is mainly matured in ex-bourbon casks in one of the 13 dunnage warehouses.
Bottlings from the new production are not expected before 2009, but some official bottlings of stored whisky have been released. These include *13 to 16 year olds* with the Beltie and the Sheep labels and the easiest obtainable right now is probably the *15 year old* at 55%. There is also a peated Bladnoch on its way but this is not expected for a few years yet. One of the more recent bottlings is a *15 year old rum finish*. The old official Flora & Fauna bottling from Diageo is also available on the market.
Recent independent bottlings include a Cadenhead 1989 (16 years), Douglas Laing 1991 (14 years) and Signatory 1992 (14 years).

15 years old

Blair Athol

Owner:
Diageo

Region/district:
Eastern Highlands

Founded:
1798

Status:
Active

Tel:
01796 482003

Visitor centre:
Yes (5/7)

website:
www.malts.com

Capacity:
2 000 000 litres

% sold as malt whisky:
10% unofficiall

Included in blended (past and/or present):
Bell´s, Johnnie Walker Blue Label

History:

1798 – John Stewart and Robert Robertson found Aldour Distillery, the predecessor to Blair Athol. The name is taken from the adjacent river Allt Dour.

1825 – The distillery is expanded by Robert Robertson and takes the name Blair Athol Distillery.

1826 – The Duke of Atholl leases the distillery to Alexander Connacher & Co.

1832 – The distillery closes.

1860 – Elizabeth Connacher runs the distillery.

1882 – Peter Mackenzie & Company Distillers Ltd of Edinburgh (future founders of Dufftown Distillery) buys Blair Athol and expands it.

1932 – The distillery is mothballed.

1933 – Arthur Bell & Sons takes over by acquiring Peter Mackenzie & Company.

1949 – Production restarts.

1973 – Stills are expanded from two to four.

1985 – Guinness Group buys Arthur Bell & Sons.

1987 – A visitor centre is built.

2003 – A 27 year old cask strength from 1975 is launched in Diageo's Rare Malts series.

Blair Athol is one of a select few active distilleries founded in the 18th century. Despite its name, the distillery is not situated in Blair Atholl but rather a few miles south in Pitlochry, very near to Edradour. The Gaelic names of Scottish distilleries often tell something about the surrounding nature, but in Blair Athol's case a lesson in history is given; The name Blair Athol is shortened from Blar ath Fhodla which translates to 'Plain of the new Ireland', Blar being plain and ath second or next. But what about Ireland? This derives from the 6th century when many Irish headed east from Ulster, finally settling in the area of Pitlochry. Fhodla is an old, poetic name for Ireland.

Blair Athol distillery can be considered the home of Bell's Whisky as it contributes strongly to this blend. The two enterprises have been associated long before Bell's takeover of Blair Athol in 1933. Arthur Bell had been employed by Thomas Sandman in his shop in Perth already in 1837 and he started using Blair Athol malt for blending in the late 1850s.

The distillery obtains its water from nearby Allt Dour which is translated as 'Burn of the Otter'. This also explains the otter picture on the official Flora & Fauna bottling.

Official bottlings are scarce. Except for the *12 year old* in the *Flora & Fauna* series and a *27 year old* that appeared in the *Rare Malts* series in 2003, it may still be possible to obtain an *18 year old* bottling from 1998 commemorating the bi-centenary of the distillery.

Independent bottlings are rarely encountered. Among the most recent are two 12 year old from Gordon & MacPhail and Douglas Laing respectively and a 29 year old from Signatory which was released in 2005.

Flora & Fauna 12 years old

Bowmore distillery. Photo: © Morrison Bowmore

Bowmore

Owner:
Morrison Bowmore Distillers (Suntory)

Region/district:
Islay

Founded:
1779

Status:
Active

Tel:
01496 810441

Visitor centre:
Yes (7/7)

website:
www.bowmore.com

Capacity:
2 000 000 litres

% sold as malt whisky:
n/a

Included in blended (past and/or present):
Rob Roy

History:

1779 – Bowmore Distillery is founded by John Simpson and becomes the oldest Islay distillery.

1837 – The distillery is sold to James and William Mutter of Glasgow. James was the Ottoman, Portuguese and Brazilian Vice-Consul.

1892 – After additional construction, the distillery is sold to Bowmore Distillery Company Ltd, a consortium of English businessmen.

1925 – J. B. Sheriff and Company takes over (they also own Dallas Dhu).

1929 – Distillers Company Limited (DCL) takes over.

1950 – William Grigor & Son, Inverness, takes over.

1963 – Stanley P. Morrison buys the distillery for £117 000 and forms Morrison Bowmore Distillers Ltd.

1989 – Japanese Suntory buys a 35% stake in Morrison Bowmore.

1993 – The famous, legendary Black Bowmore is launched. The recommended price is £100 (today it is at least ten times that if it can be found). Another two versions are released 1994 and 1995.

1994 – Suntory now controls all of Morrison Bowmore.

Bowmore Distillery is the flagship of the Bowmore group and its sales are three times that of Auchentoshan and Glen Garioch combined. Sales have been on a steady increase in recent decades. The same applies for Laphroaig which, however, still is a touch ahead as the most sold Islay single malt. The strategy for Bowmore is now to focus on single malts and to play down bulk and blended sales.

Bowmore is one of few Scottish distilleries with its own malting floor. As much as 40% of the malt requirement is produced in-house making Bowmore the distillery that malts the largest quantity in tonnes. The peat is gathered from the nearby Laggan moss. The malt has a specification of 25 ppm and the finished spirit around 10 ppm.

The distillery has two pairs of stills and six washbacks of Oregon Pine. Some decades ago they replaced wooden washbacks with stainless steel. In 1990 they reverted to wood as it was considered more beneficial to the character of the spirit. Laphroaig and Kilchoman are today the only remaining users of stainless steel washbacks on Islay. 27 000 casks are stored in two dunnage and one racked warehouse. The proportion of sherry butts is now lower than before, down to 15%. Bowmore has created a wide product range thanks to experiments with wood finishes and uses a large share of ex-bourbon casks. It has also re-enforced the Islay-character which some malt drinkers previously thought of as disappearing.

Bowmore decided to make a contribution both to the environment and the local community in 1990. They donated the number 3 warehouse to the community, which was then rebuilt into a swimming pool. The water is now heated using hot water from the condensers in the stillroom. The distillery also won the Green Apple award for its environmental work.

Bowmore's assortment is among the greatest on the market (see list on next page) and they have launched a couple of limited expressions quite recently.

There are also a number of independent bottlings. Duncan Taylor 1966, Cadenhead 1991 (14 years), Dewar Rattray 1991, Signatory 1982 (23 years) and a white wine finish from 1995 by Murray McDavid were all bottled in 2006.

History (continued):
1995 – Bowmore is nominated 'Distiller of the Year' in the International Wine and Spirits competition.

1996 – A Bowmore 1957 (38 years) is bottled at 40,1% but is not released until 2000 (861 bottles).

1999 – Bowmore Darkest with three years finish on oloroso barrels is launched. A limited edition Claret cask strength is also released in 12 000 bottles.

2000 – Bowmore Dusk with two years finish in Bordeaux barrels is launched.

2001 – Bowmore Dawn with two years finish on port pipes is launched. A bottle from 1890 is sold at an auction in Glasgow and brings in £14 300 which is a new world record. The Manager Jim McEwan moves to Bruichladdich.

2002 – A 37 year old Bowmore from 1964 and matured in fino casks is launched in a limited edition of 300 bottles (recommended price £1 500).

2003 – Another two expressions complete the wood trilogy which started with 1964 Fino - 1964 Bourbon and 1964 Oloroso.

2004 – Morrison Bowmore buys one of the most outstanding collections of Bowmore Single Malt from the private collector Hans Sommer. It totals more than 200 bottles and includes a number of Black Bowmore. Bowmore is awarded The Green Apple Award for its environmental commitment, exemplified by using warm waste water for heating.

2005 – Bowmore 1989 Bourbon (16 years) and 1971 (34 years) are launched .

2006 – Bowmore 1990 Oloroso (16 years) and 1968 (37 years) are launched.

Bowmore range

Standard
Bowmore 12 years old
Bowmore Dusk
Bowmore Darkest
Bowmore Dawn
Bowmore Cask Strength
Bowmore Mariner 15 years old
Bowmore 17 years old
Bowmore 25 years old

Limited editions
Bowmore 1971 34 years
Bowmore 1989 16 years
Bowmore 1990 16 years
Bowmore 1968 37 years

Duty Free
Bowmore Surf
Bowmore Enigma

Dawn

Darkest

1990 Oloroso

12 years old

17 years old

25 years old

Braeval

Owner:
Chivas Brothers Ltd
(Pernod Ricard)

Region/district:
Speyside

Founded:
1973

Status:
Mothballed

Tel:
01542 783042

Visitor centre:
No

website:
-

Capacity:
-

% sold as malt whisky:
-

Included in blended (past and/or present):
Chivas Regal, 100 Pipers, Passport

History:

1973 – The Chivas and Glenlivet Group founds Braes of Glenlivet, the name which will be used for the first 20 years. The Glenlivet, Tomintoul and Tamnavulin are the only other distilleries situated in the Livet Glen valley. Production starts in October.

1975 – Three stills are increased to five.

1978 – Five stills are further expanded to six.

1994 – The distillery changes name to Braeval.

2001 – Pernod Ricard takes over Chivas Brothers.

2002 – Braeval is mothballed in October.

Braeval, situated in the southernmost part of Speyside with Tamnavulin as closest neighbour, is one of the most isolated distilleries in Scotland. The region, called Braes of Glenlivet, is wild and beautiful and was one of the last refuges of moonshiners, i. e. illicit producers of spirits.

Braeval prides itself with a record, despite its fairly anonymous existence: The highest situated Scottish distillery. According to the Crown Estates Office Braeval is at an altitude of 1665 feet above medium sea level and thereby beats Dalwhinnie with almost 100 feet.

The distillery is equipped with no less than 15 washbacks, two wash stills and four spirit stills. Production ceased four years ago and there are no signs that the new owners, Chivas Brothers, are planning to put it on stream again.

Official bottlings of Braeval do not exist and independent bottlings are also difficult to find. Among the more recent ones are Gordon & MacPhail (Connoisseurs Choice) 1975 which appeared in 2001 and Signatory 1974 released in late 2004. Despite this, Braeval is obtainable albeit under a different name. Aberko Ltd, a small and relatively new spirits company in Glasgow has acquired the rights to the name Deerstalker which was established already in 1880. There are three versions of Deerstalker, the 12 and 18 years old were first and consisted of Balmenach whisky. They were followed by a 10 year old which contains Braeval. Aside from these single malts, Aberko has also a blended whisky called Black Top with main sales in South America.

Deerstalker 10 year old

Brora

Owner:
Diageo

Region/district:
Northern Highlands

Founded:
1819

Status:
Closed

Tel:
-

Visitor centre:
-

website:
www.malts.com

Capacity:
-

% sold as malt whisky:
-

Included in blended (past and/or present):
-

History:

1819 – The Marquis of Stafford, 1st Duke of Sutherland, founds the distillery as Clynelish Distillery.

1827 – The first licensed distiller, James Harper, files for bankruptcy and John Matheson takes over.

1828 – James Harper is back as licensee.

1834 – Andrew Ross takes over the license.

1846 – George Lawson & Sons takes over.

1896 – James Ainslie & Heilbron takes over and rebuilds the facilities.

1912 – James Ainslie & Co. narrowly escapes bankruptcy and Distillers Company Limited (DCL) takes over together with James Risk.

1916 – John Walker & Sons buys a stake of James Risk's stocks.

1925 – DCL buys out Risk.

1930 – Scottish Malt Distillers (SMD) takes over.

1931 – The distillery is mothballed.

1939 – Production restarts.

1960 – The distillery becomes electrified (until now it has been using locally mined coal from Brora).

1967 – A new distillery is built adjacent to the first one, it is also named Clynelish and both operate in parallel from August.

1968 – 'Old' Clynelish is mothballed in August.

1969 – 'Old' Clynelish is reopened as Brora and starts using a very peaty malt over the next couple of years

1983 – Brora is closed in March.

1995 – Brora 1972 (20 years) and Brora 1972 (22 years) are launched as Rare Malts.

1996 – Brora 1975 (20 years) is launched as a Rare Malt.

1998 – Brora 1977 (21 years) is launched as a Rare Malt.

2001 – Brora 1977 (24 years) is launched as a Rare Malt.

2002 – A 30 year old cask strength is released in a limited edition.

2003 – Brora 1982 (20 years) is launched as a Rare Malt.

2006 – The fifth release of Brora 30 year old.

Brora single malt, so appreciated by Islay-fans today, has not always been peated as it was a traditional Highland malt before 1968/69. The reason for the change of the 'recipe' was DCL fears for a shortage of peaty Islay-whisky, essential in the blend of Johnnie Walker. Ideas on expanding capacity on Islay were raised but it was decided to try out 'old' Clynelish instead which had been replaced by a new distillery on the same site. It was renamed Brora and produced heavily peated malt from 1969 to 1973. Since then peatiness was reduced, even if single peated batches turned up until the late seventies.

Brora closed permanently in 1983 but the buildings still stand next to the new Clynelish. The two stills, the feints receiver, the spirit receiver and the brass safe remain while the warehouses are used for storage from Clynelish. The last Brora casks here were recently sent away for bottling or storage elsewhere. Apparently, Diageo only holds Brora from 1972, 1979 and 1982 to which can be added the share which independent bottlers have.

The distillery was built in the time referred to as the Highland Clearances. Many land-owners wished to increase the yield of their lands and consequently went into large-scale sheep farming. Thousands of families were ruthlessly forced away and the most infamous of the large land-owners was the Marquis of Stafford who founded Clynelish (Brora) in 1819.

Since 1995 Diageo has regularly released different expressions of Brora in the Rare Malts series. The latest, which also became the last, appeared in 2003. A *30 year old* was released for the first time in 2002 and a new variety has appeared annually since then.

Douglas Laing is known among the independents for some exceptional Broras. They recently released two new ones: a 23 year old from 1982 and a 22 year old from 1983. Quite recent independent bottlings include a Signatory 1981 (23 years old) and a 1981 (23 years old) from Duncan Taylor.

30 year old cask strength, 5th release

Bruichladdich

Owner:
Bruichladdich Distillery Co

Region/district:
Islay

Founded:
1881

Status:
Active

Tel:
01496 850221

Visitor centre:
Yes (6/7)

website:
www.bruichladdich.com

Capacity:
1 500 000 litres

% sold as malt whisky:
n/a

Included in blended (past and/or present):
Black Bottle

History:

1881 – Barnett Harvey builds the distillery with money left by his brother William III to his three sons William IV, Robert and John Gourlay. The Harvey family already owns the distilleries Yoker and Dundashill.

1886 – Bruichladdich Distillery Company Ltd is founded and reconstruction commences.

1889 – William Harvey becomes Manager and remains on that post until his death in 1937.

1929 – Temporary closure.

1936 – The distillery reopens.

1938 – Joseph Hobbs, Hatim Attari and Alexander Tolmie purchase the distillery for £23 000 through the company Train & McIntyre.

1938 – Operations are moved to Associated Scottish Distillers.

1952 – The distillery is sold to Ross & Coulter from Glasgow.

1960 – A. B. Grant buys Ross & Coulter.

1961 – Own maltings ceases and malt is brought in from Port Ellen.

Bruichladdich is doing well, to say the least, under the management of Mark Reynier, Production Director Jim McEwan and Distillery Manager Duncan McGillivray. Profits doubled during 2005 and sales volumes continue to increase rapidly. The distillery is equipped with six washbacks of Oregon Pine and two pairs of stills. All casks are stored either at Bruichladdich or at the old Port Charlotte site in both dunnage and racked warehouses. The whisky is matured partly (two thirds) in ex-bourbon casks while the rest (one third) distributed between ex-sherry and various wine casks. Bruichladdich differs from other Islay distilleries in having its own bottling line which was recently expanded to enable greater capacity.

All whisky produced at the distillery is based on Scottish barley. There is, however, some room to manoeuvre and experiments with organic barley took place already in 2003. The traditional Bere variety, low in yield and not that easy to handle during the process, was used for the first time in 2005. The malt used today is exclusively taken from Bairds near Inverness.

The will to experiment and the desire to continuously surprise the market results in endless new bottlings. There can be said to be three main lines in Bruichladdich's production; Bruichladdich and the more heavily peated Port Charlotte and Octomore. In addition to them a triple-distilled variety called Trestarig has also been produced and quite recently they took one more step forward when they, for the first time in centuries, produced a quadruple distilled spirit with an alcohol content of 92%. Approximately 5 000 bottles will be for sale in around eight years.

The core range consists of *10, 12, 15, 17* and *20 years old*. A large number of limited releases, such as *Infinity*, *3D*, *The Forty* and *Rocks* (single malt designed for drinking with ice!) also occur. 2005 saw *The Fifteen second edition*, *Legacy Series IV*, *The Twenty* (nick-named Islands), *WMDII* (also called the Yellow Submarine) and *Turnberry*, yet another variety in the golf-series Links. Among several new releases in 2006, the first official bottling of Port Charlotte was probably the most anticipated among fans. It is a five year old cask strength named *PC5* and only released in 6 000 bottles. This is also the first official bottling of a whisky produced by the new owners. Other, new, releases in autumn 2006 are *1986 Blacker Still*, a *125th Anniversary bottling* from 1970 with a Pinot Gris finish, the second edition of *Infinity*, the third edition of *3D* where the heavily peated *Octomore* plays a small part for the first time and a young Bruichladdich (just 7 years) called *Waves*.

History (continued):

1968 – Invergordon Distillers take over.

1975 – The number of stills increases from two to four.

1983 – Temporary closure.

1993 – Whyte & Mackay buys Invergordon Distillers.

1995 – The distillery is mothballed in January.

1998 – In production again for a few months, and then mothballed.

2000 – After several years of attempts, Murray McDavid buys the distillery from JBB Greater Europe (previously Whyte & Mackay Group) for £6.5 million. 1.4 million litres of whisky from 1964 and younger is included in the purchase.

2001 – Jim McEwan from Bowmore becomes Production Director. The official opening is on 29th May and the first distillation at 08.26 is a Port Charlotte (40 ppm). Distilling of the first ´traditional´ Bruichladdich (10 ppm) starts in July. In September the owners' first bottlings from the old casks are released, 10, 15 and 20 years old. They all show the characteristics of Murray McDavid, i. e. reduced to 46%, not chill-filtered and no colourings. Bruichladdich is named Distillery of the Year by Malt Advocate.

2002 – The world's most heavily peated whisky is produced on 23rd October when Octomore (80ppm) is distilled.

2003 – Bruichladdich becomes the only distillery on Islay bottling on-site. It is awarded Distillery of the Year for the second time and launches the golf series, Links, 14 years old.

2004 – Time for the second edition of the 20 year old. This time the two decades of maturing in bourbon casks is rounded off with five weeks in red wine (Mourvèdre) barrels. The slightly pink-tinged whisky is named Flirtation.
3D, also called The Peat Proposal, is launched.

2005 – Several new expressions are launched - the second edition of 3D, Infinity (a mix of 1989, 1990, 1991 and Port Charlotte), Rocks, Legacy Series IV, The Yellow Submarine and The Twenty 'Islands'.

2006 – Included in a number of new releases in autumn is the first official bottling of Port Charlotte; PC5.

3D3 (third edition)

Blacker Still

125th Anniversary

PC5

Infinity (second edition)

Waves

Bunnahabhain

Owner:
Burn Stewart Distillers (CL Financial)

Region/district:
Islay

Founded:
1881

Status:
Active

Tel:
01496 840646

Visitor centre:
Yes (5/7)

website:
www.bunnahabhain.com

Capacity:
2 500 000 litres

% sold as malt whisky:
5% unofficial

Included in blended (past and/or present):
Cutty Sark, Famous Grouse, Black Bottle

History:

1881 – William Robertson of Robertson & Baxter, founds the distillery together with the brothers William and James Greenless. The Greenless brothers co-founded the Islay Distillers Company Ltd in 1879 with James Ford.

1883 – Production starts in earnest in January.

1887 – Islay Distillers Company Ltd merges with William Grant & Co. in order to form Highland Distilleries Company Limited. Glenrothes-Glenlivet is also included in the merger.

1930 – The distillery closes.

1937 – The distillery reopens.

1963 – The two stills are augmented by two more.

1982 –The distillery closes.

1984 – The distillery reopens. Highland Distilleries releases a 21 year old distilled in 1963 to commemorate the 100th anniversary of Bunnahabhain.

1999 – Edrington takes over Highland Distillers and mothballs Bunnahabhain but allows for a few weeks of production a year.

2001 – A 35 year old from 1965 is released in a limited edition of 594 bottles during Islay Whisky Festival.

2002 – William Grant & Sons shows interest in buying Bunnahabhain, but the deal does not materialize. As in the previous year, Islay Whisky Festival features another Bunnahabhain – 1966, a 35 year old in sherry casks and limited to 401 bottles. Auld Acquaintance 1968 (33 years, 2002 bottles) is launched at the Islay Jazz Festival. It is also named Hogmanay (after the Scottish New Year) as it was filled on 31st December 1968.

2003 – In April Edrington sells Bunnahabhain and Black Bottle to Burn Stewart Distilleries (C. L. World Brands) at the princely sum of £10 million. A 40 year old from 1963, matured in sherry casks, is launched.

2004 – The distillery experimented in the late 90s with a peated whisky and the first limited edition sample is a 6 year old cask strength called Moine.

2005 – Three limited editions are released - 34 years old, 18 years old and 25 years old.

2006 – 14 year old Pedro Ximenez and 35 years old are launched.

Bunnahabhain is perhaps the lightest of the Islay whiskies and it is consequently marketed as 'the gentle taste of Islay'. The malt originates from both Port Ellen (peated at 1-2 ppm) and the mainland (unpeated). The unusual and heavily peated Moine is made of malt at 38 ppm. To keep Bunnahabhain as light as possible, the stillman uses a considerably smaller part of the 'middle cut' than other Islay distilleries do. They have seven warehouses (both dunnage and racked) with a full 20 000 casks in store.

Burn Stewart Distillers has made Bunnahabhain the spiritual home of the respected blend Black Bottle. This brand had dominated their website completely but a new, excellent site focusing on single malt was launched in 2006.

The *12 year old* has been the only component of the core range for many years. Two limited editions of older Bunnahabhain (1500 bottles of an *18 year old* and 400 bottles of a *25 year old*) were therefore warmly welcomed when they entered the scene in December 2005. There will be more batches to be found in the regular range in the future. Two limited editions appeared in 2006; a *14 year old Pedro Ximinez* (761 bottles) released during the Islay festival and a *35 year old vintage from 1971*, celebrating the 125th anniversary.

Older limited editions include *Hogmanay 1968*, *Moine* (a 6 year old peated version), *34 years* and *40 years*. Several independent bottlers have also released Bunnahabhain. Some of the more recent are Duncan Taylor 1968, 37 years old (2006) and Murray McDavid 1966 (2006).

18 years old *25 years old*

Bushmills

Owner:
Irish Distillers Group (Diageo)

Region:
N Ireland (Co. Antrim)

Founded:
1784

Status:
Active

Tel:
028 20731521

Visitor centre:
Yes (7/7)

website:
www.bushmills.com

Capacity:
3 000 000 litres

% sold as malt whisky:
n/a

Included in blended (past and/or present):
Bushmills Irish Whiskey, Black Bush, Special Reserve

History:

1608 – James I issues Sir Thomas Philips a licence for whiskey distilling.

1784 – The distillery is formally registered.

1885 – Fire destroys part of the distillery.

1972 – Bushmills joins Irish Distillers Group which was formed in 1966. Floor maltings ceases.

1987 – Pernod Ricard acquires Irish Distillers.

1996 – Bushmills 16 years old is launched.

2005 – Bushmills is sold to Diageo at a price tag of €295,5 million as a result of Pernod Ricard's acquisition of Allied Domecq.

Bushmills often insists, arguably, that it is the world's oldest distillery. Sir Thomas Philips was issued a licence from James I to distill whiskey in large parts of County Colraine and County Antrim in 1608 which is the year mentioned on the distillery's labels, but it was first in 1784 that the distillery was formally registered. This makes it the oldest functioning distillery in Ireland. Bushmills uses two kinds of malt, one unpeated and one slightly peated, in production. The distillery uses triple distillation, which is the traditional Irish way, contrary to Cooley which uses double distillation. They have four wash stills and five spirit stills and the whisky is matured and bottled on site. Bushmill's core range consists of a *10 year old*, a *16 year old Triple Wood* with a finish in port pipes and a *21 year old* finished in Madeira casks. There is also a *12 year old Distillery Reserve* which is sold exclusively at the distillery. A great number of single casks have also been launched. Black Bush, Original and 1608 are the blended whiskeys available from the distillery.

Midleton Distillery in County Cork is the third Irish whiskey distillery and belongs to Irish Distillers together with Bushmills. It is the largest distillery and produces famous brands such as Jameson, Tullamore Dew and Paddy. Apart from pot-still Irish whiskey (a combination of both malted and unmalted barley in the still) and grain whiskey, there is also a small share of single malt produced for its blended whiskeys. Their 6 year old single malt Erin go Bragh (Ireland Forever) can be found with some degree of luck but it is rare and not an official bottling. Midleton produces grain whiskey for the different blended Bushmills.

10 years old

21 years old

Caol Ila

Owner: Diageo
Region/district: Islay
Founded: 1846
Status: Active
Tel: 01496 302760
Visitor centre: Yes (5/7)
website: www.malts.com
Capacity: 3 600 000 litres
% sold as malt whisky: 3% unofficial

Included in blended (past and/or present):
Bell´s, Johnnie Walker, White Horse, Black Bottle, Compass Box Eleuthra

History:

1846 – Hector Henderson founds Caol Ila.

1852 – Henderson, Lamont & Co. is subjected to financial difficulties and Henderson is forced to sell Caol Ila. The buyer is Norman Buchanan, owner of the Isle of Jura Distillery.

1863 – Norman Buchanan encounters financial troubles and sells to the blending company Bulloch, Lade & Co. from Glasgow.

1879 – The distillery is rebuilt and expanded.

1920 – Bulloch, Lade & Co. is liquidated and the distillery is taken over by Caol Ila Distillery co-owned by Robertson & Baxter, Dewar's and Distillers Company Limited (DCL).

1927 – DCL becomes sole owners.

1930 – DCL transfers administration to Scottish Malt Distillers (SMD). The distillery closes.

1937 – Operations recommence.

1972 – All the buildings, except for the warehouses, are demolished and rebuilt.

1974 – The renovation, which totals £1 million, is complete and six new stills are installed.

1989 – A 15 year old is launched in the Flora & Fauna series.

1999 – Experiments with a completely unpeated malt are performed.

2002 – The first official bottlings since Flora & Fauna/Rare Malt appear; 12 years, 18 years and Cask Strength (c. 10 years).

2003 – A 25 year old cask strength from 1978 is launched.

2005 – A 25 year old Special Release from Diageo is launched.

2006 – Unpeated 8 year old and 1993 Moscatel finish are released.

Caol Ila is the largest distillery on Islay and one of the largest distilleries belonging to Diageo. The refurbishment in 1974 saw several old buildings replaced by new, modern-style ones. The distillery cannot aspire to the title 'Islay's most beautiful distillery' but the view from the stillroom's large panorama windows over the Sound of Islay is unrivalled. The malt comes from Port Ellen and keeps c 30 – 35 ppm except on those occasions when an unpeated version is produced (Caol Ila Highland) for blending. The whole production is shipped for filling and maturing on the mainland.
Interest was great when Diageo presented three new bottlings at the Islay Festival 2002 – *12 years old*, *18 years old* and *Cask Strength*. Currently they make up the core range of Caol Ila. After a few years' wait, the followers of Caol Ila had another occasion to rejoice: A limited edition (6 000 bottles) of a *25 year old* was released, the oldest version released by Diageo. Another two versions, unique in themselves, were released in 2006; the first *unpeated Caol Ila (8 years old)* and the first owner-released wood finish version, a *1993 Distiller´s Edition Moscatel finish*. The latter is targeted at the Duty Free market. The first wood finished Caol Ila was probably a 14 year old with 4 years of second maturation in a cognac cask and released by Swedish Symposion in February 2006.
Independent bottlers simply love Caol Ila. Among the most recent are Douglas Laing 10 years old and 25 years old, Dewar Rattray 1991, Ian MacLeod 16 years old and a 12 year old rum finish, Cadenhead 11 years old and a 1991 red wine finish from Murray McDavid.

8 years old Unpeated

1993 Distiller´s Edition

Caperdonich

Owner:
Chivas Brothers
(Pernod Ricard)

Region/district:
Speyside

Founded:
1897

Status:
Mothballed

Tel:
01542 783000

Visitor centre:
-

website:
-

Capacity:
-

% sold as malt whisky:
-

Included in blended (past and/or present):
Chivas Regal

History:

1897 – The distillery is founded by James Grant and is named Glen Grant Number 2 Distillery after the neighbouring sister distillery Glen Grant.

1902 – The Pattison crash shakes the industry and the distillery closes.

1965 – It reopens with The Glenlivet & Glen Gant Distilleries as owners. According to law two distilleries cannot bear the same name so it is changed to Caperdonich.

1967 – The number of stills are increased from two to four.

1977 – Seagrams buys The Glenlivet Distilleries Ltd (the new, shortened name) and forms Chivas and Glenlivet Group. Longmorn, Benriach, Glen Grant and The Glenlivet are also included in the deal.

2001 – Pernod Ricard and Diageo take over Seagram Spirits & Wine, the Chivas Group becomes part of Pernod Ricard.

2002 – The distillery is mothballed.

2005 – A 16 year old from 1988 is launched.

One distillery in Rothes, Glenrothes, lies to the west of the road next to the old castle ruin while another, Glen Grant, has a huge and lovely garden as its neighbour. A third lies in much less vivid surroundings in the industrial area to the east of the road and that is Caperdonich. Its closest neighbours are Forsyth's Coppersmiths and Fabricators, world famous for their copper stills which are supplied to distilleries worldwide, and a huge dark grains plant.
Caperdonich distillery started off without any major encouragement when it was given the rather unimaginative name Glen Grant Number 2. Major James Grant (see p. 130) decided that the newly built distillery should operate as a complement to the already established Glen Grant across the road rather than on its own. The two distilleries were also connected with a pipeline for transporting whisky between them.
Five years later the distillery complex lay dormant, only to be revived after another 60 years as Caperdonich. The stills were active for another 37 years until it was decommissioned along with Benriach, Braeval and Allt-a-Bhainne. After many years without official bottlings time was ripe again for one in 2005. A *16 year old* from 1988 was launched as Chivas Brothers Cask Strength Edition. There will probably not be a new, official bottling as the remaining supplies will be used in different blended whiskies.
There are, however, more to be found among independent bottlings. Some more recent are Gordon & MacPhail 1995 with a Marsala finish, a Duncan Taylor 1968 (37 years), a Dewar Rattray 1980 and a Murray McDavid 1966 Madeira finish.

16 years old

Cardhu

Owner:
Diageo

Region/district:
Speyside

Founded:
1824

Status:
Active

Tel:
01340 872555 (vc)

Visitor centre:
Yes (5/7)

website:
www.malts.com

Capacity:
2 300 000 litres

% sold as malt whisky:
n/a

Included in blended (past and/or present):
Johnnie Walker

History:

1811 – The whisky smuggler John Cumming founds an illicit distillery.

1824 – John Cumming applies for and obtains a licence for Cardhu Distillery.

1846 – John Cumming dies and his son Lewis takes over.

1872 – Lewis dies and his wife Elizabeth, nicknamed 'The Queen of the Whisky Trade', takes over.

1884 – A new distillery is built to replace the old.

1893 – John Walker & Sons purchases Cardhu for £20 500 but the Cumming family continues operations. The whisky changes name from Cardow to Cardhu.

1908 – The name reverts to Cardow.

1925 – John Walker & Sons joins Scottish Malt Distillers (SMD).

1930 – Administration is transferred to Scottish Malt Distillers (SMD).

1960-61 – Reconstruction and expansion of stills from four to six.

1981 – The name changes to Cardhu once again.

1998 – A visitor centre is constructed.

2002 – The popularity of Cardhu leads to supply problems for Diageo. They decide to change Cardhu single malt to a vatted malt with contributions from other distilleries in it.

2003 – The whisky industry protests sharply against Diageo's plans. Diageo negotiates a compromise with Scotch Whisky Association (SWA).

2004 – Further protests from the whisky industry and Diageo withdraws Cardhu Pure Malt.

2005 – The 12 year old Cardhu Single Malt is relaunched and a 22 year old is released.

Cardhu's main market is without doubt Spain where it ranks as the most sold malt whisky. France, Portugal and Greece are other countries where its malt is greatly appreciated. This popularity was the cause of animated deliberations a few years ago. Demand simply outgrew supply and as Cardhu single malt was also an important ingredient in Johnnie Walker, Diageo decided to mix some of the produce with other Speyside malts thus creating Cardhu Pure Malt. Many industry insiders feared that this would dilute the term 'single malt' and protested loudly. Eventually Diageo withdrew the Pure Malt (see also under History).

This is all now history and Cardhu 12 years old single malt is once again a big seller in southern Europe. It is, in fact, difficult to obtain elsewhere. Cardhu's popularity with Spanish customers is easily proven by the official, elegant Spanish-language website at www.sensacionescardhu.com.

Johnnie Walker Green Label became the replacement for Cardhu Pure Malt and was quickly launched as Diageo's vatted malt. In principal this was just a relaunch of Johnnie Walker Pure Malt, available on a few markets and as a duty-free item since 1997.

Cardhu distillery's location is unrivalled; on a small hill with a view over Ben Rinnes and with Knockando and Tamdhu as its closest neighbours.

It has three pairs of stills and is one of Diageo's smallest distilleries. It also has a visitor centre welcoming around 7 000 visitors a year.

The core range consists of the *12 year old* and a *22 year old Special Release* which was released for the Spanish and French markets in 2005. Cardhu has appeared twice as a Rare Malt, in 1998 and 2000.

The only independent bottling is a 27 year old from Signatory which appeared in 1999.

22 years old

Clynelish

Owner:
Diageo

Region/district:
Northern Highlands

Founded:
1967

Status:
Active

Tel:
01408 623000

Visitor centre:
Yes (4/7)

website:
www.malts.com

Capacity:
3 400 000 litres

% sold as malt whisky:
1% unofficial

Included in blended (past and/or present):
Johnnie Walker Gold Label,
Compass Box Eleuthra

History:
Before 1966- see Brora.

1967 – Scottish Malt Distillers (SMD) builds a new distillery a few hundred metres from the old. The latter closes and reopens as Brora.

2002 – A 14 year old is released as a Hidden Malt, replacing the old in the Flora & Fauna series.

2006 – A Distiller´s Edition 1991 finished in Oloroso casks is released.

There is both a long and a short story of this distillery. The long one dates back to founding in 1819 but is now attached to the distillery Brora (which see) while the short one begins in the 1960s. Distillers Company Limited (DCL) raised a new Clynelish distillery made of glass, steel and concrete next to the old, more traditionally built, one.
Clynelish is considerably larger than Brora with three pairs of stills instead of one and there are only three Diageo distilleries with a higher capacity than Clynelish. Unusually, the spirit stills are slightly larger than the wash stills. They also have eight beautiful washbacks made from Larch. Wooden washbacks are still quite common in Scottish distilleries and can be found in around 65% of active distilleries. The topic of whether wood rather than stainless steel has a positive impact on the final whisky has often been discussed but it is difficult to give a definite answer. Undoubtedly, wooden washbacks are more demanding during the cleaning process.
Despite this uncertainty Diageo has decided to install stainless steel washbacks in three of their distilleries: Dufftown, Glen Spey and Strathmill. Auchroisk had steel washbacks put into place when it was built. The spirit from Clynelish is stored in its own warehouses or in the old warehouses of Brora.
When the old Clynelish opened up again as Brora, the character of the whisky had changed to a heavily peated whisky. Clynelish is much less peated and uses medium peated malt from Glen Ord maltings.
Official bottlings include a *14 year old Flora & Fauna* which was replaced in 2002 by another *14 year old* launched as a *Hidden Malt*. There have also been a handful of *Rare Malts*, the latest a *23 year old* in 1998. The latest official bottling is a *Distiller´s Edition 1991*, released in 2006. Involvement with Clynelish is popular among independent bottlers. Four recent examples are Cadenhead 1993 (12 years old), Ian Macleod 1992 (13 years old), Douglas Laing 1989 (17 years old) and a Sauternes finish from 1990 released by Murray McDavid.

1991 Distiller´s Edition

Coleburn

Owner:
Diageo

Region/district:
Speyside

Founded:
1897

Status:
Dismantled

Tel:
-

Visitor centre:
-

website:
www.malts.com

Capacity:
-

% sold as malt whisky:
-

Included in blended (past and/or present):
Johnnie Walker

History:

1897 – John Robertson & Son in Dundee founds the distillery. The famous architect Charles Doig is called in.

1913 – The distillery closes.

1916 – The distillery is bought by the consortium Clynelish Distillery Company (consisting of Distillers Company Ltd, John Risk and John Walker) and reopens.

1917 – Production is licensed to J. & G. Stewart Ltd, a subsidiary of Distillers Company Limited (DCL).

1930 – DCL buys Clynelish Distillery Company and becomes owners to Coleburn. Operations are transferred to the subsidiary Scottish Malt Distillers (SMD).

1985 – The distillery is mothballed.

1992 – From now on the distillery lacks a license.

1996 – United Distillers plans to build apartments in the distillery and local authorities approve though no further developments take place.

2000 – A 21 year old cask strength from 1979 is released in the Rare Malt series.

2004 – The brothers Dale and Mark Winchester buy the distillery from Diageo. The plans are to transform it into an activity centre with a hotel, restaurants, shops and concert venues.

Coleburn distillery is embedded in greenery halfway to Rothes from Elgin, between the A491 and Morayshire Railway. In the old days, before the railway was decommissioned in 1966, the distillery even had its own railway station.
Coleburn was founded in the late 1890s with Charles Doig as the architect. Rather than becoming a distillery in its own right it produced malt whisky for Andrew Usher blends and, at a later date, for Johnnie Walker. Coleburn's main contribution to the whisky world in its early days were new, experimental production methods.
Diageo sold the distillery to brothers Dale and Mark Winchester in 2004. Apart from other career interests, the brothers have been involved in Scottish folk music since they were children and also starred in the film 'Local Hero' where Dale played accordion and Mark the fiddle. They submitted plans for development of Coleburn that very same year to Moray Council, applying for permission to 'change of use of distillery to travel lodge, restaurants, shops, music studios and entertainment centre'. Not much more has happened and the situation in spring 2006 was that the application was on hold pending receipt of further information from the Winchester brothers.
Coleburn has appeared in the *Rare Malt* series once, a *21 year old* from 1979 released in 2000. This is the only existing official bottling available. Independent bottlings are almost as rare; a 34 year old from Douglas Laing and a 20 year old from Gordon & MacPhail appeared in 2002. After that it took until 2006 when Signatory released a 36 year old from 1970, matured in a wine treated puncheon.

Gordon & MacPhail (Connoisseurs Choice) 1972

Convalmore

Owner:
Diageo

Region/district:
Speyside

Founded:
1894

Status:
Dismantled

Tel:
-

Visitor centre:
-

website:
www.malts.com

Capacity:
-

% sold as malt whisky:
-

Included in blended (past and/or present):
Grant´s

History:

1893 – Founded by the Convalmore–Glenlivet Distillery Company. Architect is Donald Mackay from Dufftown.

1894 – Production starts in February.

1904 – Convalmore-Glenlivet is purchased by the blending company W. P. Lowrie & Co. from Glasgow for £6 000.

1906 – The new owner runs into financial troubles and James Buchanan, a major customer to Lowrie, buys the company including Convalmore Distillery.

1909 – Large parts of the distillery are destroyed by a fire in October.

1910 – The distillery is back in operation. Experimental distilling of malt whisky in continuous stills, i. e. the same method as used in production of grain whisky, takes place.

1916 – The continuous still experiments are abandoned.

1925 – Distillers Company Limited (DCL) buys the distillery from James Buchanan & Co.

1930 – DCL transfers operations to Scottish Malt Distillers (SMD).

1962 – Direct heating of the stills from a coal fire is abandoned for indirect heating by steam.

1964 – The number of stills is increased from two to four.

1985 – The distillery is mothballed.

1990 – United Distillers sells the buildings to William Grant & Sons who uses them for storing their own malts Glenfiddich and Balvenie.

2003 – Diageo launches a 24 year old Convalmore from 1978 in the Rare Malts series.

2005 – A 28 year old is launched as a Special Release from Diageo

Convalmore distillery was founded by the whisky blender Peter Dawson. In 1896 he continued by building Towiemore distillery which was situated between Keith and Dufftown but closed in 1930. Dawson's blended whisky received a degree of popularity, amongst other customers he supplied whisky to was the British Antarctic Expedition in 1910 led by Robert F. Scott. Unfortunately, the whisky did not help the expedition succeed. Amundsen beat Scott to the South Pole and the members of the British expedition all died on the return journey.

Unlike many other dormant distilleries, Convalmore was spared transformation into a cark park, housing estate or shopping centre and has retained its looks despite having been out of production since 1985. There will never be another distillery on the site but the beautiful pagoda roofs still alludes to its former glory. Since 1990 William Grant & Sons uses Convalmore as storage for Glenfiddich and Balvenie which are situated nearby. A dark grains plant used for turning pot ale and grist into cattle feed was closed in 1995.

A sidetrack in the history of Convalmore were attempts to produce malt whisky in continuous stills. Simultaneous trials also took place at Lochruan Distillery in Campbeltown (closed c. 1925) and Glentauchers with the objective of finding cost-effective procedures. The disappointing outcome was uneven maturation and the trials were therefore discontinued.

Diageo kept the rights to issue bottlings of Convalmore when the distillery was sold but have not taken advantage of this to a great extent. The first bottling was a *Rare Malts 24 years* from 1978 that appeared in 2003 and the second, a *28 year old Special Release*, that was launched in 2005.

Independent bottlings are rare. The two latest were from 1975 and were launched in 2004 by Ian Macleod and Speyside Distillers (Scott's Selection).

28 years old

Cooley

Owner:
Cooley Distillery plc

Region/district:
Ireland (County Louth)

Founded:
1987

Status:
Active

Tel:
++353 (0)42 9376102

Visitor centre:
No

website:
www.cooleywhiskey.com

Capacity:
3 250 000 litres

% sold as malt whisky:
n/a

Included in blended (past and/or present):
Inishowen, Kilbeggan, Millar´s

History:

1987 – John Teeling purchases Ceimici Teo Distillery in Dundalk. Previously it has produced spirits in column stills (e. g. vodka) and is now renamed Cooley Distillery.

1988 – Willie McCarter acquires part of A. A. Watt Distillery and the brand Tyrconnell and merges with Teeling. Teeling simultaneously buys decommissioned Locke's Kilbeggan Distillery which will be used for storage of whiskey from Cooley.

1989 – A pair of pot stills is installed for production of both malt and grain whiskey.

1992 – Locke's Single Malt, without age statement, is launched as the first single malt from the distillery. Cooley encounters financial troubles and Pernod Ricard, via Irish Distillers, offers to purchase the company for £24.5 million.

1994 – The Competition Authority establishes that Irish Distillers cannot acquire Cooley as they then would be dominating the Irish whiskey market.

1995 – Finances improve and production resumes.

1996 – Connemara is launched. It is the first peated Irish whiskey for a couple of decades.

1998 – Cooley Distillery is awarded a prize at the International Wine and Spirits Competition for its outstanding achievement to the spirit industry.

2000 – Locke's 8 year old single malt is launched.

2003 – The Connemara 12 year old is launched.

2006 – Five Connemara Single Casks from 1992 are released.

Ireland could pride itself on some 1000 licensed distilleries in the 19th century. In the beginning of the 20th century, they had decreased to 30 and by the late eighties they were further diminished to two, both owned by Irish Distillers. Entrepreneur John Teeling and partners then decided to start a third, independent distillery. The financial troubles of Cooley nearly put an end to the venture but Cooley's American and German agents entered the scene and agreed to pre-buy £2 million of stock provided the owners contributed cash. When the distillery was running again the next clever move came with the decision to enter the retailer own brand sector, producing whisky for Sainsbury´s and Waitrose. Around 95% of production is exported and the distillery also has the capacity to produce 10 million litres of grain whiskey a year.
There are currently three different single malts in Cooley's product range: *Locke's 8 years old*, *Tyrconnell* with *no age* and *1992 single cask* and *Connemara* with *no age*, *12 years old* and *Cask Strength*. Spring 2005 saw the release of five single casks of Connemara, handpicked by Master Blender Noel Sweeney. Distilled in 1992 this is the oldest Connemara whiskey to date. A special release for the American market is *Michael Collins Single Malt*, named after the legendary Irish hero who fought for independence. It is also available as a blended.
A number of blended whiskeys are also produced: Inishowen (lightly peated), Kilbeggan and Millar's Special Reserve. A single grain called Greenore 8 years old can also be found, with 10, 16 and 18 years old coming up in the future. A huge number of independent bottlings exist. The prestigious Knappouge Castle deserves a mention among these as it has contained single malt from Cooley in 1990, 1991 and 1992.

Connemara 12 years

Tyrconnell no age

Locke´s 8 years

Cragganmore

Owner: Diageo

Region/district: Speyside

Founded: 1869

Status: Active

Tel: 01479 874700

Visitor centre: Yes (6/7)

website: www.malts.com

Capacity: 1 600 000 litres

% sold as malt whisky: n/a

Included in blended (past and/or present):
Old Parr, Haig, White Horse, Compass Box Asyla

History:

1869 – John Smith, who already runs Ballindalloch and Glenfarclas Distilleries, founds Cragganmore. He has also held managerial positions at Macallan and Glenlivet.

1886 – John Smith dies and his brother George takes over operations.

1893 – John's son Gordon, at 21, is old enough to assume responsibility for operations.

1901 – The distillery is refurbished and modernized with help of the famous architect Charles Doig.

1912 – Gordon Smith dies and his widow Mary Jane supervises operations.

1917 – The distillery closes.

1918 – The distillery reopens and Mary Jane installs electric lighting.

1923 – The distillery is sold to the newly formed Cragganmore Distillery Co. where Mackie & Co. (later to become White Horse Distillers) and Peter Mackie share half ownership. The remaining half is owned by Sir George Macpherson-Grant and Ballindalloch Estate.

1927 – White Horse Distillers is bought by DCL who thus obtains 50% of Cragganmore.

1931 – The distillery closes.

1934 – The distillery reopens.

1964 – The number of stills is increased from two to four.

1965 – DCL buys the remainder of Cragganmore.

1988 – Cragganmore 12 years succeeds in being one of six selected for United Distillers´ Classic Malts.

1998 – Cragganmore Distillers Edition Double Matured (port) is launched for the first time.

2002 – A visitor centre opens in May.

2006 – A 17 year old from 1988 is released.

In contrast to its closest neighbour Tormore Distillery which rises impressively next to the A95, Cragganmore lies in a more secluded setting in the valley of River Spey on the other side of the road. The surrounding grounds are owned by Ballindalloch Estate with Ballandilloch Castle nearby which is certainly worth a visit. The castle has belonged to the Macpherson – Grant family since the 16th century and Sir George Macpherson-Grant gave John Smith permission to construct the distillery. Cragganmore has always enjoyed great respect as a classic Speyside and it is also to be found on the Blender's List from 1974 as one of twelve Top Class distilleries. Cragganmore was chosen by United Distillers to represent Speyside in their Classic Malts in 1988 in stiff competition with the three other Top Class distilleries: Mortlach, Linkwood and Glen Elgin. Many consider Cragganmore the most complex of all single malts but it is still relatively unknown.

The distillery has a rather unusual set of equipment with flat tops on the stills, T-shaped lyne arms on the spirit stills and two rectangular worm tubs made of cast iron. Ex-sherry casks are used for the single malt and a mix of sherry and bourbon for blends. It is one of Diageo's smaller distilleries and a visitor centre, which has been closed but re-opened in summer 2006, receives around 1000 visitors annually.

The core range is made up of a *12 year old* and a *Distiller's Edition*. There has also been five limited bottlings since 2000 – a *14 year old* destined for 'Friends of Classic Malts', a *1973 29 year old*, a *10 year old cask strength* in 2004, a *1993 Bodega Cask* the same year and, finally, a *17 year old* released in 2006.

Recent independent bottlings include Dewar Rattray 1993, Cadenhead's 1989 and a 1985 Syrah finish from Murray McDavid.

1992 Distiller´s Edition

17 years old

Craigellachie

Owner: John Dewar & Sons (Bacardi)

Region/district: Speyside

Founded: 1891

Status: Active

Tel: 01340 872971

Visitor centre: No

website: -

Capacity: 2 700 000 litres

% sold as malt whisky: less than 1%

Included in blended (past and/or present): Dewar´s White Label

History:

1891 – The distillery is built by Craigellachie-Glenlivet Distillery Company which has Alexander Edward and Peter Mackie as part-owners. The famous Charles Doig is the architect.

1898 – Production does not start until this year.

1916 – Mackie & Company Distillers Ltd takes over.

1924 – Peter Mackie dies and Mackie & Company changes name to White Horse Distillers.

1927 – White Horse Distillers are bought by Distillers Company Limited (DCL).

1930 – Administration is transferred to Scottish Malt Distillers (SMD), a subsidiary of DCL.

1964 – Refurbishing takes place and two new stills are bought, increasing the number to four.

1998 – United Distillers & Vintners (UDV) sells Craigellachie, together with Aberfeldy, Brackla and Aultmore and the blending company John Dewar & Sons to Bacardi Martini.

2004 – The first official versions from the new owners are a new 14 year old which replaces UDV's Flora & Fauna and a 21 year old cask strength from 1982 produced for Craigellachie Hotel.

Craigellachie distillery is not easily missed as it sits just north of Craigellachie village by the A491 in the direction of Rothes and Elgin. The whisky is however, more unobtrusive. During virtually all of the distillery's lifetime it has produced malt whisky for blendeds, first White Horse and more recently Dewar's.

It looks modern despite being over 100 years of age. The refurbishing in 1964 modernised most of the facilities leaving only the kiln with its pagoda roof and one warehouse still in original condition. Craigellachie has eight washbacks made of larch wood, two pairs of stills and a very modern full lauter mash tun installed in 2001.

If Craigellachie is mentioned in whisky contexts it is often in association with the four-star hotel bearing the same name. The hotel, Danish-owned for many years, was sold in June 2006 to London & Edinburgh Inns, the largest hotel chain in Scotland and number 5 in the UK. In addition to hundreds of pubs they also run around 150 hotels in the UK. It remains to be seen whether this will affect the famous Quaich Bar with its selection of over 600 whiskies. On the other hand, if one is interested in good whisky and a nice meal as well, The Highlander Inn a few hundred metres from the hotel is worth a visit. There one can find Duncan Elphick and Tatsuya Minagawa, who ran Craigellachie Hotel earlier.

New owner Bacardi's decision to launch a *14 year old* Craigellachie in 2004 as an official bottling was a welcome step into the limelight. This is, so far, the only official bottling. Recent independent bottlings include a 10 year old from Douglas Laing and a 1970 from Murray McDavid finished in white wine casks from Guigal, both of which were bottled in 2006.

14 years old

Dailuaine

Owner:
Diageo

Region/district:
Speyside

Founded:
1852

Status:
Active

Tel:
01340 872500

Visitor centre:
No

website:
www.malts.com

Capacity:
3 200 000 litres

% sold as malt whisky:
2% unofficial

Included in blended (past and/or present):
Johnnie Walker

History:

1852 – The distillery is founded by William Mackenzie.

1865 – William Mackenzie dies and his widow leases the distillery to James Fleming, a banker from Aberlour.

1879 – William Mackenzie's son forms Mackenzie and Company with Fleming.

1884 – Rebuilding transforms the distillery into one of the largest in the Highlands.

1889 – Charles Doig builds his and Scotland's first pagoda roof on Dailuaine.

1891 – Dailuaine-Glenlivet Distillery Ltd is founded.

1898 – Dailuaine-Glenlivet Distillery Ltd merges with Talisker Distillery Ltd and forms Dailuaine-Talisker Distilleries Ltd. Imperial Distillery, built by Thomas Mackenzie the previous year, and a grain distillery in Aberdeen are also incorporated.

1915 – Thomas Mackenzie dies without heirs.

1916 – Dailuaine-Talisker Company Ltd is bought by the previous customers John Dewar & Sons, John Walker & Sons and James Buchanan & Co.

1917 – A fire rages and the pagoda roof collapses. The distillery is forced to close.

1920 – The distillery reopens.

1925 – Distillers Company Limited (DCL) takes over.

1930 – Operations are transferred to Scottish Malt Distillers (SMD).

1960 – Refurbishing. The stills increase from four to six and a Saladin box replaces the floor maltings.

1965 – Indirect still heating through steam is installed.

1983 – On-site maltings is closed down and malt is purchased centrally.

1991 – The first official bottling, a 16 year old, is launched in the Flora & Fauna series.

1996 – A 22 year old cask strength from 1973 is launched as a Rare Malt.

1997 – A cask strength version of the 16 year old is launched.

2000 – A 17 year old Manager´s Dram matured in sherry casks is launched.

Dailuaine distillery is situated a few miles south-west of Aberlour, adjacent to the small community of Carron, with Imperial Distillery as its closest neighbour across River Spey. The magnificent granite warehouse is the first that one sees upon leaving the A95. Due to the approach road's incline the impression is of imminent landing on the roof! The warehouses are, regrettably, not used for storage anymore as all spirit is tankered away for filling and maturing elsewhere.

Dailuaine was one of many distilleries using the railway for receiving barley and coal and for sending casks of whisky to waiting customers. The distillery was connected by a siding to the Strathspey Railway (opened in 1863) in 1905. The railway finally closed in 1971 but train enthusiasts have opened up a steam railway on the stretch from Boat of Garten to Aviemore.

Dailuaine has secured a position in whisky history thanks to a roof constructed in 1889 which was destroyed in a fire in 1917. This was the first eye-catching pagoda roof by the famous architect Charles Doig, a roof type that would become commonplace in many distilleries.

A small proportion of the production (2%) is sold as single malt. It is stored on sherry butts, while the whisky produced for blending is stored on ex-bourbon casks. Except for a *16 year old* in the *Flora & Fauna* series, only a couple of limited versions have been released by the owners. Independent bottlings are rare. Some of the more recent ones are Gordon & MacPhail 1991 and Ian MacLeod 1994, both released in 2005, and Cadenhead 1994 (12 years) released in 2006.

Flora & Fauna 16 years old

Dallas Dhu

Owner:
Diageo (administered by Scotland's Historic Buildings and Monument Directorate)

Region/district:
Speyside

Founded:
1898

Status:
Closed

Tel:
01309 676548

Visitor centre:
Museum

website:
www.historic-scotland.gov.uk

Capacity:
-

% sold as malt whisky:
-

Included in blended (past and/or present):
Roderick Dhu

History:

1898 – The blending company Wright & Greig in Glasgow, with Alexander Edward as one part-owner, founds the distillery. The 'Distillery Architect' Charles Doig does the drawings and it is first named Dallasmore.

1899 – Production starts and the name is changed to Dallas Dhu.

1919 – Dallas Dhu is sold to the blending company J. P. O´Brien & Co.

1921 – Benmore Distilleries Ltd buys the distillery.

1929 – Distillers Company Limited (DCL) takes over.

1930 – Operations are transferred to SMD and the distillery closes.

1937 – The distillery reopens.

1939 – The stillhouse is completely destroyed by a fire and the distillery is forced to close.

1947 – The distillery reopens.

1983 – DCL discontinues production in March.

1986 – Historic Scotland purchases the facilities.

1988 – The distillery opens as a tourist attraction managed by Historic Scotland.

1995 – Dallas Dhu 1970 (24 years) is launched as a Rare Malt.

1997 – Dallas Dhu 1975 (21 years) is launched as a Rare Malt.

One of the founders, Alexander Edwards, was an energetic man. He was also involved in the establishment of Aultmore, Benromach and Craigellachie and owned Benrinnes and Oban for some years. He owned large expanses of land around Forres and both Dallas Dhu and Benromach on the other side of A96 between Elgin and Inverness, were built on his lands. The blending company Wright & Greig's intention with Dallas Dhu was to safeguard supplies of malt whisky to their main blend, Roderick Dhu. It sold well in the 1880s and 1890s, especially in India, Australia and New Zealand. Roderick Dhu was named after the character in Sir Walter Scott's poem 'The Lady of the Lake'.

For the past 20 years Dallas Dhu in Forres has been an interactive museum managed by Historic Scotland, an agency within the Scottish Executive Education Department. One may wonder whether a distillery decommissioned back in 1983 really can provide an experience on a par with those on offer at neighbouring, active, distilleries such as Benromach. Historic Scotland has certainly succeeded in this and maintained an atmosphere of a Victorian era model distillery. Since no production takes place, visitors are unrestrained by safety, security or excise rules and can thus become truly interactive. For example, one can test his/her skills at operating the spirit safe or climb into the mash tun.

Apart from two releases in the *Rare Malts* series, the owners have released three bottlings for Historic Scotland in recent years. The first one was in 1998, followed by Centenerary 15 years old (1999) to commemorate the 100th anniversary of the first distilling and Millenium 25 years old (1999). Independent bottlings include Signatory 1982 (2005) and 1975 (2005), Gordon & MacPhail 1982 (2005), Douglas Laing 1972 (2005) and the most recent one, a 1979 white wine finish released by Murray McDavid in May 2006.

Gordon & MacPhail Dallas Dhu 1980

Dalmore

Owner:
Whyte and Mackay Ltd

Region/district:
Northern Highlands

Founded:
1839

Status:
Active

Tel:
01349 882362

Visitor centre:
Yes (6/7)

website:
www.thedalmore.com

Capacity:
3 200 000 litres

% sold as malt whisky:
n/a

Included in blended (past and/or present):
Whyte and Mackay, Claymore

History:

1839 – Alexander Matheson founds the distillery and lets it to the Sunderland family.

1850 – Margaret Sunderland takes over operations.

1867 – The brothers Charles, Andrew and Alexander Mackenzie run the distillery.

1870 – Dalmore becomes the first malt whisky to be exported to Australia.

1874 – The number of stills is increased by two to four.

1886 – Alexander Matheson dies.

1891 – Sir Kenneth Matheson sells the distillery for £14 500 to the Mackenzie brothers.

1917 – The Royal Navy moves in to start manufacturing of American mines

1920 – The Royal Navy moves out and leaves behind a distillery partly damaged by an explosion.

1922 – The distillery is in production again. Andrew Mackenzie and the Royal Navy disagree on compensation for the damages.

1925 – The dispute between Mackenzie and the navy moves into the House of Lords.

1956 – Floor malting is replaced with a Saladin box.

1960 – Mackenzie Brothers (Dalmore) Ltd merges with Whyte & Mackay and forms the company Dalmore-Whyte & Mackay Ltd.

1966 – The number of stills is increased from four to eight.

1982 – The Saladin box is abandoned.

1990 – American Brands buys Whyte & Mackay.

1996 – Whyte & Mackay changes name to JBB (Greater Europe).

2001 – Through management buy-out, JBB (Greater Europe) is bought from Fortune Brands and changes name to Kyndal Spirits.

2002 – A 62 year old Dalmore is sold at McTear's auction for £25 877.50 and becomes the world's so far most expensive bottle of whisky. Kyndal Spirits changes name to Whyte & Mackay.

2004 – A new visitor centre with exhibition and screening rooms, a sampling bar and a shop opens.

2005 – Black Pearl, with six months on Madeira barrels, is launched

Dalmore is still the star in the Whyte & Mackay group (of single malts that is!). It doubled its sales in the five years from 1998 to 2003 while sales at Jura, the other major distillery in the group, virtually was stagnant. With the re-launch of the Jura brand in 2005 sales started to pick up. A similar re-launch is also imminent for Dalmore, likely to take place in October 2006. There is, however, some uncertainty over this as rumours have circulated for some time that Indian United Breweries may acquire Whyte & Mackay which could affect this.
Another re-launch occurred in August 2006; of the Whyte & Mackay blend which as been around 20th place on the sales list since some time. Three new expressions, 13, 19 and 22 years old, now augment the range.
Part of Dalmore's success can be attributed to Richard Paterson of Whyte & Mackay. He is a third-generation Master Blender and one of the great whisky profiles. He began working at Whyte & Mackay in 1970 and became, at 26 years of age, the youngest Master Blender in Scotland.
The *12 year old* whisky was the only one on the market for some time until a *21 year old* and *The Cigar Malt* (and also a *30 year old* for the North American market) appeared in 2002 to complete the core range. Limited editions include '*The Dalmore 1973 Vintage Gonzales Byass Sherry Cask Finish*', introduced in 2003 followed by *Black Isle* in 2004 and *Black Pearl* in 2005. Two extremely rare and old bottlings of Dalmore are the 50 year old and the 62 year old. Only 12 bottles were released of the latter. One can probably expect new expressions in the future bearing Paterson's interest for experimenting with different casks in mind.
Independent bottlings are not commonly found. Among the latest are a Cadenhead 1992 (14 years) and a 1995 (10 years) from Douglas Laing.

12 years old

Dalwhinnie

Owner:
Diageo

Region/district:
Speyside

Founded:
1897

Status:
Active

Tel:
01540 672219 (vc)

Visitor centre:
Yes (6/7)

website:
www.malts.com

Capacity:
1 300 000 litres

% sold as malt whisky:
n/a

Included in blended (past and/or present):
Buchanan, Haig

History:

1897 – John Grant, George Sellar and Alexander Mackenzie from Kingussie commence building the facilities. The first name is Strathspey and the construction work amounts to £10 000.

1898 – Production starts in February. The owners encounter financial troubles after a few months and John Somerville & Co and A P Blyth & Sons take over in November and change the name to Dalwhinnie. The architect Charles Doig is called in to make some improvements.

1905 – America's largest distillers, Cook & Bernheimer in New York, buys Dalwhinnie for £1 250 at an auction. This marks the first time a foreign company takes ownership of a Scottish distillery. The administration of Dalwhinnie is placed in the newly formed company James Munro & Sons.

1919 – Macdonald Greenlees & Willliams Ltd headed by Sir James Calder buys Dalwhinnie.

1926 – Macdonald Greenlees & Williams Ltd is bought by Distillers Company Ltd (DCL) which licences Dalwhinnie to James Buchanan & Co.

1930 – Operations are transferred to Scottish Malt Distilleries (SMD).

1934 – The distillery is closed after a fire in February

1938 – The distillery opens again.

1968 – The maltings is decommissioned.

1986 – A complete refurbishing takes place.

1987 – Dalwhinnie 15 years becomes one of selected six in United Distillers´ Classic Malts.

1991 – A visitor centre is constructed.

1992 – The distillery closes and goes through a major refurbishment costing £3.2 million.

1995 – The distillery opens in March.

1998 – Dalwhinnie Distillers Edition 1980 (oloroso) is introduced for the first time. The other five in The Classic Malts, each with a different finish, are also introduced as Distillers Editions for the first time.

2002 – A 36 year old is released.

2003 – A 29 year old is released.

2006 – A 20 year old is released.

The Scottish whisky lands have traditionally been divided into several regions, even if these are more or less obsolete nowadays when it comes to leaving their mark on the character of the whisky. For example, Bunnahabhain is not typical Islay in its character while Benriach in Speyside is sometimes as peaty as an Islay. Dalwhinnie is also difficult to place regionally on taste alone. It lies in splendid isolation some 30 miles south of Speyside proper but is often counted to this region. Diageo, however, chose Dalwhinnie as Northern Highlands representative in their Six Classic Malts series.
Most literature recognises Dalwhinnie as being the highest situated distillery in Scotland, at 1037 ft above sea level. When Braes of Glenlivet (later Braeval Distillery) was built in 1973 it was situated at 1165 ft above sea level according to the Crown Estates Office and thereby officially claiming the altitude record. Dalwhinnie is still unique among distilleries though in having the coldest average annual temperature of 6°C.
The distillery draws its water from Allt an t'Sluic at 2000 ft above sea level. The water originates from meltwater in the Cairngorm Mountains. Dalwhinnie is one of few distilleries still using worm tubs for condensing the spirit vapours. It is also one of the smallest of Diageo's distilleries with only one pair of stills. Despite this it scores around 20th place among the most sold single malts in the world.
The core range is made up of a *15 years old* and a *Distiller's Edition*. A *36 year old* in 2002, a *29 year old* in 2003 and a *20 year old* in 2006 have also been released. It is very difficult to find an independently bottled Dalwhinnie.

1990 Distiller´s Edition

20 years old

Deanston

Owner:
Burn Stewart Distillers (C L Financial)

Region/district:
Eastern Highlands

Founded:
1965

Status:
Active

Tel:
01786 841422

Visitor centre:
No

website:
www.burnstewartdistillers.com

Capacity:
3 000 000 litres
1 600 000 litres

% sold as malt whisky:
15%

Included in blended (past and/or present):
Scottish Leader, Black Prince

History:

1965 – A weavery from 1785 is transformed into Deanston Distillery by James Finlay & Co. and Brodie Hepburn Ltd (Deanston Distillery Co.). Brodie Hepburn also runs Tullibardine Distillery.

1966 – Production commences in October.

1971 – The first single malt is named Old Bannockburn.

1972 – Invergordon Distillers takes over.

1974 – The first single malt bearing the name Deanston is produced.

1982 – The distillery closes.

1990 – Burn Stewart Distillers from Glasgow buys the distillery for £2.1 million.

1991 – The distillery resumes production.

1999 – C L Financial buys an 18% stake of Burn Stewart.

2002 – C L Financial acquires the remaining stake.

2006 – Deanston 30 years old is released.

Deanston distillery is located about two miles from the town of Doune, home of the Doune Castle built in the late 14th century. The castle might be recognised by many from the film 'Monty Python and the Holy Grail' from 1974 where it is variously known as Camelot, Castle Anthrax and Swamp Castle! Despite being a fairly young distillery, the buildings have an older history as a cotton mill. They were designed in 1785 by the Architect Richard Arkwright, the inventor of the first steam-powered spinning frame, an improvement of the famous Spinning Jenny which appeared a few years earlier and revolutionised the whole cotton industry.

Deanston dams water from the river Teith a couple of miles from the distillery. This dam and a turbine make it unique in being the only Scottish distillery that is self-sustaining with electricity.

The current owner C L Financial, founded in Trinidad Tobago in 1993, is a holding company consisting of more than 50 companies. Its business interests span insurance, real estate, media, forestry and agriculture, medical services, petrochemicals and marine services. Part of this conglomerate is known as C L World Brands and owns Angostura Bitter and Rhum, Hine cognac and Burn Stewart Distillers who they took over 2002 and which added Bunnahabhain, Tobermory and Deanston to the group.

Apart from a *6 year old* targeted for the French market, there are only three official bottlings of Deanston, a *12 year old*, a *17 year old* and the newly released *30 year old*. A *35 year old* limited edition from 1967 released in 2003 is the oldest Deanston whisky still available. Independent bottlings are not easy to come by. One recent is an 11 year old from 1994 released by Douglas Laing in 2006.

12 years old

Dufftown

Owner:
Diageo

Region/district:
Speyside

Founded:
1896

Status:
Active

Tel:
01340 822100

Visitor centre:
No

website:
www.malts.com

Capacity:
4 000 000 litres

% sold as malt whisky:
1% unofficial

Included in blended (past and/or present):
Bell´s

History:

1895 – Peter Mackenzie, Richard Stackpole, John Symon and Charles MacPherson build the distillery Dufftown-Glenlivet in an old mill.

1896 – Production starts in November.

1897 – The distillery is owned by P. Mackenzie & Co., who also owns Blair Athol in Pitlochry.

1933 – P. Mackenzie & Co. is bought by Arthur Bell & Sons for £56 000.

1968 – The floor maltings is discontinued and malt is bought from outside suppliers.

1974 – The number of stills is increased from two to four.

1979 – The stills are increased by a further two, to six.

1985 – Guinness buys Arthur Bell & Sons.

1997 – Guinness and Grand Metropolitan merge to form Diageo.

2006 – The Singleton of Dufftown is launched as a special duty free bottling.

There are a handful of villages in Speyside such as Elgin, Rothes and Keith which have several distilleries, but Dufftown can certainly be labelled 'whisky town no. 1' with no fewer than six active distilleries, including Glenfiddich. The town, initially called Balvenie, was founded in 1817 by James Duff, the 4th Earl of Fife, in order to secure work opportunities for soldiers returning from the Napoleonic wars. Six years later Mortlach was founded as the first distillery. Dufftown and Mortlach had many disputes over the water source, Jock's Well, which resulted in Mortlach workers trying to lead the water away by digging canals before they eventually had to give up the battle. Dufftown distillery is a modern distillery even if it was built in the late 19th century, and expansion has been contained within the old buildings. The two last stills were installed in 1979 and had to be placed in the stillroom with a degree of planning as it is probably one of Scotland's most cramped. The original wooden washbacks were replaced by stainless steel in 1998 and the traditional, ubiquitous red Porteus mill was replaced already in 1979 with one of the industry's few Vicker's mills. Fermentation is very long at Dufftown, lasting from 75 hours up to 120 hours over weekends. The whisky from the distillery, Diageo's largest, has been an important part of the blended Bell's (number one in the UK) since the 1930s and only a slight percentage is bottled as single malt.

The only official bottling used to be the *15 year old* in the *Flora & Fauna* series. In 2006, however, Diageo launched a special duty free version called *Singleton of Dufftown* (cf. Singelton of Glen Ord that appeared just before).

It is also bottled as a *Rare Malt 1975 (21 years)* and as a limited *centenary bottling 20 years* which was released in 1996.

Two finishes have been released from Wilson & Morgan fairly recently, 1989 Marsala (14 years) and 1992 Port (12 years). There is also a 1993 (12 years) from Gordon & MacPhail.

Flora & Fauna 15 years old

Edradour

Owner:
Signatory Vintage Scotch Whisky Co. Ltd

Region/district:
Eastern Highlands

Founded:
1825

Status:
Active

Tel:
01796 472095

Visitor centre:
Yes (5/7)

website:
www.edradour.com

Capacity:
90 000 litres

% sold as malt whisky:
n/a

Included in blended (past and/or present):
House of Lords, Clan Campbell

History:

1825 – This is probably the year when a distillery called Glenforres is founded by farmers in Pertshire.

1837 – The first year Edradour is mentioned.

1841 – The farmers form a proprietary company, John MacGlashan & Co.

1886 – The American company J. G. Turney & Sons acquires Edradour through its subsidiary William Whitely & Co.

1922 – William Whiteley buys the distillery in order to produce its own blended whiskies, among them King's Ransom and House of Lords. The distillery is renamed Glenforres-Glenlivet.

1975 – Pernod Ricard buys Campbell Distilleries.

1982 – Campbell Distilleries (Pernod Ricard) buys Edradour and builds a visitors' centre.

1986 – Edradour's first single malt (10 years) is released.

2002 – Edradour is bought by Andrew Symington from Signatory Vintage Scotch Whisky in July for £5.4 million (£3 million consists of stocks). The product range is expanded in autumn with a 10 year old that is not chill-filtered and a 13 year old cask strength. Iain Henderson, Distillery Manager at Laphroaig, becomes Director of Operations at Edradour.

2003 – A 30 year old and a 10 year old that are non chill-filtered are released. As an experiment a heavily peated variety (50ppm) is also distilled.

2004 – A number of wood finishes (port, sauternes, burgundy and chardonnay) are launched as cask strength.

2006 – Willie McDougall replaces Iain Henderson as Distillery Manager.

Andrew Symington made a clever move when he acquired Edradour from Pernod Ricard through his company Signatory Vintage Scotch Whisky Co. in July 2002. Today, 4 years later, the distillery is responsible for 80% of the profits in the group, with Signatory independent bottlers making the other 20%. A large part of the revenue comes from the 100 000 visitors that visit the picturesque distillery in Perthshire each year.

Edradour is perfectly placed for attracting visitors, by the A9 leading directly into the Scottish highlands and it ranks as the second most visited distillery in Scotland after Glenturret.

Edradour has always attracted interest as it is Scotland's smallest distillery with an annual production corresponding to that of one week´s at the major distilleries. The ranking as Scotland's smallest distillery is now shared with newly opened Kilchoman distillery on Islay.

Iain Henderson, who joined Edradour in 2002, left in June 2006 to help the Nelstrops with their distillery establishment in Norfolk. Willie MacDougall from Lagavulin became the new Manager.

Symington and his staff have been generous in their distillery bottlings. A non chill-filtered *10 year old* and a *'Straight from the cask' 11 year old* appeared in 2002, the same year as the acquisition. Two different *30 year olds* were released in 2003 and a wide range of *finishes* on 50 cl bottles in 2004: *burgundy, chardonnay, sauternes, madeira, marsala* and *port*. A *Port Wood finish from 1983* was released in 2005 and an *11 year old Barolo finish* appeared in 2006.

An exciting experiment, inspired by Iain Henderson, commenced in 2003 with the first distilling of a heavily peated (no less than 50 ppm) malt. Its maturation takes place on different casks, among them Madeira, Port and Burgundy.

The whisky will be named *Ballechin* after a distillery in the neighbourhood which was closed in 1927. There are no recent independent bottlings.

10 years old

Fettercairn

Owner:
Whyte & Mackay Ltd

Region/district:
Eastern Highlands

Founded:
1824

Status:
Active

Tel:
01561 340205

Visitor centre:
Yes (5/7)

website:
www.whyteandmackay.co.uk

Capacity:
1 600 000 litres

% sold as malt whisky:
4%

Included in blended (past and/or present):
Whyte & Mackay, Johnnie Walker

History:

1824 – Sir Alexander Ramsay, owner of Fasque Estate, founds the distillery.

1825 – The first licensee is James Stewart & Co.

1830 – Sir Alexander Ramsay sells Fasque Estate and the distillery to Sir John Gladstone, father of the future PM William Gladstone.

1887 – A fire erupts and the distillery is forced to close for repairs.

1890 – Thomas Gladstone dies and his son John Robert takes over. A company, Fettercairn Distillery Co., is formed with several owners. The distillery reopens after the fire.

1912 – The company is close to liquidation and John Gladstone buys out the investors and forms a new company.

1926 –The distillery is mothballed.

1939 – The distillery is bought by Associated Scottish Distillers Ltd, subsidiary of Train & McIntyre which is owned by National Distillers of America. Production restarts.

1960 – The maltings discontinues.

1966 – The stills are increased from two to four.

1971 – The distillery is bought by Tomintoul-Glenlivet Distillery Co. Ltd owned by W. & S. Strong & Co. and Hay & McLeod & Co.

1973 – Tomintoul-Glenlivet Distillery Co. Ltd is bought by Whyte & Mackay Distillers Ltd through Scottish & Universal Investment Trust headed by Sir Hugh Fraser.

1974 – The mega group of companies Lonrho buys Whyte & Mackay.

1988 – Lonrho sells to Brent Walker Group plc.

1989 – A visitor centre opens.

1990 – American Brands Inc. buys Whyte & Mackay for £160 million through their subsidiary Gallaher Tobacco.

1996 – Whyte & Mackay and Jim Beam Brands merge to become JBB Worldwide.

2001 – Kyndal Spirits, a company formed by managers at Whyte & Mackay, buys Whyte & Mackay from JBB Worldwide.

2002 – The whisky undergoes a major makeover including a new bottle, new packaging, its age and the name which is changed from Old Fettercairn to Fettercairn 1824 and is relaunched.

2003 – Kyndal Spirits changes name to Whyte & Mackay.

Fettercairn is a small and not relatively well-known distillery in the Whyte & Mackay group. One feature makes it unique among Scottish distilleries: cooling water is allowed to trickle along the spirit still necks and is collected at the base for circulation towards the top again in order to increase reflux and thereby produce a lighter and cleaner spirit. A similar installation can be found at Dalmore distillery but each spirit still has a water jacket which circulates cold water between the reflux bowl and the neck of the stills. It is difficult to ascertain which distillery was first with this innovation, but according to Drew Sinclair, ex manager of Dalmore, they inspired Fettercairn.

Fettercairn takes all its water from the Cairngorm Mountains, some 40 miles to the northwest, and there are 15 dunnage warehouses on the premises.

For a decade Fettercairn was the lone representative of eastern Scotland distilleries. One after another, the distilleries between Aberdeen and Dundee (North Port, Lochside, Glenesk and Glenury Royal) were closed. Glencadam finally closed its doors in 2000 but was revived a couple of years ago.

Fettercairn is situated slightly off the main tourist routes which is reflected in the number of visitors received, roughly 7 000 a year despite its visitor centre having been established for 20 years.

The core range of Fettercairn simply consists of a *12 year old*. Some older, limited versions exist such as *Stillmans Dram 26* and *30 years* respectively. There are also two casks of *15 year old* Fettercairn that visitors can bottle when visiting the distillery.

Independent bottlings are very rare but turn up every now and then. Scott's Selection 1989, Douglas Laing 1991 (13 years) and a 25 year old Part Nan Angelen (Swedish Vin & Sprit) released in 2003 are among the more recent.

12 years old

Glen Albyn

Owner:
Diageo

Region/district:
Northern Highlands

Founded:
1844

Status:
Demolished

Tel:
-

Visitor centre:
-

website:
www.malts.com

Capacity:
-

% sold as malt whisky:
-

Included in blended (past and/or present):
-

History:

1844 – The distillery is founded by James Sutherland and inaugurated in October the same year.

1846 – Production starts in earnest.

1849 – A fire in November damages the distillery.

1850 – Production recommences in February.

1855 – James Sutherland goes bankrupt due to costly repair work and the distillery is put up for sale without success.

1866 – The building is transformed into a flour mill.

1884 – The new owners Gregory & Co. converts the mill to a distillery.

1891 – Glen Albyn Distillery Company is formed.

1892 – A sister distillery, Glen Mohr, is built by Glen Albyn's manager John Birnie and James Mackinlay.

1920 – Mackinlay & Birnie Ltd, owner of Glen Mohr, buys Glen Albyn and runs both distilleries in parallel operations.

1954 – Floor maltings is abolished and replaced by a Saladin box.

1972 – DCL buys Glen Albyn which is administered by SMD.

1983 – The distillery is taken out of production.

1986 – The distillery is demolished.

The three remaining distilleries in Inverness persevered until the mid 1980s before closing down. Millburn capitulated in 1985 while the 'twin' distilleries Glen Albyn and Glen Mhor were decommissioned two years previously. Glen Albyn was the oldest, being almost 50 years older than Glen Mhor, but in regard to quality Glen Mhor was rated higher.
The name Glen Albyn is put together from Glen, meaning valley and Alba which is an old name for Scotland. The name is also sometimes used instead of 'Great Glen' for the valleys which run from Inverness in the north to Fort William in the south.
Even if Glen Albyn's history can be dated back to 1844 when it was built on the ruins of Muirtown brewery, it was only active during 8 of its first 40 years. The largest part of the distillery and equipment was rebuilt in 1884 when the second period of its distilling history started. Glen Albyn made its contribution to the war effort during WWI when it was requisitioned by the Admiralty and used as a site for the construction of anti-submarine boom defences for Scapa Flow.
Glen Albyn was a small distillery with an annual production volume totalling 1.5 million litres in the mid 20th century.
Its whisky was used for blending and with the exception of a 10 year old from the 1970s which is reported to have been sold in Italy, there are no official bottlings except a *Rare Malt 1975* (26 years) which turned up in 2002.
Independent bottlings are not that common. Gordon & MacPhail has released two, 1966 and 1975, both bottled in 2005 and there is also a Duncan Taylor 1979 bottled in 2006.

Rare Malts 1975 26 years old

Glenallachie

Owner:
Chivas Brothers (Pernod Ricard)

Region/district:
Speyside

Founded:
1967

Status:
Active

Tel:
01542 783042

Visitor centre:
No

website:
-

Capacity:
2 800 000 litres

% sold as malt whisky:
n/a

Included in blended (past and/or present):
Clan Campbell, House of Lords

History:

1967 – The distillery is founded by Mackinlay, McPherson & Co. a subsidiary of Scottish & Newcastle Breweries Ltd. William Delmé Evans is architect.

1985 – Scottish & Newcastle Breweries Ltd sells Charles Mackinlay Ltd to Invergordon Distillers which acquires both Glenallachie and Isle of Jura.

1987 – The distillery is decommisioned.

1989 – Campbell Distillers (Pernod Ricard) buys the distillery, increases the number of stills from two to four and takes up production again.

2005 – The first official bottling for many years becomes a Cask Strength Edition from 1989.

William Delmé Evans who constructed Glenallachie is sometimes likened to the great distillery architect of the 19th century, Charles Doig. Delmé Evans was not as prolific as Doig, but on the other hand he was considerably more engaged in his projects and even a part-owner of the first two – Tullibardine and Jura. He trained as an engineer and had a knowledge and understanding of whisky production which went into great detail, as for example in still construction. Glenallachie became Delmé Evan's last distillery project. Eight years later he withdrew from his post as Managing Director of Jura Distillery. He died on 6th October 2003, 83 years old, just two months before the reopening of his first distillery Tullibardine.

The distillery, with two wash stills (23 000 litres) and two spirit stills (16 000 litres) has five employees and is operating at full capacity which entails an annual production of 3 million litres of alcohol.

There has not been an official bottling of Glenallachie for a long time but Chivas Brothers launched a series called *Cask Strength Edition* in 2005 in which a number of their distilleries (also Glenallachie) are represented. Glenallachie *16 years old* is extremely dark as it has been stored on first fill oloroso casks. Independent bottlings have also been scarce even if single versions have appeared in the Netherlands and Germany. Douglas Laing released a 31 year old in 2003 and a 12 year old in 2006 and Balmoral Hotel in Edinburgh launched a 12 year old Glenallachie as their own single malt in November 2004.

1989 16 years old

Glenburgie

Owner:
Chivas Brothers (Pernod Ricard)

Region/district:
Speyside

Founded:
1810

Status:
Active

Tel:
01343 850258

Visitor centre:
No

website:
-

Capacity:
4 000 000 litres

% sold as malt whisky:
0%

Included in blended (past and/or present):
Ballantine´s, Teacher´s

History:

1810 – William Paul founds Kilnflat Distillery. Official production starts in 1829.

1870 – Kilnflat distillery closes.

1878 – The distillery reopens under the name Glenburgie-Glenlivet, Charles Hay is licensee.

1884 - Alexander Fraser & Co. takes over.

1925 – Alexander Fraser & Co. goes bankrupt and the receiver Donald Mustad assumes control of operations.

1927 – James & George Stodart Ltd buys the distillery which by this time is inactive.

1930 – Hiram Walker buys 60% of James & George Stodart Ltd.

1936 – Hiram Walker buys Glenburgie Distillery in October. Hiram Walker then acquires the remaining 40% of James & George Stodart and adds Glenburgie to subsidiary Ballantine's. Production restarts.

1958 – Refurbishment and expansion take place, two Lomond stills are installed producing a single malt named Glencraig. Floor malting ceases and malt purchase is centralized.

1981 – The Lomond stills are replaced by conventional stills.

1987 – Allied Lyons buys Hiram Walker.

2002 – Special Distillery bottlings from Allied, 15 years.

2004 – A £4.3 million refurbishment and reconstruction takes place.

2005 – Chivas Brothers (Pernod Ricard) become new owners through the acquisition of Allied Domecq.

2006 – The number of stills are increased from four to six in May.

Glenburgie Distillery lies a few kilometres from the main road between Elgin and Forres. Despite its rather unappealing appearance it is on the cutting edge when it comes to production and technology.
Allied put much effort into Glenburgie when they decided to give it a fresh start in 2004. The old distillery was demolished rather than refurbished and only the copper stills and milling equipment were kept. The bill finished at £4.3 million and when the re-inauguration took place in June 2005 only five months of production had been lost. New owners since 2005, Chivas Brothers, kept its direction and installed another pair of stills in May 2006 enhancing capacity to no less than 4 000 000 litres which made Glenburgie the third largest distillery in the group after Glenlivet and Miltonduff.
A single malt from this distillery named Glencraig can be found with some luck. It came into being by Hiram Walker's experimenting with Lomond stills in the fifties. Glenburgie's first Lomond still was a small model, originating in Dumbarton. It was replaced in 1958 by a pair of full-size Lomond stills and it is the make from these stills that received the name Glencraig after Willie Craig, the company's Production Director. Despite Glencraig's production winding up in 1981, independent bottlings still turn up. The latest is a Duncan Taylor 1974 released in May 2006.
An official *15 year old Glenburgie* was released several years ago and has been difficult to find recently. Additional bottles of this expression were however released in summer 2006 by Chivas Brothers.
Independent bottlings are rare. Some recent are Duncan Taylor 36 years old released in 2005 and a couple of 40 year olds from Gordon & MacPhail and Signatory released in 2003.

Gordon & MacPhail Glenburgie 10 years old

Glencadam

Owner: Angus Dundee Distillers
Region/district: Eastern Highlands

Founded: 1825
Status: Active

Tel: 01356 622217
Visitor centre: No

website: www.angusdundee.co.uk

Capacity: 1 500 000 litres
% sold as malt whisky: 1%

Included in blended (past and/or present): Ballantine´s, Teacher´s Highland Cream

History:

1825 – George Cooper founds the distillery.

1827 – David Scott takes over.

1837 – The distillery is sold by David Scott.

1852 – Alexander Miln Thompson becomes the owner.

1857 – Glencadam Distillery Company is formed.

1891 – The blending company Gilmour, Thompson & Co Ltd takes over.

1954 – Hiram Walker takes over.

1959 – Refurbishing and modernization of the distillery.

1987 – Allied Lyons buys Hiram Walker Gooderham & Worts.

1994 – Allied Lyons changes name to Allied Domecq.

2000 – The distillery is mothballed.

2003 – Allied Lyons sells the distillery to Angus Dundee Distillers.

2005 – The new owner releases a 15 year old.

It seemed that Glencadam was doomed when Allied Domecq experienced a surplus of distillery capacity in the end of the 1990s. They mothballed the distillery in 2000 and made all staff except for one redundant. Three years later Angus Dundee Distillers, based in London, bought Glencadam. Family-owned Angus Dundee had over 50 years of experience of producing not only whisky, but also gin and vodka, as well as blending whisky. They produce mainly for own labels and customers' own brands and most sales are abroad. Examples are: Glen Parker (single Speyside malt), Parkers 12 year old (blended), The Dundee (blended) and Angus Dundee (blended malt). Most distilleries have stills with horizontal or descending lyne arms. Glencadam differs as the lyne arms of both the wash still and the spirit still are approximately 15 degrees ascending, which increases reflux and gives a lighter spirit. The spirit is stored on site, mainly on bourbon casks, in one dunnage and two racked warehouses.

An eagerly awaited official bottling of Glencadam from the new owners appeared in 2005 when a *15 year old* was released. This is also the only official bottling from Angus Dundee Distillers so far. Independent bottlings are rather unusual. Three recent ones are a 27 year old (1977) from Douglas Laing, a 20 year old (1985) from Ian Macleod and a 17 year old (1987) from Cadenhead. A surprise bottling appeared from Oddbins which recently introduced 'Against the Grain', a series of malt whiskies designed to highlight Scotland's lesser known distilleries. The first whisky in this series was a Glencadam 1987.

15 years old

Glendronach

Owner:
Chivas Brothers
(Pernod Ricard)

Region/district:
Speyside

Founded:
1826

Status:
Active

Tel:
01466 730202

Visitor centre:
Yes (5/7)

website:
-

Capacity:
1 400 000 litres
532 000 litres

% sold as malt whisky:
5-10%

Included in blended (past and/or present):
Teacher´s Highland Cream, Ballantine´s 17

History:

1826 – The distillery is founded by a consortium. James Allardes is one of the owners.

1837 – The major part of the distillery is destroyed in a fire.

1852 – Walter Scott (from Teaninich) takes over.

1887 – Walter Scott dies and Glendronach is taken over by a consortium from Leith. John Somerville & Co. is the main owner of the consortium.

1920 – Charles Grant, son of the founder of Glenfiddich Distillery, William Grant, buys Glendronach for £9 000 and starts production three months later.

1960 – William Teacher & Sons buys the distillery.

1966-67 – The number of stills is increased from two to four.

1976 – A visitor centre is opened.

1976 – Allied Breweries takes over William Teacher & Sons.

1991 – Glendronach is one of a select few in Caledonian Malts, launched by Allied Distillers (formerly known as Allied Breweries).

1996 – The distillery is mothballed.

2002 – Production is resumed on 14th May.

2005 – Glendronach 33 years old is launched. The distillery closes for six months to rebuild from coal to indirect firing by steam. Reopens in September. Chivas Brothers (Pernod Ricard) becomes new owner through the acquisition of Allied Domecq.

Glendronach was, for a number of years, the last Scottish distillery to fire the stills with coal. Owner Allied Domecq apparently planned a reconstruction of the distillery to suit EU directives, but then changed mind. Glendronach did close, however, between April and September 2005 in order to replace coal firing with steam.

Another sign of the old times, the malting floors, are still in existence but have not been used since 1996. Ready, unpeated malt is purchased today, but a couple of decades ago Glendronach was much peatier with up to 12-14 ppm. The whole production since the reopening in 2002 has been on bourbon casks even if Glendronach has a reputation for sherried malts.

Persistent rumours have it that Chivas, who obtained Glendronach through the acquisition of Allied as recent as 2005, has put the distillery on the sales list with independent bottlers Duncan Taylor as a possible purchaser.

When it comes to bottlings, the distillery has done their utmost to confuse followers:

Since the early 1990s a number of expressions have relieved each other. First, there was a 12 year old Original, mainly stored on bourbon casks and at the same time a 12 year old which was sherry matured. Both of them were eventually replaced by a 12 year old Traditional which was a combination of bourbon and sherry. Thereafter, 15 years 100% matured in sherry casks, appeared, only to be replaced by the existing *Original 12 years Double Matured* with 12 years on sherry butts but with a final finish of 6 months on bourbon casks. The cherry on the cake was a limited edition in spring 2005: *33 years* on ex-Spanish Oloroso sherry butts at a price of £220 and a *Vintage 1968*.

Original 12 years old

Glendullan

Owner:
Diageo

Region/district:
Speyside

Founded:
1897

Status:
Active

Tel:
01340 822100

Visitor centre:
No

website:
www.malts.com

Capacity:
3 700 000 litres

% sold as malt whisky:
n/a

Included in blended (past and/or present):
Old Parr, Cardhu (vatted version)

History:

1896-97 – William Williams & Sons, a blending company with Three Stars and Strahdon among their brands, founds the distillery.

1902 – Glendullan is delivered to the Royal Court and becomes the favourite whisky of Edward VII.

1919 – Macdonald Greenlees buys a share of the company and Macdonald Greenlees & Williams Distillers is formed.

1926 – Distillers Company Limited (DCL) buys Glendullan.

1930 – Glendullan is transferred to Scottish Malt Distillers (SMD).

1962 – Major refurbishing and reconstruction.

1972 – A brand new distillery, accommodating six stills, is constructed next to the old one and both operate simultaneously during a few years.

1985 – The oldest of the two distilleries is mothballed.

1995 – The first launch of Glendullan in the Rare Malts series becomes a 22 year old from 1972.

2005 – A 26 year old from 1978 is launched in the Rare Malts series.

The old distillery

The industrial Glendullan distillery, at the confluence of Dullan and Fiddich, is likely to disappoint if one already has visited the picturesque Glenfiddich and Balvenie a few kilometres away. But the new Glendullan was built in 1972 next to the old which is now used as a workshop for Diageo.
Glendullan is officially managed by Macdonald Greenlees, subsidiary of Diageo (DCL) since 1926, according to the sign on the façade. They had launched Old Parr just before the takeover and Glendullan malt is a significant component in this blended which has decreased in sales in recent years. It now sells c 4 million bottles a year, mainly in Japan.
Glendullan has the second largest production capacity (after Dufftown) among Diageo´s distilleries. The single malt has gained prominent followers over the years. The first was King Edward VII who ordered regular deliveries in the beginning of the century. Glendullan also received attention in 1992 when Betty Boothroyd was elected first-ever female Speaker in the House of Commons. She chose Glendullan as the Speaker's whisky.
The *12 year old* in the *Flora & Fauna* series is the most common when it comes to official bottlings but there is also an *8 year old* single malt targeted at supermarkets. A *Centenary 1998* to commemorate the distillery's 100th anniversary and *five versions of Rare Malts* (the last in October 2005) also deserve mention.
Independent bottlings are rare but a couple of Platinum Old and Rare from Douglas Laing appeared a few years back. They are interesting as they were distilled in the old stillhouse in the early 70s.

Flora & Fauna 12 years old

Glen Elgin

Owner:
Diageo

Region/district:
Speyside

Founded:
1898

Status:
Active

Tel:
01343 862100

Visitor centre:
No

website:
www.malts.com

Capacity:
1 800 000 litres

% sold as malt whisky:
n/a

Included in blended (past and/or present):
White Horse, Compass Box Asyla

History:

1898 – The bankers William Simpson (former manager of Glenfarclas distillery) and James Carle found Glen Elgin. The famous Charles Doig is called in as architect.

1900 – Production starts in May but the distillery closes just five months later.

1901 – In February, the distillery is auctioned for £4 000 to the Glen Elgin-Glenlivet Distillery Co. and is mothballed.

1904 – Production restarts.

1905 – Production ceases.

1906 – The wine producer J. J. Blanche & Co. buys the distillery for £7 000 and production resumes.

1929 – J. J. Blanche dies and the distillery is put up for sale again.

1930 – Scottish Malt Distillers (SMD) buys it and the license goes to White Horse Distillers.

1964 – Expansion from two to six stills plus other refurbishing takes place.

1977 – The first official version (12 years).

1992 – The distillery closes for refurbishing and installation of new stills.

1995 – Production resumes in September.

2001 – A 12 year old is launched in the Flora & Fauna series.

2002 – The Flora & Fauna series malt is replaced by a Hidden Malt 12 years.

2003 – A 32 year old cask strength from 1971 is released in a limited edition of 1 500 elegant carafes.

Glen Elgin lies hidden by the village Fogwatt along the A941 between Rothes and Elgin. There are not many miles between the distilleries in this area; Coleburn neighbouring to the south, Longmorn and Benriach to the north and Glenlossie and Mannochmore to the west.

One of the main attractions for the whisky connoisseur is the six worm tubs, neatly placed in the yard. Only some ten distilleries use this type of tub for condensing the alcohol. Those of Glen Elgin have only been used for the past two years, replacing six old worm tubs, and they are very beautiful. Three rather small pairs of stills limit production and the whisky is stored at Glenlossie and Auchroisk. The older production is stored in dunnage warehouses on site.

Construction of Glen Elgin started at the time when great optimism in the whisky business was replaced by chaos after the Pattison crash. The next Speyside distillery to become established was Glen Keith 60 years later, in 1957. Some sources consider Glen Elgin as the last distillery constructed for six decades in all of Scotland, but in 1908 Malt Mill next to Lagavulin was built.

Glen Elgin became closely associated with White Horse for so many years that its own identity almost vanished. The previous official bottling of Glen Elgin *12 years old* was withdrawn from the *Flora & Fauna* series in 2002 when Diageo launched their series of *Hidden Malts*. This series has now been abandoned by Diageo for an expanded group of *Classic Malts*, launched in autumn 2005. Glen Elgin is represented in it together with 12 other distilleries, including the original six Classic Malts. Two limited editions have also been released – a *19 year old* in 2000 (750 bottles) and a *32 year old* launched in 2003.

Recent independent bottlings include a 20 year old from Douglas Laing released in December 2005 and a white wine finish (Viognier) from 1991 released by Murray McDavid in April 2006.

Hidden Malts 12 years old

Glenesk

Owner:
Diageo

Founded:
1897

Tel:
-

website:
www.malts.com

Capacity:
-

Region/district:
Eastern Highlands

Status:
Dismantled

Visitor centre:
-

% sold as malt whisky:
-

Included in blended (past and/or present):
VAT 69

History:

1897 – The distillery is founded by James Isles. The first name is Highland Esk Distillery.

1898 – The distillery is sold to Septimus Parsonage & Co. Ltd in London.

1899 – The distillery is bought by J. F. Caille Heddle and the name changes to North Esk Distillery.

1910 – A fire breaks out and the distillery has to be rebuilt.

1919 – Thomas Bernard & Co. buys the distillery but only uses the maltings under the name North Esk Maltings.

1938 – Production restarts headed by Joseph Hobbs and Associated Scottish Distillers. The distillery is converted into a grain distillery and the name is changed to Montrose Distillery.

1954 – The distillery is bought by Distillers Company Limited (DCL) who uses the facilities for storage and malting.

1959 – DCL resumes grain distilling.

1964 – DCL transfers operations to Scottish Malt Distillers (SMD) who starts malt distilling. The name changes to Hillside.

1968 – A large drum maltings is built adjacent to the distillery.

1980 – Name changes to Glenesk Distillery & Maltings.

1985 – The distillery closes in December.

1995 – Hillside 1969 is launched as a Rare Malt.

1996 – The last pieces of equipment are taken down. Hillside 1970 (25 years) is launched as a Rare Malt.

1997 – Hillside 1971 is launched as a Rare Malt. The maltings is sold to Paul´s Malt.

Highland Esk, North Esk, Montrose, Glenesk and Hillside all have in common that they refer to this single distillery and its chequered past. It closed slightly more than 20 years after opening, and then it took 45 years until it was re-opened again as a malt distillery. During this time Glenesk was used for malting, grain distilling or just storage.
Glenesk has never enjoyed success as a single malt. Virtually all production has been used in blends such as Vat 69. Even though Glenesk was closed in 1985 the facilities have continued to be active as the drum maltings installed in 1968 are still in production. The maltings was expanded in 1973 and now consists of 24 germination drums. Paul's Malt, who bought the maltings from United Distillers in 1997, belongs to the conglomerate Greencore Malt since 1998. They are currently the sixth largest malt producers in the world with annual production in Glenesk Maltings amounting to around 46 000 tonnes.
It is extremely difficult to find official bottlings. Diageo has released *Hillside* as a *Rare Malt* on three occasions, the last one in 1997. There has also been a *24 year old Glenesk*. It was released in 1993 to celebrate the 25th anniversary of Glenesk maltings.
Among recent independent bottlings are two from Douglas Laing (1971 32 years and 1974 30 years), Duncan Taylor (Peerless) from 1983 (20 years) and Gordon & MacPhail 1984 (20 years). Aside from well-known independent bottlers in the UK, there is also a bottling of a Glenesk 1971 by Swedish Vin & Sprit in the series Part Nan Angelen ('Angel's share' in gaelic).

Gordon & MacPhail (Connoisseurs Choice) 1985

Glenfarclas distillery

Glenfarclas

Owner:
J. & G. Grant

Region/district:
Speyside

Founded:
1836

Status:
Active

Tel:
01807 500257

Visitor centre:
Yes (5/7)

website:
www.glenfarclas.co.uk

Capacity:
3 000 000 litres

% sold as malt whisky:
50% unofficial

Included in blended (past and/or present):
Glen Dowan (J & G Grant), Isle of Skye

History:

1836 – Robert Hay founds the distillery on the original site since 1797.

1865 – Robert Hay passes away and John Grant and his son George buy the distillery for £511.19s on 8th June. They lease it to John Smith at The Glenlivet Distillery.

1870 – John Smith resigns in order to start Cragganmore and J. & G. Grant Ltd takes over.

1889 – John Grant dies and George Grant takes over.

1890 – George Grant dies and his widow Barbara takes over the license while sons John and George control operations.

1895 – John and George Grant take over and form The Glenfarclas-Glenlivet Distillery Co. Ltd with the infamous Pattison, Elder & Co.

Glenfarclas was voted 'Distiller of the Year 2006' by persons in the industry for 'being consistently good and staying true to its core values'. That motivation sums up this second oldest family-owned malt distillery in Scotland well. The Grant family has followed a conscious line since 1865 saying no to wood finishes, restricting sales to independent bottlers and showing a weakness for sherry butts for maturation despite the tenfold higher price for these than for bourbon casks.
Glenfarclas is large in many aspects of production. The mill is a modern Buhler with a capacity of 8 tonnes per hour, the two mash tuns measure 10 metres in diameter, and the three wash stills hold 25 000 litres each and are, as the spirit stills, direct fired by gas, which is unusual. As many as13 persons work in production at the distillery. One reason for the number of staff is that all labour in the ten dunnage warehouses which hold over 60 000 casks is done manually without the aid of lifts. The casks are rolled by hand on rail tracks between the buildings.
Glenfarclas was one of the first distilleries to open a visitor centre. 'The Ship's Room', where each tour is ended with a dram is unique and very beautiful. The decorations were taken from an ocean liner, the 'Empress of Australia' which had a colourful history from 1913 to 1952.
Glenfarclas have a number of expressions in their product range; *10, 12, 15, 21, 25* and *30 years old*. Furthermore, there is *Glenfarclas 105*, one of the first cask strengths in the business, limited editions of *40* and *50 years old* and a number of *vintages*. Since Glenfarclas is lucky in having an unbroken succession of vintages from 1952 onwards they have decided to release a number of these annually. The following were released in 2006: *1989, 1987, 1982, 1977, 1972, 1968, 1967, 1962, 1957* and *1952*. Another new item which is restricted to the German market: *Quarter Cask* distilled in 1987 which is made up of six 125 litre sherry casks that have been vatted together and bottled in 2006.
The rumours that there are two versions of Glenfarclas 15 years old (one new 100% sherry and one old sherry/bourbon) are not true. True however, is that the supplier of sherry butts was changed 15 years ago and this is now reflected in the end product. The 15 year old is always a mix of 60% sherry butts and 40% bourbon casks.
A few independent bottlings have been released recently by Cadenhead; 1972 (33 years) and 1988 (18 years).

History (continued):

1898 – Pattison becomes bankrupt. Glenfarclas encounters financial problems after a major overhaul of the distillery but survives by mortgaging and selling stored whisky to R. I. Cameron, a whisky broker from Elgin.

1914 – John Grant leaves due to ill health and George continues alone.

1948 – The Grant family celebrates the distillery's 100th anniversary, a century of active licensing. It is 9 years late, as the actual anniversary coincided with WW2

1949 – George Grant senior dies and sons George Scott and John Peter inherit the distillery.

1960 – Stills are increased from two to four.

1968 – Glenfarclas is first to launch a cask-strength single malt. It is later named Glenfarclas 105.

1972 – Floor maltings is abandoned and malt is purchased centrally.

1973 – A visitor centre is opened.

1976 – Enlargement from four stills to six.

2001 – Glenfarclas launches its first Flower of Scotland gift tin which becomes a great success and increases sales by 30%.

2002 – George S Grant dies and is succeeded as company chairman by his son John L S Grant

2003 – Two new gift tins are released (10 years old and 105 cask strength).

2005 – A 50 year old is released to commemorate the bi-centenary of John Grant´s birth.

2006 – Ten new vintages are released.

10 years old

12 years old

105 Cask Strength

21 years old

25 years old

Glenfiddich

Owner:	***Region/district:***
William Grant & Sons	Speyside
Founded:	***Status:***
1886	Active
Tel:	***Visitor centre:***
01340 820373 (vc)	Yes (6/7)
website:	
www.glenfiddich.com	
Capacity:	***% sold as malt whisky:***
10 000 000 litres	n/a

Included in blended (past and/or present):
Grant´s

History:

1886 – The distillery is founded by William Grant, 47 years old, who had learned the trade at Mortlach Distillery. The equipment is bought from Mrs. Cummings of Cardow Distillery. The construction totals £800.

1887 – The first distilling takes place on Christmas Day.

1892 – William Grant builds Balvenie.

1898 – The blending company Pattisons, largest customer to Glenfiddich, files for bankruptcy and Grant decides to blend their own whisky. Standfast becomes one of their major brands.

1903 – William Grant & Sons is formed.

1957 – The famous, three-cornered bottle is introduced.

1958 – The floor maltings is closed.

1963 – Glennfiddich becomes the first whisky to be marketed as single malt in the UK and the rest of the world.

Glenfiddich paved the way for the global malt whisky charge. Their conscious marketing of the triangular-shaped bottle on export markets worldwide in the 1960s created an interest which the rest of the business eventually could profit from. The worldwide, annual, sales of 10 million bottles corresponding to approximately 18% of the market, makes Glenfiddich the most sold malt whisky in the world. Demand is still increasing and has forced Glenfiddich to move part of its bottling to new facilities at Bellshill near Glasgow. Although most of Glenfiddich will still be bottled at Dufftown, the bottling of Special Reserve will be moved to Bellshill though water from the Robbie Dhu spring is still used for reducing the whisky to bottling strength.

Glenfiddich is an impressive distillery and has the largest number of stills in the world (no less than 11 wash stills and 18 spirit stills). They are direct-fired by gas which is quite unusual nowadays. They also have 24 washbacks made of Oregon Pine and 43 warehouses which can house 800 000 casks. With their own cooperage, coppersmiths and bottling line they are more or less self-sustaining although they lack their own maltings. Malt is therefore purchased and mixed with a small share of the sister distillery Balvenie's floor maltings.

Glenfiddich was the second distillery, after Mortlach, to be founded in Dufftown and are still owned by the founding family Grant. The two other distilleries in the group, Balvenie and Kininvie, are situated on the premises. It may come as a surprise that Glenfiddich, which was first among distilleries in building a visitor centre, received their five-star attraction status from VisitScotland first 37 years later! Three million visitors have found their way to it over the years.

Glenfiddich´s core range consists of *Special Reserve 12 years*, *Caoran Reserve 12 years*, *Solera Reserve 15 years*, *Ancient Reserve 18 years*, *Gran Reserva 21 years* and *Glenfiddich 30 years*. A number of limited editions, such as *40 and 50 years old*, also exist on top of the standard range. The new *Vintage Reserve* for 2006, a *33 year old* from 1973, was released in June. This was the first time two second-fill sherry butts were chosen for Vintage Reserve. When it comes to the 15 year old, Glenfiddich uses the Solera method from the sherry industry. Large vats are filled with 15 year old whisky. Only half of them are tapped for marrying and later bottling. The Solera vat is then filled up, thus mixing the malt but retaining a diminishing share of the original whisky. Independent bottlings do not exist.

History (continued):

1964 – A version of Standfast's three-cornered bottle is launched for Glenfiddich in green glass.

1969 – Glenfiddich becomes the first distillery in Scotland to open a visitor centre.

1974 – 16 new stills are installed.

2001 – 1965 Vintage Reserve is launched in a limited edition of 480 bottles. Glenfiddich 1937 is bottled (61 bottles).

2002 – Glenfiddich Gran Reserva 21 years old, finished in Cuban rum casks is launched. Sales in the US are not possible due to the trade embargo between the US and Cuba. Caoran Reserve 12 years, an attempt to recreate the peaty Glenfiddich produced during the war years, is launched. Glenfiddich Rare Collection 1937 (61 bottles) is launched at a recommended price of £10 000 each and becomes the oldest Scotch whisky on the market.

2003 – 1973 Vintage Reserve (440 bottles) is launched.

2004 – 1991 Vintage Reserve (13 years) and 1972 Vintage Reserve (519 bottles) are launched.

2005 – Circa £1.7 million is invested in a new visitor centre.

2006 – 1973 Vintage Reserve, 33 years (861 bottles) is released.

Glenfiddich Vintage Reserve 1973

Ancient Reserve 18 years old

Gran Reserva 21 years old

Glenfiddich 30 years old

Special Reserve 12 years old

Caoran Reserve 12 years old

Solera Reserve 15 years old

Glen Garioch

Owner:
Morrison Bowmore (Suntory)

Region/district:
Eastern Highlands

Founded:
1797

Status:
Active

Tel:
01651 873450

Visitor centre:
Yes

website:
www.glengarioch.com

Capacity:
1 000 000 litres
400 000 litres

% sold as malt whisky:
100%

Included in blended (past and/or present):
Rob Roy, Vat 69

History:

1797 – The distiller Thomas Simpson founds Glen Garioch.

1827 – Ingram, Lamb & Co. takes over the distillery.

1837 – The distillery is bought by John Manson & Co., owner of Strathmeldrum Distillery.

1884 – The distillery is bought by J. G. Thompson & Co. from Leith.

1908 – Glengarioch Distillery Company, owned by William Sanderson, buys the distillery.

1933 – Sanderson & Son merges with the gin maker Booth's Distilleries Ltd.

1937 – Booth´s Distilleries Ltd is acquired by Distillers Company Limited (DCL).

1943 – Glen Garioch is transferred to Scottish Malt Distillers (SMD).

1968 – Glen Garioch is decommissioned.

1970 – Sold to Stanley P. Morrison Ltd.

1973 – Reconstruction and production starts again. A more peaty whisky is produced.

1978 – Stills are increased from two to four.

1982 – Becomes the first distillery to use gas from the North Sea for heating.

1994 – Suntory controls all of Morrison Bowmore Distillers Ltd.

1995 – The distillery is mothballed in October.

1997 – The distillery reopens in August.

2004 – 336 bottles of the oldest ever Glen Garioch is released, a 46 year old from 1958.

2005 – 15 year old Bordeaux Cask Finish is launched. A visitor centre opens in October.

2006 – An 8 year old is released.

The time seems finally to have come for this beautiful, urban distillery in the small village of Oldmeldrum to enter the same stage as its fellow Morrison Bowmore distilleries Auchentoshan and Bowmore. The old cooperage has been turned into a visitor centre which opened officially in 2006. The proximity to Aberdeen will probably attract many visitors and if they decide to reopen the malting floors (closed in 1993) the attraction will certainly increase. Only six people work a five-day week and it closes for two to three weeks over Christmas. Just one pair of stills (one of the wash stills is gone and the other spirit still is not in use at the moment) produces just 400 000 litres of alcohol a year of which 100% is sold as single malt. The spirit is tankered to Glasgow, tapped on casks and is then returned to be stored in the distillery´s four warehouses. The main export markets are Taiwan and the USA.

The core range consists of *10, 12, 15* and *21 years old*. An *8 year old* was released in summer 2006 and marks the first bottling from the new production started in 1997. Glen Garioch's first wood finish, launched in 2005, is found among the limited editions. The *15 year old Bordeaux Cask Finish* spent the last seven years on casks from the Grand Cru vineyard St. Julien in Médoc and only 1 800 bottles were released. There is now a new *16 year old* version of this bottling. An even rarer bottling was the *46 year old* from 1958 that was released in 2004. *Highland Tradition* is also available on the duty free market. One of the more recent independent bottlings comes from Douglas Laing; an 11 year old from 1994 released in March 2006. Two older expressions from the same company stand out among independents: 1967 (36 years) and 1968 (36 years) rum cask finish. Murray MacDavid has also released a 1993 (10 years) Pinot Noir finish.

8 years old

Glenglassaugh

Owner:
Edrington Group

Region/district:
Speyside

Founded:
1875

Status:
Mothballed

Tel:
-

Visitor centre:
No

website:
-

Capacity:
-

% sold as malt whisky:
-

Included in blended (past and/or present):
Famous Grouse, Laing´s, Cutty Sark

History:

1873-75 – The distillery is founded by Glenglassaugh Distillery Company consisting of, among others, Thomas Wilson, James Moir, and brothers Alexander and William Morrison. The total cost was £10 000.

1887 – Alexander Morrison embarks on renovation work including new stills and other equipment.

1892 – Alexander Morrison, the sole survivor of the original founders, sells the distillery to one of his customers, Robertson & Baxter. They in turn sell it on to Highland Distilleries Company for £15 000.

1908 – The distillery closes.

1931 – The distillery reopens.

1936 – The distillery closes.

1957-59 – Substantial reconstruction, including acquisition of new stills, takes place. Own maltings are abandoned and the malt is bought from Tamdhu Distillery instead.

1960 – The distillery reopens.

1986 – Glenglassaugh is mothballed in November.

2005 – A 22 year old is released.

2006 – Two limited editions are released - 19 years old and 44 years old.

Photo: © 2005 www.thewhiskystore.de

The history of Glenglassaugh distillery spans short periods of production interspersed with longer periods of inactivity. After the latest refurbishment, the distillery produced malt for the blending industry for 26 years before it was mothballed. A couple of months´ production in 1998 raised hopes for the friends of Glenglassaugh, but the distillery was closed soon after and it is doubtful whether it will ever re-open. The distillery is still intact however with all its equipment in place. The only activities today are in the warehouses which are used by Edrington.
The first official bottling since closure came in 1998 when Highland Distillers released a Glengassaugh from 1973 in their 'Family Silver' series. It is very difficult to find today. Nobody had expected Edrington to release three new limited editions in half a year, but that is what happened in late 2005 when a *22 year old* appeared. A *19 year old* was released in spring 2006, shortly followed by a *44 year old* from 1960. The latter consists of the distiller´s last two oldest casks, with a yield of 351 bottles. The first bottle was presented at Balmoral (the Queen's castle in Scotland), while the rest have been distributed to whisky specialists in the UK, the USA and Asia.
Recent independent bottlings include a 27 year old (1978) from Douglas Laing, a 38 year old (1967) from Signatory and a 1978 Syrah finish from Murray McDavid.

Gordon & MacPhail
Glenglassaugh 1986 (bottled 2000)

Glengoyne

Owner: Ian Macleod Distillers
Region: Southern Highlands

Founded: 1833
Status: Active

Tel: 01360 550254 (vc)
Visitor centre: Yes (6/7)

website: www.glengoyne.com

Capacity: 1 100 000 litres
840 000 litres
% sold as malt whisky: 11%

Included in blended (past and/or present):
Famous Grouse, Lang´s, Cutty Sark

History:

1833 – The distillery is licensed under the name Burnfoot Distilleries by the Edmonstone family.

1851 – George Connell is replaced as licensee by John MacLelland.

1867 – Archibald C. McLelland takes over.

1876 – Lang Brothers buys the distillery and changes the name to Glenguin.

1905 – The name changes to Glengoyne.

1910 – Own floor maltings ceases.

1965-66 – Robertson & Baxter takes over Lang Brothers and the distillery is refurbished. The stills are increased from two to three.

2001 – Glengoyne Scottish Oak Finish (16 years old) is launched as the first single malt stored in Scottish oak casks

2003 – Ian MacLeod Distillers Ltd buys the distillery plus the brand Langs from the Edrington Group (formerly Roberston & Baxter) for £7.2 million.

2004 – The first release after Ian Macleod's acquisition, a 12 year old cask strength.

2005 – Relaunch of Scottish Oak Finish (15 years old). Limited editions of a 19 year old, a 32 year old and a 37 year old cask strength are launched.

2006 – Nine "choices" from Stillmen, Mashmen and Manager are released.

Glengoyne is the southernmost of the Highland distilleries, just a few kilometres north of the imaginary Highland line. In fact, the owners claim that the line divides the distillery itself so that the whisky is distilled in the Highlands but matured in the Lowlands. The Glengoyne single malt reminisces more of a Lowland malt than that of its northern neighbours and once upon a time they used triple distillation. Glengoyne is, along with Macallan, one of few distilleries that still uses the barley variety called Golden Promise.

The owner, bottler and blender Ian MacLeod announced in 2005 that they will increase output by 130 000 litres which means that production will be doubled from when they took over in April 2003.

The core range consists of *10, 12, 17* and *21 year old* with limited editions including the *28 year old* and *Scottish Oak*. The launch of *Scottish Oak Finish* in 2005 was a repeat of the previous owners' innovation from autumn 2001. They produced 31 hogsheads of Scottish oak which were filled with grain spirit from North British for 16 months. Thereafter they were depleted and filled with a 15 year old Glengoyne which was finished for 13 months. A large number of single cask bottlings have been launched recently. The *19, 32* and *37 years old* from late 2005 were followed up by the three stillmen (Duncan, Ewan and Ronnie) selecting their *Stillmen's Choices* (*15, 19* and *22 years old*). Three *Mashmen's Choice* followed suite in 2006, followed by three *Manager's Choice* single casks.

The visitor centre receives some 40 000 visitors annually and new features have recently been added to raise the quality. There are now opportunities for cask tasting and creating your own whisky blend.

12 years old

Glen Grant distillery

Glen Grant

Owner:
Campari Group

Region/district:
Speyside

Founded:
1840

Status:
Active

Tel:
01340 832118

Visitor centre:
Yes (7/7)

website:
www.chivas.com

Capacity:
5 900 000 litres

% sold as malt whisky:
40%

Included in blended (past and/or present):
Chivas Regal, Islay Mist

History:

1840 – The brothers James and John Grant, managers of Dandelaith Distillery, found the distillery.

1861 – The distillery becomes the first to install electric lighting.

1864 – John Grant dies.

1872 – James Grant passes away and the distillery is inherited by his son, James junior (Major James Grant).

1897 – James Grant decides to build another distillery across the road; it is named Glen Grant No. 2.

1902 – Glen Grant No. 2 is mothballed.

1931 – Major Grant dies and is succeeded by his grandson Major Douglas Mackessack.

Despite being number two or three (challenged by Glenlivet and Macallan over the position) in world sales, aficionados rarely mention Glen Grant single malt. Perhaps this is because the number of official bottlings is low or that little of the whisky is sold outside Europe. The winds of change are, however, blowing. Italian Campari made their debut on the whisky market when they acquired Glen Grant from Pernod Ricard. The sell-out was the result of Pernod Ricard's obligation to sell off certain drink brands under orders of the EU when they acquired Allied in summer 2005. Old Smuggler and Braemar blends were thus thrown in when Campari acquired Glen Grant.
Campari seems serious over the future of the distillery and expansion in important but currently small Glen Grant-markets such as the US and Asia are top on the agenda. Today's largest market is Italy where Glen Grant 5 year old is the number one selling single malt since long.
Dennis Malcolm has been called in as distillery manager to master the change. It is difficult, not to say impossible, to find somebody with more experience of Glen Grant as he worked there between 1961 and 1970 and again from 1983 to 1999. His most recent employment was at Balmenach which he revived during his five years as manager.
The development of Glen Grant is greatly due to James Grant (the Major) son of one of the founders. As a major entrepreneur he was appreciated not just for his work for the distillery but also for the whole area around Rothes. He was also the person behind 'The Garden', which today is an additional attraction to the distillery itself.
The four pairs of stills are somewhat peculiar in that they have vertical sides at the base of the neck and are all fitted with purifiers. This gives an increased reflux and creates a light and pale whisky. Ex-bourbon casks are usually used for maturing and the share of sherry butts is less than 10%, mostly used for the 10 year old. According to an agreement, Chivas buys 60% of produce the coming years to use in mainly Chivas Regal.
The Glen Grant core range consists of a *5 year old*, a *10 year old* and a *no age statement.* Recent, limited editions include a *14 year old cask strength*. Most independent bottlers have been involved with Glen Grant. Gordon & MacPhail in particular have specialised in very old expressions with the latest a 50 year old from 1956. Other recent independent bottlings include Duncan Taylor 35 years old, Berry Brothers 32 years old, Ian MacLeod 50 years old and a wine finish from Douglas Laing (12 years old).

History (continued):

1953 – J. & J. Grant merges with George & J. G. Smith who runs Glenlivet distillery, forming The Glenlivet & Glen Grant Distillers Ltd.

1961 – Armando Giovinetti and Douglas Mackessak found a friendship that eventually leads to Glen Grant becoming the most sold malt whisky in Italy.

1965 – Glen Grant No. 2 is back in production, but renamed Caperdonich.

1972 – The Glenlivet & Glen Grant Distillers merges with Hill Thompson & Co. and Longmorn-Glenlivet Ltd to form The Glenlivet Distillers. The drum maltings ceases.

1973 – Stills are increased from four to six.

1977 – The Chivas & Glenlivet Group (Seagrams) buys Glen Grant Distillery. Stills are increased from six to ten.

2001 – Pernod Ricard and Diageo buy Seagrams Spirits and Wine; with Pernod acquiring the Chivas Group.

2006 – Campari buys Glen Grant for €115 million in a deal that includes the acquisition of Old Smuggler and Braemar for another €15 million.

The Major's spirit safe in the garden.

5 years old

No age

Glen Keith

Owner:
Chivas Brothers (Pernod Ricard)

Region/district:
Speyside

Founded:
1957

Status:
Mothballed

Tel:
01542 783042

Visitor centre:
No

website:
-

Capacity:
-

% sold as malt whisky:
-

Included in blended (past and/or present):
Chivas Regal, Passport, 100 Pipers

History:

1957 – The Distillery is founded by Chivas Brothers (Seagrams).

1958 – Production starts.

1970 – The first gas-fuelled still in Scotland is installed, the number of stills increases from three to five.

1976 – Own maltings (Saladin box) ceases.

1983 – A sixth still is installed.

1994 – The first official bottling, a 10 year old, is released as part of Seagram's Heritage Selection.

2000 – The distillery is mothballed.

2001 – Pernod Ricard takes over Chivas Brothers from Seagrams.

Glen Keith, usually an anonymous distillery, has featured on the whisky lovers' grapevine in recent years. The subject was two very special bottlings released by independent bottler Signatory - Craigduff and Glenisla and whether they were distilled at Glen Keith or at Strathisla. Signatory, who initially depicted Strathisla as the producer now claim with support from previous employees, that both were in fact distilled at Glen Keith. Other sources uphold that at least Craigduff is from Strathisla. Both are peated malts although Craigduff is the more peated of the two. The peat in Craigduff is said to stem from an experiment with peated water brought in from Stornoway on Isle of Lewis and added to the wash charge, while the considerably milder Glenisla is claimed to having been produced by using peat from Shetland and possibly distilled in column stills installed at Glen Keith in the 70s. Be that as it may, Glen Keith has served as an experimental laboratory for Chivas during its short lifespan. It started with triple distillation which was abandoned in 1970. That year Glen Keith became the first to use gas-fired stills. The next innovation appeared in 1980 when microprocessors were installed to control mashing, milling and distilling. Today, Glen Keith accommodates a technical centre and the laboratory from Miltonduff was also moved there when Allieds' distilleries were taken over. The distillery itself has been closed since 2000 and it is highly unlikely that it will produce whisky again although the stills can clearly be seen through the large windows. The official *10 year old* is difficult to obtain but there are independent bottlings. Among the most recent are two from Gordon & MacPhail (1967 and 1993), a 33 year old (1971) from Duncan Taylor as well as a 32 year old (1973) and a 14 year old (1991) from Douglas Laing.

10 years old

Glenkinchie

Owner:
Diageo

Region/district:
Lowlands

Founded:
1837

Status:
Active

Tel:
01875 342004

Visitor centre:
Yes (6/7)

website:
www.malts.com

Capacity:
1 700 000 litres

% sold as malt whisky:
10% unofficially

Included in blended (past and/or present):
Haig Gold Label, Johnnie Walker

History:

1825 – A distillery known as Milton is founded by John and George Rate.

1834 – Production probably stops this year.

1837 – The Rate brothers are registered as licensees of a distillery named Glenkinchie.

1840 – James Gray takes over operations.

1852 – John Rate is once again licensee.

1853 – John Rate sells the distillery to a farmer Christie who converts it to a sawmill.

1881 – The buildings are bought by a consortium from Edinburgh made up of wine merchants, whisky blenders and brewers.

1890 – Glenkinchie Distillery Company is founded with Major James Gray as General Manager. Reconstruction and refurbishment is on-going for the next few years.

1914 – Glenkinchie forms Scottish Malt Distillers (SMD) with four lowland distilleries, Rosebank, Clydesdale, St. Magdalene and Grange.

1925 – Distillers Company Limited (DCL) buys SMD.

1939-45 – Glenkinchie is one of few distilleries allowed to maintain a small production during the war.

1968 – Floor maltings is decommissioned.

1969 – The maltings is converted into a museum.

1988 – Glenkinchie 10 years becomes one of selected six in the Classic Malt series.

1996 – The visitor centre is modernized.

1998 – A Distiller's Edition with amontillado finish is launched.

There are two reasons for Glenkinchie having survived as a distillery when so many others, in the Lowlands in particular, were decommissioned. One was the formation of Scottish Malt Distillers with four other distilleries which took it through the hard years after the First World War. The other is the proximity to Edinburgh which obviously makes it an attractive distillery to visit and which also perhaps contributed to Glenkinchie being selected as one of six Classic Malts.

Glenkinchie is also unique in having the Museum of Malt Whisky Production, opened already in 1969 in the old maltings. A distillery model scale 1:6 (18 metres long) which was built for the British Empire Exhibition in 1924 became one of the main attractions. It lay dismantled at different distilleries (e. g. Glenlossie and Mortlach) for many years but was reassembled in 1974 and now stands in the museum which was renovated in 1995.

Glenkinchie only has two stills, with the wash still (30 963 litres) being one of the industry's largest. They also use worm tubs for cooling the spirits but these are unusually enough made from cast iron rather than wood.

Diageo cannot be accused of flooding the market with new versions of Glenkinchie. The product range consists of a *10 year old* and a *Distillers' Edition* previously 12 years but now *14 years*. A *Special Edition cask strength* for 'Friends of Classic Malts' has also been produced. Independent bottlings are extremely rare. A couple of the latest are Signatory 1987 17 years old and an 18 year old from the same year released by Cadenhead in 2006.

1991 Distiller's Edition

Glenlivet

Owner:
Chivas Brothers (Pernod Ricard)

Region/district:
Speyside

Founded:
1824

Status:
Active

Tel:
01340 821720 (vc)

Visitor centre:
Yes (7/7)

website:
www.theglenlivet.com

Capacity:
5 900 000 litres

% sold as malt whisky:
n/a

Included in blended (past and/or present):
Chivas Regal, Royal Salute

History:

1817 – George Smith inherits the farm distillery Upper Drummin from his father Andrew Smith who has been distilling on the site since 1774.

1840 – George Smith buys Delnabo farm near Tomintoul and leases Cairngorm Distillery. His son William takes over operations at Upper Drummin.

1845 – George Smith leases three other farms, one of which is situated on the river Livet and is called Minmore.

1846 – William Smith develops tuberculosis and his brother John Gordon moves back home to assist his father. Sales of Smith's Glenlivet increases steadily and neither Upper Drummin nor Cairngorm Distillery can meet demand.

1858 – George Smith buys Minmore farm, which he has leased for some time, and obtains permission from the Duke of Gordon to build a distillery.

1859 – Upper Drummin and Cairngorm close and all equipment is brought to Minmore which is renamed The Glenlivet Distillery.

Two objectives have been set up by Pernod Ricard since autumn 2004. One is to let Chivas Regal take back its position as most sold premium blended from Johnnie Walker Black Label who attained it in 2000. They seem well on their way of achieving that. The other is to increase sales of Glenlivet to challenge the current top seller Glenfiddich. Much remains to be done to reach the second objective even if Glenlivet increased global sales by 9% during 2004 and by another 14% in 2005/06.
Stiff competition is likely to be encountered from Glen Grant which Pernod Ricard have recently sold to Campari. Glenlivet is number one in the USA, Mexico and Hungary today.
Despite being a large distillery, Glenlivet is run by few employees and only six people work in production. The reason for this is that casks are never filled on site. Instead they are sent to Chivas bonded warehouses in Keith for filling. Nor do they have warehousemen at the distillery; instead they are assisted by a central team which alternates between the different distilleries in the group. 62 000 casks are stored on-site in both dunnage and racked warehouses. The rest is stored at other distilleries.
A new feature at the distillery is the small, 12 gallon still which HM Revenue & Customs have granted special license to use twice a year. The size is way below the minimum legally required, 40 gallons, in The Small Stills Act of 1816 and reminisces of the many illegal stills in use in the area in the old days.
Glenlivet's core range is the *12 year old*, matured in bourbon casks, the *French Oak 15 years* (with 6-9 months finish in new Limousin Oak casks) and the *18 year old* (matured in ex-sherry casks). Limited editions include the re-launched *21 year old Archive* and the recently released *1972 Cellar Collection*. Earlier versions of the Cellar Collection include *1964* (40 years old) and *1983* (20 years old). The Glenlivet *16 year old cask strength*, a limited edition launched in 2004, is still available.
Three expressions are earmarked for the Duty Free market: *First Fill Sherry Cask 12 years old* (replaced American Oak 12 years), *15 years old* and *Nadurra* (16 years old and non-chill filtered). A *cask strength* version of *Nadurra* was released in the U.S. in autumn 2006.
Gordon & MacPhail which has launched a considerable number of vintage under the name of George & J. G. Smith's stand out among independents. Douglas Laing has recently released two bottlings; a 20 year old from 1985 and a 25 year old from 1980 and 2006 saw the release of a Duncan Taylor 1968 (37 years) and a Cadenhead 1976 (30 years).

History (continued):

1864 – George Smith cooperates with the whisky agent Andrew P. Usher and exports the whisky with great success.

1871 – George Smith dies and his son John Gordon takes over.

1880 – John Gordon Smith applies for and is granted sole rights to the name The Glenlivet. Only Glenlivet Distillery may thus use the name. All distilleries wishing to use Glenlivet in their names must from now hyphenate it with their brand names.

1890 – A fire breaks out and some of the buildings are replaced.

1896 – Another two stills are installed.

1901 – John Gordon Smith dies.

1904 – John Gordon's nephew George Smith Grant takes over.

1921 – Captain Bill Smith Grant, son of George Smith Grant, takes over.

1953 – George & J. G. Smith Ltd merges with J. & J. Grant of Glen Grant Distillery and forms the company Glenlivet & Glen Grant Distillers Ltd.

1966 – Floor maltings closes.

1970 – Glenlivet & Glen Grant Distillers Ltd merges with Longmorn-Glenlivet Distilleries Ltd and Hill Thomson & Co. Ltd to form The Glenlivet Distillers Ltd.

1978 – Seagrams buys The Glenlivet Distillers Ltd. A visitor centre opens.

1996/97 – The visitor centre is expanded, and a multimedia facility installed.

2000 – French Oak 12 years and American Oak 12 years are launched

2001 – Pernod Ricard and Diageo buy Seagram Spirits & Wine. Pernod Ricard thereby gain control of the Chivas group.

2004 – This year sees a lavish relaunch of Glenlivet, the objective is to overtake Glenfiddich as number one on the sales lists. French Oak 15 years replaces the previous 12 year old.

2005 – Two new duty-free versions are introduced – The Glenlivet 12 year old First Fill and Nadurra, a 16 year old non chill-filtered matured in first-fill bourbon casks. The 1972 Cellar Collection (2 015 bottles) is launched.

2006 – Nadurra 16 year old cask strength is released.

21 year old Archive

Nadurra cask strength

1972 Cellar Collection

12 years old

18 years old

15 years old
French Oak Reserve

Glenlochy

Owner:
Diageo

Region:
Western Highlands

Founded:
1898

Status:
Demolished

Tel:
-

Visitor centre:
-

website:
www.malts.com

Capacity:
-

% sold as malt whisky:
-

Included in blended (past and/or present):
-

History:

1898 – The distillery is founded by Glenlochy Fort William Distillery Co. headed by David McAndies.

1901 – Production starts.

1919 – The distillery closes.

1925 – In production again.

1926 – The distillery closes.

1937 – Train & McIntyre buys the distillery.

1938 – In production again. The distillery is incorporated in Associated Scottish Distilleries.

1953 – Distillers Company Limited (DCL) buys Train & McIntyre from American company National Distillers and transfers Glenlochy to Scottish Malt Distillers (SMD).

1983 – The distillery is taken out of operation.

1986 – SMD applies for permission to demolish the distillery but it is not granted.

1992 – The premises are sold to the hotel group West Coast Inns Ltd which obtains permission to demolish everything excepting the kiln with its pagoda roof which is declared a historic building.

1995 – Glenlochy 1969 (25 years) is launched as a Rare Malt.

1996 – Glenlochy 1969 (26 years) is launched as a Rare Malt.

2001 – Old Malt Cask Glenlochy 49 years is launched by Douglas Laing.

2003 – Another Old Malt Cask (38 years) is launched.

Fort William once had three contemporary distilleries but today only one remains; Ben Nevis Distillery. Glenlochy is closed and Nevis distillery founded in 1878 as an extension of Ben Nevis merged with its parent in 1908. The warehouses of Nevis were used for a few decades, but currently there are only residential buildings on the premises.

There is, however, more to see in Glenlochy. Parts of the buildings have been reconstructed into a guest house, but the kiln with its pagoda roof and the malt barn are both B-listed and therefore protected from demolition. Lochaber Housing is in the process of building 16 flats in the malt barn and Grid Construction Ltd has applied for permission to convert the maltings to 7 flats.

Some distilleries are not fully appreciated until after their decommissioning, and Glenlochy certainly falls into this category. It was established during the turbulent years of the Pattison crash and did not exactly get off the ground easily. The production was always low as there were only two stills and several long interruptions eventually led to its closing in 1983.

One interesting character turns up in the history of Glenlochy, the Canadian millionaire Joseph W. Hobbs. He came to Scotland already in 1931 searching for distilleries that could be purchased for the American company National Distillers. Glenury Royal, Bruichladdich, Fettercairn, Benromach and Glenlochy were some of the distilleries he managed to lay his hands on. He also safeguarded his own business and purchased Ben Nevis in 1941 as a private venture.

Official bottlings have occurred twice in the *Rare Malts* series (released *1995* and *1996*). Douglas Laing (Old Malt Cask) released a 49 year old in 2003 and that same year Gordon & McPhail (Rare Old) released a 37 year old. More recent independents come from Signatory and Duncan Taylor, both 24 years old and bottled in 2005.

Gordon & MacPhail, Rare Old 1965

Glenlossie

Owner:
Diageo

Region/district:
Speyside

Founded:
1876

Status:
Active

Tel:
01343 862000

Visitor centre:
No

website:
www.malts.com

Capacity:
1 100 000 litres

% sold as malt whisky:
0.5% unofficial

Included in blended (past and/or present):
Haig Gold Label

History:

1876 – John Duff, former manager at Glendronach Distillery, founds the distillery. Alexander Grigor Allan (to become part-owner of Talisker Distillery), the whisky trader George Thomson and Charles Shirres (both will co-found Longmorn Distillery some 20 years later with John Duff) and H. Mackay are also involved in the company.

1895 – The company Glenlossie-Glenlivet Distillery Co. is formed. Alexander Grigor Allan passes away.

1896 – John Duff becomes more involved in Longmorn and Mackay takes over management of Glenlossie.

1919 – Distillers Company Limited (DCL) takes over the company.

1929 – A fire breaks out and causes considerable damage.

1930 – DCL transfers operations to Scottish Malt Distillers (SMD).

1962 – Stills are increased from four to six.

1971 – Another distillery, Mannochmore, is constructed by SMD on the premises. A dark grains plant is installed.

1990 – A 10 year old is launched in the Flora & Fauna series.

The blender's list from 1974 categorizes malt and grain whiskies according to the characteristics appropriate to a blended whisky. Glenlossie, relatively anonymous for the general single malt buyer, steps into the limelight in this list as it is rated 'top class', i. e. among the 12 top single malts.
The by-products of the distillation of whisky has to be disposed of carefully in order not to cause environmental pollution. During the 1990s United Distillers spent £4.7 million on a large scale project in the management of harmful waste disposal.
A dark grains plant, was constructed at Glenlossie, with the purpose of transforming draff and pot ale into cattle feed. The plant is huge and is, on a weekly basis, able to process 2 600 tonnes of draff and 8 million litres of pot ale to produce 1 000 tonnes of dark grains. The unit also serves some ten other distilleries in the vicinity. The whole Scottish whisky industry produces 750 000 tonnes of animal feed annually. The quantity is so large that a proportion is exported to other European countries via Trident Feeds - who, incidentally, handle 80% of the whisky industry's dried by-products.
Scottish Malt Distillers (SMD), the owners at the time, built another distillery, Mannochmore, on the premises in 1971 and both are now operating with the same, alternating workforce. This means that Glenlossie is only operating between October and March. Both distilleries share a number of warehouses, both dunnage and racked, which together have a total capacity of 200 000 casks.
Glenlossie is Diageo's third smallest distillery after Oban and Royal Lochnagar in capacity.
The only official bottling available today is a *10 year old* in the *Flora & Fauna* series. Glenlossie´s high quality has, however, inspired several independent bottlers. The two most recent are a Gordon & MacPhail (Connoisseurs Choice) 1978 released in 2005 and a 12 year old from Douglas Laing released in 2006.

Flora & Fauna 10 years old

Glen Mhor

Owner:
Diageo

Founded:
1892

Tel:
www.malts.com

website:
-

Capacity:
-

Included in blended (past and/or present):
-

Region/district:
Northern Highlands

Status:
Demolished

Visitor centre:
-

% sold as malt whisky:
-

History:

1892 – John Birnie, Manager of Glen Albyn distillery, and James Mackinlay in Inverness are commissioned by Charles Mackinlay & Co. to set up the distillery. The architect is Charles Doig.

1894 – Production starts in December.

1906 – John Walker & Co. buys part of the company.

1920 – Mackinlay & Birnie Ltd buys Glen Mhor and neighbouring Glen Albyn.

1954 – A Saladin box replaces floor maltings which makes Glen Mhor one of the first distilleries to introduce mechanical malting.

1972 – The distillery is bought by Distillers Company Limited (DCL).

1980 – Own maltings is decommissioned.

1983 – The distillery closes.

1986 – The buildings are demolished.

2001 – A 22 year old from 1979 is launched in the Rare Malts series.

2005 – A 28 year old from 1976 is launched in the Rare Malts series.

Glen Mhor in Inverness was closed the ill-fated year of 1983 when United Distillers wound up so many of their smaller distilleries. This hit Inverness especially hard as neighbouring Glen Albyn was also closed down. Millburn, the third distillery in Inverness, was spared until 1985. Glen Mhor still has followers mourning the closure until this day, but its biggest fan was probably Neil Gunn, famous author who also worked as an Excise Officer at several distilleries. He was established at Glen Mohr since 1924. According to Brian Townsend in *Scotch Missed*, Gunn became so inspired by Glen Mhor that he stated 'Until a man has had the luck to chance upon a perfectly matured malt, he does not really know what whisky is'.

The Birnie family was well known and respected in Inverness and John Birnie was even a Provost. He worked for a time as Distillery Manager at Glen Albyn but when he was not allowed to buy in to it he set about building Glen Mhor. Revenge came in 1920 when he bought Glen Albyn with James Mackinlay. Birnie's son William took over from him and he was 80 years old when both distilleries were sold to DCL in 1972. Today there is a supermarket where Glen Mhor once was active.

The only official bottlings of Glen Mhor are a couple of *Rare Malts, 22 years old* from *1979* and *28 years old* from *1976*.

Independent bottlings have become increasingly rare. The most recent are Signatory (Silent Stills) from 1965 (released 2003), Gordon & MacPhail 1979 (released 2004) and Duncan Taylor 1975 (released 2005).

Rare Malts 1976 28 years old

Glenmorangie distillery. Photo: © Glenmorangie Co

Glenmorangie

Owner:
The Glenmorangie Co (Moët Hennessy)

Region/district:
Northern Highlands

Founded:
1843

Status:
Active

Tel:
01862 892477 (vc)

Visitor centre:
Yes (5/7)

website:
www.glenmorangie.com

Capacity:
4 000 000 litres

% sold as malt whisky:
70% unofficial

Included in blended (past and/or present):
The Bailie Nicol Jarvie, Highland Queen, Martins

History:

1843 – William Mathesen, formerly part-owner of Balblair Distillery, and brother John apply for a license for a farm distillery called Morangie, which is rebuilt by them. Production took place here in 1738, and possibly since 1703.

1849 – Production starts in November.

1880 – Exports to foreign destinations such as Rome and San Francisco commence.

1887 – The distillery is rebuilt and Glenmorangie Distillery Company Ltd is formed.

1918 – 40% of the distillery is sold to GDCL´s largest customer, Macdonald & Muir Ltd and 60 % to the whisky dealer Durham. Macdonald & Muir takes over Durham's share by the late thirties.

1931 – The distillery closes due to the depression and prohibition in the US.

1936 – Production restarts in November.

1980 – Number of stills increases from two to four and own maltings ceases.

1990 – The number of stills is doubled to eight.

Dr. Bill Lumsden, Master Distiller at Glenmorangie.

No other distillery takes wood as seriously as Glenmorangie. The distillery has even bought oak forests in the Ozark Mountains of Missouri in order to secure a high-quality supply for their casks. The casks are used for storing bourbon for the first four years before being sent overseas to Scotland. Glenmorangie have set the standards for the now so popular wood finishes. Their first malt that finished its maturation on ex port casks appeared already in 1994.
Glenmorangie is highly protective of their whisky and when they sell to the blending industry they always mix in a small amount of Glen Moray. This practice prevents casks from reaching independent bottlers who could then release Glenmorangie single malt out of the distillery's control.
The company's headquarters lie in Broxburn west of Edinburgh. A huge bottling plant, where most of the company's employees work, is also situated there.
Glenmorangie is the best-selling malt in Scotland covering roughly 15% of the market and they aim at becoming number one in the UK as well. They are currently number two and closing in on Glenfiddich. On the world list of best-selling malt whiskies, Glenmorangie takes place five with c. 6% of the world market.
The core range consists of *10 years old*, *15 years old*, *18 years old* and four *wood finishes*; *Port*, *Sherry*, *Madeira* and *Burgundy*. There are also a large number of wood finishes and vintages with more recent ones such as *Artisan Cask*, *1993 Truffle Oak Reserve* and a *30 year old Oloroso finish*.
An extra dimension to the wood finishes is added when one is aware that the Sauternes finish is obtained by casks from Chateau d'Yquem, the Cote de Nuits finish by casks from Domaine de la Romanée-Conti and the Bordeaux finish by casks from Chateau Mouton Rotschild.
Recent rumour has it that owners LVMH are not content with the large volumes of Glenmorangie sold as own-label whiskies by chains Asda and Sainsbury's. Management fears that such large volumes of low-priced Glenmorangie may harm the brand.

History (continued):

1994 – A visitor centre opens. September sees the launch of Glenmorangie Port Wood Finish which marks the start of a number of different wood finishes.

1995 – Glenmorangie´s Tain l´Hermitage (Rhone wine) is launched

1996 – Two different wood finishes are launched, Madeira and Sherry. Glenmorangie plc is formed.

1997 – A museum opens.

2001 – A limited edition of a cask strength port wood finish is released in July, Cote de Beaune Wood Finish is launched in September and Three Cask (ex-Bourbon, charred oak and ex-Rioja) is launched in October for Sainsbury's.

2002 – A Sauternes finish, a 20 year Glenmorangie with two and a half years in Sauternes casks, is launched.

2003 – Burgundy Wood Finish is launched in July and a limited edition of cask strength Madeira-matured (i. e. not just finished) in August.

2004 – Glenmorangie buys the Scotch Malt Whisky Society which has 27 000 members worldwide. The Macdonald family decides to sell Glenmorangie plc (including the distilleries Glenmorangie, Glen Moray and Ardbeg). Bidding is frantic and the buyer is Moët Hennessy (owned by Diageo and LVMH) at £300 million. A new version of Glenmorangie Tain l´Hermitage (28 years) is released and Glenmorangie Artisan Cask is launched in November.

2005 – A 30 year old is launched.

Wood finishes – Port, Sherry, Burgundy, Madeira

10 years old

18 years old

Glen Moray

Owner: The Glenmorangie Co (Moët Hennessy)

Region/district: Speyside

Founded: 1897

Status: Active

Tel: 01343 542577

Visitor centre: Yes (6/7)

website: www.glenmoray.com

Capacity: 2 000 000 litres

% sold as malt whisky: 5-10%

Included in blended (past and/or present):
Highland Queen

History:

1897 – West Brewery, dated 1828, is reconstructed as Glen Moray Distillery.

1910 – The distillery closes.

1912 – The distillery reopens, but soon closes again.

1920 – Financial troubles force the distillery to be put up for sale. Buyer is Macdonald & Muir.

1923 – Production restarts.

1932 – No whisky is produced this year.

1958 – A reconstruction takes place and the floor maltings are replaced by a Saladin box.

1976 – The first official bottling is released.

1978 – Own maltings are terminated.

1979 – The number of stills is increased from two to four.

1992 – Two old stills are replaced by new.

1996 – Macdonald & Muir Ltd changes name to Glenmorangie plc.

1999 – Three wood finishes are introduced - Chardonnay (no age) and Chenin Blanc (12 and 16 years respectively).

2004 – Louis Vuitton Moët Hennessy buys Glenmorangie plc for £300 million. Glen Moray becomes a member of the The Malt Whisky Trail. A new visitor centre is inaugurated and 276 bottles of Glen Moray 1986 cask strength are released. A 20 and a 30 year old are released late in the year. Wood finishing ceases.

2005 – The Fifth Chapter (Manager's Choice from Graham Coull) is released. Jim Murray announces Glen Moray 1986 Commemorative Bottling to Single Scotch Malt of the Year in Whisky Bible 2006.

2006 – Two vintages, 1963 and 1964, and a new Manager's Choice from Graham Coull are released.

Glen Moray and Glen Garioch have one thing in common; both have a 'little brother'-relationship to two other distilleries. Glen Garioch has Auchentoshan and Bowmore to squabble with and within Glenmorangie Co, to which Glen Moray belongs; it is Glenmorangie and Ardbeg that receive most attention. Still, Glen Moray is now making itself heard.
For the last few years, Glen Moray has stopped wine-finishing their malt and are now strictly into ex-bourbon and a few ex-sherry casks. A dapper visitor centre has grown up and exciting vintage expressions have recently been launched.
Glen Moray is where Macdonald & Muir started their experiments with wood finishes which were later commercialised through Glenmorangie. Glen Moray became famous for its wine finishes in Chardonnay and Chenin Blanc casks which started in 1999.
A new manager, Graham Coull who is only the fifth since starting in 1897, has been appointed. He has previously worked at Glenfiddich and Balvenie and now manages 17 people of which eight are in production and three in warehouses. They work in three-shifts and the distillery only closes for a couple of weeks around Christmas. Two indirectly heated wash stills (10 000 litres) and two spirit stills (6 000 litres) account for full production. Around 50 000 casks are stored on site in nine dunnage warehouses and one palletized.
The core range consists of *Classic* (no age statement), *12 years old* and *16 years old*. Limited editions include *1992 The Fifth Chapter* (Manager's Edition) which will be replaced by a 1989 first fill bourbon called *Signature*. There are also *20* and *30 years old* as well as several vintages. New vintages during 2006 are *1963* (50 bottles) and *1964* (100 bottles). A special version called *Mountain Oak Malt* has also been released (800 bottles) which has a combination of both charred and toasted casks. Glen Moray single malt is number 4 on the UK sales list.

16 years old

Glen Ord

Owner:
Diageo

Region/district:
Northern Highlands

Founded:
1838

Status:
Active

Tel:
01463 872004 (vc)

Visitor centre:
Yes (5/7)

website:
www.malts.com

Capacity:
3 400 000 litres

% sold as malt whisky:
n/a

Included in blended (past and/or present):
Dewar´s, Johnnie Walker

History:

1838 – Thomas Mackenzie founds the distillery and licenses it to Ord Distillery Co. (Robert Johnstone and Donald MacLennan).

1847 – Robert Johnstone, by now single owner of Ord Distillery Co., becomes bankrupt and the distillery is put up for sale.

1855 – Alexander MacLennan and Thomas McGregor buy the distillery.

1870 – Alexander MacLennan dies and the distillery is taken over by his widow who eventually marries the banker Alexander Mackenzie.

1877 – Alexander Mackenzie leases the distillery.

1878 – Alexander Mackenzie builds a new stillhouse and barely manages to start production before a fire destroys it on 8th November.

1882 – Mackenzie registers the name Glenoran to be used for whisky from Glen Ord.

1896 – Alexander Mackenzie dies and the distillery is sold to the blending company James Watson & Co. for £15 800.

1923 – John Jabez Watson, James Watson's son and the only remaining family member, dies and the distillery is sold to John Dewar & Sons. The name is changed from Glen Oran to Glen Ord.

1925 – Dewar's joins Distillers Company Limited.

1930 – Glen Ord is transferred to Scottish Malt Distillers (SMD).

1961 – Substantial renovation takes place; floor maltings is abandoned in favour of a Saladin box.

1966 – The two stills are increased to six.

1968 – To augment the Saladin box a drum maltings is built.

1983 – Malting in the Saladin box ceases.

1988 – A visitor centre is opened.

2002 – A 12 year old in the Hidden Malt series is launched.

2003 – A limited-edition cask strength, 28 years, is launched.

2004 – A 25 year old is launched.

2005 – A 30 year old is launched as a Special Release from Diageo.

2006 – A 12 year old Singleton of Glen Ord is launched.

Glen Ord is situated in the fertile Black Isle, north of Inverness. Surrounded by barley fields it is perhaps not so surprising that Diageo decided to keep and expand the maltings at Glen Ord. Glen Ord's malt is produced in drum maltings since 1996 and it also supplies the likes of Talisker, Clynelish and Teaninich.
Only three of Diageo's distilleries have a greater production capacity than Glen Ord, but despite this the whisky is among Diageo's more unknown. The frequent name changes (Glenordie, Ord, Ordie, Muir of Ord) have not helped to imprint the whisky in the mind of malt fanatics.
Large amounts of waste water from the distilling process and maltings are generated at Glen Ord. This problem is shared with many other distilleries, but Glen Ord became unique in being the first UK company trying out a new method for treating the effluent problem. The process is called Biobed MP and cleans biologically with the help of bacteria.
Despite its comparatively anonymous existence, the visitor centre receives 20 000 visitors annually.
The distillery itself is an interesting blend of modern and old. The large windows from floor to ceiling are comparable to those of Caol Ila but lack the latter´s fantastic view.
Besides the *12 year old* in *Hidden Malts*, Glen Ord has been bottled as a *Rare Malt,* the last time in 1998. Even more interesting is a *28 year old* which appeared in November 2003, a *25 year old* which was launched in 2004 and a *30 year old*, the oldest release to be offered by the distillery, launched in 2005.
A special version, *The Singleton of Glen Ord*, was launched in 2006. It is a 12 year old mainly targeted at selected Asian markets.
Independent bottlings of Glen Ord are rarely encountered but one of the latest was a Cadenhead 22 year old from 1983 released in 2006.

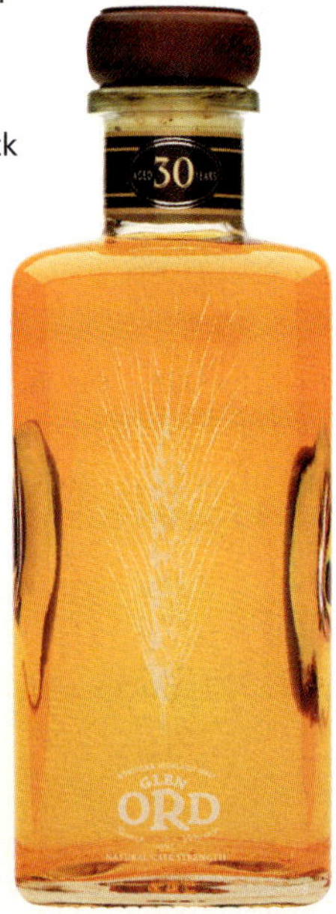

30 years old

Glenrothes

Owner:
The Edrington Group

Region/district:
Speyside

Founded:
1878

Status:
Active

Tel:
01340 872300

Visitor centre:
No

website:
www.glenrotheswhisky.com

Capacity:
5 600 000 litres

% sold as malt whisky:
2%

Included in blended (past and/or present):
Cutty Sark, Famous Grouse

History:

1878 – James Stuart & Co., licensees of Macallan since 1868, begins planning a new distillery in Rothes. Robert Dick and William Grant, both from Caledonian Bank and the lawyer John Cruickshank are partners in the company. Stuart has financial problems so Dick, Grant and Cruickshank terminate the partnership and form William Grant & Co. while James Stuart focuses on Macallan. William Grant & Co. takes over the building of the distillery in Rothes.

1879 – Production starts in May.

1884 – The distillery changes name to Glenrothes-Glenlivet.

1887 – William Grant & Co. joins forces with Islay Distillery Co. (owners of Bunnahabhain Distillery) and forms Highland Distillers Company.

1897 – A fire ravages the distillery in December.

1898 – Capacity doubles.

1903 – An explosion causes substantial damage.

1922 – A fire breaks out in one of the warehouses.

1963 – Expansion from four to six stills.

1980 – Expansion from six to eight stills.

1989 – Expansion from eight to ten stills.

1999 – Edrington and William Grant & Sons buy Highland Distillers.

2002 – Four single cask malts from 1966 and 1967 are launched.

2005 – A 30 year old is launched together with Select Reserve and Vintage 1985.

2006 – 1994 Vintage is launched.

Glenrothes sits quietly at the end of a street in central Rothes. But production-wise it is certainly not anonymous as its five stills give it a capacity close to that of Macallan.
Sales of Glenrothes have more than quadrupled thanks to renowned, London-based wine merchants Berry Brothers & Rudd (BBR) who are licensed to tap official bottlings of the Edrington-owned Glenrothes.
Glenrothes contributes to many blended whiskies, especially Cutty Sark. Today Cutty Sark is among the Top 10 of blended whiskies and sells in 24 million bottles annually worldwide.
For some years BBR have only produced bottlings of the single malt when a cask is determined to be mature and shows a sufficiently high quality. Glenrothes surprised the market in autumn 2005 as vintages and some occasional single casks have been trademarks of the distillery. First came a *30 year old* which consisted of three casks from the early seventies which had been vatted together at the beginning of the eighties. The purpose was to launch a 12 year old Glenrothes, but minds were changed and the whisky was not bottled until in 2004.
The next expression was *Select Reserve* without age statement, devised to provide continuity in the product range as vintages come and go.
A couple of weeks later *Vintage 1985* appeared in a second edition (the first came in 1997). The most recent official bottling was *Vintage 1994* released in August 2006.
Among other later vintages from Glenrothes, *1972* (bottled in 2004) and *1992* (bottled in 2005) deserve mention. Berry Brothers also launched four *single cask bottlings* (from 1966 and 1967) for the first time in 2002.
Several independent bottlers have also released Glenrothes. More recent (2006) releases include a Murray McDavid from 1968 with a finish in Mouvedre casks and a 14 year old and a 19 year old from Douglas Laing.

Select Reserve

Glen Scotia

Owner:
Loch Lomond Distillery Co.

Region/district:
Campbeltown

Founded:
1832

Status:
Active

Tel:
01586 552288

Visitor centre:
No

website:
www.lochlomonddistillery.com

Capacity:
750 000 litres

% sold as malt whisky:
n/a

Included in blended (past and/or present):
Black Prince, Royal Escort

History:

1832 – The family Galbraith founds Scotia Distillery (the year 1835 is mentioned by the distillery themselves on their labels).

1895 – The distillery is sold to Stewart Galbraith & Company.

1919 – The distillery is sold to West Highland Malt Distillers.

1924 – West Highland Malt Distillers goes bankrupt and one of their Directors, Duncan MacCallum, buys the distillery.

1928 – The distillery closes.

1930 – Duncan MacCallum commits suicide and the Bloch brothers, who eventually buy Scapa Distillery in 1936, take over.

1933 – Production restarts.

1954 – Hiram Walker takes over Glen Scotia and Scapa.

1955 – A. Gillies & Co. becomes new owners.

1970 – A. Gillies & Co. becomes part of Amalgated Distillers Products.

1979–82 – Reconstruction, totalling £1 million, takes place.

1984 – The distillery closes.

1989 – Amalgated Distillers Products is taken over by Gibson International and production restarts.

1994 – Glen Catrine Bonded Warehouse Ltd takes over and the distillery is mothballed.

1999 – Production restarts from 5th May through J. A. Mitchell & Co., owners of Springbank.

2000 – Loch Lomond Distillers runs operations with its own staff from May onwards.

2005 – An official bottling of a 12 year old is released.

Photo: © 2005 www.thewhiskystore.de

Campbeltown, once the most important whisky town in Scotland and a proud, independent whisky region along with Highlands, Lowlands and Islay, has seen its distilleries reduced to three, of which one was commissioned as recently as in 2004 (Glengyle). During a few years in the 1980s not a single distillery was up and running, as both Springbank and Glen Scotia were temporarily closed. Since then Springbank has flourished and established itself as one of the largest while Glen Scotia has had a more chequered past. The owners of Loch Lomond took up Glen Scotia's cause and with some help from neighbouring Springbank got production going in 2000.
Glen Scotia is one of Scotland's smallest distilleries. They only have one pair of stills and still use worm tubs for cooling the spirit vapours. The six washbacks are, unusually, made of cast iron rather than the more common wood or stainless steel.
SWA (Scotch Whisky Association) made a controversial decision a few years ago when they decided that Campbeltown should no longer be treated as a whisky region of its own. Something must have happened since then as SWA fairly recently reinstated Campbeltown as a region in its own right.
A new, official bottling was released in 2005 when the old 14 and 8 year olds were replaced by a *12 year old*. Rumour has it that a heavily peated version also is on the way. Older versions include a *17 year old* and an occasional vintage.
There are only a small number of independent bottlers to chose from in recent times; Cadenhead 1991 (14 years), Ian MacLeod (Chieftain's) 1974 (30 years), Gordon & MacPhail 1992 (12 years) and Signatory 1974 (31 years).

12 years old

Glen Spey

Owner:
Diageo

Region/district:
Speyside

Founded:
1878

Status:
Active

Tel:
01340 831215

Visitor centre:
No

website:
www.malts.com

Capacity:
1 400 000 litres

% sold as malt whisky:
n/a

Included in blended (past and/or present):
J&B, Spey Royal

History:

1878 – James Stuart & Co. founds the distillery which becomes known by the name Mill of Rothes.

1886 – James Stuart buys Macallan.

1887 – W. & A. Gilbey buys the distillery for £11 000 thus becoming the first English company to buy a Scottish malt distillery.

1920 – A fire breaks out.

1962 – W. & A. Gilbey combines forces with United Wine Traders and forms International Distillers & Vintners (IDV).

1970 – The stills are increased from two to four.

1972 – IDV is bought by Watney Mann who are then acquired by Grand Metropolitan.

1997 – Guiness and Grand Metropolitan merge to form Diageo.

2001 – A 12 year old is launched in the Flora & Fauna series.

The whisky town Glenrothes, between Craigellachie and Elgin in Speyside, has four active distilleries, Glen Grant, Glenrothes, Speyburn and Glen Spey. Glen Spey is comparatively anonymous. In fact, it is so little known that Alfred Barnard did not manage to write more than a half page on it in his groundbreaking book 'Whisky Distilleries in the United Kingdom' from 1887.
In common with Glenrothes, Glen Spey distillery is situated in the middle of the town at the foot of the hill where the ruins of Castle Rothes is to be found. This was the home of the Leslie family (Earl of Rothes) for four hundred years until 1662 when it was destroyed in a fire. Only a fragment of the outer walls remain on site, but many of the stones were used for building houses in Rothes.
Those with a technical interest in whisky distilling should take note of some features. First, the distillery has two pairs of stills where the spirit stills are equipped with purifiers. Second, a special type of Semi-Lauter mash tun was installed in the renovation of 1970. When it was used in other distilleries it was known as the Glen Spey mash tun. Finally, an unusual four roller Buhler mill is used rather than the traditional Porteus mill.
Glen Spey is mainly found as a component in different versions of J & B. There are no other official bottlings apart from the *12 year old Flora & Fauna*. A small number of independent bottlings are available. Two of these released in 2005 are Gordon & MacPhail (Connoisseurs Choice) 1995 and Adelphi Distillery 1977 (28 years). In 2006 Douglas Laing released a 28 year old from 1977.

Flora & Fauna 12 years old

Glentauchers

Owner:
Chivas Brothers (Pernod Ricard)

Region/district:
Speyside

Founded:
1897

Status:
Active

Tel:
01542 860272

Visitor centre:
No

website:
-

Capacity:
3 500 000 litres

% sold as malt whisky:
0%

Included in blended (past and/or present):
Ballantine´s, Teacher´s

History:

1897 – James Buchanan and W. P. Lowrie, a whisky merchant from Glasgow, found the distillery. A company named Glentauchers Distillery Co. is also formed at the same time.

1898 – Production starts.

1902 – Buchanan offers to buy out Lowrie who is in financial difficulties.

1906 – James Buchanan & Co. takes over the whole distillery and acquires an 80% share in W. P. Lowrie & Co.

1915 – James Buchanan & Co. merges with Dewars.

1923-25 – Mashing house and maltings are rebuilt.

1925 – Buchanan-Dewars joins Distillers Company Limited (DCL).

1930 – Glentauchers is transferred to Scottish Malt Distillers (SMD).

1965 – The number of stills is increased from two to six.

1969 – Floor maltings is decommissioned.

1985 – DCL mothballs the distillery.

1989 – United Distillers (formerly DCL) sells the distillery to Caledonian Malt Whisky Distillers, a subsidiary of Allied Distillers.

1992 – Production recommences in August.

2000 – A 15 year old Glentauchers is released.

2005 – Chivas Brothers (Pernod Ricard) become new owners through the acquisition of Allied Domecq.

Blenders and brokers enthusiastically started building distilleries in the late 19th century. Dewar, Mackie, Teachers and Haig all established themselves in the Highlands. One of the greatest whisky personalities, James Buchanan also did so with Glentauchers. He had previously had much success in London when he introduced his blended whiskies adapted for the English taste. In 1898 he joined forces with his old benefactor from poorer days, W. P. Lowrie, and founded Glentauchers, the only distillery he actually built himself (he acquired more distilleries later). Lord Woolavington, the title he was given later, died in 1935 but by then Glentauchers and his company had been absorbed by the huge Distillers Company Limited and he himself had retired. His Black & White blended whisky still flourishes and sells 5 million bottles a year.

Glentauchers was built by a blender and still today, over 100 years later, its produce is destined exclusively for blended whiskies which may be the reason for its survival. The distillery was expanded in 1965 and its modern stillhouse with its six stills is clearly visible from the A95 between Keith and Dufftown. When Allied Distillers took over the closed distillery in the late eighties the purpose was to produce single malt for their top seller, Ballantine's.

An official *15 year old* was released several years ago and has been difficult to obtain recently. Chivas Brothers did, however, release more bottles in summer 2006.

The number of independent bottlings have not been impressive until a few years ago when four expressions, all from 1990, appeared from Duncan Taylor (Whisky Galore), Gordon & MacPhail, James MacArthur and Wilson & Morgan (the latter rum-finished). The most recent bottling comes from Douglas Laing, a 15 year old also from 1990.

Gordon & MacPhail Glentauchers 1990

Glenturret

Owner:
The Edrington Group

Region/district:
Eastern Highlands

Founded:
1775

Status:
Active

Tel:
01764 656565

Visitor centre:
Yes (7/7)

website:
www.famousgrouse.co.uk

Capacity:
340 000 litres

% sold as malt whisky:
n/a

Included in blended (past and/or present):
Famous Grouse

History:

1775 – Whisky smugglers establish a small illicit farm distillery named Hosh Distillery.

1818 – John Drummond is licensee, until 1837.

1826 – A distillery in the vicinity is named Glenturret, but is decommissioned before 1852.

1852 – John McCallum is licensee until 1874.

1875 – Hosh Distillery takes over the name Glenturret Distillery and is managed by Thomas Stewart.

1903 – Mitchell Bros Ltd takes over.

1921 – Production ceases and the buildings are used for whisky storage only.

1929 – Mitchell Bros Ltd is liquidated, the distillery dismantled and the facilities are used as storage for agricultural needs.

1957 – James Fairlie buys the distillery and re-equips it.

1959 – Production restarts.

1981 – Remy-Cointreau buys the distillery and invests in a visitor centre which becomes one of the most popular destinations in Scotland.

1987 – The distillery's cat, Towser, dies after almost 24 years having killed precisely 28 899 mice! A number which warrants her a mention in the Guinness Book of Records.

1990 – Highland Distillers takes over.

1999 – Edrington and William Grant & Sons buys Highland Distillers for £601 million. The purchasing company, 1887 Company, is a joint venture between Edrington (70%) and William Grant (30%).

2002 – The Famous Grouse Experience, a visitor centre costing £2.5 million, is inaugurated on 10th June.

2003 – A 10 year old Glenturret replaces the 12 year old as the distillery´s standard release.

The Famous Grouse blended whisky has a long history dating back to 1896 when it was introduced as 'The Grouse' by Matthew Gloag & Son though Glenturret has an even longer story. Founded in 1775 it is considered by many the oldest still active distillery in Scotland. The two are closely intertwined today through the visitor centre, the most visited in Scotland, which bears the name 'The Famous Grouse Experience'.
The relationship is, however, only a few years old: The present day existence of Glenturret is probably thanks to James Fairlie, a whisky enthusiast who resurrected Glenturret to a living distillery after a 40 year break. Fairlie cherished a dream of creating a visitor's distillery long before these were commonplace.
He put in great effort and when Remy-Cointreau took over in 1981 they continued their work on that track. The Fairlie family was still engaged in the realisation of this project when the father died, then his son Peter took over and became one of the directors at the same time as Highland Distillers became owners. In 2002, Famous Grouse and Glenturret became further entangled when the owners decided to make it the spiritual home of the world famous blend, thus resulting in the birth of 'Famous Grouse Experience'.
The production of Glenturret is very small and there is only one official bottling today (there used to be more); the *10 year old*. Famous Grouse, on the other hand, have released a number of vatted malts as a supplement to their blended whiskies: 12, 18 and 30 years old, various vintages and the recently introduced 10 years old.
Recent independent bottlings of Glenturret include two from Douglas Laing (15 and 27 years old), a Rioja finish from 1980 by Murray McDavid and a 27 year old bottled by The Whisky Exchange.

10 years old

Glenury Royal

Owner:
Diageo

Region/district:
Eastern Highlands

Founded:
1825

Status:
Demolished

Tel:
-

Visitor centre:
-

website:
www.malts.com

Capacity:
-

% sold as malt whisky:
-

Included in blended (past and/or present):
-

History:

1824-1825 – Captain Robert Barclay, MP and Laird of Ury, founds the distillery which is named Glenurie.

1835 – Captain Barclay receives permission to use the word Royal by William IV.

1854 – Captain Barclay dies.

1857 or 58 – The distillery is put up for auction and it is bought by William Ritchie of Glasgow. The Ritchie family retain ownership until 1936.

1928-37 – No production takes place.

1936 – The owner Lord Stonehaven, who probably was the real owner while the Ritchie family leased the distillery, sells the distillery to the Glenury Distillery Company, with Joseph William Hobbs in it, for £7 500.

1938 – Glenury Distillery Company sells the distillery for £18 500 to Associated Scottish Distillers (ASD), where J. W. Hobbs is one of the owners.

1940 – American National Distillers buys ASD.

1953 – Distillers Company Limited (DCL) buys ASD from National Distillers and transfers Glenury Royal to Scottish Malt Distillers.

1965 – Substantial refurbishing takes place and the number of stills double to four.

1968 – Own maltings cease.

1983 – The distillery is mothballed.

1992 – United Distillers decides not to open Glenury Royal for production and sells the buildings to an estate company.

1999 – A 29 year old cask strength is launched in the Rare Malts series.

2003 – 498 bottles of a 50 year old Glenury Royal are launched.

2005 – A 36 year old is launched as a Special Release from Diageo.

Glenury Royal did not have a lucky start. Already a few weeks after inception, on the 20th April 1825, a fire destroyed the whole kiln, the greater part of the grain lofts and the malting barn as well as the stock of barley and malt. The distillery part was, however, spared. Just two weeks later, distillery worker James Clark, fell into the boiler and died a few hours later. With such a catastrophic start it was fortunate that the energetic entrepreneur Captain Robert Barclay Allardyce was at the helm. He was the first to walk 1000 miles in 1000 hours in 1809 and was inducted into the Scottish Sports Hall of Fame for his achievement. He was also an excellent middle-distance runner and boxer. There are many stories about this somewhat eccentric man. When he was invited to dinner at Brechin Castle in 1844, aged 65, he sent his butler by horse with his dinner clothes while he ran the 25 miles himself. The following day he ran the 25 miles back home. To be able to use 'Royal' in the name, he used a contact in the Royal Court he simply referred to as Mrs. Windsor.

Production ceased already in 1983 and most of the old distillery buildings have been demolished with the remaining ones converted into flats.

A couple of spectacular official bottlings have been released in recent years - a *50 year old* in 2003 and a *36 year old* in 2005. In addition to them, Glenury Royal occurred three times in the Rare Malts series.

Independent bottlings are few. Among recent ones are a 31 year old (1973) from Signatory, a 20 year old (1984) from Duncan Taylor and a 32 year old (1972) from Douglas Laing.

36 years old

Highland Park

Owner:
Edrington Group

Region/district:
Highlands (Orkney)

Founded:
1798

Status:
Active

Tel:
01856 874619

Visitor centre:
Yes (7/7)

website:
www.highlandpark.co.uk

Capacity:
2 500 000 litres

% sold as malt whisky:
60%

Included in blended (past and/or present):
Cutty Sark, Famous Grouse

History:

1798 – David Robertson founds the distillery. The local smuggler and businessman Magnus Eunson previously operated an illicit whisky production on this site.

1816 – John Robertson, an Excise Officer who arrested Magnus Eunson, takes over production.

1826 – Highland Park obtains a license and the distillery is taken over by Robert Borwick.

1840 – Robert´s son George Borwick takes over but the distillery deteriorates.

1869 – The younger brother James Borwick inherits Highland Park and attempts to sell it as he does not consider the distillation of spirits as compatible with his priesthood.

1876 – Stuart & Mackay becomes involved and improves the business by exporting to Norway and India.

Highland Park faces an exciting future: The owners, Edrington, are determined to ascertain that Highland Park obtains a place among the top ten most selling single malts worldwide in five years. This implies that sales have to double. In order to obtain that, £18 million will be invested in the trademark and the starting point for this was in early September 2006 when a new packaging was launched.

Highland Park is one of few distilleries malting part of their barley themselves. As the barley currently grown on Orkney is not suitable for whisky, it is bought from the mainland instead. The peat, around 350 tonnes a year, is dug out from own supplies at Hobbister Hill. It is cut in April and left to dry during the summer. The malt is peated at 20 ppm which corresponds to that of Bowmore. Around 20% of the malt requirement is produced locally in the distillery with the remaining brought in from Tamdhu Distillery in the Highlands.

Highland Park matures in both ex-sherry and ex-bourbon casks. The proportions of sherry casks vary from 20% first fill for the 12 year old to 50% in the 25 year old. The new 30 year old has as much as 75% second fill sherry casks.

The core range of Highland Park consists of *12, 18* and *25 years old* and a *15 year old* produced especially for Sainsbury's. Limited editions include a range of vintages. A *30 year old* was new for 2005 as was their first *Ambassador's Cask* (selected by Gerry Tosh) *21 years old* and distilled in 1984. Other news in 2005 were Highland Park's first duty free exclusive (*16 years old*) and that was the first combination of first fill and re-fill sherry casks with bourbon casks. Summer 2006 saw the release of the second edition of the Ambassador´s Cask. This time it was a younger expression, just *10 years old from 1996.*

Independent bottlers are often involved with Highland Park and some of the latest are Signatory 1992 (13 years), Douglas Laing 1995 (10 years) and 1990 (16 years), Murray McDavid 1967 and 1979 finished in a Syrah cask and Cadenhead 1989 (16 years). Highland Park has recently decided not to sell to independent bottlers as their own sales are so high.

Highland Park is still the northernmost distillery in Scotland as Blackwood on the Shetlands is not expected to be operational in the near future.

History (continued):
1895 – James Grant (of Glenlivet Distillery) buys Highland Park.

1898 – James Grant expands capacity from two to four stills.

1937 – Highland Distilleries buys Highland Park.

1979 – Highland Distilleries invests considerably in marketing Highland Park as single malt which increases sales markedly.

1986 – A visitor centre, considered one of Scotland's finest, is opened.

1997 – Two new Highland Park are launched, an 18 year old and a 25 year old.

1999 – Highland Distillers are acquired by Edrington Group and William Grant & Sons.

2000 – Visit Scotland awards Highland Park "Five Star Visitor Attraction". The distillery has spent over £2 million on the visitor centre and distillery.

2005 – Highland Park 30 years old is released, first in the US and in the autumn in UK. A 16 year old for the Duty Free market and Ambassador´s Cask 1984 are released.

2006 – The second edition of Ambassador´s Cask, a 10 year old from 1996, is released. New packaging is introduced.

18 years old

25 years old

30 years old

Ambassador´s Cask 1984

12 years old

Imperial

Owner:
Chivas Brothers (Pernod Ricard)

Region/district:
Speyside

Founded:
1897

Status:
Closed

Tel:
-

Visitor centre:
-

website:
-

Capacity:
-

% sold as malt whisky:
-

Included in blended (past and/or present):
Teachers, Long John, Ballantine´s, Old Smuggler

History:

1897 – Thomas Mackenzie, who already owns Dailuaine and Talisker, founds the distillery helped by architect Charles Doig. The distillery's name hints at Queen Victoria's Diamond Jubilee this year.

1898 – The distillery is inaugurated in the summer and is administered by Thomas Mackenzie's company Dailuaine-Talisker Distilleries Limited.

1899 – The Pattison whisky crash forces the distillery to close.

1916 – Imperial is bought by Distillers Company Limited (DCL), Dewar's, Johnnie Walker and W. P. Lowrie.

1919 – Production restarts.

1925 – The distillery becomes fully owned by DCL and closes again although the maltings remains active.

1955 – Imperial, now administered by Scottish Malt Distillers (SMD), reopens.

1965 – The number of stills is doubled from two to four and a Saladin box is installed for malting.

1985 – The distillery closes.

1989 – Allied Distillers buys Imperial from United Distillers and starts refurbishing.

1991 – Once again in operation.

1998 – Imperial is mothballed.

2005 – Chivas Brothers (Pernod Ricard) become new owners through the acquisition of Allied Domecq.

A more than 100 year old distillery which has been out of production for 60% of the time cannot be considered reliable. It has often been said that the problem with Imperial is that the large stills (2 pairs) cannot be run flexibly.
Since its latest closure, in 1998, rumours of a resurrection have flourished now and then. The kiss of death for Imperial, we thought, came in 2005 when estate agents Bell Ingram were commissioned to sell the buildings and convert them into apartments. Imperial has however been removed from Bell Ingram's listings and those who want to can start hoping again. Chivas Brothers have not released any news on the future fate of the distillery.
Even with its run-down appearance one can imagine how impressive it must have been in its heyday, situated by the River Spey with the surrounding pine forests and the large lawns which are still well-manicured to this very day. The cottages at the entrance used to be homes for employees but have now been sold to private individuals.
At times (even when it was not producing whisky) Imperial supplied other distilleries with malt and along with Aultmore they were leaders in recycling by-products from the distillation process by turning it into cattle feed.
An official *15 year old* was released several years ago and has been difficult to obtain recently. Chivas Brothers did, however, release more bottles in summer 2006.
Independent bottlers, especially Gordon & MacPhail, have begun picking up on Imperial more recently. One of the latest was from 1993 and bottled in 2004 for La Maison du Whisky. Another recent bottling from Signatory was a 28 year old from 1976 released in 2005.

Gordon & MacPhail Imperial 1991

Inchgower

Owner:
Diageo

Region/district:
Speyside

Founded:
1871

Status:
Active

Tel:
01542 836700

Visitor centre:
No

website:
www.malts.com

Capacity:
2 200 000 litres

% sold as malt whisky:
1% unofficial

Included in blended (past and/or present):
Bell´s, Johnnie Walker, White Horse

History:

1871 – Alexander Wilson & Co. founds the distillery. Equipment from the disused Tochieneal Distillery, also owned by Alexander Wilson, is installed.

1936 – Alexander Wilson & Co. becomes bankrupt and Buckie Town Council buys the distillery and the family's home for £1 600.

1938 – The distillery is sold on to Arthur Bell & Sons for £3 000.

1966 – Capacity doubles to four stills.

1985 – Guinness acquires Arthur Bell & Sons.

1987 – United Distillers is formed by a merger between Arthur Bell & Sons and DCL.

1997 – Inchgower 1974 (22 years) is released as a Rare Malt.

2004 – Inchgower 1976 (27 years) is released as a Rare Malt.

Inchgower belongs to a small group of three distilleries that are situated in Speyside but can make use of the unofficial epithet 'coastal'. Inchgower is situated near the small fishing port of Buckie, Glenglassaugh outside Portsoy and Macduff adjacent to Banff.

Inchgower is a beautiful distillery and since it was not acquired by United Distilleries until the 1980s it managed to avoid SMD's frantic reconstruction and renovation boom that hit so many distilleries in the 1960s and 1970s. The distillery's size is considered middle range among Diageo's distilleries and it has been a true workhorse quietly producing malt for Bell's blended whiskies.

The distillery is equipped with six washbacks made from Oregon Pine and two pairs of stills. Most of the production is matured elsewhere, but the share sold as single malt is stored on site. All malt comes from Diageo's own facility in Burghead c 20 miles further west along the coast. This maltings, which is Diageo's and Scotland's largest, was built in 1966 and has been expanded since then to cater for a capacity of 85 000 tonnes per annum.

The legendary Grant Carmichael was manager of Burghead maltings before he became Distillery Manager of, among others, Lagavulin, Port Ellen and Caol Ila. He was also involved in introducing Classic Malts.

Aside from the *Flora & Fauna 14 years old* there are two *Rare Malt* bottlings, *1974* (22 years) and *1976 (27 years)*. Independent bottlings are not so common. Two of the most recent are Duncan Taylor 1968 (36 years) and Dewar Rattray 1980, the latter released in May 2006.

Flora & Fauna 14 years old

Rare Malts 1976 27 years old

Jura

Owner:
Whyte & Mackay Ltd

Region/district:
Highlands (Jura)

Founded:
1810

Status:
Active

Tel:
01496 820240

Visitor centre:
Yes (5/7)

website:
www.isleofjura.com

Capacity:
2 500 000 litres

% sold as malt whisky:
30%

Included in blended (past and/or present):
Whyte & Mackay, Stewart´s, Claymore, Cluny

History:

1810 – Archibald Campbell founds a distillery named Small Isles Distillery.

1831 – William Abercombie obtains the first licence for Isle of Jura Distillery.

1832 – The license is taken over by Archibald Fletcher.

1853 – Richard Campbell leases the distillery to Norman Buchanan from Glasgow.

1867 – Buchanan files for bankruptcy and J. & K. Orr takes over the distillery.

1876 – The licence is transferred to James Ferguson & Sons.

1901 – The distillery closes due to a dispute between Ferguson and the land-owner Colin Campbell. Ferguson dismantles the distilling equipment.

1920 – Campbell removes the roofs of the buildings to avoid tax.

1960 – Charles Mackinlay & Co. embarks on reconstruction and extension of the distillery. The famous architect William Delmé-Evans is called in. Newly formed Scottish & Newcastle Breweries acquires Charles Mackinlay & Co.

1962 – Scottish & Newcastle forms Mackinlay-McPherson for the operation of Isle of Jura.

1963 – The first distilling after reconstruction takes place and Isle of Jura Distillery Co. Ltd is founded.

1974 – The first single malt from the new owners is launched.

1978 – Stills are doubled from two to four.

1985 – Invergordon Distilleries acquires Charles Mackinlay & Co., Isle of Jura and Glenallachie from Scottish & Newcastle Breweries.

1993 – Whyte & Mackay (Fortune Brands) buys Invergordon Distillers.

1996 – Whyte & Mackay changes name to JBB (Greater Europe).

2001 – The management of JBB (Greater Europe) buys out the company from the owners Fortune Brands and changes the name to Kyndal. A new visitor centre opens in May.

2002 – Isle of Jura Superstition is launched in December.

2003 – Kyndal reverts back to its old name, Whyte & Mackay. Isle of Jura 1984 (19 years) is launched.

2004 – Two cask strengths (15 and 30 years old) are released in limited numbers.

Only walls remain of the first Jura distillery founded in 1810. Today's Jura is the result of two Jura Estate owners, Tony Riley-Smith and Robin Fletcher, who wished to trigger the island's local economy. They joined forces with the architect William Delmé-Evans and built a new distillery on the same site as the ancient one in 1963.

The single malt from Jura led a secluded existence until the mid 1990s when Whyte & Mackay entered the scene as owners. Their Master Blender Richard Paterson and Distillery Manager Michael Heads put much effort into raising Juras profile to new heights. In contrast to Dalmore, Paterson's other favourite project, bourbon casks are almost exclusively used at Jura as the malt is sensitive to sherry maturation. Most of the malt is brought in from Port Ellen on Islay and there are around 27 000 casks maturing in five warehouses.

The core range consists of *10, 16* and *21 years old*. For those wishing to sample a peatier Jura, *Superstition 2002* was released, containing a mix of heavily peated younger and older malt. Several limited editions, such as a *15 year old cask strength*, a *30 year old* from *1973*, a *36 year old* from *1965* and a *19 year old* from *1984*, have also been released. The latter was launched to commemorate the memory of George Orwell who wrote his book '1984' while staying on the island.

Independent bottlings appear from time to time. Among the most recent are two from May 2006; Cadenhead 1992 (14 years old) and Ian MacLeod 1987 (18 years old).

Isle of Jura 10 years old

Knockando

Owner: Diageo
Region/district: Speyside
Founded: 1898
Status: Active
Tel: 01340 882000
Visitor centre: No
website: www.malts.com
Capacity: 1 300 000 litres
% sold as malt whisky: 8% unofficial
Included in blended (past and/or present): J&B, Spey Royal

History:

1898 – John Thompson founds the distillery which is administered by Knockando-Glenlivet Distillery Company. The architect is Charles Doig.

1899 – Production starts in May.

1900 – The Pattison crash forces the distillery to close in March and J. Thompson & Co. takes over administration.

1904 – W. & A. Gilbey purchases the distillery for £3 500 and production restarts in October.

1962 – W. & A. Gilbey merges with United Wine Traders (including Justerini & Brooks) and forms International Distillers & Vintners (IDV).

1968 – Floor maltings is decommissioned.

1969 – The number of stills is increased from two to four.

1972 – IDV is acquired by Watney Mann who, in its turn, is taken over by Grand Metropolitan.

1978 – Justerini & Brooks launches a 12 year old Knockando.

1997 – Grand Metropolitan and Guinness merge and form Diageo; simultaneously IDV and United Distillers merge to United Distillers & Vintners.

Knockando has been signature malt in J & B Rare for a long time and it was during the seventies and eighties that IDV put most effort into the single malt. Back in 1977 and before the great interest for single malt whisky had started, Knockando was launched on the export market. This early launch has earned it a place as one of the most popular single malts in Spain. Even though the interest for Knockando whisky has diminished since the nineties it is still on the top 20 sales list. The distillery is situated in beautiful surroundings on a small hill overlooking River Spey. The name Knockando means 'small, black hill'. The distillery has two pairs of stills and four washbacks made of Oregon Pine. The share of production destined as single malt is stored on site while the rest is shipped to different distilleries in the Diageo group.

Distillery jobs are often inherited in Scotland. Knockando exemplifies this practice well as the great grandfather of current Distillery Manager Innes Shaw was one of the men that built the distillery in the late 1880s.

Knockando has traditionally, since the 1970s, bottled their whisky according to vintage and without any age statement. Only in the US, where whisky age is important in marketing, have both age and year been depicted on the labels. This practice has, however, now also been applied to other markets. Around 400 casks are vatted together for each release.

A *21 year old* is sometimes bottled which then is called *Knockando Extra Old Master Reserve*.

Independent bottlings are virtually impossible to find. A recent exception is a 25 year old from Duncan Taylor bottled in 2005.

1991 12 years old

Knockdhu

Owner:
Inver House Distillers (Pacific Spirits)

Region/district:
Speyside

Founded:
1893

Status:
Active

Tel:
01466 771223

Visitor centre:
No

website:
www.inverhouse.com

Capacity:
900 000 litres

% sold as malt whisky:
8%

Included in blended (past and/or present):
Haig, McArthur´s, Blairmhor

History:

1893 – Distillers Company Limited (DCL) starts construction of the distillery which is named Knockdhu. Architects are Gordon & Macbey from Elgin.

1894 – Production starts in October.

1924 – Management of the distillery is transferred to Distillers Agency.

1930 – Scottish Malt Distillers (SMD) takes over production.

1931 – The distillery closes.

1933 – The distillery opens up again.

1983 – The distillery closes in March.

1988 – Inver House buys the distillery from United Distillers.

1989 – Production restarts on 6th February.

1990 – First official bottling of Knockdhu.

1993 – First official bottling of An Cnoc, the new name to avoid confusion with Knockando.

2001 – Pacific Spirits (Great Oriole Group) purchases Inver House Distillers at a price of $85 million.

2003 – Reintroduction of An Cnoc 12 years, with new, contemporary packaging.

2004 – A 14 year old from 1990 is launched.

2005 – Two limited editions, a 30 year old from 1975 and a 14 year old from 1991 are launched.

The richest man in Thailand, Charoen Sirivadhanabhakdi, took over Knockdhu with the rest of Inver House Distillers in 2001. Supported by previous Thai governments, Charoen built up a monopoly-reminiscent position in Thailand with 90% of the Thai liquor market and 60% of the beer market with the brand Chang as big-seller. His great interest for football also led to his becoming principal sponsor of the Premier League football team Everton in 2004. The two most recent governments have opened up the beer and spirit market to more competition. Although still a dominant player on the market, Charoen's business group has diverted interest into acquiring a strong position in other areas such as the insurance business.
Distillers Company Limited (DCL) set up Knockdhu as their first distillery in 1893. Many count this as the only distillery DCL started themselves, but two more were founded by their subsidiary Scottish Malt Distillers (SMD): Clynelish II in 1967 and Mannochmore in 1971.
Knockdhu has one pair of stills and is one of few remaining distilleries still using worm tub condensers. Five warehouses can hold c 7 500 ex-bourbon casks.
The core range consists of a *12 year old* since 2004, but the owner has also launched a few limited editions; a *14 year old* (the latest version from 1991) and a *30 year old* from 1975.
Independent bottlings are scarce and when they do occur it is always under the name Knockdhu. The most recent ones were released in 2005; Cadenhead 16 years old and Douglas Laing 10 years old from 1994.

1975 30 years old *1991 (bottled 2004)*

Sunlight on the malting floor.

Lagavulin

Owner:
Diageo

Region/district:
Islay

Founded:
1816

Status:
Active

Tel:
01496 302749 (vc)

Visitor centre:
Yes (6/7)

website:
www.malts.com

Capacity:
2 400 000 litres

% sold as malt whisky:
85% unofficial

Included in blended (past and/or present):
White Horse, Haig

History:

1816 – John Johnston founds the distillery.

1825 – John Johnston takes over the adjacent distillery Ardmore founded in 1817 by Archibald Campbell and closed in 1821.

1835 – Production at Ardmore ceases.

1837 – Both distilleries are merged and operated under the name Lagavulin by Donald Johnston.

1852 – The brother of the wine and spirits dealer Alexander Graham, John Crawford Graham, purchases the distillery.

1867 – The distillery is acquired by James Logan Mackie & Co. and refurbishment starts.

1878 – Peter Mackie is employed.

1889 – James Logan Mackie passes away and nephew Peter Mackie inherits the distillery.

1890 – J. L. Mackie & Co. changes name to Mackie & Co. Peter Mackie launches White Horse onto the export market with Lagavulin included in the blend. White Horse blended is not available on the domestic market until 1901.

Lagavulin ruled supreme as the number one seller among Islay distilleries but since 1998 sales have gone down by 50% while Laphroaig have increased by 50% and have taken over the top spot. In addition to this, Bowmore climbed to the number two spot a few years ago, forcing Lagavulin down to third place. The reason for this began 15 years ago. Two day shifts were in force at Lagavulin during a large part of the 1980s. The 16 year old was introduced as a Classic Malt in 1989 and simultaneously interest in Islay whisky took off completely. Five-day shifts were reintroduced first in 1991 and today operations run in seven-day shifts 24 hours a day. Demand thus surpassed output for a large number of years and this affected mainly the 16 year old of which there is a certain shortage today. Lagavulin could be ready to fight for the number one spot one or two years from now.

Some perceive Lagavulin as the peatiest Islay whisky, but in fact both Laphroaig and Ardbeg contain more phenols than Lagavulin which has 16 ppm in finished spirit. All malt has been brought from Port Ellen maltings since 1974. The lion's share of Lagavulin production is stored on bourbon casks on the mainland with the rest spread between Lagavulin, Port Ellen and Caol Ila. Around 85% of production is exported.

There has been some managerial turbulence during the last year. Donald Renwick resigned as manager to pick up the same position at Lochnagar distillery where he succeeded another former Lagavulin manager, Mike Nicholson. Renwick's successor was John Thomson from Port Ellen maltings who went to Knockando after just a few weeks. Willie MacDougall from Oban was meant to replace him but he changed his mind and replaced Iain Henderson at Edradour. To be on the safe side, a true Ileach was selected, Graham Logie, who came from Talisker.

Lagavulin was bottled at 12 years until 1989; thereafter the classic 16 year old was introduced. Today, the core range of Lagavulin consists of *12 years old cask strength*, *16 years* and the *Pedro Ximenez sherry finish*. A limited edition of a *25 year old* was released in 2002 and a *30 year old* was launched in 2006.

Independent bottlings are rarely encountered. A few recent ones come from Murray McDavid, Ian MacLeod and Signatory.

History (continued):

1908 – Peter Mackie uses the old distillery buildings to build a new distillery, Malt Mill, on the site. Mackie had previously been agent for Laphroaig but the owners were not content and terminated the contract. Malt Mill was an attempt by Mackie to compete and force Laphroaig out of the market.

1924 – Peter Mackie passes away and Mackie & Co. changes name to White Horse Distillers.

1927 – White Horse Distillers becomes part of Distillers Company Limited (DCL).

1930 – The distillery is administered under Scottish Malt Distillers (SMD).

1952 – An explosive fire breaks out and causes considerable damage.

1960 – Malt Mills distillery closes and today it houses Lagavulin's visitor centre.

1974 – Floor maltings are decommisioned and malt is bought from Port Ellen instead.

1988 – Lagavulin 16 years becomes one of six Classic Malts.

1998 – A Pedro Ximenez sherry finish is launched as a Distillers Edition.

2002 – Two cask strengths (12 years and 25 years) are launched.

2006 – A 30 year old is released.

12 years old

16 years old

Distiller's Edition

25 years old

30 years old

Laphroaig

Owner:
Beam Global Spirits & Wine

Region/district:
Islay

Founded:
1810

Status:
Active

Tel:
01496 302418

Visitor centre:
Yes (6/7)

website:
www.laphroaig.com

Capacity:
2 400 000 litres
2 220 000 litres

% sold as malt whisky:
50%

Included in blended (past and/or present):
Islay Mist, Ballantine

History:

1810 – Brothers Alexander and Donald Johnston, already proprietors of Tallant Distillery, found Laphroaig.

1815 – Official year of starting.

1836 – Donald buys out Alexander and takes over operations.

1837 – James and Andrew Gairdner found the distillery Ardenistiel a stone's throw from Laphroaig.

1847 – Donald Johnston is killed in an accident in the distillery when he falls into a kettle of boiling hot burnt ale. The Manager of neighbouring Lagavulin, Walter Graham, takes over.

1857 – Operation is back in the hands of the Johnston family when Donald's son Dugald takes over.

circa 1860 – Ardenistiel Distillery merges with Laphroaig.

1877 – Dugald, being without heirs, passes away and his sister Isabella, married to their cousin Alexander takes over.

1907 – Alexander Johnston dies and the distillery is inherited by his two sisters Catherine Johnston and Mrs. William Hunter (Isabella Johnston).

1908 – Ian Hunter arrives in Islay to assist his mother and aunt with the distillery.

1923 – The two stills are increased to four.

1927 – Catherine Johnston dies and Ian Hunter takes over.

Laphroaig has been part of American Jim Beam Brands (now Beam Global Spirits & Wine) since summer 2005. They are the fourth largest spirits company in the world with brands such as Jim Beam, Canadian Club and Teacher's in their portfolio.
It is obvious that the new owners pay careful attention to their new acquisition. They will switch to seven-day production for part of the year and the total annual output will be increased by 300 000 litres. Their position as one of the great malt whiskies will be strengthened further by a new campaign and new bottlings are likely to appear, probably in 2007.
Laphroaig has not only got new owners, for the first time they also have an Ileach (a person born on Islay) as Distillery Manager. John Campbell is, at 35 years, the youngest distiller on the island.
Laphroaig is one of very few distilleries with their own maltings. Two malting floors produce around 20% of the requirement while the rest comes from Port Ellen maltings on Islay. The malt specification is set to 40-45 ppm which results in a finished spirit down to 25 ppm. The distillery uses an unusual combination of three wash stills and four spirit stills. The last one which was installed in 1972 is twice the size of the others. The owner at the time, Schenley, considered it more economical to install one big still rather than two small. Many consider that Laphroaig, although still robust and powerful, went in a lighter direction associated with the new spirit still. The latest decade has seen Laphroaig switch to maturing exclusively in ex-bourbon casks (Maker's Mark).
The core range of Laphroaig is a *10 year old*, a *10 year old cask strength*, *Quarter Cask*, a *15 year old* and a *30 year old*. Limited editions include the *40 year old* and special versions often launched in connection with Feis Isle. One of the latest was a *12 year old* from 1994 released in spring 2006. A 1987 (19 years) was released for Maison du Whisky in September 2006. The Quarter Cask, first released in 2004, is finished for seven months in a quarter cask (105 litres) of a type which was used in the old days. Thanks to the small casks, 30% more of the contents come into contact with the oak which affects the taste.
Recent independent bottlings include a 17 year old (1988) rum finish from Douglas Laing, a 15 year old (1990) from Cadenhead, a 12 year old (1993) from Ian MacLeod, a 13 year old (1992) from Signatory and a 12 year old (1993) from The Whisky Exchange (Single Malts of Scotland).

History (continued):

1928 – Isabella Johnston dies and Ian Hunter becomes sole owner.

1950 – Ian Hunter forms D. Johnston & Company Ltd.

1954 – Ian Hunter passes away and management of the distillery is taken over by Elisabeth "Bessie" Williamson, who was previously Ian Hunters PA and secretary. She becomes Director of the Board and Managing Director.

1967 – Seager Evans & Company buys the distillery through Long John Distillery, having already acquired part of Laphroaig in 1962.

1968 – The number of stills is increased from four to six.

1972 – Bessie Williamson, married name Campbell, retires. Another spirit still is installed bringing the total to seven.

1975 – Whitbread & Co. buys Seager Evans (now renamed Long John International) from Schenley International.

1989 – The spirits division of Whitbread is sold to Allied Distillers.

1991 – Allied Distillers launches its equivalent to United Distillers' Classic Malts called Caledonian Malts. Laphroaig is one of the four malts included; Miltonduff, Glendronach and Tormore (later to be replaced by Scapa) being the others.

1993 – A severe gale blows the pagoda roof off the kilns, but it is repaired.

1994 – HRH Prince Charles gives his Royal Warrant to Laphroaig. Friends of Laphroaig is founded and eventually number more than 200 000 members.

1995 – A 10 year old cask strength is launched.

2001 – 4 000 bottles of a 40 year old, the oldest-ever Laphroaig, are released.

2002 – The legendary distillery manager Iain Henderson retires.

2004 – Quarter Cask, a 5 year old Laphroaig matured for 7 months in a quarter cask (i. e. 105 litres) is launched in a limited edition.

2005 – Fortune Brands becomes new owner.

Quarter Cask

10 years old

10 years old cask strength

Linkwood

Owner:
Diageo

Region/district:
Speyside

Founded:
1821

Status:
Active

Tel:
01343 862000

Visitor centre:
No

website:
www.malts.com

Capacity:
2 300 000 litres

% sold as malt whisky:
2% unofficiall

Included in blended (past and/or present):
White Horse, Bell´s, Haig Gold Label, Compass Box Asyla

History:

1821 – Peter Brown founds the distillery.

1825 – Linkwood comes on stream.

1868 – Peter Brown passes away and his son William inherits the distillery.

1872 – William demolishes the distillery and builds a new one.

1874 – The new distillery is inaugurated.

1897 – Linkwood Glenlivet Distillery Company Ltd takes over operations.

1902 – Innes Cameron, a whisky trader from Elgin, joins the Board and eventually becomes the major shareholder and Director.

1932 – Innes Cameron dies and Scottish Malt Distillers takes over in 1933.

1962 – Major refurbishment takes place.

1971 – The two stills are increased by four. Technically, the four new stills belong to a new distillery sometimes referred to as Linkwood B.

1982 – Distillers Company Limited (DCL) launches their series The Ascot Malt Cellar which includes Linkwood 12 years.

1985 – Linkwood A (the two original stills) closes.

1990 – Linkwood A is in production again for a few months each year.

2002 – A 26 year old from 1975 is launched as a Rare Malt.

2005 – A 30 year old from 1974 is launched as a Rare Malt.

Linkwood distillery lies on the southern outskirts of Elgin, just a mile off the A941. The new stillhouse, built in 1971, with its panoramic windows and four stills is visible as one enters the courtyard. The old stillhouse with two stills is situated by the road and is used on and off today. A rectangular worm tub is still being used for cooling the spirit vapours while the new stills are equipped with shell and tube condensers. The two productions are vatted together before filling the casks.
Another aspect of the distillery, totally unconnected to whisky, is the gardens. They have been reverentially looked after by Hilary Lamont who worked as a full-time gardener at the distillery until her retirement a year ago.
Her work has contributed to no less than 530 species of live creatures having been recorded on the premises. A surprise visit was even made by an otter which was seen fishing in the dam containing cooling water.
Linkwood has always enjoyed a good reputation among blenders and is often included in lists of top class distilleries – especially suited for top dressings (flavouring malts) in a blend. The owners, however, have chosen not to promote Linkwood to a great extent, save for a *12 year old Flora & Fauna* and a number of *Rare Malts* (the most recent in 2005, *30 years old*).
Independent bottlers have provided a wider selection. Among later bottlings are Dewar Rattray 1985, Gordon & MacPhail 15 years old, Cadenhead 1989 (16 years old), Douglas Laing 1989 (16 years old), Ian MacLeod 1995 (11 years old and Port finished) and a Madeira finish from 1983 released by Murray McDavid.

Flora & Fauna 12 years old

Littlemill

Owner:
Loch Lomond Distillery Co. Ltd

Region/district:
Lowlands

Founded:
1772

Status:
Closed

Tel:
-

Visitor centre:
-

website:
-

Capacity:
-

% sold as malt whisky:
-

Included in blended (past and/or present):
-

History:

1772 – The distillery is founded.

1823 – Jane MacGregor is licensee and thereby one of the first females in the business.

1843 – Hector Henderson sells Littlemill and commences building Caol Ila.

1931 – The American Duncan G. Thomas buys the distillery and founds Littlemill Distillery Company Ltd with the Argyll Group. Saladin boxes are installed for maltings.

1959 – Barton Brands Inc. from Chicago becomes part-owners.

1971 – Duncan Thomas and Argyll Group are bought out and the company is restructured as Barton Distilling (Scotland) Ltd.

1972 – Production of the experimental whiskies Dunglas and Dumbuck stops.

1984 – The distillery closes.

1988 – Barton International becomes Gibson International.

1989 – Production resumes.

1992 – Production stops.

1994 – Gibson International files for bankruptcy and Glen Catrine Bonded Warehouse Ltd (sister company to Loch Lomond Distillery Company Ltd) buys Littlemill.

1996 – The equipment is dismantled and part of the buildings are demolished.

2003 – Loch Lomond Distillery Co. shelves plans to convert Littlemill into a working distillery/ musem.

2004 – Newstead Properties buys the facility to build 61 apartments. A fire, started by youngsters, destroys much of the remaining buildings.

2005 – The owners obtain permission from the Procurator Fiscal to demolish the remaining buildings except the two towers. A 12 year old Littlemill is released.

Photo: © 2005 www.thewhiskystore.de

Until 1992 Littlemill was Scotland's oldest working malt distillery and could trace its roots back to 1772 (possibly even back to the 1750s).
Triple distilling was abandoned in 1930. The year after, Duncan Thomas took over and replaced much of the equipment. Saladin boxes were installed to replace the old floor maltings, and he created new stills with rectifying columns instead of the ordinary swan-necks customary on pot stills. The stills were also isolated with aluminium. Thomas hoped to create a hybrid whisky which would mature quicker with the rectifier.
He also thought that this construction would facilitate adapting production to various types of whisky. One of these, distilled in 1967, was named Dunglas and is probably one of the rarest whisky bottlings in the world. The Whisky Exchange in London surprisingly released 102 bottles of a 36 year old Dunglas in 2003. But this was not its first time on the market, as already in 1990 Signatory were selling a 22 year old Dunglas in their Dun Eideann range.
Another experimental whisky, the peated Dumbuck, is not yet bottled. The experimental distilling stopped in 1972 and since then there has only been Littlemill flowing through the pipes.
For many years Littlemill has been put on the market at *8 years old* but this has recently been changed to *12 years old*. The bottle also has a new design, shared with the new 12 year olds from Glen Scotia and Loch Lomond (Inchmurrin).
Recent independent bottlings include a 16 year old from 1989 released by Cadenhead and a Murray McDavid 1991.

12 years old

Loch Lomond

Owner:
Loch Lomond Distillery Co.

Region/district:
Western Highlands

Founded:
1965

Status:
Active

Tel:
01389 752781

Visitor centre:
No

website:
www.lochlomonddistillery.com

Capacity:
2 500 000 litres

% sold as malt whisky:
n/a

Included in blended (past and/or present):
Loch Lomond, Scots Earl

History:

1965 – The distillery is built by Littlemill Distillery Company Ltd owned by Duncan Thomas and American Barton Brands.

1966 – Production commences.

1971 – Duncan Thomas is bought out and Barton Brands reforms as Barton Distilling (Scotland) Ltd.

1984 – The distillery closes.

1985 – Glen Catrine Bonded Warehouse Ltd with Alexander Bulloch at the helm buys Loch Lomond Distillery.

1987 – The distillery resumes production.

1993 – Grain spirits are also distilled.

1997 – A fire destroys 300 000 litres of maturing whisky.

1999 – Two more stills are installed.

2005 – Inchmoan and Craiglodge are officially launched for the first time. Both are 4 years old from 2001. Inchmurrin 12 years is launched.

2006 – Inchmurrin 4 years, Croftengea 1996 (9 years) and Glen Douglas 2001 (4 years) are launched.

Loch Lomond Single Blend and Single Malt

Loch Lomond Distillery, situated at the southern end of the Loch bearing the same name, is a virtually self-sufficient distillery. They have their own grain distillery and cooperage but lack their own malt production. The owner Sandy Bulloch has always gone his own way concerning whisky and except for a few tough years at the beginning of the millenium, they generate a healthy profit (£700 000 pre-tax in 2005).

The actual history of Loch Lomond can be said to have begun when the Bulloch family become owners. The main problem for Sandy Bulloch, who was both retailer and wholesaler, in the mid 1980s was obtaining sufficient stocks of whisky. The purchase of Loch Lomond Distillery from Barton Distilling in 1985 was one way of mitigating the shortage.

They have their own bottling plant (Glen Catrine Bonded Warehouse) which is one of the largest independent bottlers of spirit in Scotland today.

The distillery has two normal stills with traditional swan necks and four stills with adjustable rectifying columns. This makes it possible to vary the whisky character and widen the product range further.

The Coffey Still installed in 1993 contributes to Loch Lomond's uniqueness in being the only Scottish distillery producing both malt and grain whisky at the same site.

Loch Lomond produces a broad range of whiskies not found in other Scottish distilleries:

Single malt: Loch Lomond no age, Loch Lomond 21 years, Old Rhosdhu 5 years, Old Rhosdhu 1967 32 years, Inchmurrin 4 and 12 years, Inchmoan 2001 4 years, Craiglodge 2001 4 years, Croftengea 1996 9 years, Glen Douglas 2001 4 years.
Single blended: Loch Lomond **Blended:** Scots Earl **Single grain:** Loch Lomond

Croftengea is the most peated (40 ppm) followed by Craiglodge and Inchmoan (both 20 ppm) and, finally, Glen Douglas which is the least peated. Annual production at Loch Lomond is 10 million litres of grain alcohol and 2.5 million litres of malt alcohol.

Inchmurrin 12 years old

Lochside

Owner:
Chivas Brothers
(Pernod Ricard)

Region/district:
Eastern Highlands

Founded:
1957

Status:
Demolished

Tel:
-

Visitor centre:
-

website:
-

Capacity:
-

% sold as malt whisky:
-

Included in blended (past and/or present):
Macnab´s

History:

1957 – The legendary Joseph W. Hobbs starts production at Lochside Distillery, housed in the old brewery James Deuchar Brewery. Macnab Distillery Ltd is responsible for operations and uses the whisky in their blended Sandy Macnab's. Only grain whisky is produced the first years.

1961 – Malt whisky is also distilled.

1964 – Joseph Hobbs passes away and his son Joe takes over.

1971 – Production stops.

1973 – The Spanish company Destilerias y Crianza del Whisky (later to be acquired by Pedro Domecq) buys the distillery and restarts production.

1974 – Grain whisky production ceases.

1992 – The last distillation takes place in May and the distillery is then mothballed.

1994 – Allied Lyons buys Pedro Domecq and changes name to Allied Domecq.

1997 – All equipment and stored whisky is removed from the buildings.

2005 – The facilities are partly destroyed by a fire. Chivas Brothers (Pernod Ricard) become new owners through the acquisition of Allied Domecq.

Photo: © 2005 www.thewhiskystore.de

Lochside had operated as a brewery for nearly two centuries before it became a comparatively short-lived whisky distillery. The man behind it all was the energetic Joseph W. Hobbs who was involved with a large number of distilleries at the time. He seemed to have taken a special liking to producing both grain and malt whisky at the same distillery, as this was the procedure at both Ben Nevis and Lochside at the time. The idea was to blend whisky on site and then let it mature in casks as blended whisky. Obviously these ideas were his babies as grain distilling quickly ceased after his demise. A couple of years later Lochside became the first and so far only Spanish-owned Scottish distillery and output was mainly produced for a Spanish blended whisky.

The destiny of Lochside holds much in common with other distilleries that closed during the 1980s and 90s. The buildings were found to be in too poor condition so demolition work commenced in late 2004. A fire erupted in late January 2005 and eventually the landmark at the northern entrance to Montrose, the distillery tower, was demolished. The distillery site is now owned by Muir Homes, who have permission to build 37 flats on the premises.

Official bottlings of Lochside have occurred but they are virtually impossible to get hold of.

Independent bottlings are also rare. Some of the most recent are Douglas Laing 15 years old from 1990 and Cadenhead 24 year old from 1981, both which were released in autumn 2005. Douglas Laing has also recently released an unusual version of Lochside - a single grain from 1963 (42 years).

Gordon & MacPhail Lochside 1991

Longmorn

Owner:
Chivas Brothers (Pernod Ricard)

Region/district:
Speyside

Founded:
1894

Status:
Active

Tel:
01343 554139

Visitor centre:
No

website:
-

Capacity:
3 500 000 litres

% sold as malt whisky:
n/a

Included in blended (past and/or present):
Chivas Regal, Queen Anne, Something Special

History:

1893 – John Duff & Company, which founded Glenlossie already in 1876, starts construction. John Duff, George Thomson and Charles Shirres are involved in the company. The total cost amounts to £20 000.

1894 – First production in December.

1897 – John Duff buys out the others and founds Longmorn Distillery.

1898 – John Duff builds another distillery next to Longmorn which is called Benriach (at times aka Longmorn no. 2). The Pattison crash hits John Duff hard and he is forced to pawn shares in the bank. As he cannot pay his mortgages, the shares are sold by the bank to James R. Grant. Eventually, Grant's both sons and Tommy Dewar become part-owners.

1970 – The distillery company is merged with The Glenlivet & Glen Grant Distilleries and Hill Thomson & Co. Ltd. Own floor maltings ceases.

1972 – The number of stills is increased from four to six.

1974 – Another two stills are added (in total eight).

1978 – Seagrams takes over through The Chivas & Glenlivet Group.

1994 – Seagrams introduces The Heritage Selection and tries in vain to copy United Distillers´ success The Classic Malts. Apart from Longmorn, Glen Keith, Benriach and Strathisla are included.

2001 – Pernod Ricard buys Seagram Spirits & Wine together with Diageo and Pernod Ricard takes over the Chivas group.

2004 – A 17 year old cask strength is released.

Despite being placed some distance from the A941 between Rothes and Elgin, it is possible to see Longmorn if one pays attention. The pagoda roof is of course visible, but the words Longmorn Distillery are painted with huge letters on the warehouse roof. It seems contradicting to promote the distillery in this obvious way, when the owners do their best not to cause any major rumblings over the whisky. Almost all of the large production is destined for blending, especially in Chivas Regal, and the blenders love it.
Longmorn was one of the last distilleries to abandon coal firing of the stills (in 1994) and whisky purists are now eagerly awaiting to see how this has affected the whisky. A 'before and after' comparison should be possible around 2008. The eight stills, strangely enough situated in two separate stillhouses, are now heated using steam coils. The spirit is tankered away to Keith for filling. Some of the casks (a mix of bourbon and sherry) are stored there while the rest are returned to the distillery for storing in their dunnage warehouses or the three new racked warehouses situated on the grounds of Benriach.
Longmorn was the first distillery to welcome the father of Japanese whisky, Masataka Taketsuru, who was a student in 1919 on a visit from Japan to learn whisky production. Despite only staying for ten days at the distillery he was so impressed he used Longmorn as a model when he founded his first own distillery, Yoichi, on Hokkaido in 1934.
The only official bottlings so far are the *15 year old* and a *17 year old cask strength* released in 2004.
Recent independent bottlings include Douglas Laing 18 years old (1987), Gordon & MacPhail 1973 and a 1990 wine finish (Tempranillo) from Murray McDavid. From WoodWinters, a wine and whisky shop north of Stirling, comes a 15 year old Longmorn simply called The One.

15 years old

Macallan distillery

Macallan

Owner: Edrington Group

Region/district: Speyside

Founded: 1824

Status: Active

Tel: 01340 871471

Visitor centre: Yes (6/7)

website: www.themacallan.com

Capacity: 6 000 000 litres

% sold as malt whisky: n/a

Included in blended (past and/or present):
-

History:

1824 – The distillery is licensed to Alexander Reid under the name Elchies Distillery.

1847 – Alexander Reid passes away and James Shearer Priest and James Davidson take over.

1868 – James Stuart takes over the licence. He founds Glen Spey distillery a decade later.

1896 – James Stuart buys the distillery.

1892 – Stuart sells the distillery to Roderick Kemp from Elgin who has previously worked at and been part-owner of Talisker. Kemp expands the distillery and names it Macallan-Glenlivet.

1909 – Roderick Kemp passes away and the Roderick Kemp Trust is established to secure the family's future ownership.

1965 – The number of stills is increased from six to twelve.

1966 – The trust is reformed as a private limited company.

1968 – The company is introduced on the London Stock Exchange.

1974 – The number of stills is increased to 18.

1975 – Another three stills are added, now making the total 21.

Macallan is a community of its own almost like in the old days. Several of the 45 employees live on the premises with their families. 23 of them are warehousemen responsible for 70 000 casks spread in 25 dunnage warehouses with a further 80 000 in a gargantuan racked warehouse. The road to the distillery is bordered by fields of Golden Promise, making up a few percent of the barley requirements, which are malted at Tamdhu. The rest are Optic and Chariot bought malted from Simpsons in Berwick upon Tweed. Macallan has 21 stills but only five wash stills and ten spirit stills are in use. The last six are in a separate stillhouse but can be utilised if a need arises. The wash stills are directly fired with gas, while the spirit stills are indirectly fired using steam coils. The cooling water for the alcohol comes from Spey while distilling water is taken from three bore holes on the grounds.
The excellent Macallan tour was expanded in summer 2006 with 'The story of Wood', an interactive exhibition on the second floor of warehouse no. 7.
Macallan has always been known for concentrating on whisky matured in sherry wood. With the launch in 2004 of the Macallan Fine Oak series, a mix of sherry and bourbon matured whisky; they extended the brand to attract new customers. Recent new bottlings have been dedicated to limited editions. A *50 year old* in a crystal decanter from Lalique was launched in America, Russia and Asia in just 470 bottles. *The Macallan Woodland Estate*, a 12 year old is sold together with a newly planted tree on the grounds. Proceeds will be invested in ongoing woodland regeneration. Another version in the *Fine Oak* range (*17 years old*) was launched in the US and a new Vintage was added to the *Fine and Rare* range (*1975*, Bourbon matured). There is also rumour of an as yet unnamed Summer edition will be released, a follow-up to Winter Reserve (the 14 year old puncheon cask sold at the distillery).
Macallan puts effort into new export markets which have resulted in great increases in sales in Russia in recent years. Edrington has also opened a sales office in China.

The current range is great and can be divided into:

Sherry Oak: 10 years, 12 years, Elegancia, 18 years, 25 years and 30 years old.

Fine Oak: 8, 10, 12 15, 17, 18, 21, 25 and 30 years old.

Special releases: Cask Strength, 1841 Replica, 1876 Replica, Exceptional V, Exceptional VI, 20's Vintage Travel, 30's Vintage Travel, 40's Vintage Travel and 50's Vintage Travel.

Fine and Rare: A range of vintages from 1926 to 1975.

History (continued):

1979 – Allan Schiach, descendant of Roderick Kemp, becomes the new chairman of the board after Peter Schiach.

1980 – The name changes to Macallan and a large launch campaign takes place in the UK.

1984 – The first official 18 year old single malt is launched.

1986 – Japanese Suntory buys 25% of Macallan-Glenlivet plc stocks.

1996 – Highland Distilleries buys the remaining stocks and terminate the Kemp family's influence on Macallan. 11 000 bottles of 1874 Replica are launched.

1999 – Edrington and William Grant & Sons buys Highland Distilleries (where Edrington, Suntory and Remy-Cointreau already are shareholders) for £601 million. They form the 1887 Company which owns Highland Distilleries with 70% held by Edrington and 30% by William Grant & Sons (excepting the 25% share held by Suntory).

2000 – The first single cask from Macallan (1981) is named Exceptional 1.

2001 – A new visitor centre is opened and 1861 Replica (17 400 bottles) are introduced.

2002 – Macallan Elegancia replaces Macallan 12 years in the duty-free assortment. 1841 Replica, Exceptional II and Exceptional III, from 1980, are also launched during the year.

2003 – 1876 Replica (19 800 bottles) and Exceptional IV, single cask from 1990 (864 bottles) are launched.

2004 – Exceptional V, single cask from 1989 (858 bottles) is launched as well as Exceptional VI, single cask from 1990 (816 bottles). The Fine Oak series is launched and Macallan 18 years old takes first place in Whisky Magazine's 'Best Malts of the World'.

2005 – New expressions are Macallan Woodland Estate, Winter Edition and the 50 year old.

2006 – Fine Oak 17 years old and Vintage 1975 are launched.

40 years old

50 years old

10 years old

Fine Oak 17 yo

1975 vintage

Woodland Estate

18 years old

25 years old

Elegancia

Macduff

Owner:
John Dewar & Sons Ltd (Bacardi)

Region/district:
Highlands

Founded:
1962

Status:
Active

Tel:
01261 812612

Visitor centre:
No

website:
-

Capacity:
2 400 000 litres
1 600 000 litres

% sold as malt whisky:
10%

Included in blended (past and/or present):
William Lawson (Scottish Gold, Founders Reserve)

History:

1962 – The distillery is jointly founded by the Duff family, Marty Dyke, George Crawford and Brodie Hepburn (who is also involved in Tullibardine and Deanston). Macduff Distillers Ltd is the name of the company.

1963 – Production starts.

1965 – The number of stills is increased from two to three.

1967 – Stills now total four.

1972 – William Lawson Distillers buys the distillery from Glendeveron Distilleries.

1980 – William Lawson is bought by Martini Rossi through the subsidiary General Beverage Corporation.

1990 – A fifth still is installed.

1992 – Bacardi buys Martini Rossi (including William Lawson) and transfers Macduff to the subsidiary John Dewar & Sons.

Macduff is Speyside's easternmost distillery, situated in Macduff opposite Banff on the Deveron's outflow in Banff Bay. Together with Inchgower and the now decommissioned Glenglassaugh, Macduff is by many reckoned as one of the Coastal Speysiders. The owners, on the other hand, count it as a Highland, period. Many appreciate Glen Deveron, the official bottling, for its pure and mild taste. Part of this character can be traced to the fact that the lyne arm of the stills has a rather unusual raised angle which creates more reflux (re-distillation of the vapours) giving a lighter spirit. There are two wash stills and three spirit stills at the distillery.

Saying has it that Macduff was first to use a mash tun made of metal and there was a cooperage at Macduff but it has since long closed. A rare form of maturation took place in the sixties when firkin casks, usually associated with ale and not whisky, were used.

Macduff was built mainly for the purpose of delivering malt whisky for blending, principally to William Lawson. Still, it is the one out of Dewar's five distilleries which produces most single malt. 450 000 bottles a year are produced more or less exclusively for export.

A bottle of single malt bearing the name Glen Deveron is an official bottling from Macduff Distillery. If the name on the label is Macduff, it is an independent bottling.

A *5 year old* is produced for the Italian market (cf. Glen Grant) while the most common Glen Deveron is *10 years*. Some old versions of *8 year* and *12 year olds* are also available.

Independent bottlings include Douglas Laing (Platinum) 1967 (35 years), Cadenhead 16 years old, Duncan Taylor (Peerless) 1969 (35 years) and another Duncan Taylor (Rare Auld) 1969 (35 years) released in 2006.

10 years old

Mannochmore

Owner:
Diageo

Region/district:
Speyside

Founded:
1971

Status:
Active

Tel:
01343 862000

Visitor centre:
No

website:
www.malts.com

Capacity:
1 300 000 litres

% sold as malt whisky:
n/a

Included in blended (past and/or present):
Haig Dimple

History:

1971 – Scottish Malt Distillers (SMD) founds the distillery on the site of their sister distillery Glenlossie. It is managed by John Haig & Co. Ltd.

1985 – The distillery is mothballed.

1989 – In production again.

1992 – A Flora & Fauna series 12 years old becomes the first official bottling.

1997 – United Distillers launches Loch Dhu – The Black Whisky which is a 10 year old Mannochmore. A 22 year old Rare Malt from 1974 and a sherry-matured Manager´s Dram 18 years are also launched.

Mannochmore is one of many distilleries located around the A941 between Rothes and Elgin. Its nearest neighbours are Longmorn and Benriach. Even closer, almost next door is Glenlossie. It is often considered as a sister distillery to the latter, even if it was built 100 years later in the early 1970s. Its main purpose was to contribute to Haig's blends. The same staff man both distilleries, so when one is temporarily closed the other is up and running. Both distilleries share the cask warehouse and the huge dark grains plant which processes draff and pot ale from 21 different distilleries. It produces no less than 1 000 tonnes of dark grains per week from 2 600 tonnes of draff and 8 million litres of pot ale.

A special, dark-coloured, Mannochmore named Loch Dhu was launched in 1996. It quickly became a cult whisky, especially in Denmark. The Loch Dhu has now become a collector's item with prices ranging between £120 and 150. When production of Loch Dhu ceased in 2000 the Danish whisky importer Mac Y decided to find a replacement. They invented Cu Dhub, a Speyside distillery bottling, with plenty of caramel added giving the whisky its dark colour.

Aside from the *12 year old* there is another bottling from Diageo, *Rare Malts 1974,* which appeared in 1997. Independent bottlings are not very common, recent ones include a Signatory 1991 (13 years) and a Douglas Laing (Old Malt Cask) 1990 (14 years).

Flora & Fauna 12 years old

Millburn

Owner:
Diageo

Region/district:
Northern Highlands

Founded:
1807

Status:
Dismantled

Tel:
-

Visitor centre:
-

website:
www.malts.com

Capacity:
-

% sold as malt whisky:
-

Included in blended (past and/or present):
-

History:

1805 – A Mr. Welsh founds the distillery on the outskirts of Inverness and names it Inverness Distillery.

1825 – Alexander Macdonald and James Rose operate the distillery.

1829 – The company Macdonald & Rose is wound up.

1853 – The corn dealer David Rose buys the distillery but probably uses it for purposes other than distilling.

1876 – Inverness Distillery is reconstructed in order to function as a distillery again.

1881 – David Rose's son George takes over.

1892 – Andrew Haig & Co. buys the distillery.

1904 – The distillery is renamed Millburn and Millburn Distillery Company is formed.

1921 – Booth's Distillers Limited (distiller of gin) from London acquires the distillery.

1922 – A raging fire destroys most of the distillery, but it is rebuilt the same year.

1935 – Booth's Distillers merges with William Sanderson & Co.

1937 – Sanderson & Booth's joins Distillers Company Limited (DCL).

1943 – Administration is transferred to Scottish Malt Distillers (SMD).

1985 – Production ceases and the distillery closes.

1988 – The equipment is removed and the facilities are rebuilt as the steakhouse 'The Auld Distillery' by the restaurant chain Beefeater.

1995 – Millburn 1975 (18 years) is the first official bottling in the Rare Malts series.

2001 – Another Rare Malt is launched; Millburn 1975 (25 years).

2005 – A 35 year old is launched in the Rare Malt series.

There have been a number of distilleries in Inverness during the last two centuries, but none exists today. The only three that survived into modern times were Glen Mhor, Glen Albyn and Millburn.
The trend in the malt industry of the 1970s and 1980s was large-scale production and many smaller units were therefore closed. Millburn was one of these as it was not feasible to expand it. Sandwiched between a river and the streets of an expansive Inverness it had to close in 1985, although most of the buildings remain. Whitbread opened a Beefeater Restaurant, 'The Auld Distillery', in one of them in 1989. Whitbread are still the owners of the restaurant which has since changed name to 'Slice' and is part of the largest hotel chain in the UK, Premier Travel Inn.
Millburn was the oldest of the three remaining Inverness distilleries and the last one to close. It may come as some consolation for fans of Millburn to know that at least one part of the distillery, the spirit safe, still functions and has been installed at Benromach distillery.
A couple of *Rare Malts* have been released by Diageo (the most recent and last in 2005, *35 years old*).
Independent bottlings are not that common and are increasingly rare to encounter. Three of the most recent ones are Cadenhead 1974 (31 years), Douglas Laing 1969 (36 years) and a Signatory 1979 (26 years).

Rare Malts 1969 (35 years)

Miltonduff

Owner:
Chivas Brothers (Pernod Ricard)

Region/district:
Speyside

Founded:
1824

Status:
Active

Tel:
01343 547433

Visitor centre:
No

website:
-

Capacity:
5 500 000 litres

% sold as malt whisky:
0%

Included in blended (past and/or present):
Ballantine´s, Teachers, Old Smuggler

History:

1824 – Andrew Peary and Robert Bain obtain a licence for Miltonduff Distillery. It has previously operated as an illicit farm distillery called Milton Distillery but changes name when the Duff family buys the site it is operating on.

1866 – William Stuart buys the distillery.

1895 – Thomas Yool & Co. becomes new part-owners.

1936 – Thomas Yool & Co. sells the distillery to Hiram Walker Gooderham & Worts. The latter transfers administration to the newly acquired subsidiary George Ballantine & Son.

1964 – A pair of Lomond stills is installed to produce the rare Mosstowie.

1974-75 – Major reconstruction of the distillery.

1981 – The Lomond stills are decommissioned and replaced by two ordinary pot stills; the number of stills now totalling six.

1986 – Allied Lyons buys 51% of Hiram Walker.

1987 – Allied Lyons acquires the rest of Hiram Walker.

1991 – Allied Distillers follow United Distillers´ example of Classic Malts and introduce Caledonian Malts where Tormore, Glendronach and Laphroaig are included in addition to Miltonduff. Tormore is later replaced by Scapa.

2005 – Chivas Brothers (Pernod Ricard) become new owners through the acquisition of Allied Domecq.

While many distilleries are hidden away in glens, Miltonduff is well visible as it rises over the plains a few miles southwest of Elgin. It is large, in fact the second largest complex after Glenlivet in the Chivas group. Previous owners Allied chose to locate the major part of their whisky-associated activities to Miltonduff. Since the laboratories moved to Glen Keith, the engineering department and a dark grains plant remain.
A danger in the old days was the carbon dioxide that was formed in connection with fermentation. A traditional solution to this was mesh flooring and a good flow-through of air. Miltonduff was first with using extractor fans to lead away the dangerous gas from its 18 washbacks.
Miltonduff is one of a handful of distilleries which used Lomond stills for a period of time. The idea behind them was to produce several types of malt whisky with the same still. Miltonduff had Lomond stills installed in 1964, but by 1981 they were rebuilt as ordinary stills as the trials had not been completely successful. Cleaning of the Lomond stills was complicated and demand on the standard produce, Miltonduff, had increased. The Lomond still malt was named Mosstowie and is still available. Gordon & MacPhail released a 25 year old in 2004 and during 2005 a 26 year old was launched by Signatory and a 29 year old by Duncan Taylor (Rarest of the Rare).
An official *15 year old* Miltonduff was released several years ago and has been difficult to obtain recently. Chivas Brothers did, however, release more bottles in summer 2006.
Otherwise Gordon & MacPhail are more or less fully responsible for official bottlings from Miltonduff. A 10 year old and two limited editions – cask strength from 1993 and a 1968 vintage are the current ones.

Gordon & MacPhail 1993 Cask Strength

Mortlach

Owner:
Diageo

Region/district:
Speyside

Founded:
1823

Status:
Active

Tel:
01340 822100

Visitor centre:
No

website:
www.malts.com

Capacity:
2 800 000 litres

% sold as malt whisky:
n/a

Included in blended (past and/or present):
Johnnie Walker Black Label

History:

1823 – The distillery is founded by James Findlater.

1824 – Donald Macintosh and Alexander Gordon become part-owners.

1831 – The distillery is sold to John Robertson for £270.

1832 – A. & T. Gregory buys Mortlach.

1837 – James and John Grant of Aberlour become part-owners. No production takes place at Mortlach as the equipment probably is dismantled and used in building Glen Grant Distillery.

1842 – The distillery is now owned by John Alexander Gordon and the Grant brothers.

1851 – Mortlach is once again an up and running distillery after having been used as a church and a brewery for some years. The whisky is sold under the name The Real John Gordon.

1853 – George Cowie joins as part-owner with Gordon.

1867 – John Alexander Gordon dies and Cowie becomes sole owner.

1895 – George Cowie Jr. joins the company.

1897 – The number of stills is increased from three to six.

1923 – Alexander Cowie sells the distillery to John Walker & Sons.

1925 – John Walker becomes part of Distillers Company Limited (DCL).

1930 – The administration is transferred to Scottish Malt Distillers (SMD).

1964 – Major refurbishment.

1968 – Floor maltings ceases.

1995 – Mortlach 1972 (22 years) is released as a Rare Malt.

1996 – Mortlach 1972 (23 years) is released as a Rare Malt. The distillery is renovated at a cost of £1.5 million.

1998 – Mortlach 1978 (20 years) is released as a Rare Malt.

2004 – Mortlach 1971, a 32 year old cask strength is released.

When Mortlach was founded in 1823 it was the first of the famous seven Dufftown distilleries. Among the employees was one man who would eventually become one of the great men of the whisky world, William Grant. He began as book keeper in 1866 and ended his career there as manager in 1886 when he left in order to set up Glenfiddich a few miles to the north. The stillhouse at Mortlach is a peculiar and unique sight with six stills of various shapes and formats. Neither does the process resemble any other distillery's. No. 3 spirit still and no. 3 wash still are operated in pairs. 80% of the low wines run from no. 1 and no. 2 wash stills to no. 2 spirit still for a traditional distilling while the remaining 20% is led to no. 1 spirit still called Wee Witchie. The spirit in Wee Witchie is distilled three times before collecting the middle cut. At that moment there are three varieties of spirit of different strengths and flavours which are mixed. The process is usually called partial triple distillation and is a variation of the method used at Benrinnes and Springbank. The aim is to achieve a robust and flavour-rich whisky and the still combination is one of the prerequisites in achieving this. Another success factor is the use of worm tubs for a quick condensation with as little contact as possible with the copper. By using this procedure more of the sulphury compounds are retained instead of becoming neutralised by the copper.

The official bottling of Mortlach (*Flora & Fauna*) is *16 years* but in 2004 a *32 year old cask strength* from 1971 was released as a limited edition of 2 160 bottles. Mortlach has always been popular with blenders and independent bottlers. Gordon & MacPhail in particular have released very old versions of up to 60 years of age. Recent bottlings include a 12 year old from Douglas Laing, a 37 year old from Gordon & MacPhail, a 1988 and 1993 from Duncan Taylor and a port finish from 1993 released by Ian Macleod.

Flora & Fauna 16 years old

North Port

Owner:
Diageo

Region/district:
Eastern Highlands

Founded:
1820

Status:
Demolished

Tel:
-

Visitor centre:
-

website:
www.malts.com

Capacity:
-

% sold as malt whisky:
-

Included in blended (past and/or present):
-

History:

1820 – David Guthrie founds the distillery and names it Townhead Distillery.

1823 – David, John and Alexander, three of David Guthrie's sons, help their father with operations. The name is changed to Brechin Distillery.

1825 – Guthrie, Martin & Co. is formed to operate the distillery.

1922 – The distillery is acquired by Distillers Company Limited (DCL) together with W. H. Holt Ltd.

1928 – The distillery closes.

1937 – The distillery is in production again.

1939 – The distillery changes name from Brechin to North Port.

1983 – North Port is mothballed.

1993 – The buildings are demolished.

1995 – North Port 1971 (23 years) is launched as a Rare Malt.

1998 – North Port 1979 (19 years) is launched as a Rare Malt.

1999 – North Port 1979 (20 years) is launched as a Rare Malt.

2005 – A 28 year old is launched as a Special Release from Diageo.

Production increased markedly in the Scottish distilleries from the end of World War II to the 1970s. Consumers´ tastes changed in the 1980s, especially in the American market where many began to prefer vodka, white rum and wine to whisky. This resulted in whisky availability far exceeding demand. At the same time, whisky was affected by heavier taxation than that of wines. Therefore, Diageo was forced to close 21 of their 45 distilleries between 1983 and 1985. Only five of these have been resurrected today.

North Port, also known as Brechin, does not belong to the existing ones. It was dismantled piece by piece in the 1980s and 1990s. The last remnants disappeared in 1994 when a supermarket was built on the site.

North Port used a peculiar worm tub technique for cooling the spirits. Alexander Guthrie dammed Den Burn which flowed past the distillery and dug a canal in the mountain where the copper worms were cooled by the passing water. The hard construction work was made with only a hammer and a chisel and is commemorated on the packaging of the newly released 28 year old.

North Port and Brechin are used interchangeably on the whisky labels. Brechin is the name of the city and North Port comes from a gate in the wall which surrounded the city.

The first two official bottlings of North Port were released as *Rare Malts; 1971* (*23 years old*) and *1979* (*20 years old*). It was therefore an opportunity to rejoice when a *28 year old* Brechin appeared in 2005 as a Special Release. The number of bottles was low (2 040) and it was priced accordingly.

Independent bottlings include Signatory 1975 (29 years), Douglas Laing (Old Malt Cask) 1976 (26 years), Gordon & MacPhail 1981 (21 years) and Duncan Taylor (Rarest of the Rare) 1981 (23 and 24 years respectively).

Brechin 28 years

Oban

Owner: Diageo

Region/district: Western Highlands

Founded: 1794

Status: Active

Tel: 01631 572004 (vc)

Visitor centre: Yes (6/7)

website: www.malts.com

Capacity: 700 000 litres

% sold as malt whisky: n/a

Included in blended (past and/or present): Old Mull

History:

1793 – Brothers John and Hugh Stevenson found the distillery on premises previously used for brewing. Their company is named Oban Brewery Company.

1794 – Start of operations.

1820 – Hugh Stevenson dies.

1821 – Hugh Stevenson's son Thomas, having recently returned from Buenos Aires, takes over.

1822 – Thomas Stevenson acquires the remaining shares in Oban Brewery Company.

1829 – A series of unsuccessful business investments force Thomas Stevenson into bankruptcy with debts of over £8 000. His eldest son John takes over operations at the distillery.

1830 – John buys the distillery from his father's creditors for £1 500.

1866 – Peter Cumstie from Oban buys the distillery.

1883 – Cumstie sells Oban to James Walter Higgins who refurbishes and modernizes it.

1898 – The Oban & Aultmore-Glenlivet Co. takes over with Alexander Edwards at the helm A consortium made up of John Dewar & Sons, James Buchanan & Company and White Horse Distillers is also involved in the company.

1923 – The Oban Distillery Co. owned by Buchanan-Dewar takes over.

1925 – Buchanan-Dewar becomes part of Distillers Company Limited (DCL).

1930 – Administration is transferred to Scottish Malt Distillers (SMD).

1931 – Production ceases.

1937 – In production again.

1968 – Floor maltings ceases and the distillery closes for reconstruction.

1972 – Reopening of the distillery.

1979 – Oban 12 years is on sale.

1988 – United Distillers launches Classic Malts. Oban 14 year is selected to represent Western Highlands.

1989 – A visitor centre is built.

1998 – A Distillers' Edition, with a montilla fino finish, is launched.

2002– The, so far, oldest Oban (32 years) is launched in a limited edition of 6 000 bottles.

2004 – A 20 year old cask strength from 1984 (1 260 bottles) is released.

Oban is unusual in that it is an urban distillery. When the distillery was built the area was hardly more than a small fisherman's village, but the Stevenson brothers who founded the distillery put in at least the same effort to build up the whole village. A city quickly grew up surrounding the distillery and now counts 8 500 inhabitants.

Oban is one of only nine distilleries founded in the 18th century which are still active. It is also one of few distilleries still using worm tubs for cooling the vapours. At Oban these are rectangular and built into the roof.

The distillery is interesting, but it is not the most famous building in Oban. Instead, that building is found on the hill just behind the distillery and is called McCaig's Tower (sometimes McCaig's Folly) after the man who started building it, John Stuart McCaig. He was a local banker who started to build a monument to his family in 1897. He was a great admirer of Roman architecture and the resulting building resembled the Colosseum in Rome. McCaig died in 1902 and nobody wanted to complete the monument; therefore it still only consists of the outer walls.

Official bottlings are few; a *14 year old*, a *Distiller's Edition* and some limited editions, among them a *32 year old* and a *20 year old*.

It is virtually impossible to find independent bottlings of Oban. The latest from Cadenhead appeared in the early nineties.

14 years old

1991 Distiller's Edition

Pittyvaich

Owner:
Diageo

Region/district:
Speyside

Founded:
1974

Status:
Demolished

Tel:
-

Visitor centre:
-

website:
www.malts.com

Capacity:
-

% sold as malt whisky:
-

Included in blended (past and/or present):
Bell´s

History:

1974 – Arthur Bell & Sons founds the distillery as a sister distillery to Dufftown-Glenlivet.

1975 – Production starts.

1985 – Guinness Group acquires Bell's

1987 – United Distillers is formed by merging Bell´s and Distillers Company Limited (DCL) - which Guinness bought in 1986.

1991 – The first official bottling is launched, a 12 year old in the Flora & Fauna series.

1993 – The distillery is mothballed.

1994 – Gordon's begins gin distilling on a trial basis in November to evaluate the feasibility of Pittyvaich backing up the Laindon facility.

2002 – The distillery closes and part of the equipment is sent to Clynelish.

The purpose of Bell´s opening Pittyvaich distillery on the outskirts of Dufftown was to secure malt whisky for the blending industry. Pittyvaich became one of four signature malts in Bell's blended whisky. Bell's had been sold as a blended whisky since 1896 but it was in 1925 that the by now world-famous slogan 'Afore ye go' was coined. It is said to have originated during the First World War when the Bell family sent crates of whisky to the docks so the soldiers could get a dram '...afore ye go'.
There were already plenty of malt distilleries in the group when Bell's came into the Guinness and United Distiller's family so the requirement for Pittyvaich malt diminished over time. It was suggested within UD at the time that Gordon's Gin could be distilled by using the great capacity of Cameronbridge rather than that in Laindon in Essex. More conservative forces within the company were dismayed at the thought of making gin north of the Scotland border. Compromising, the solution became to first distill gin on a trial basis at Pittyvaich. The trials at Pittyvaich were successful and since the end of the 1990s all production of Gordon´s Gin had been moved to Cameronbridge.
The last official malt distilling at Pittyvaich took place in 1993. Staff from Dufftown-Glenlivet distillery has used the facilities since to evaluate distilling techniques and different sorts of barley. The end came in 2002 when part of the equipment was dismantled and sent away and the buildings demolished.
The only official bottling of Pittyvaich is the *12 year old Flora & Fauna*. Independent bottlings are becoming rarer. An example of recent ones being Gordon & MacPhail 1993, Douglas Laing 1990 (15 years) and Duncan Taylor 1979 (26 years).

Flora & Fauna 12 years old

Port Ellen

Owner: Diageo	***Region:*** Islay
Founded: 1825	***Status:*** Dismantled
Tel: -	***Visitor centre:*** -
website: www.malts.com	
Capacity: -	***% sold as malt whisky:*** -

Included in blended (past and/or present):
-

History:

1825 – Alexander Kerr Mackay assisted by Walter Campbell founds the distillery. Mackay runs into financial troubles after a few months and his three relatives John Morrison, Patrick Thomson and George Maclennan take over.

1833 – John Ramsay, a cousin to John Morrison, comes from Glasgow to take over.

1836 – Ramsay is granted a lease on the distillery from the Laird of Islay.

1892 – Ramsay dies and the distillery is inherited by his widow, Lucy.

1906 – Lucy Ramsay dies and her son Captain Iain Ramsay takes over.

1920 – Iain Ramsay sells to Buchanan-Dewar who transfers the administration to the company Port Ellen Distillery Co. Ltd.

1925 – Buchanan-Dewar joins Distillers Company Limited (DCL).

1929 – No production.

1930 – Administration is transferred to Scottish Malt Distillers (SMD) and the distillery is mothballed.

1967 – In production again after reconstruction and doubling of the number of stills from two to four.

1973 – A large drum maltings is installed.

1980 – Queen Elisabeth visits the distillery and a commemorative special bottling is made.

1983 – The distillery is mothballed.

1987 – The distillery closes permanently but the maltings continue to deliver malt to all Islay distilleries.

1998 – Port Ellen 1978 (20 years) is released as a Rare Malt.

2000 – Port Ellen 1978 (22 years) is released as a Rare Malt.

2001 – Port Ellen cask strength first edition is released.

When Port Ellen closed in 1983 it was one of three Islay distilleries owned by Diageo (then DCL). The other two were Lagavulin and Caol Ila who had been operating uninterrupted for many years. Port Ellen, mothballed since 1930, had only been operating for 16 years since re-opening, which made it easy for the owners to single out which Islay distillery to close when malt whisky demand decreased. It was also the smallest of the three, with an annual output of c 1 700 000 litres alcohol per year.
The stills were shipped abroad early in the 1990s, possibly destined for India, and the distillery buildings were destroyed shortly afterwards, but the whisky from Port Ellen is so beloved that rumours of distilling starting up again flourish from time to time.
Today the site is associated with the huge drum maltings that was built in 1973. It supplies all Islay distilleries and a few others, with a large proportion of their malt.
1-10 tonnes of peat (depending on the ppm specifications) are required for each batch of 46 tonnes of produced malt. This means that 2 000 tonnes of peat are required each year. The peat was taken from Duich Moss until 1993 when conservationists managed to obtain national nature reserve status on the area to protect the thousands of Barnacle Geese that make a stop-over there during their migration. Nowadays the peat is taken from nearby Castlehill.
Besides a couple of versions in the *Rare Malts* series from *1978*, the owners began releasing one official bottling a year in 2001 when a *22 year old cask strength* was released in an edition of 6 000 bottles. This was followed in 2002 and 2003 by two *24 years old*, in 2004 and 2005 by two *25 years old* and in 2006 by a *27 year old*.
Port Ellen is a favourite with independent bottlers. Douglas Laing has been the most industrious and released four new (22, 23, 25 and 27 years old) in 2006. Ian MacLeod 23 years old and Signatory 30 years old are other recent bottlings.

1978 27 years old
6th release

Pulteney

Owner:
Inver House Distillers (Pacific Spirits)

Region/district:
Northern Highlands

Founded:
1826

Status:
Active

Tel:
01955 602371

Visitor centre:
Yes (4/7)

website:
www.oldpulteney.com

Capacity:
1 000 000 litres

% sold as malt whisky:
23%

Included in blended (past and/or present):
Ballantine´s

History:

1826 – James Henderson founds the distillery. It claims to be the only distillery named after a person, Sir William Johnstone Pulteney, although Glen Grant also comes to mind in this context.

1920 – The distillery is bought by James Watson & Co.

1923 – Buchanan-Dewar takes over.

1925 – Buchanan-Dewar becomes part of Distillers Company Limited (DCL).

1930 – Production ceases.

1951 – In production again after being acquired by the solicitor Robert Cumming, who also buys Balblair.

1955 – Cumming sells to James & George Stodart Ltd, a subsidiary to Hiram Walker & Sons.

1958 – The distillery is rebuilt.

1959 – The floor maltings close.

1961 – Allied Breweries buys James & George Stodart Ltd.

1981 – Allied Breweries changes name to Allied Lyons after the acquisition of J Lyons in 1978.

1994 – Allied Lyons acquires Pedro Domecq and changes name to Allied Domecq plc.

1995 – Allied Domecq sells Pulteney to Inverhouse Distillers.

1997 – Old Pulteney 12 years is launched.

2001 – Pacific Spirits (Great Oriole Group) buys Inverhouse at a price of $85 million.

2004 – A 17 year old is launched (4 200 bottles).

2005 – A 21 year old is launched (3 000 bottles).

In recent years attention has been drawn to the Scottish whisky industry's impact on the environment. Adverse effects include the release of carbon dioxide into the atmosphere and habitat changes due to peat extraction. Several distillery owners have reacted to the problems driven by laws and regulation issues while some have seen them as drivers for innovation.
An example of the latter is the project started by Pulteney distillery and Pulteney town together with the Highland Council. The idea is to make use of the excess thermal energy that is derived from cooling the spirit by building a wood-fuelled combustion boiler adjacent to the distillery. It will boost the heat from the distillation process to a higher temperature before pumping it to the surrounding houses. 500 homes will be able to make use of the heat in phase 1, and some of the steam will be re-circulated into the distillery itself. An enhanced boiler will be installed in phase 2, making it possible for another 1000 customers to take advantage.
Pulteney is a small distillery with only one pair of stills. The wash still is large (21 700 litres) with a huge ball creating added reflux. Its top is quaintly chopped off as the still apparently was too tall for the stillroom when it was installed. The spirit still (17 300 litres) is equipped with a purifier.
Pulteney is one of few distilleries still using worm tubs as condensers and they are unusually enough made of stainless steel. Old Pulteney, as the whisky is called, is the best seller of the five Inver House distilleries. The core range is a *12 year old* with limited editions of a *17 year old* and a *21 year old*. A Pulteney 1969 bottled in 2006 from Gordon & MacPhail and an 8 year old from Douglas Laing, also in 2006, are among the most recent independent bottlings.

12 years old

Rosebank

Owner:
Diageo

Region:
Lowlands

Founded:
1798

Status:
Closed

Tel:
-

Visitor centre:
-

website:
www.malts.com

Capacity:
-

% sold as malt whisky:
-

Included in blended (past and/or present):
-

History:

1798 – According to legend, the Stark brothers operate a distillery by the name Rosebank.

1817 – James Robertson runs a distillery named Rosebank which may be identical to that of the Stark brothers´.

1840 - James Rankine builds the present distillery buildings. He has taken over the maltings of Camelon Distillery, situated on the nearby eastern bank of the Forth-Clyde canal.

1845 – The distillery expands.

1861 – Rankine buys Camelon Distillery, on the west bank of the Forth-Clyde canal.

1864 – James Rankine's son, R. W. Rankine, rebuilds Rosebank distillery.

1865 – Rankine demolishes Camelon Distillery but keeps the maltings and connects the two sites by a swing bridge.

1894 – Rosebank Distillery Company is formed.

1914 – Rosebank, with Clydesdale, Glenkinchie, St. Magdalene and Grange form Scottish Malt Distillers (SMD).

1919 – Scottish Malt Distillers (SMD) becomes part of Distillers Company Limited (DCL).

1968 – The old Camelon maltings is closed and partly demolished.

1982 – DCL launches the series The Ascot Malt Cellar with Rosebank (8 years), Linkwood (12 years), Talisker (8 years), Lagavulin (12 years) and two vatted malts, Strathconnan and Glenleven.

1993 – The distillery closes in June.

2002 – The buildings are bought in May by British Waterways for the building of a restaurant, offices and flats.

One can ponder over which fate Rosebank would have encountered back in 1988 if it had been selected as one of six Classic Malts. Although Rosebank was considered equal to Glenkinchie quality-wise, United Distillers selected the latter to represent the Lowlands. Perhaps highly appreciated Rosebank had still been in operation if the decision had been more favourable.

After Rosebank was mothballed in 1993, rumours were that it might reopen, but they were killed in 2002 when the facilities were sold to British Waterways, a public corporation responsible for the care and enhancement of the network of canals and rivers in the UK. By that time, the Camelon maltings across the canal had already been turned into a Beefeater Restaurant. This maltings, in use as recently as in 1968, was the last remaining part of the old Camelon distillery. British Waterways and Scottish & Newcastle Pub Enterprises made an agreement in 2005 to establish and develop pubs and restaurants at over 100 sites across British Waterways canals and rivers. The enterprise is called Waterside Pub partnership and the idea is to convert the old malt stores into a canal side bar/ restaurant, possibly in 2007. The bonded warehouses, facing the canals have now been rebuilt into offices. The plans for the old stillhouse, facing the road, are still unclear but three stills remain inside. An additional number of buildings on the premises are sold to Westpoint Homes who are well underway with the development of 72 flats.

Apart from a number of official bottlings in the *Rare Malts* series (the last being a *1981, 22 years* released in 2004) and *Flora & Fauna 12 years*, several independent bottlers have shown their interest. Among the latter are Douglas Laing 15 years old (1990), Adelphi 14 years old (1991), Signatory from 1991 and a white wine finish 1989 from Murray McDavid.

Flora & Fauna 12 years old

Royal Brackla

Owner:
John Dewar & Sons (Bacardi)

Region:
Highlands

Founded:
1812

Status:
Active

Tel:
01667 402002

Visitor centre:
No

website:
-

Capacity:
2 500 000 litres
2 700 000 litres

% sold as malt whisky:
less than 1%

Included in blended (past and/or present):
Johnnie Walker, Dewar´s

History:

1812 – The distillery is founded by Captain William Fraser.

1835 – Brackla becomes the first of three distilleries (Royal Lochnagar and Glenury Royal are the other two) allowed to use 'Royal' in the name. This is thanks to William IV who takes a delight in this particular whisky.

1852 – Robert Fraser & Co. takes over the distillery.

1898 – The distillery is rebuilt and Royal Brackla Distillery Company Limited is founded.

1919 – John Mitchell and James Leict from Aberdeen purchase Royal Brackla.

1926 – John Bisset & Company Ltd takes over.

1943 – Scottish Malt Distillers (SMD) buys John Bisset & Company Ltd and thereby acquires Royal Brackla.

1966 – The maltings closes.

1970 – Two stills are increased to four.

1985 – The distillery is mothballed.

1991 – Production resumes.

1993 – A 10 year old Royal Brackla is launched in United Distillers´ Flora & Fauna series.

1997 – UDV spends more than £2 million on improvements and refurbishing.

1998 – Bacardi–Martini buys Dewar´s from Diageo. United Distillers releases a 20 year old Brackla in their Rare Malts series.

2004 – A new 10 year old is launched.

Diageo made a thorough renovation of Royal Brackla in the latter half of the nineties. The result was a light and elegant stillhouse with a view towards Cawdor Castle, renowned from William Shakespeare's Macbeth. Although Cawdor Castle was built in the end of the 14th century and Macbeth was born around 1005, it apparently did not deter Shakespeare from linking the castle to Macbeth for ever.
When the giant Diageo owned Brackla virtually all of its production went into blending, with the malt whisky itself not receiving much attention except for a 10 year old in the Flora & Fauna series and a Rare Malt. Hopes were therefore high when Bacardi took over Royal Brackla and some other distilleries in 1998. Not much has happened though. Focus has been on Dewars blended whisky and the visitor centre of Aberfeldy.
Bacardi is the largest family-owned spirit company and was founded already in 1862 in Cuba by Don Facundo Bacardi. It has been close to being listed on the stock market a couple of times (most recently in 2003), but the majority of share-owners (i. e. the 450 family members) have vetoed this. Not even a suggestion of letting the family's shares be worth ten times more in votes made an impact on the conservative family members. A large part of Bacardi's assets on Cuba were confiscated by Fidel Castro in 1960 and the family therefore works from a US office in Miami, Florida.
Today's core range consists of a *10 year old* and a limited edition of a *25 year old*. All of production is matured elsewhere as the warehouses at Brackla are on a long-term lease to Diageo.
Several independent bottlers have shown interest in Royal Brackla. Recent samples include an 11 year old distilled in 1993 and released in 2004 by Signatory. Two old Royal Bracklas were also released in 2004 from Gordon & McPhail, 1964 (40 years) and Scott's Selection 1976 (28 years).

10 years old

Royal Lochnagar

Owner:
Diageo

Region/district:
Eastern Highlands

Founded:
1845

Status:
Active

Tel:
01339 742700

Visitor centre:
Yes (4/7)

website:
www.malts.com

Capacity:
400 000 litres

% sold as malt whisky:
-

Included in blended (past and/or present):
Vat 69, Johnnie Walker (Black and Blue Label)

History:

1823 – James Robertson from Crathie founds a distillery in Glen Feardan on the north bank of River Dee.

1826 – The distillery is burnt down by competitors but Robertson decides to establish a new distillery near the mountain Lochnagar which lends it its name.

1841 – This distillery is also burnt down, although some sources say Robertson built a third distillery which remained until 1860.

1845 – A new distillery is built by John Begg, this time on the south bank of River Dee, It is named New Lochnagar. This is today considered as the official opening year of Royal Lochnagar.

1848 – Lochnagar obtains a Royal Warrant and the epithet Royal is added to the name.

1882 – John Begg passes away and his son Henry Farquharson Begg inherits the distillery.

1896 – Henry Farquharson Begg dies.

1902 – The distillery is converted into the company John Begg Ltd.

1906 – The children of Henry Begg rebuild the distillery.

1916 – When Henry Begg's only son Albert dies, the distillery is sold to John Dewar & Sons.

1925 – John Dewar & Sons becomes part of Distillers Company Limited (DCL).

1930 – Administration of the distillery is transferred to Scottish Malt Distillers (SMD).

1963 – A major reconstruction takes place.

1967 – The distillery undergoes further reconstruction.

1990 – A visitor centre is built.

2004 – A 30 year old cask strength from 1974 is launched in the Rare Malts series (6000 bottles).

Royal Lochnagar is one of three distilleries allowed to use the word Royal in its name. Royal Brackla and Glenury Royal are the other two. At Lochnagar this is thanks to Queen Victoria. In 1848 Queen Victoria and Prince Albert took over the lease of the castle Balmoral which is situated in the area. They eventually bought it in 1852. The distillery owner at that time, John Begg, was daring enough to send an invitation to his new royal neighbours to visit the distillery and they unexpectedly turned up on 12th September 1848. The Queen apparently took a liking to the whisky as Lochnagar received a Royal Warrant already the same year.

The distillery is situated on the outskirts of the Grampians without other distilleries in the vicinity. Its proximity to Balmoral is probably one explanation as to why 12 000 visitors find their way there each year.

Royal Lochnagar is considered to produce a light whisky despite the production process. The fermentation takes an unusually long time of 75-120 hours, but the two stills are very small and the cooling takes place in worm tubs, two factors which should produce a more heavy spirit.

The official version is *12 years old* and annual sales total 60 000 bottles. A more unusual expression is *Selected Reserve* of which 3 000 bottles a year is produced. It is a vatting of four selected casks (half sherry and half bourbon), usually around 20 years of age. There have also been three releases (most recently in 2004) in the *Rare Malts* series.

The distillery is Diageo's smallest and not much is left for independent bottlers with such a small production. Douglas Laing seems to have good connections though and has released a number of bottlings in recent years. The two latest are a 34 year old from 1971 and a 12 year old from 1993. There is also a McGibbon's Provenance (12 years old) from 1993.

Rare Malts 1974 30 years old

St Magdalene

Owner: Diageo

Region: Lowlands

Founded: 1795

Status: Dismantled

Tel: -

Visitor centre: -

website: www.malts.com

Capacity: -

% sold as malt whisky: -

Included in blended (past and/or present): -

History:

1795 – Sebastian Henderson founds the distillery.

1797 – Adam Dawson, proprietor of the distillery Bonnytoun in Linlithgow, buys the distillery.

1894 – A. & J. Dawson is formed and the distillery is expanded.

1912 – A. & J. Dawson goes into liquidation and Distillers Company Limited (DCL) purchases St. Magdalene.

1914 – St. Magdalene is one of the five founders of Scottish Malt Distillers (SMD). The others are Clydesdale, Glenkinchie, Rosebank and Grange,

1927 – Extensive repair work takes place.

1968 – Floor maltings is closed.

1983 – The distillery closes.

1995 – St. Magdalene 1970 (23 years) is released as a Rare Malt.

1998 – St. Magdalene 1979 (19 years) is released as a Rare Malt.

The two communities Linlithgow and Falkirk are situated a few miles west of Edinburgh and have roughly 10 000 inhabitants each. These two small towns housed several distilleries from the 18th century onwards. Seven were established in Linlithgow, including St. Magdalene. It was closed, in common with many others, by Distillers Company Limited's (DCL) purging in 1983. Only ten years later Falkirk was deprived of its last distillery when Rosebank closed. After the closure of St Magdalene, the buildings were untouched for nearly ten years until the mid 1990s when some of them were converted into luxury flats. Further reconstruction totalling £3 million, led to another 30 flats being built in 2002.

St. Magdalene was perfectly situated as far as production and transport was concerned. It lay next to the main road between Stirling and Edinburgh, had its own railway sidings and was close to the Union Canal from which it could take water for cooling and the water wheel. The canal was built in 1822 to connect Edinburgh and Glasgow. A full 30 years previously the Forth & Clyde canal which ran coast to coast between Grangemouth by the Firth of Fort and Bowling at the Firth of Clyde had been completed. The Union Canal connected at Falkirk and was of great importance, e. g. in facilitating coal transports to Edinburgh. The canals were closed in 1963 but were reopened in 2001-2002.

St. Magdalene was never a prominent malt with blenders, but it aged very well on its own. A *19 year Rare Malt* from 1979 has been praised by many. The owners, Diageo, have released four bottlings the last couple of years, three as *Rare Malts* and a *30 year old Linlithgow* from 1973.

The whisky can be difficult to obtain but a 30 year old from Gordon & McPhail released in 2005 and a Signatory from 1975 released in 2004 can be mentioned as samples of more recent independent bottlings.

Gordon & MacPhail Rare Old 1982 (bottled 2001)

Scapa

Owner:
Chivas Brothers (Pernod Ricard)

Region/district:
Highlands (Orkney)

Founded:
1885

Status:
Active

Tel:
01856 876585

Visitor centre:
No

website:
www.scapamalt.com

Capacity:
1 000 000 litres
200 000 litres

% sold as malt whisky:
100%

Included in blended (past and/or present):
Ballantine´s, Teacher´s

History:

1885 – Macfarlane & Townsend founds the distillery with John Townsend at the helm.

1919 – Scapa Distillery Company Ltd takes over.

1934 – Scapa Distillery Company goes into voluntary liquidation and production ceases.

1936 – Production resumes.

1936 – Bloch Brothers Ltd (John and Sir Maurice) takes over and uses Scapa in their blend Ambassador. The brothers are already owners of Glen Scotia and Glengyle.

1954 – Hiram Walker & Sons takes over.

1959 – A Lomond still is installed.

1962 – Maltings closes.

1978 – The distillery is modernized.

1994 – The distillery is mothballed.

1997 – Production takes place a few months each year using staff from Highland Park.

2004 – Extensive refurbishing and new construction takes place in March, the cost being £2.1 million. Scapa 14 years is launched. The first new spirit flows in November.

2005 – Production ceases in April and phase two of the refurbishment programme starts. Chivas Brothers (Pernod Ricard) become new owners through the acquisition of Allied Domecq. Scapa 1980 (25 years) is released in September.

2006 – Scapa 1992 (14 years) is launched.

Bryan Ross and his crew have been quite busy for the last two years since Allied Domecq decided to resurrect Scapa in March 2004. The distillery was rather run-down and production was irregular during the last six years, taking place only when workers from neighbouring Highland Park came in and fuelled the stills for a few weeks each year.
The extensive renovation included a new mash tun and a new stillhouse. The old stills were used although the main body of the spirit still was sent to Speyside for refurbishment.
There are six warehouses, three dunnage and three racked, and the distillery is fully operational since January 2006. What is really needed now with everything else being in place is a visitor centre, but perhaps this is in the pipeline.
The majority of people arriving in Orkney would probably visit both Scapa and the nearby Highland Park.
Scapa's wash still is of Lomond type and the distillery is unique for using this kind of still. It was developed by Alistair Cunningham at Hiram Walker in 1955 with the intention of creating a still with greater flexibility for different kinds of whisky. The Lomond still was equipped with internal rectifying plates which could be set vertically and horizontally to affect the reflux in order to achieve this flexibility. The plates have been removed from Scapa's still, but on the other hand Scapa does not aim at producing different types of whisky. One other distillery, Bruichladdich, owns a Lomond still (purchased in 2002 from Dumbarton/Inverleven) but it is not used in production.
The Scapa range is very limited with a *14 year old* and a limited edition of a *25 year old* from 1980. A *vintage version* of the *14 year old* from 1992 was launched in 2006. Recent independent bottlings, all from 2005, include Duncan Taylor 1977, Gordon & MacPhail 1993 and two expressions from Douglas Laing (11 and 14 years old).

14 years old

Speyburn

Owner:
Inver House Distillers (Pacific Spirits)

Region/district:
Speyside

Founded:
1897

Status:
Active

Tel:
01340 831213

Visitor centre:
No

website:
www.inverhouse.com

Capacity:
2 700 000 litres

% sold as malt whisky:
17%

Included in blended (past and/or present):
Glen Talloch

History:

1897 – Brothers John and Edward Hopkin and their cousin Edward Broughton found the distillery through John Hopkin & Co. They already own Tobermory. The architect is Charles Doig. Building the distillery costs £17 000 and the distillery is transferred to Speyburn-Glenlivet Distillery Company.

1916 – Distillers Company Limited (DCL) acquires John Hopkin & Co. and the distillery.

1930 – Production stops.

1934 – Productions restarts.

1962 – Speyburn is transferred to Scottish Malt Distillers (SMD).

1968 – Drum maltings closes.

1991 – Inver House Distillers buys Speyburn.

1992 – A 10 year old is launched as a replacement for the 12 year old in the Flora & Fauna series.

2001 – Pacific Spirits (Great Oriole Group) buys Inver House for $85 million.

2005 – A 25 year old Solera is released.

As one has passed Glen Grant and is driving away from Rothes towards Elgin, Speyburn lies on the right side down at Glen of Rothes. Many a tourist has stopped by the roadside to take pictures and Speyburn is probably one of the most photographed distilleries in Scotland. A line of recently grown up birch trees now obscures the view.
The only method of malting the barley was floor malting until the end of the 19th century. More or less at the same time two new methods were invented, Saladin box and drum malting. Speyburn was the first distillery to install a drum maltings and Glen Grant and St. Magdalene soon followed suit. The maltings have now been closed for years but Speyburn is still one of few distilleries using worm tubs for cooling the distillation.
The core range consists of a *10 year old* launched by Inver House to replace the previous owners' 12 year old. They have also launched a number of limited editions throughout the years. A *21 year old* of several different vintages was replaced by a *25 year old*, the most recent being from 1977. Inver House introduced a series called Highland Selection in 2001 whereby all of their five distilleries were represented. A *16 year old* from 1986 and a *27 year old* from 1973 can be found among Speyburn single malts in this series which now has been abandoned by Inver House.
The latest, official, bottling is a *25 year old Solera* which was released in late 2005. It is a marriage between American casks, used for fino sherry, and bourbon casks selected by Bobby Anderson, the distillery manager.
Independent bottlings, e. g. from Gordon & MacPhail occur but are not common. Even if Speyburn is small on the domestic market where only 10 000 bottles are sold annually, sales are bigger across the Atlantic in the USA to which almost 350 000 bottles are exported.

10 years old

Speyside

Owner: Speyside Distillers Co.

Region/district: Speyside

Founded: 1976

Status: Active

Tel: 01540 661060

Visitor centre: No

website: www.speysidedistillery.co.uk

Capacity: 600 000 litres
500 000 litres

% sold as malt whisky: 20%

Included in blended (past and/or present):
Speyside, Scottish Prince, Scotch Guard, Murdoch´s

History:

1962 – The whisky blender George Christie (founder of Speyside Distillery Group in the fifties) commissions the drystone dyker Alex Fairlie to build a distillery in Drumguish.

1986 – Scowis assumes ownership.

1987 – The distillery is completed.

1990 – The distillery is on stream in December.

1993 – The first single malt, Drumguish, is launched.

1999 – Speyside 8 years is launched.

2000 – Speyside Distilleries is sold to a group of private investors.

2001 – Speyside 10 years is launched.

The whisky blender and perhaps the last of the true whisky barons, George Christie, was in for long-term planning when he founded his Speyside Distillery. The land was purchased in 1956 at Drumguish near Kingussie. The building of the distillery began six years later, in 1962, and took 25 years to complete, it being yet another three years before the first whisky was distilled. In total it took 34 years from idea to whisky. Speyside was not the former submarine captain's first distillery as he started a grain distillery near Alloa in 1957. He sold the distillery in the 1980s to DCL who decommissioned it.
Owners have come and gone over the years. In 1986 financial troubles forced the selling to Scowis, a Swiss investment group. They owned it until 2000 when Ricky Christie, who worked for Scowis then, bought it with, amongst others, Sir James Ackroyd and Ian Jerman. Ricky Christie was Sales Director and as such responsible for exports to over 60 countries until he left the company in 2005.
Speyside distillery is equipped with four stainless steel washbacks and one pair of stills. They store some 40 000 casks in their warehouse at Rutherglen, Glasgow.
Aside from the distillery at Drumguish, there is a diverse range of activities at the base in Rutherglen, Glasgow. Cask warehousing, a bottling plant and a blending operation are all found there.
Apart from what is produced at the distillery, the company also owns some 20 brands of blended whiskies and two ranges of cask strength single malts; Scott's Selection and Private Cellar.
The distillery's own range of single malts consists of *Drumguish (no age)* and *Speyside 8, 10 and 12 years.*
A blended (vatted) malt named Glentromie is also produced.
A special, very dark version of Speyside is the Cu Dhub produced for the Danish whisky importer Mac Y.

12 years old

Springbank distillery. Photo: © Springbank Distillers

Springbank

Owner: Springbank Distillers (J & A Mitchell)
Region/district: Campbeltown
Founded: 1828
Status: Active
Tel: 01586 552085
Visitor centre: Yes (6/7)
website: www.springbankdistillers.com
Capacity: 750 000 litres *140 000 litres*
% sold as malt whisky: 100%
Included in blended (past and/or present): Mitchell´s, Campbeltown Loch

History:

1828 – The Reid family, in-laws of the Mitchells (see below), founds the distillery as the fourteenth in Campbelltown.

1837 – The Reid family encounters financial difficulties and John and William Mitchell buy the distillery.

1897 – J. & A. Mitchell Company Ltd is founded. William Mitchell founded Glengyle in 1872 and when he and John parted ways, John Mitchell continued operating Springbank first alone and then with his son Archibald.

1926 – The depression forces the distillery to close.

1933 – The distillery is back in production.

1960 – Own maltings ceases.

1969 – J. & A. Mitchell buys the independent bottler Cadenhead.

1973 – The first distillation of Longrow.

1979 – The distillery closes.

1985 – A 10 year old Longrow is launched as an experiment.

1987 – Limited production restarts.

1989 – Production restarts.

1990 – Longrow becomes a standard label.

1992 – Springbank takes up its own maltings again.

1997 – First distillation of Hazelburn, a triple distilled and unpeated malt.

Springbank is Scotland's oldest, continuously family-owned distillery and one may think that it quietly rests on antiquated traditions and values. Nothing could be more wrong. It is the only distillery in Scotland producing three distinctively (as regards both taste and production methods) different whiskies, they have recently opened up a new distillery, are unafraid of testing new wood finishes and have experimented with both organic whiskies and new strains of barley.

The production process however, adheres strictly to traditions. Own barley is malted using peat from a bog at the nearby Machrihanish and from Tomintoul in the Highlands. All whisky is matured on-site and they have their own bottling line. There are five washbacks made of Scandinavian Larch, one wash still and two spirit stills. The wash still is unique in Scotland as it is fired by both an open fire and internal steam coils. The spirit stills are heated using steam coils. The water used for bottling comes from the same source as for production, Crosshill Loch. The water is passed through a reversed osmosis filter prior to being used to reduce the whisky. Like Bruichladdich, Springbank has experimented with traditional Bere barley. The barley was grown locally and distilled in February 2006 giving 23 casks of spirit. The drawback of Bere is that spirit yields are low compared with e. g. Optic and Chariot.

The legendary manager Frank McHardy has now taken the role of director of production for Springbank and Glengyle and left the daily work as distillery manager to Stuart Robertson from Cragganmore.

Springbank distillery produces three distinctive single malts with different phenol contents in the malted barley: Springbank which is distilled two and a half times (12-15ppm), Longrow, distilled two times (50-55 ppm) and finally Hazelburn, distilled three times (unpeated).

The core range of Springbank distillery is a *Springbank 10* and *15 years, Springbank 10 years 100 proof, Longrow 10 years, Longrow 100 proof* and *Hazelburn 8 years old*. There are also a number of limited releases, among them their *Wood Expression series*. Aside from Longrow 100 proof, new releases 2006 include *Springbank 25 years old* from 1971, *9 years old Marsala finish, 11 years old Madeira finish* and a new edition of *Hazelburn 8 years old*.

Two different blended whiskies are also produced - Mitchell's 12 years and Campbeltown Loch 5 years. Very small amounts of Springbank are used for the blends but there are plans to use Kilkerran (from Glengyle) in Mitchell's from 2007 and remove the age statement.

History (continued):

1998 – Springbank 12 years is launched.

1999 – Dha Mhile (7 years) is the world's first organic single malt and is released as a limited supply of 1000 bottles in a joint venture between Springbank and John Savage-Onstwedder.

2000 – A 10 year old is launched.

2001 – Springbank 1965 'Local barley' (36 years), 741 bottles, is launched. Barley, coal, peat and water are all obtained locally.

2002 – Number one in the series Wood Expressions is a 12 year old with five years on Demerara rum casks. Next is a Longrow sherry cask (13 years). A relaunch of the 15 year old replaces the 21 year old.

2003 – 50 sets of six 20 cl bottles aged 25, 30, 35, 40, 45 and 50 years are launched to commemorate the 175th anniversary of the distillery.

2004 – J. & A. Mitchell's main owner, Hedley Wright, opens Glengyle Distillery which has been closed since March 1925. Springbank 10 years 100 proof is launched as well as Springbank Wood Expression bourbon, Longrow 14 years old, Springbank 32 years old and Springbank 14 years Port Wood.

2005 – 2 400 bottles of Springbank 21 years old take the market by surprise when they are released in March. The next batch will not appear until in 2011. The first version of Hazelburn (8 years old) is released 5th September. Longrow Tokaji Wood Expression is launched.

2006 – Longrow 10 years 100 proof, Springbank 25 years (1 200 bottles), Springbank 9 years Marsala finish, Springbank 11 years Madeira finish and a new Hazelburn 8 year old are released.

Springbank 25 years old

Springbank 10 years old 100 proof

Longrow 10 years old 100 proof

Strathisla

Owner:
Chivas Brothers (Pernod Ricard)

Region/district:
Speyside

Founded:
1786

Status:
Active

Tel:
01542 783044 (vc)

Visitor centre:
Yes (7/7)

website:
www.chivas.com

Capacity:
2 400 000 litres

% sold as malt whisky:
5%

Included in blended (past and/or present):
Chivas Regal, Royal Salute, 100 Pipers

History:

1786 – Alexander Milne and George Taylor found the distillery under the name Milltown, but soon change it to Milton. The whisky, however, is called Strathisla.

1825 – MacDonald Ingram & Co. purchases the distillery.

1830 – William Longmore acquires the distillery.

1870 – The name of the distillery changes to Strathisla.

1876 – The distillery is badly damaged by fire.

1879 – Another accident strikes; a dust explosion in the malt mill.

1880 – William Longmore retires and hands operations to his son-in-law John Geddes-Brown. William Longmore & Co. is formed.

1882 – William Longmore dies.

1890 – The distillery changes name to Milton.

1940 – Jay (George) Pomeroy acquires majority shares in William Longmore & Co. Pomeroy is jailed as a result of dubious business transactions and the distillery goes bankrupt in 1949.

1950 – Chivas Brothers buys the run-down distillery at a compulsory auction for £71 000 and starts restoration.

1951 – The name reverts to Strathisla.

1965 – The number of stills is increased from two to four.

1970 – A heavily peated whisky, Craigduff, is produced but production stops later.

1994 – Seagrams introduces The Heritage Selection with Strathisla, Longmorn, Glen Keith and Benriach.

1995 – The visitor centre is renovated.

2001 – The Chivas Group is acquired by Pernod Ricard.

Established in 1786, Strathisla is not just the oldest working distillery in the Highlands but also one of the most beautiful of Scottish distilleries with its stately pagoda roofs. When visiting Strathisla one strongly experiences the notion of how a classic distillery should be, a feeling which is further reinforced when sinking into one of the armchairs of the library with a dram after the tour.
Strathisla is a lot about Chivas Regal. It has been the heart of this blend for more than half a century and the owners are reluctant to let the distillery or new bottlings steal attention. Chivas Regal is a story in itself. Introduced as a brand already in 1801 it is today the world's leading premium blend. It increased by 10% the last year and is now selling 40 million bottles a year. The main part (95%) is a 12 year old while the 18 year old and 21 year old (Royal Salute) are sold in much smaller quantities. Chivas Regal contains 40% malt whisky of which Strathisla makes up c 4%. The distillery is equipped with 10 (formerly 11, but one has been remade into a pot ale tank) washbacks of Oregon Pine, two wash stills (13 600 litres) and two spirit stills (10 900 litres). A small amount is stored on-site in a dunnage and a racked warehouse. The rest is sent to the huge Chivas warehouses just outside Keith.
Pernod Ricard have only released two official bottlings - the *12 year old* and a *15 year old cask strength*. Recent independent bottlings include a 1967 from Murray McDavid with a red wine finish (Banyul/Grenache) and a 38 year old sherry cask from 1967 released by Duncan Taylor. Strathisla has been a member of the malt whisky trail for a number of years and the visitor centre attracts around 12 000 people a year.

12 years old

Strathmill

Owner:
Diageo

Region/district:
Speyside

Founded:
1891

Status:
Active

Tel:
01542 883000

Visitor centre:
No

website:
www.malts.com

Capacity:
1 700 000 litres

% sold as malt whisky:
n/a

Included in blended (past and/or present):
J&B Rare, Dunhill, Old Master, Gentleman´s Speyside

History:

1891 – The distillery is founded in an old mill from 1823 and is named Glenisla-Glenlivet Distillery.

1892 – The inauguration takes place in June.

1895 – The gin company W. & A. Gilbey buys the distillery for £9 500 and names it Strathmill.

1962 – W. & A. Gilbey merges with United Wine Traders (including Justerini & Brooks) and forms International Distillers & Vintners (IDV).

1968 – The number of stills is increased from two to four and purifiers are added.

1972 – IDV is bought by Watney Mann which later the same year is acquired by Grand Metropolitan.

1993 – Strathmill becomes available as a single malt for the first time since 1909 as a result of a bottling (1980) from Oddbins.

1997 – Guinness and Grand Metropolitan merge and form Diageo.

2001 – The first official bottling is a 12 year old in the Flora & Fauna series.

Strathmill distillery is beautifully situated in a valley next to a river in Keith, one of the major whisky towns of Speyside. Two stately pagoda roofs together with a couple of beautiful, traditional dunnage warehouses (with an additional two racked) gives the right distillery atmosphere. The distillery was closed for maintenance since June 2005 but reopened again in June 2006.
The intention was not to make a name as a single malt producer, despite Strathmill being sold as single malt since 1909. Instead it has always been (and still is) an important component in J & B blended whisky. J & B is the second best selling blended today after Johnnie Walker and sales amount to 70 million bottles a year of four different versions: Rare (standard variety and tailored for the American market during prohibition), Reserve (15 years old), Jet (12 years old) and -6°C, a quite bizarre, extremely pale version introduced in spring 2005. The billionth bottle of J & B was received by Margaret Thatcher at a ceremony already in 1985. J & B Rare is the most sold whisky in Spain and holds 25% of the market there.
Strathmill is one of a select few distilleries using a facility called purifier on their two pairs of stills. It is mounted between the lyne arm and the condensers and its purpose is to produce a lighter whisky with fruity notes.
The only official bottling, from Diageo, turned up in 2001, and was a *12 year old* in the *Flora & Fauna* series. Except for the two butts (*25 years old*) that were bottled in 1992 to celebrate the centenary of the distillery there are no other official bottlings. As that release was only sold to the distillery's staff and some guests, encountering it at an auction appears to be the only way to get hold of it.
Recent independent bottlings include Gordon & MacPhail 1991, Signatory 1986 (16 years), Duncan Taylor (Peerless) 1975 (28 years) and a very old from Douglas Laing; 1963 (40 years).

Flora & Fauna 12 years

Talisker

Owner: Diageo

Region/district: Highlands (Skye)

Founded: 1830

Status: Active

Tel: 01478 614308 (vc)

Visitor centre: Yes (6/7)

website: www.malts.com

Capacity: 1 900 000 litres

% sold as malt whisky: n/a

Included in blended (past and/or present):
Johnnie Walker, White Horse

History:

1830 – Hugh and Kenneth MacAskill, sons of the local doctor, found the distillery.

1848 – The brothers transfer the lease to North of Scotland Bank and Jack Westland from the bank runs the operations.

1854 – Kenneth MacAskill dies.

1857 – North of Scotland Bank sells the distillery to Donald MacLennan for £500.

1863 – MacLennan experiences difficulties in making operations viable and puts the distillery up for sale.

1865 – MacLennan, still working at the distillery, nominates John Anderson as agent in Glasgow.

1867 – Anderson & Co. from Glasgow takes over.

1879 – John Anderson is imprisoned after having sold non-existing casks of whisky.

1880 – New owners are now Alexander Grigor Allan and Roderick Kemp.

1892 – Kemp sells his share and buys Macallan Distillery instead.

1894 – The Talisker Distillery Ltd is founded.

Talisker is the sole distillery on Skye and will probably remain so for some time. Sir Iain Noble, with a background in banking, oil and insurance has, however, plans for opening a distillery in Torabhaig, but the plans have not been approved by the local authorities yet. Sir Iain hopes that the distillery, manned by Gaelic-speaking staff, will be realized during 2008.
Talisker followers are undoubtedly among the most dedicated and the whisky is one of the most highly-awarded. The distillery practiced triple distillation until 1928 and this is the reason for the slightly different arrangement of the stills with two wash stills feeding three spirit stills. The wash stills have a remarkable appearance dating back to the construction of the original stills in 1830, with their u-shaped lyne arms. Thin copper pipes under the arms lead back to the still. Talisker is also equipped with five worm tubs instead of the more modern shell/tube variety used for condensing. The whisky is quite heavily peated with a strong island character. The malt is peated to c. 25 ppm.
Talisker's core range consists of a *10 year old*, an *18 year old* and a *Distiller's Edition* with an amoroso sherry finish. Additionally, a number of *25 year old* cask strengths have been launched, the most recent in 2006. Two *20 year olds* from 1981 and 1982, one *28 year old* from 1973 and the recent *Talisker 175th Anniversary* bottling are examples of limited versions. The latest contribution to the range was a *30 year old* released in 2006.
A more unusual variety to keep a watch for is The Isle of Eigg Heritage Trust which was launched in 2001. Isle of Eigg is south of the Isle of Skye and it was from here the brothers MacAskill returned in 1825 and subsequently founded Talisker five years later. In 1997 the inhabitants bought the Isle of Eigg to secure the future for the island and themselves. In commemoration of this and as support to the inhabitants, Talisker released 252 bottles, 102 were destined for each family on the island and the rest were sold with the profit going to The Trust.
Independent bottlings of Talisker are rare and when they do occur the names do not reveal their origin. The two most recent are Tactical from Douglas Laing, 23 years old from 1982 (a previous variety is from 1977, 25 years old) and Secret Stills 01.01 from Gordon & MacPhail; a Talisker distilled in 1955 and bottled in 2005.

History (continued):
1895 – Allan dies and Thomas Mackenzie, who has been his partner, takes over.

1898 – Talisker Distillery merges with Dailuaine-Glenlivet Distillers and Imperial Distillers to form Dailuaine-Talisker Distillers Company.

1916 – Thomas Mackenzie dies and the distillery is taken over by a consortium consisting of, among others, John Walker, John Dewar, W. P. Lowrie and Distillers Company Limited (DCL).

1928 – The distillery abandons triple distillation.

1930 – Administration of the distillery is transferred to Scottish Malt Distillers (SMD).

1960 – On 22nd November the distillery catches fire and substantial damage occurs.

1962 – The distillery reopens after the fire with five new identical copies of the destroyed stills.

1972 – Malting ceases and malt is now purchased from Glen Ord Central Maltings.

1988 – United Distillers introduce Classic Malts, Talisker 10 years included. A visitor centre is opened.

1998 – A new stainless steel/copper mash tun and five new worm tubs are installed. Talisker is launched as a Distillers Edition with an amoroso sherry finish.

2004 – Two new bottlings appear, an 18 year old and a 25 year old.

2005 – To celebrate the 175th birthday of the distillery, Talisker 175th Anniversary is released (60 000 bottles). The third edition of the 25 year old cask strength is released (15 600 bottles).

2006 – A 30 year old and the fourth edition of the 25 year old are released.

1982 20 years old

25 years old

30 years old

10 years old

18 years old

Distiller´s Edition 1992

Tamdhu

Owner:
Edrington Group

Region/district:
Speyside

Founded:
1896

Status:
Active

Tel:
01340 872200

Visitor centre:
No

website:
-

Capacity:
4 000 000 litres

% sold as malt whisky:
n/a

Included in blended (past and/or present):
Famous Grouse, Cutty Sark, Lang´s, J & B, Dunhill, The Rich and Spicy One

History:

1896 – The distillery is founded by Tamdhu Distillery Company, a consortium of whisky blenders with William Grant as the main promoter. Charles Doig is the architect.

1897 – The first casks are filled in July.

1898 – Highland Distillers Company, which has several of the 1896 consortium members in managerial positions, buys Tamdhu Distillery Company.

1911 – The distillery closes.

1913 –The distillery reopens.

1928 – The distillery is mothballed.

1948 – The distillery is in full production again in July.

1950 – The floor maltings is replaced by Saladin boxes when the distillery is rebuilt.

1972 – The number of stills is increased from two to four.

1975 – Two stills augment the previous four.

1976 – Tamdhu 8 years is launched as single malt.

Tamdhu is in the heart of Speyside with Cardhu and Knockando as nearest neighbours. The impression is lasting even if it lacks the charm of many other distilleries. Tamdhu was one of the first (North British was first in 1948) to install a Saladin box for malting, an invention of Charles Saladin in the 1890s. Today it is the only distillery still using Saladin boxes, ten of them to be precise. This gives a capacity enough to supply the other distilleries in the Edrington group (especially Glenrothes) with malt.
Tamdhu belongs to the distilleries who, in the 70s and 80s, tried to use the surplus warm water from distillation to some kind of profitable bi-product. Tamdhu tried breeding salmon, Tomatin started an eel-farm and Glen Garioch grew tomatoes. All these experiments have long since been terminated.
Tamdhu sells well as a malt in the Mediterranean countries and the United States but the lion's share still goes to blended whiskies. Since 1997 Dunhill is one of them and a sign at Tamdhu distillery states 'Home of Dunhill'.
There is only one *official bottling* on the market today, *without age*. Two independent bottlings from Douglas Laing appeared quite recently, a 10 year old from 1994 and a 29 year old. Ian Macleod have also launched a couple of Tamdhus in their Dun Bheagan range such as 13 years sherry finish and 14 years Medoc finish. Gordon & MacPhail, Duncan Taylor and Adelphi have also bottled Tamdhu which, despite its anonymity is appreciated among connoisseurs.

Gordon & MacPhail Tamdhu 8 years old

Tamnavulin

Owner:
Whyte & Mackay

Region/district:
Speyside

Founded:
1966

Status:
Mothballed

Tel:
-

Visitor centre:
-

website:
-

Capacity:
-

% sold as malt whisky:
-

Included in blended (past and/or present):
Mackinlay

History:

1966 – Tamnavulin-Glenlivet Distillery Company, a subsidiary of Invergordon Distillers Ltd, founds Tamnavulin.

1993 – Whyte & Mackay buys Invergordon Distillers.

1995 – The distillery closes in May.

1996 – Whyte & Mackay changes name to JBB (Greater Europe).

2001 – Company management buy out operations for £208 million and rename the company Kyndal.

2003 – Kyndal changes name to Whyte & Mackay.

Tamnavulin is situated in a very scenic part of the Highlands with Glenlivet, Tomintoul and mothballed Braeval as closest neighbours.
Many distilleries wishing to bask in the glory of The Glenlivet added it to their names. Tamnavulin did this in the beginning too, though perhaps with a greater right as the distillery is actually considered to be the only distillery situated by the River Livet. This is, however not completely true as the distillery is actually built on the banks of Allt a Choire, a tributary of the Livet.
The distillery has only had around 30 years of regular production and has been mothballed by the owner Whyte & Mackay for the last ten years. Neither do there appear to be any imminent plans to reopen. Whyte & Mackay has undergone restructuring in recent years and has three other large distilleries to concentrate on: Dalmore, Jura and Fettercairn.
Tamnavulin had the impressive annual production capacity of 4 million litres during its heyday. There are eight washbacks made of stainless steel and three pairs of stills. The visitor centre closed around the millennium, i. e. a few years after production ceased.
The standard release of Tamnavulin is a *12 year old* but there are also a number of aged *Stillman's Dram* on the market, the most recent a *30 year old*.
Gordon & MacPhail and Douglas Laing belong to independent bottlers which have released versions of Tamnavulin. A truly old Tamnavulin appeared in 2005 from Duncan Taylor, 1967 (37 years) and Cadenhead released a 14 year old in 2006.

12 years old

Teaninich

Owner:
Diageo

Region/district:
Northern Highlands

Founded:
1817

Status:
Active

Tel:
01349 885001

Visitor centre:
No

website:
www.malts.com

Capacity:
2 700 000 litres

% sold as malt whisky:
n/a

Included in blended (past and/or present):
Mackinlay, Johnnie Walker

History:

1817 – Captain Hugh Monro, owner of the estate Teaninich, founds the distillery.

1845 – Captain Munro's son (or younger brother) Lieutenant General John Munro takes over after the death of his father.

1850 – John Munro, who spends most of his time in India, leases Teaninich to the infamous Robert Pattison from Leith.

1869 – John McGilchrist Ross takes over the licence.

1895 – Munro & Cameron takes over the licence.

1898 – Munro & Cameron buys the distillery.

1904 – Robert Innes Cameron becomes sole owner of Teaninich. He has had interests in Linkwood Distillery since 1902.

1932 – Robert Innes Cameron dies.

1933 – The estate of Robert Innes Cameron sells the distillery to Distillers Company Limited (DCL).

1970 – A new distillation unit with six stills is commissioned and becomes known as the A side.

1975 – A dark grains plant is built.

1984 – The B side of the distillery is mothballed.

1985 – The A side is also mothballed.

1991 –The A side is in production again

1992 – United Distillers launches a 10 year old Teaninich in the Flora & Fauna series.

1999 – The B side is decommissioned.

2000 – A mash filter is installed.

Alness village, a 30 minute drive north of Inverness, is best known in whisky contexts for Dalmore Distillery. Unbeknown to the general public though is that Teaninich is also situated here.
There is a picture of a dolphin on the official bottle of Teaninich and the choice of motif has its story. The Moray Firth is home to the northernmost resident population of Bottlenose dolphins in the world. They number up to 130 at peak times.
Two elements in the production process of Teaninich differ from that of other distilleries. Firstly, the malt is ground in an Asnong hammer mill from Asnong BVA in Belgium rather than in traditional roller mills such as Porteus and Boby. The process is done by revolving hammers pounding against a perforated grate. This process is more common in the USA where for example Buffalo Trace Distillery uses hammer mills. Once the grist has been mixed with water the mash passes through a filter press and the wort is collected. Water is added a second time in the filter and a second run of mash is obtained. The procedure is repeated three times until a washback is filled. Mash filters have been used in breweries for many years but it was first in 2000 that a whisky distillery used it. Some of the advantages are less mechanical wear and quicker turnover times.
Many will have come in contact with its malt as it is an important component of Johnnie Walker blended whiskies.
The first official bottling, a *10 year old*, appeared as late as 1992 in the *Flora & Fauna* series. In 1996, 1997 and 2000 respectively it appeared as a *Rare Malt*, 1996 and 1997 as a *23 year old* and 2000 as a *27 year old*. A *Manager's Dram 17 years old* was launched in September 2001.
There are independent bottlings from Gordon & MacPhail and Ian Macleod. The latter have also bottled a 16 year old Double Wood on port casks. The most recent bottling is a 1975 from Dewar Rattray which was released in May 2006.

Flora & Fauna 10 years old

Tobermory

Owner: Burn Stewart Distillers (C L Financial)

Region/district: Highland (Mull)

Founded: 1798

Status: Active

Tel: 01688 302647 (vc)

Visitor centre: Yes (4/7)

website: www.burnstewartdistillers.com

Capacity: 1 000 000 litres

% sold as malt whisky: 15%

Included in blended (past and/or present): Scottish Leader, Black Prince

History:

1798 – John Sinclair founds the distillery named Ledaig Distillery. (It was possibly founded already in 1795).

1837 – The distillery closes.

1878 – The distillery reopens.

1890 – John Hopkins & Company buys the distillery.

1916 – Distillers Company Limited (DCL) takes over John Hopkins & Company.

1930 – The distillery closes and is used as both a canteen and a power station

1972 – A shipping company in Liverpool and the sherrymaker Domecq buy the buildings and embark on refurbishment. When work is completed it is named Ledaig Distillery Ltd.

1975 – Ledaig Distillery Ltd files for bankruptcy and the distillery closes again.

1979 – The estate agent Kirkleavington Property Company of Cleckheaton buys the distillery, forms a new company, Tobermory Distillers Ltd and starts production.

1982 – No production. Some of the buildings are converted into flats and some are rented to a dairy company for cheese storage.

1989 – Production resumes.

1993 – Burn Stewart Distillers buys Tobermory for £600 000 and pays an additional £200 000 for the whisky supply.

2002 – Trinidad-based venture capitalists CL Financial buys Burn Stewart Distillers for £50 million.

2005 – A 32 year old from 1972 is launched.

10 years old

Mull is the third largest of the Hebrides and the easiest to reach from the mainland. It only takes 45 minutes by ship from Oban. If one wishes to visit the single distillery on the island it is necessary to take the bus or car to Tobermory town, which has lent its name to the distillery, at the northernmost part of the island.

Tobermory is one of the oldest distilleries in existence and the only legal distillery that has existed on the island. After 1930 production has been sporadic, but with more continuity since Burn Stewart Distillers acquired it in 1993. The distillery has two pairs of stills and the malt is bought from Port Ellen maltings. The former owners sold the warehouses which have now been converted into flats. Since then the whisky has been stored at Deanston on the mainland while some casks are also sent to Bunnahabhain on Islay for storage. It will be interesting to see whether these different storage places will affect the future character of the whisky.

A couple of years back there were three different varieties of Tobermory on the market at the same time; single malt, vatted malt and blended whisky. After Burn Stewarts' take-over the brand names have been made distinctive. Today Tobermory (30% of the production) is an unpeated single malt and sold as a *10 year old* with a *32 year old* as a limited version. The peated share (35ppm) of the distillation is sold as Ledaig (70% of the production), a name which earlier was reserved for the whisky distilled between 1972-74 and again for a short period in the late seventies. Ledaig from this era is much sought-after among connoisseurs. Ledaig has been launched in many different versions. Current ones are *Peated*, *Sherry Finish* and a *32 year old* finished in Oloroso butts, all released in 2004. Earlier releases have included a *7 year old*, a *15 year old*, a *20 year old* and several vintages. Three recent independent bottlings of Ledaig are Ian MacLeod 1973 (32 years old), Signatory 1974 (30 years old) and Cadenhead 1992 (14 years old).

No age

Sherry finish

Tomatin

Owner:
Tomatin Distillery Co (Marubeni Europe plc)

Region/district:
Highland

Founded:
1897

Status:
Active

Tel:
01808 511444 (vc)

Visitor centre:
Yes (3/7)

website:
www.tomatin.com

Capacity:
5 000 000 litres
2 000 000 litres

% sold as malt whisky:
30%

Included in blended (past and/or present):
Big-T, Antiquary, The Talisman

History:

1897 – The Inverness businessmen behind Tomatin Spey Distillery Company found Tomatin.

1906 – Production ceases.

1909 – Production resumes through Tomatin Distillers Co. Ltd.

1956 – Stills are increased from two to four.

1958 – Another two stills are added.

1961 – The six stills are increased to ten.

1964 – One more still is installed.

1974 – The stills now total 23 and the maltings closes.

1985 – The distillery company goes into liquidation.

1986 – Two long-time customers, Takara Shuzo Co. and Okara & Co., buy Tomatin through Tomatin Distillery Co. Tomatin thus becomes the first distillery to be acquired by Japanese interests.

1997 – Tomatin Distillery Co buys J. W. Hardie and the brand Antiquary.

1998 – Okara & Co, owners of 20% of Tomatin Distillery, is forced to sell its share to Takara Shuzo Co. which now is part of the Marubeni group.

2004 – Tomatin 12 years is launched.

2005 – A 25 year old and a 1973 Vintage are released.

2006 – An 18 year old and a 1962 Vintage are launched.

Photo: © 2005 www.thewhiskystore.de

It is difficult to miss Tomatin Distillery when driving on the A9 towards Inverness. The buildings lack the classic whisky distillery design and look more like those of a modern, large-scale process industry instead. The distillery was founded at the end of the 19th century but it was from 1956 and 20 years onwards that it expanded most rapidly. The number of stills increased at a pace similar to that of the former Soviet Union's five-year plans' and had reached 23 by 1974. By then it was Scotland's largest distillery with a production of 12 million litres of alcohol. Today the capacity is lower with 5 million litres as 11 of the original stills were dismantled in 2002.

The 15 warehouses of the traditional dunnage type and Tomatin's own cooperage staffed by a cooper and his apprentice are in contradiction to the distillery's modern appearance.

In 1986 Tomatin was the first Scottish Distillery to be fully owned by Japanese interests.

The larger part of production is for blending of its own brands The Antiquary, The Talisman, Big T and – for the Japanese market – Ancient Clan.

Tomatin's industrial appearance may give the impression that a visit is not worthwhile, but 30 000 visitors finding their way annually tell a different story. The visitor centre has recently been refurbished and was awarded four stars from Visit Scotland.

Today's official standard bottling is the *12 year old* which has replaced the 10 year old. Limited releases of a *25 year old* and a *1973 vintage* were made in 2005 and the year after an *18 year old* and a *1962 Vintage* were added to the range.

Recent independent bottlings include one from Duncan Taylor and one from Douglas Laing respectively, both distilled in 1965 and bottled in 2006.

12 years old

Tomintoul

Owner:
Angus Dundee Distillers plc

Region/district:
Speyside

Founded:
1964

Status:
Active

Tel:
01807 590274

Visitor centre:
No

website:
www.tomintouldistillery.co.uk

Capacity:
3 300 000 litres

% sold as malt whisky:
1,6%

Included in blended (past and/or present):
Whyte & Mackay, Parker´s, Dundee

History:

1964 –The distillery is founded by Tomintoul Distillery Ltd, which is owned by Hay & MacLeod & Co. and W. & S. Strong & Co.

1965 – On stream in July.

1973 – Scottish & Universal Investment Trust owned by the Fraser family, buys the distillery. They buy Whyte and Mackay the same year and transfer Tomintoul to that company.

1974 – The two stills are increased to four and Tomintoul 12 years is launched.

1978 – Lonhro buys Scottish & Universal Investment Trust.

1989 – Lonhro sells Whyte and Mackay to Brent Walker.

1990 – American Brands buys Whyte & Mackay.

1996 – Whyte and Mackay changes name to JBB (Greater Europe).

2000 – Angus Dundee plc buys Tomintoul.

2002 – Tomintoul 10 year is launched as the first bottling after the change of ownership.

2003 – Tomintoul 16 years is launched.

2004 – Tomintoul 27 years is launched.

2005 – A young, peated version called Old Ballantruan is launched.

Let us first establish the fact that Tomintoul is not a beautiful distillery, built in the 60s with efficient production in the mind. The surrounding scenery is, however, among the most beautiful in Speyside, with Tomintoul town just to the south of the distillery. It is the highest situated village in the Highlands (with Wanlockhead 30 miles north of Dumfries in the southwest as Scotland's highest).

Tomintoul was the first distillery owned by Angus Dundee and it was followed by the acquisition of Glencadam in 2003. The distillery is twice the size of Glencadam, but only a diminutive share of their whisky is sold as single malt. The rest is used in different blended whiskies from Angus Dundee, e. g. Parker's and Dundee.

A team of 21 people led by Distillery Manager Robert Fleming operate the distillery at full capacity meaning 3 300 000 litres of pure alcohol a year. The two pairs of stills are quite large and some of the whisky is matured on-site in four, racked warehouses.

There have been quite a number of distillery bottlings. The first was a *10 year old* which appeared in 2002, followed by a *16 year old* in 2003 and a *27 year old* in 2004. Then the odd *Old Ballantruan* appeared in autumn 2005, a peaty expression distilled in 2001. The name comes from the source in Cromdale Hills from which the distillery takes its water. Independent bottlings are unusual and with the new owners being independents themselves (MacKillop's Choice and several blends) it seems unlikely that they will become more common. Adelphi Distillery 1967, which appeared in 2003, is one of the more recent.

10 years old

27 years old

Tormore

Owner:
Chivas Brothers (Pernod Ricard)

Region/district:
Speyside

Founded:
1958

Status:
Active

Tel:
01807 510244

Visitor centre:
No

website:
www.tormore.com

Capacity:
3 600 000 litres
2 160 000 litres

% sold as malt whisky:
7%

Included in blended (past and/or present):
Long John, Ballantine´s, Teachers

History:

1958 – Schenley International, owners of Long John, founds the distillery.

1960 – The distillery is ready for production.

1972 – The number of stills is increased from four to eight.

1975 – Schenley sells Long John and its distilleries (including Tormore) to Whitbread.

1989 – Allied Lyons (to become Allied Domecq) buys the spirits division of Whitbread.

1991 – Allied Distillers introduce Caledonian Malts where Miltonduff, Glendronach and Laphroaig are represented besides Tormore. Tormore is later replaced by Scapa.

2004 – Tormore 12 year old is launched as an official bottling.

2005 – Chivas Brothers (Pernod Ricard) becomes new owners through the acquisition of Allied Domecq.

Architecturally, Tormore is undoubtedly the most original distillery in Speyside and probably all of Scotland. When driving the A95 towards Aberlour and Craigellachie it appears just by the road with a view towards Spey and is impossible to miss. And as if the original buildings themselves were not enough to attract attention, the distillery is surrounded by plenty of bushes trimmed in imaginative figures and shapes. A number of buildings to the right of the distillery used to house staff but were made into private residences in 2005.
Tormore was intended to be a showpiece distillery when construction commenced in 1958. The great architect Sir Albert Richardson, who had been president of the Royal Academy, was commissioned for the undertaking. Tormore was built in light granite with copper roofs and the building was considered so smart that a model of it was constructed for the exhibition at the Scotch Whisky Heritage Centre in Edinburgh.
The four pairs of stills are fitted with purifiers resulting in a lighter spirit. Maturation is in ex-bourbon casks with only a small share sold as single malt.
The official bottling is a *12 year old* introduced in 2004/05. An official *15 year old* was released several years ago and has been difficult to obtain recently. Chivas Brothers did, however, release more bottles in summer 2006
Independent bottlings of Tormore are rare, but two expressions from 1989 were released from Signatory and Douglas Laing. There is also a 1990 14 year old from Blackadder.

12 years old

Tullibardine

Owner:
Tullibardine Distillery Ltd

Region/district:
Highlands

Founded:
1949

Status:
Active

Tel:
01764 682252

Visitor centre:
Yes

website:
www.tullibardine.com

Capacity:
2 000 000 litres
120 000 litres

% sold as malt whisky:
100%

Included in blended (past and/or present):
-

History:

1949 – The architect William Delmé-Evans founds the distillery with C. I. Barret. The buildings originate from a 15th century beer brewery.

1953 – Delmé-Evans sells Tullibardine to Brodie Hepburn Ltd.

1971 – Invergordon Distillers buys Brodie Hepburn Ltd.

1973 – The number of stills doubles from two to four.

1993 – Whyte and Mackay (owned by Fortune Brands) buys Invergordon Distillers.

1994 – Tullibardine is mothballed.

1996 – Whyte and Mackay changes name to JBB (Greater Europe).

2001 – JBB (Greater Europe) is bought out from Fortune Brands by management and changes name to Kyndal (Whyte and Mackay from 2003).

2003 – A consortium including Michael Beamish buys Tullibardine in June for £1.1 million. The distillery is in production again by December. The first official bottling from the new owners is a 10 year old from 1993.

2004 – Three new vintage malts, from 1964, 1973 and 1988 respectively, are launched. Tullibardine 1488 Shop and 1488 Café opens.

2005 – Three wood finishes from 1993, port, muscatel and marsala are launched together with a 1986 John Black selection.

2006 – Vintage 1966 (plus a special World Cup version), Sherry Wood 1993 and a new John Black selection are launched.

It is difficult to say whether Tullibardine is a distillery with a shopping complex attached to it or the other way round. However, the new owner's idea since 2003 is to offer a total experience for visitors to the small village of Blackford north of Stirling on the A9: a working distillery and a huge shopping centre in one location.
The whole current range of malts from Tullibardine builds on produce from the previous owners (Brodie Hepburn and Invergordon Distillers) since the distillery was mothballed between 1995 and 2003. At the take-over in 2003, 3 000 casks from 1952 to 1993 were bought from Whyte & Mackay. The owners state that the whisky from the new production will be available in 2014 in time for Ryder's Cup at nearby Gleneagles.
The core range can be said to be a number of *vintages from 1993* and *1988*. A number of different finishes from *1993 (port, marsala, sherry* and *moscatel* with plans for a sauternes) are included in limited editions.
The latter include the *40 years series*, started in 2004 with *1964* and with *1965* and *1966* the following years. Distillery Manager John Black also has chosen a single cask *1986* (released in 2005) and a *1987* released in 2006. A *World Cup* version of *vintage 1966* was released in 2006 to celebrate the World Cup in football (marking both 1966 when England won and the 2006 event in Germany). The latter release has set emotions flowing among Scots who consider it unpatriotic by a Scottish company to commemorate the football victory of their archrivals. A micro-brewery producing beer has been installed as a 'first' for Scottish whisky distilleries. The beer, and the newly built visitor centre, has been named 1488. That was the year of the coronation of King James IV at which beer made in the brewery situated at the site was served. The 1488 Whisky Ale is made using distillery worts and yeast and is matured in ex-bourbon casks. Only 10% of Tullibardine's production is sold on the domestic market, with the rest for exports to more than 40 countries.

1988 vintage

The almost forgotten ones...

There are a handful of distilleries whose whisky is rarely encountered. All have in common the fact that they have been closed or demolished for a long time. Most, like Ladyburn, in production for only eight years, had a short lifespan whilst others, such as Glenugie, founded in the 19th century, had a longer period of activity (150 years). All except for Glenugie were also examples of a special trend in the 1950s and 1960s when distillery owners embraced the seemingly excellent concept of building malt distilleries adjacent to already existing grain distilleries. That concept apparently looked better on paper than in reality as none of these distilleries lasted for long.

Ben Wyvis

Owner: Whyte & Mackay Ltd

Region/district: Northern Highlands

Founded: 1965

Status: Dismantled

Tel: -

Visitor centre: -

website: -

Capacity: -

% sold as malt whisky: -

Included in blended (past and/or present):
-

History:

1965 – Invergordon Distillers opens a malt distillery on the same grounds where they already run a grain distillery. The malt whisky is intended for exclusive use in Invergordon's blended whiskies.

1974 – Rumours have it that a barrel of Ben Wyvis is exported to the United States of America.

1976 – Production stops.

1977 – The distillery closes.

1999 – The first version of a Ben Wyvis Single Malt (except for the possible American version) is released by Invergordon. It was distilled in 1972, 27 years old, and 658 bottles are released.

2000 – The independent bottler Signatory causes a sensation when it announces that it has come across five casks of Ben Wyvis. Two are in a condition not allowing release while the other three are released as 31 year olds.

2002 – Kyndal releases what will probably be the last from Ben Wyvis, a 37 year old distilled in 1965.

Ben Wyvis is highly sought after among collectors of rare single malts. There have been only a few occasions of filling after its decommissioning. The last was in 2002 when it was said that it was the last bottling available, on the other hand the same was also said in 1999... Bottles of Ben Wyvis are likely to be sold for slightly over £1 000.

Glen Flagler/Killyloch

Owner: Inver House Distillers (Pacific Spirits)

Region/district: Lowlands

Founded: 1964

Status: Demolished

Tel: -

Visitor centre: -

website: -

Capacity: -

% sold as malt whisky: -

Included in blended (past and/or present):
Mackinlay, Johnnie Walker

History:

1964 – The American company Publicker Industries buys and rebuilds Moffat Paper Mills in Airdrie creating three co-located distilleries: Garnheath (grain) and Glen Flagler and Killyloch (both malt). Moffat Maltings are also built.

c. 1975 – Killyloch closes.

1978 – Moffat Maltings is sold to Associated British Maltsters.

1985 – Glen Flagler closes in July.

1986 – Garnheath closes in July.

1988 – Inver House is bought out from Publicker by management.

2001 – Pacific Spirits (owned by Great Oriole Group) buys Inver House Distillers for $85 million.

2003 – Inver House releases Glen Flagler 1973 (931 bottles) and Killyloch 1967 (371 bottles).

Both Glen Flagler and Killyloch had a short involvement with the whisky market. The American market for blended whisky was growing and the American company Publicker considered having a grain distillery (Garnheath) and two malt distilleries (Gen Flagler and Killyloch) on the same premises a good business incentive. Business went well in the beginning and Glen Flagler was also sold as single

malt in the 1960s and 1970s to Italy among other countries. However, the demand for blended whisky grew smaller in the US in the late 1970s and Killyloch, which had been used exclusively for blending purposes, was closed followed by Glen Flagler and Garnheath a few years later.
There were actually two versions of Glen Flagler as the wash still was replaced by a continuous still in 1969 in order to better produce a whisky which was more adapted to the American market.
Glen Flagler and Killyloch are two major rarities on the whisky scene today. Signatory launched two Glen Flagler in the mid 1990s but everything went quiet until 2003 when Inver House surprisingly released a Glen Flagler 1973 and a Killyloch 1967. These were possibly the last two bottlings ever made. Some caution is advised if one encounters the name Glen Flagler. Inver House has sold blended malt named Glen Flagler Pure Malt Special Reserve since the 1980s. Another Glen Flagler version is the peated version which was produced until 1970 and named Islebrae.

Glenugie

Owner:
Whitbread/Long John

Region/district:
Eastern Highlands

Founded:
1831

Status:
Dismantled

Tel:
-

Visitor centre:
-

website:
-

Capacity:
-

% sold as malt whisky:
-

Included in blended (past and/or present):
-

History:

1831 – The distillery is founded by Donald, McLeod & Co. as Invernettie Distillery.

1837 – The name changes to Glenugie Distillery and it is converted into a brewery.

1875 – The brewery is bought by Scottish Highland Distillers Company Ltd which restarts the distillery.

1879 – The distillery closes.

1882 – Glenugie is bought by George Whyte & Co. which becomes bankrupt the same year.

1915 – Production ceases.

1923 – The distillery begins production once more.

1925 – Production stops.

1937 –Seager Evans & Company Ltd takes over and resumes production.

1956 – Seager Evans is bought by Schenley Industries Inc. The number of stills doubles to four.

1963 – Own floor maltings discontinues.

1971 – Seager Evans changes name to Long John International Ltd.

1975 – Schenley sells Long John International to Whitbread & Company.

1983 – The distillery closes and the buildings are sold.

Glenugie, which disappeared during the great cleansing of distilleries in 1983, was situated in an area aptly named 'oil country'. The oil industry nowadays dominates these coastal tracts and no whisky distilleries remain here. Companies associated with the oil business have been seeking property and two of these have finally established themselves on the grounds of Glenugie.
No official bottling of Glenugie exists but a handful of independent bottlings occur. Among recent ones are Gordon & MacPhail 1968 (36 years), Douglas Laing 1984 (20 years) and Murray McDavid 1977 (26 years).

Inverleven

Owner:
Chivas Brothers
(Pernod Ricard)

Region/district:
Lowlands

Founded:
1938

Status:
Partly demolished

Tel:
-

Visitor centre:
-

website:
-

Capacity:
-

% sold as malt whisky:
-

Included in blended (past and/or present):
Ballantine´s, Long John, Teacher´s

History:

1938 – The distillery is founded by Hiram Walker & Son as part of Dumbarton Distillery, a complex with grain distilling, warehousing and a bottling plant.

1956 – Hiram Walker constructs a 'distillery within the distillery' by inventing the Lomond still, which makes whisky that differs in character from Inverleven. The same type of still is introduced at Glenburgie, Miltonduff and Scapa.

1987 – Allied Lyons buys Hiram Walker Gooderham & Worts.

1991 – The distillery is mothballed.

2002 – Dumbarton Distillery closes.

2003 – The site is bought by the construction company Carvill.

Inverleven was constructed within the Dumbarton Distillery complex and equipped with a Lomond still. The Lomond still was developed by Alistair Cunningham at Hiram Walker with the purpose of acquiring a greater flexibility to produce different kinds of whisky with the same equipment.
When Dumbarton closed in 2002 production was moved to Strathclyde but by then Inverleven had already been closed for ten years. When Dumbarton finally closed in 2002, Bruichladdich took the opportunity of buying some of the equipment including the old Lomond still.
The whisky from the Lomond still, Lomond single malt, was only bottled in 1992 in two versions of 19 and 20 years respectively by the Scotch Malt Whisky Society. Inverleven single malt cannot be obtained as an official bottling, but there are recent releases from independent bottlers such as Duncan Taylor 1977, Douglas Laing 1989 (16 years) and Signatory 1977 (27 years).

Kinclaith

Owner:
Whitbread/Long John

Region/district:
Lowlands

Founded:
1957

Status:
Demolished

Tel:
-

Visitor centre:
-

website:
-

Capacity:
-

% sold as malt whisky:
-

Included in blended (past and/or present):
Long John

History:

1957 – Seager Evans Ltd builds the distillery on the site of the grain distillery Strathclyde.

1958 – Production starts.

1971 – Seager Evans Ltd changes name to Long John International.

1975 – Schenley sells Long John International to Whitbread & Co. and the distilleries are dismantled and closed down. Strathclyde continues to produce grain whisky.

Kinclaith was the last malt distillery to be built in Glasgow. As there are no official bottlings, one has to turn to independents to find a bottle. One of the most recent and perhaps final bottlings, 217 bottles of 35 years old cask strength, was released by Signatory. Another 35 year old was released by Duncan Taylor in their 'Rarest of the Rare' series.

Ladyburn

Owner:
William Grant & Sons

Region/district:
Lowlands

Founded:
1966

Status:
Dismantled

Tel:
-

Visitor centre:
No

website:
-

Capacity:
-

% sold as malt whisky:
-

Included in blended (past and/or present):
Grant´s Standfast

History:

1963 – William Grant & Sons builds the grain distillery Girvan.

1966 – The malt distillery Ladyburn is built on the premises of Girvan.

1975 – The distillery closes in November.

1976 – The equipment is dismantled.

2000 – A 27 year old (1973) from William Grant and a 30 year old from Gordon & MacPhail are launched.

Of the experimental 'malt distilleries within a grain distillery', Ladyburn Distillery, built by William Grant, was the shortest lived, closing after only nine years. Two official and a couple of independent bottlings have been released since 2000, the most recent one being a Duncan Taylor 1973 (31 years) and Wilson & Morgan 1975 (30 years). Independent labels will often mention Ayrshire Distillery rather than Ladyburn.

Ladyburn 1973

Glen Flagler 1973

...and the really new ones!

Permanent closure of distilleries is sadly commonplace. A number of them are doomed through demolition or the selling of buildings for other purposes. Examples of these are Lochside, Littlemill and Coleburn. There may be hope for some others, like Braeval, Glenglassaugh and Glen Keith, but it is questionable whether they will ever produce again. There are, however, a number of mothballed Scottish distilleries which have been started up again in recent years.
Happily enough, the handful of newly established distilleries counter-balance those doomed to closure. Persistent efforts by enthusiastic whisky-lovers, indefatigable entrepreneurs and established persons in the business have resulted in new distilleries. Some units will be small-scale, farm house distilleries while other harbour more grandiose plans.
One of them, Glengyle, opened already in 2004 and another two, Kilchoman and Daftmill, started producing in 2005.
There are even plans for new distilleries outside Scotland, for example in England, and you can read more about them in the chapter 'Distilleries across the globe'.

Blackwood

Owner:
Blackwood Distillers

Region/district:
Highlands (Shetland)

Founded:
2002

Status:
Not yet opened

Tel:
01595 694455

Visitor centre:
-

website:
www.shetlandwhisky.com,
www.blackwooddistillers.com

Capacity:
-

% sold as malt whisky:
-

Caroline Whitfield, previously advisor for, among others, Diageo, raised the idea of building the first whisky distillery in the Shetlands in 2002. She is currently CEO of Blackwood Distillers.
Blackwood did not have a trouble-free start. Planning permission was granted by Shetland Council in June 2004, but a survey found the original site unsuitable so it was moved 60 metres and a new application had to be sent in. After that there was a long wait for building warrants and when they finally came through, Shetland Council approached Blackwood to discuss moving it to one of the most northerly Shetland islands, Unst, which had recently lost the RAF airbase at Saxa Vord. Some 40 jobs were lost and the idea was to use the site for building the distillery. MAM (Military Asset Management), which specialises in transforming ex military sites into commercial ventures, plan to start a combined distillery and hotel enterprise with Blackwood. Caroline Whitfield hopes production will now start in 2007.
The financing of Blackwood Distillers was obtained by selling shares in the company to private investors at a price of £1.6 million. To keep money flowing until the first whisky is ready for sale a range of branded products, including gin, vodka and cream liqueur, was launched in October 2003. The range is produced on license from Inver House.
When it comes to whisky the plans are to produce 40 000 cases of single malt a year. They will be offering peated malt, as well as unpeated in different versions. They claim the peated will remind of Caol Ila whilst the unpeated will be closer to a Glenrothes or Speyside in flavour.

Kilchoman

Owner:
Kilchoman Distillery Co.

Region/district:
Islay

Founded:
2005

Status:
Active

Tel:
01496 850011

Visitor centre:
Yes

website:
www.kilchomandistillery.com

Capacity:
90 000 litres

% sold as malt whisky:
-

When Kilchoman Distillery was inaugurated on 3rd June 2005 it was the first distillery to open on Islay since Malt Mill opened on Lagavulin Distillery's premises in 1908. Anthony Wills and Mark French started the project in 2002 by selecting Rockside farm, a few miles from Port Charlotte and Bruichladdich Distillery on the west coast of Islay as the site. As consultants, Wills and French selected Jim Swan, previously involved as an advisor at Blackwood Distillery on Shetland and Gwalia Distillery in Wales and John McDougall, legendary through his work with no less than 19 distilleries.

The first distillation took place in late 2005 and production is expected to be 40 000 litres of alcohol the first year which will increase to 90 000 litres within five years. They plan to launch a 5 year old in 2010, gradually increasing the range with 8, 10 and 12 year olds. For maturation fresh bourbon and refill barrels are used but other casks such as sherry, port, rum and wine also occur. There is one wash still (2 700 litres), one spirit still (1 500 litres) and two washbacks (with two more being added in 2007).
Kilchoman is a typical farm distillery with the whole production carried out on site. The barley is grown at Rockside Farm, malted, distilled, matured and eventually bottled at the distillery. The plans are to use 50% own-produced malt and 50% ready-peated malt from Port Ellen.
A fire started in the distillery on 12th February 2006 but damages were limited and only caused a few weeks of stoppage.
There is also a visitor centre with a café and a shop where one can buy miniatures of Kilchoman 'New Spirit' among other items.

Daftmill

Owner: Cuthbert family	***Region/district:*** Lowlands
Founded: 2005	***Status:*** Active
Tel: -	***Visitor centre:*** -
website: -	
Capacity: -	***% sold as malt whisky:*** 100%

Permission was granted in autumn 2003 for a disused steading at Daftmill Farmhouse near Cupar in Fife to be converted into a distillery. Contrary to most other new distilleries selling shares in their enterprise, Francis and Hazel Cuthbert have quietly established the distillery. It will be run as a typical farmhouse distillery and they do not have plans to open it to the public. Distilling began in late 2005 and it was officially opened in the beginning of August 2006. There is one wash still (3 000 litres) and one spirit still (2 000 litres). The establishment of Daftmill increased the number of Lowland distilleries from three to four.

Ladybank

Owner: Ladybank Company of Distillers Club	***Region/district:*** Lowlands
Founded: 2003	***Status:*** Not yet opened
Tel: 0845 450 1885	***Visitor centre:*** -
website: www.whisky.co.uk	
Capacity: 25 000 litres	***% sold as malt whisky:*** -

Ladybank represents a completely new type of distillery regarding ownership. It is organised as a private club with roughly 300 members, many of whom live overseas. James Thomson is the founder. He managed a travel and events company for many years before starting work with whisky companies developing their online marketing.
Ladybank is in Cugar, Fife, not far away from Daftmill Distillery. It consists of a converted, old, stone mill building. Construction of the distillery started in summer 2006 and the relatively small production, which is likely to begin in 2008, is sufficient to provide for the club's members and ensure that some produce is saved for greater ageing. The objective is to produce three types of whisky, a distinctly peated, an un-peated and one using a novel, aromatic wood-smoked recipe. Annual capacity will be 35 000 litres.

Glengyle

Owner: Mitchell´s Glengyle Ltd	***Region/district:*** Campbeltown
Founded: 2004	***Status:*** Active
Tel: 01586 552009	***Visitor centre:*** -
website: www.kilkerran.com	
Capacity: 750 000 litres	***% sold as malt whisky:*** -

Glengyle Distillery was the first distillery to open in the new millennium and the first to open in Campbeltown for 125 years though its heritage is old. Glengyle was founded by William Mitchell in 1872. Mitchell owned Springbank with his brother John for a period of years before the two brothers went separate ways. Glengyle closed in 1925.
Nearly 80 years later Hedley Wright, owner of Springbank and great great nephew of William Mitchell, founded a new company, acquired the run-down buildings and embarked on a painstaking renovation. Stills were bought from the closed Ben Wyvis Distillery in 2002 and were rebuilt to fulfil the needs of Glengyle. A left-over malt mill from Craigellachie's expansion was purchased and installed at Glengyle. The new Glengyle was finally inaugurated on 25th March 2004.
The name of the whisky will be Kilkerran as Glengyle was already in use by a vatted Highland malt and the name could not be taken over. Intending buyers signed up for six bottles to be delivered in ten years at the commissioning. All bottles, which were priced at £950, come from different casks; Oloroso, Fino, Rum, Madeira, Port and Bourbon.
The malt comes from Springbank maltings and is malted to the same recipe as Springbank. They have one wash still (18 000 litres) and one spirit still (11 000 litres). The estimated production will be 50-60 000 litres of alcohol per annum and will be stored in Springbank's warehouses.

Distilleries per owner

c = closed, d = demolished, mb = mothballed, dm = dismantled

Diageo
Auchroisk
Banff (d)
Benrinnes
Blair Athol
Brora (c)
Bushmills
Caol Ila
Cardhu
Clynelish
Coleburn (dm)
Convalmore (dm)
Cragganmore
Dailuaine
Dallas Dhu (c)
Dalwhinnie
Dufftown
Glen Albyn (d)
Glendullan
Glen Elgin
Glenesk (dm)
Glenkinchie
Glenlochy (d)
Glenlossie
Glen Mhor (d)
Glen Ord
Glen Spey
Glenury Royal (d)
Inchgower
Knockando
Lagavulin
Linkwood
Mannochmore
Millburn (dm)
Mortlach
North Port (d)
Oban
Pittyvaich (d)
Port Ellen (dm)
Rosebank (c)
Royal Lochnagar
St Magdalene (dm)
Strathmill
Talisker
Teaninich

Pernod Ricard
Aberlour
Allt-a-Bhainne
Braeval (mb)
Caperdonich (mb)
Glenallachie
Glenburgie
Glendronach
Glen Keith (mb)
Glenlivet
Glentauchers
Imperial (c)
Inverleven (d)
Lochside (d)
Longmorn
Miltonduff
Scapa
Strathisla
Tormore

Edrington Group
Glenglassaugh (mb)
Glenrothes
Glenturret
Highland Park
Macallan
Tamdhu

Inver House (Pacific Spirits)
Balblair
Balmenach
Glen Flagler (d)
Knockdhu
Pulteney
Speyburn

John Dewar & Sons (Bacardi)
Aberfeldy
Aultmore
Craigellachie
Macduff
Royal Brackla

Whyte & Mackay
Dalmore
Fettercairn
Jura
Tamnavulin (mb)

William Grant & Sons
Balvenie
Glenfiddich
Kininvie
Ladyburn (dm)

Glenmorangie Co. (Moët Hennessy)
Ardbeg
Glenmorangie
Glen Moray

Morrison Bowmore (Suntory)
Auchentoshan
Bowmore
Glen Garioch

Burn Stewart Distillers (CL Financial)
Bunnahabhain
Deanston
Tobermory

Loch Lomond Distillers
Glen Scotia
Littlemill (d)
Loch Lomond

Angus Dundee Distillers
Glencadam
Tomintoul

Long John Whitbread
Glenugie (dm)
Kinclaith (d)

J & A Mitchell
Glengyle
Springbank

Beam Global Spirits & Wine
Ardmore
Laphroaig

Campari Group
Glen Grant

Isle of Arran Distillers
Arran

Signatory Vintage Scotch Whisky Co.
Edradour

Ian Macleod Distillers
Glengoyne

Tomatin Distillery Co. (Marubeni Europe plc)
Tomatin

J & G Grant
Glenfarclas

Bruichladdich Distillery Co. (Murray McDavid)
Bruichladdich

Co-ordinated Development Services
Bladnoch

Gordon & MacPhail
Benromach

Benriach Distillery Co.
Benriach

Ben Nevis Distillery Ltd (Nikka)
Ben Nevis

Tullibardine Distillery Ltd
Tullibardine

Speyside Distillers Co.
Speyside

Cooley Distillery plc
Cooley

Kilchoman Distillery Co.
Kilchoman

Cuthbert family
Daftmill

Single malts

from Japan

By Hideo Yamaoka
and Taylor Smisson

Yoichi Distillery

The old No. 1 spirit still of Yamazaki

Introduction to Japanese malt whisky

Traditionally, 'whisky' in Japan had two distinctive images. One image was of very expensive Scotch blends (and, maybe, the occasional Scotch single malt) you gave to your boss to impress him during the two traditional Japanese gift-giving seasons or, if you were lucky, drank yourself on an expense account at a Ginza bar. The other image was of the 'mizuwari' (literally meaning 'with water added') – inexpensive, usually Japanese but often unidentified whisky drowned in plenty of water and ice and drunk by Japanese 'sarariiman' in crowded, smoky bars.

In recent years, however, the image of whisky in Japan has started to coalesce into a somewhat more consistent less schizophrenic image. Four reasons for this transformation come to mind. *First*, changes in tax rates in 1989 and increases in 'parallel imports' (imports through channels other than those officially sanctioned by the brand) over the years thereafter lowered the prices of premium Scotch blends and malts to much more reasonable levels, making them less impressive as gifts and more affordable to those not on expense accounts. *Second*, the wine boom in Japan from several years ago got people into the habit of not only actually choosing the brand they would drink but also nosing and sipping it from a special glass. *Third*, recognition of Japanese blends and malts in tasting competitions overseas and the release of bottlings of several Japanese distilleries by the Scotch Malt Whisky Society went a long way towards convincing the Japanese consumer that the Japanese distillers could also produce a world-class quality product. *Finally*, extensive advertising by Suntory, especially through creative tie-up articles with a wide variety of magazines (including some women's magazines) over the past year or so, often show Suntory's Yamazaki and Hakushu single malts interwoven together with its affiliated Scotch single malts in the same ads and articles. Thus, recognition of malts and of the quality of Japanese malts (and relative equality with Scotch malts) has increased among a relatively large spectrum of Japanese consumers, an increasing number of whom, instead of choosing if they will have a 'mizuwari' or a 'beeru', now contemplate whether they will have a Laphroaig or a Yamazaki.

What is Japanese malt whisky?

There are currently 6 working malt whisky distilleries in Japan: *Yamazaki* and *Hakushu* owned by Suntory, *Yoichi* and *Miyagikyo* owned by Nikka (an affiliate of the Asahi Brewery Group), *Fuji-Gotemba* owned by Kirin Brewery and *Karuizawa* owned by Mercian. Each Japanese distillery/company has its own style of making whisky, so generalizing about what is Japanese malt whisky is difficult but, more often than not, the following can be said:

- Japanese malt whisky is distilled in pot stills using basically Scottish techniques with some Japanese innovations.
- It is made mainly with imported malt, especially from Scotland, some of which is peated.
- It is filled in both cask types traditionally used in Scotland as well as cask types unique to Japan such as Japanese oak. Japanese-made American oak casks are probably the most popular choice for new casks these days.
- It is matured in a climate much more similar to that of Kentucky and Tennessee than that of Scotland; i.e. the summers of Japan are much hotter than those of Scotland, and the difference in temperature of the hottest and coldest months of the year is roughly twice that of Scotland. The fact that Japanese malt whiskies tend to show more of the influence of the wood than Scotch malt whiskies, sometimes to the point of being bourbon-like, is probably due to these higher temperatures and the increased expansion and contraction of the whisky in the casks due to the larger variations in temperature.
- It tends to mature more quickly than Scotch malt whisky, due mainly to the higher temperatures it is matured at.
- It's flavors tend to be cleaner, fruitier, more estery and less malty than a typical Scotch malt.
- Japanese whisky companies do not share whisky stocks with each other, so Japanese blended whisky is made only from the production of each company's own distilleries, often supplemented with overseas (mainly Scotch) whisky. This has resulted in Japanese distilleries tending to make whiskies with a relatively wide range of flavors to enable production of blended whisky with only a single or a couple of distilleries. To accomplish this, a variety of pot still shapes, pot still heating methods (direct and steam), casks, yeast types, peat levels, etc. tend to be used.

Born in Tokyo, Japan, Hideo Yamaoka is an editor, writer and translator. He writes for the regular whisky tasting column in Japan, "The Whisky World", and has also translated some of Michael Jackson's books. He has won the malt whisky nosing contest three times at the Speyside Festival and once at the Islay Festival.

Taylor Smisson is an American who has lived most of his life in Japan. He is the author of the "Malt Drinker's Diary in Tokyo", www.scotchclub.org/mdd/mdd.htm and has written whisky-related articles for publications in both Japan and the UK. Over the years, Taylor has tried a total of around 5,000 different single malts, including around 100 Japanese single malts.

Fuji-Gotemba

Owner:
Kirin Brewery

Tel:
+81-(0)550-89-3131

Founded:
1973

Capacity:
12 000 000 litres
(including grain whisky)

Cask types:
First fill and refill American oak barrels seasoned with grain whisky

Present malt whisky range:
The Fuji-Gotemba Single Malt 18yo, 43%
Fuji Sanroku Single Malt 18yo, 43%

History:

1973 - The distillery is founded by Kirin-Seagram.

1993 - Fuji-Gotemba Pure Malt Whisky is released.

2002 - Kirin Brewery becomes the sole owner.

2004 - The Fuji-Gotemba Single Malt Whisky 18yo is released.

2005 - Fuji Sanroku Single Malt 18yo is released.

Fuji-Gotemba is one of few distilleries in the world which not only has malt whisky stills but also grain whisky stills, a bottling plant and a cooperage. It was founded by Kirin-Seagram in 1973. Kirin-Seagram was a joint venture of Kirin Brewery Company Ltd. (Japan), JE Seagam Company Ltd. (USA) and Chivas Brothers (UK). The premium blend 'Evermore', versions of which have been released every year since 1999, used to contain the same vatted malt as that used in Chivas Regal, but matured in Japan and blended with malt and grain whisky produced at Fuji-Gotemba.

The distillery aims at producing a clean and estery malt well-influenced by the wood it was aged in. One important factor that contributes to this desired clean and estery flavour is the slight upward slant of the lyne arms of the pot stills, which is said to make it difficult for heavier compounds to make it to the condenser. Also, the selection of the distillery´s site was aimed at making the whisky rounded and fruity. Some of the factors which led to this site´s selection were the fact that the average annual temperature is around 13°C and the often foggy weather maintains relatively high humidity. Also, the air is clean due to the vast forest around the distillery, and the water, which started as snow on Mt. Fuji and flows underground to the distillery, is pure and relatively soft.

This distillery´s whisky was originally used almost exclusively in blended whisky, however, since 2002 when Kirin Brewery became the sole owner, the distillery has been releasing more single malts. The oldest component of Fuji Sanroku 18yo is 27 years.

Fuji Sanroku 18 years old

Fuji-Gotemba 18 years old

Hakushu

Owner:
Suntory

Tel:
+81-(0)551-35-2211

Founded:
1973

Capacity:
3 000 000 litres

Cask types:
Mainly hogsheads and bourbon barrels, but also a small number of first fill and refill American oak puncheons seasoned with grain whisky, sherry butts and Japanese oak butts

Present malt whisky range:
The Hakushu Single Malt Whisky 10yo, 40%
The Hakushu Single Malt Whisky 12yo, 43%

New releases:
The Hakushu Single Malt Whisky 18yo, 43%

History:

1973 - The distillery is built.

1981 - Hakushu East Distillery is built.

1983 - Yatsugatake Aging Warehouse is built.

1988 - Hakushu East Original Pure Malt Whisky is released.

1994 - Hakushu 12yo Pure Malt is released.

1998 - Hakushu 10yo Pure Malt is released.

2003 - 'The Cask of Hakushu' series is released.

2004 - 'The Owner´s Cask' series is released.

2006 - Hakushu 18yo Single Malt Whisky is released.

Hakushu is located in the foothills of the Southern Alps of Japan. There is also a plant which bottles Suntory´s 'Southern Alps Natural Water'. It is this very soft water that is used for making Hakushu malt whisky.

Hakushu is situated 700 metres above sea level and for that reason, so-called low pressure distillation occurs naturally. That is, since the distillation takes place at a lower temperature, it is more difficult for oily compounds with high boiling points to be distilled. For this reason, the resulting distillate tastes light and estery.

Hakushu was started in 1973 and, in 1981, a new distillery, Hakushu East, was built and only that distillery is currently working. Although the original lantern-shaped pot stills of Hakushu East were smaller than those of the original distillery, now known as Hakushu West, some have been replaced with even smaller pot stills. Hakushu East now has a wide variety of pot stills enabling it to produce many different styles of spirit. There are pots stills with different sizes, shapes and lyne arm configurations. Although most of its stills are direct-fired, it also has one indirect-heated still. In 2006, the core range was expanded with the 18 yo at 43%, in addition to the existing 10yo and 12yo. The 18yo is very clean with some fruit, mint and peat notes.

Hakushu 10 years old

Hakushu 12 years old

Hakushu 18 years old

Karuizawa

Owner:
Mercian

Tel:
+81-(0)267-32-2006

Founded:
1955

Capacity:
150 000 litres

Cask types:
Roughly 90% are sherry butts and the remainder are mainly bourbon and wine casks

Present malt whisky range:
Karuizawa Single Malt 12yo, 40%
Karuizawa Single Malt 15yo, 40%
Karuizawa Single Cask 17yo, 40%

New releases:
Karuizawa Vintage series (single cask whiskies which were distilled from 1974 to 1993).

History:

1955 - The distillery is built by Mercian.

1958 - The distillery becomes the first Japanese distillery to use malted barley imported from Scotland.

1976 - The malt whisky Karuizawa is released.

1987 - Karuizawa Single Malt Ageing series 10yo, 12yo and 17yo are released.

2002 - Karuizawa Vintage series of single cask malt whisky bottlings are released.

The Karuizawa distillery uses spring water that flows underground from Mt. Asama. It´s water is classified as soft but it is somewhat on the hard side.

The distillery´s fermentation process is unique. When they transfer the wort (6 000 litres) from the mash tun to the washback, they first put only 400 litres of the wort in a tank and add 20 kg of yeast. After a few hours they transfer this to the washback and then add the rest of the wort and an additional 10 kg of yeast. This process is similar to that used in the brewing of Japanese sake.

The washback runs 48-50 hours and the wash is then distilled in a small 4 000 litres pot still. The stillhouse has two wash stills of the same size and two spirit stills, but only one of the spirit stills is used.

Karuizawa uses Golden Promise barley imported from the UK, and the resulting spirit is clean and sweet.

The whisky is matured mainly in sherry casks, many of which are remade with shortened staves resulting in a capacity of around 400 litres in order to better fit Karuizawa´s warehouse racks.

At the distillery, 20 bottlings of the single cask Karuizawa Vintage series distilled from 1974 to 1993 are for sale. On the label of each bottle, written by hand, are the year of distillation, the date of bottling, the cask number and the signature of the 'Malt Master'.

Karuizawa Vintage 1993

Karuizawa 15 years old

Karuizawa Vintage 1974

Miyagikyo (Sendai)

Owner:
Nikka
(an affiliate of the
Asahi Brewery Group)

Tel:
+81-(0)22-395-2865

Founded:
1969

Capacity:
5 000 000 litres
(including grain whisky)

Cask types:
Hogsheads, first fill and refill new wood American oak puncheons (i.e. not seasoned with other spirits, wines, etc. before the first fill), bourbon barrels and sherry butts

Present malt whisky range:
Single Malt Miyagikyo 10yo, 45%
Single Malt Miyagikyo 12yo, 45%
Single Malt Miyagikyo 15yo, 45%

New releases:
Nikka Single Cask Malt Whisky 1987, 61%
Nikka Single Cask Malt Whisky 1991, 64%

History:

1969 - The distillery is built by Nikka.

1976 - Two additional pairs of stills are installed.

1990 - Single Malt Miyagikyo 12yo is released.

1999 - The Coffey stills are moved from the Nishinomiya Distillery to Miyagikyo Distillery.

2003 - Single Malt Miyagikyo 10yo and 15yo are released.

Miyagikyo Distillery (also known as Sendai Distillery) is near Sendai, a city in the northern part of Japan´s main island of Honshu. Since Nikka´s other distillery, Yoichi, is farther north, on the island of Hokkaido, Miyagikyo has been called Nikka´s lowland malt and Yoichi its highland malt. In fact, Miyagikyo Distillery stands in a valley surrounded by mountains and near the Nikkawa river, giving it the feel of a Speyside distillery.

The malt is flowery and fruity. This is said to be due in part to the fact that the pot stills have boil balls and the lyne arms are slanted slightly upward. All the stills are steam-heated and use shell-and-tube condensers. In contrast, the malt of Yoichi is rich and powerful. The necks of Yoichi´s pot stills are straight and the lyne arms slant downward. Also, they are direct-fired with coal and use worm-tubs.

Miyagikyo has 24 warehouses by the Nikkawa river. They are all built of red brick and most of them are of dunnage type.

Miyagikyo also has Coffey stills, which are now rare even in Scotland. They were moved from the Nishinomiya distillery in 1999. Sometimes they are used to distill wash which is made using only malted barley. After aging, this is blended with 'regular' (twice distilled in pot stills) Miyagikyo malt whisky. This is sold as 'All Malt', which is inexpensive and tastes smooth and soft.

Miyagikyo 10 years old

Miyagikyo 15 years old

Miyagikyo 1990

Yamazaki

Owner:
Suntory

Tel:
+81-(0)75-962-1423

Founded:
1923

Capacity:
3 500 000 litres

Cask types:
Hogsheads, first fill and refill American oak puncheons seasoned with grain whisky, bourbon barrels, sherry butts and Japanese oak butts. Also, it has a small number of casks alternating between whisky and plum wine.

Present malt whisky range:
Suntory Single Malt Whisky Yamazaki 10yo, 40%
Suntory Single Malt Whisky Yamazaki 12yo, 43%
The Yamazaki Single Malt Whisky 18yo, 43%
The Yamazaki Single Malt Whisky 25yo, 43%

New releases:
The Yamazaki Single Malt Whisky 35yo, 43%

History:

1923 - The distillery is founded by Kotobukiya.

1924 - Production begins. Masataka Taketsuru becomes the distillery manager.

1929 - Kotobukiya changes its name to Suntory.

1988 - Major revamping of production process started in 1987 is completed, including replacement of 3 pairs of stills.

2002 - The Cask of Yamazaki series is released.

2004 - The Owner´s Cask series is released.

2005 - Yamazaki 50yo is released and sells out in a few hours.

2006 - Yamazaki Distillery receives the Visitor Centre of the Year Award at Icons of Whisky 2006. Replacement of 3 pairs of stills which was started in 2005 is completed.

Yamazaki 10 years old

Yamazaki 12 years old

Yamazaki 18 years old

Yamazaki 25 years old

Yamazaki 35 years old

Yamazaki, Japan´s first whisky distillery, was founded in 1923 and started production in 1924. Yamazaki is located on the outskirts of Osaka, nestled against bamboo-covered hills, but is right next to Kyoto and it is where the famous tea master Sen no Rikyu (1522-1591) had his tea house. It is, therefore, no surprise that this area is renowned for the high quality of its water.

From the summer of 2005, Suntory began to replace three pairs of stills and the new stills commenced distillation in February 2006. In total, Yamazaki has six pairs of stills (each pair consisting of one wash still and one spirit still). Each pair is numbered 1 to 6, and the No.1, No. 2 and No. 4 pairs were replaced. All the new stills are smaller than their predecessors. The capacity of the wash stills is now 12 000 litres (before the replacement it was 30 000 litres). The shapes of the new pots stills are all different. The necks of the No. 1 stills are straight and the lyne arm of the wash still is slanted downward at a sharp angle, resulting in a spirit with a lot of body. Each No. 2 still has a boil ball resulting in a more elegant spirit. The necks of the No. 4 pair of stills are wide and straight resulting in a well-balanced spirit. All the new wash stills are direct-fired. The overall aim of these replacements is to make malts which are rich, big and full.

This replacement was a continuation of the large-scale revamping of its production process carried out in 1987-1988. At that time, three pairs of stills were replaced by smaller-sized stills including two direct-fired wash stills. In addition, wooden washbacks were introduced and the yeast normally used was changed from just distillers yeast to a combination of distillers yeast and brewers yeast.

In 2004, Suntory began selling casks to individuals for whom they would bottle the casks under 'The Owner´s Cask' program. Potential customers can taste samples of the various casks in a special tasting room at the distillery. The price per cask runs from 500,000 yen to 30,000,000 yen (around £2 300 to £138 000).

In 2006, Suntory released Premium Soda, which is soda water made using water from Yamazaki. It is intended mainly for making whisky and soda. Although normally some minerals are added to water in order to make soda water, Premium Soda uses only natural water and CO_2 because the water of Yamazaki is relatively hard. The aftertaste is soft and slightly sweet and does not impair the flavour of malt whiskies.

Following the release in 2005 of the Yamazaki 50yo, which sold out in a few hours, the Yamazaki 35yo (200 bottles) was released in 2006. The price per bottle was 500,000 yen (about £2 300), but it also sold out quickly. It is creamy with fruity apple notes and with a finish of sandalwood incense.

Yamazaki´s visitor center, where you can taste for yourself the difference between whisky distilled in a direct-fired still and that distilled in an indirect-heated still, received the 'Visitor Centre of the Year' award at Icons of Whisky 2006, sponsored by Whisky Magazine.

Yamazaki warehouse

The new No. 2 spirit still

Yoichi (Hokkaido)

Owner:
Nikka
(an affiliate of the Asahi Brewery Group)

Tel:
+81-(0)135-23-3131

Founded:
1934

Capacity:
2 000 000 litres

Cask types:
Hogsheads, first fill and refill new wood American oak puncheons (i.e. not previously seasoned with other spirits, wines, etc. before the first fill), bourbon barrels, sherry butts and some old Japanese oak casks

Present malt whisky range:
Single Malt Yoichi 10yo, 45%
Single Malt Yoichi 12yo, 45%
Single Malt Yoichi 15yo, 45%
Single Malt Yoichi 20yo, 52%

New releases:
Single Malt "Yoichi" 1985 20yo, 55%
Nikka Single Cask Malt Whisky 1985, 58% (#250216)
Nikka Single Cask Malt Whisky 1985, 58% (#250241)
Nikka Single Cask Malt Whisky 1986, 49%
Nikka Single Cask Malt Whisky 1987, 52%
Nikka Single Cask Malt Whisky 1991, 64%

History:

1934 - The distillery is founded.

1936 - Whisky production starts.

1940 - The company´s first whisky, Nikka Whisky, a blended whisky, is released.

1952 - The company changes its name to The Nikka Whisky Distilling Co. Ltd.

1984 - Nikka Single Malt 'Hokkaido' 12yo, Yoichi´s first single malt, is released.

2001 - Nikka delists and becomes a full subsidiary of the Asahi Brewery Group.

In 1934, Masataka Taketsuru established the Dainipponkaju Co. Ltd. (Great Japan Juice Co. Ltd. – in 1952, the company was renamed Nikka, which is an abbreviation of the original Japanese name) and built its Yoichi Distillery (also known as Hokkaido Distillery) on Hokkaido, the most northern of Japan´s major islands. Before that, Taketsuru had studied whisky production in Scotland both in academia and at several distilleries, especially Longmorn and Hazelburn, and had worked at Kotobukiya (which would later change its name to Suntory) where he supervised the startup of Yamazaki, Japan´s first whisky distillery.

Yoichi is the most northern of Japan´s whisky distilleries, and its latitude is roughly in line with that of Vladivostok, Marseilles and Milwaukee. Although it is said that Taketsuru chose this location in part for its similarities to Scotland and the annual average temperature is similar to that of Scotland. The coldest month of the year averages around 7°C colder than that of Scotland and the hottest month of the year averages around 8°C hotter. For whisky matured in Yoichi´s warehouses, this results in a speeding up of the maturation process in the summer and slowing down in the winter. Yoichi is surrounded by mountains on three sides and the Sea of Japan on the fourth. Also, peat is found nearby and this peat has been used in the making of Yoichi´s malt in the past.

Initially, true to its company name, Yoichi made apple products including juices, sauces, etc. It distilled its first whisky in 1936 and sold its first whisky in 1940. Early pictures of Yoichi show mountainous piles of apples, the raw material for its fruit products, heaped around the distillery buildings. (For more information about Masataka Taketsuru in English, see *Japanese Whisky, Scotch Blend* in the Books & Magazines section, page 263).

Among Japanese whiskies, Yoichi has the image of being dry and peaty. Also, Yoichi has a reputation in Japan of sticking more to its Scottish roots than, for example, Yamazaki, which is seen as making a more Japanese whisky. An example of this emphasis on tradition is Yoichi´s investment in pollution-control equipment to enable it to continue to use traditional coal-burning direct-fired stills. It is the only distillery in Japan to have coal-fired stills and in this sense, Yoichi can be said to be more true in some ways to its Scottish roots than even Scottish distilleries. Also, it uses worm-tubs and the straight-neck shape of its pot stills is said to have been inspired by the shape of those which Taketsuru saw at Longmorn when he was there.

However, Yoichi also has developed its own original production techniques, one being the use of first fill and refill new wood American oak casks (i.e. not previously seasoned with other spirits, wines, etc. before the first fill). Yoichi chars the new casks to lower the amount of the woody pencil-shavings like flavour that is imparted to the whisky by the new wood casks. First fill new wood casks have been used for several notable single cask bottlings of Yoichi, including the bottling that received the highest rating in Whisky Magazine´s 2001 'Best of the Best' blind tasting.

Another notable innovation by Nikka can be seen in its bottles (for not only Yoichi but also Miyagikyo). To avoid the impact that corks can have on the flavour of whisky while still benefiting from the upscale image that consumers have of cork caps as opposed to screw caps, Nikka tends to use cork caps which have the corks encased in transparent, inert plastic.

For those to whom just reading about or drinking Yoichi is not enough, there is the Yoichi 'Making My Whisky' experience. Several times each year, Yoichi conducts 2-day sessions that people can attend for a reasonable fee to experience making malt whisky. The malt whisky made then is matured in casks signed by the participants, and, after 10 years, each participant gets a bottle of the whisky they helped to make.

Yoichi 10 years old

Yoichi 15 years old

Single Cask Yoichi 1988

Distilleries around the globe

You will find them in Tasmania and Turkey as well as in Sweden and South Africa. Let´s seek out the hidden malt distilleries around the world.

Mackmyra distillery, Sweden

Nowadays, single malt distilling is not restricted just to Scotland, Ireland and Japan. New distilleries can be found all over the globe. Most of them are small units or so-called micro distilleries. Some initially produced spirits based on fruit or berries, or made vodka or fortified wines, but eventually turned to whisky. Others started with whisky but came to the conclusion that financial liquidity and 3-6 years of storage without sales are not compatible. Products that are possible to sell soon after distillation have thus been important in keeping the distilleries' finances sound until 'whisky bottling day'.

There are some distilleries that are of such magnitude and are so well-organised that they are key actors on local or national markets. Tekel (Turkey), Murree Brewery (Pakistan) and McDowell´s (India) are almost exclusively targeted at the local market and maintain strong positions there, thanks to the other products in their respective ranges. Glenora (Canada) is a fully fledged whisky distillery with a comparatively large production, although the produce is mostly sold locally. James Sedgwick (South Africa) produce and annually sell some 5 million bottles of blended whisky but do not seem to be planning on expanding malt whisky production at the moment. Amrut Distillers (India) have, on the other hand, both the size and ambition. In 2004 the ball started rolling when they embarked on a major European launch attempt, interestingly enough choosing Scotland as the base for their crusade.

The highest quality is often found among the smaller distilleries. Their single malts are usually single cask, non chill-filtered and without added colourings. The whisky can often be surprisingly mature after only three or four year's storage as the casks are small, down to 30 litres in size. Among these smaller distilleries, Gwalia in Wales received much credit for their Penderyn single malt and Swedish distillery Mackmyra released their two first expressions in limited numbers during 2006 which sold out in record time. Other distilleries in, for example, Switzerland, Germany and the US produce malt whisky which is mentioned with esteem by connoisseurs. Many of the described distilleries have not yet launched their products commercially and others have not embarked on or completed construction. Two such examples are found in England which, after almost 150 years, is back on the map again with two small distilleries – one in the Lake District and one in Norfolk.

Some distilleries have become decommissioned recently though it may still be possible to obtain bottlings from some of them. Lammerlaw and Milford were both produced at Wilson's Willowbank Distillery in New Zeeland, which closed in 1996 and was dismantled in 2000. New Zealand Malt Whiskey Company with Warren Preston bought approximately 400 cases of Milford whisky and the brand is now available from specialist whisky shops around the world. Preston also has plans on building a bottling plant in New Zealand which will eventually be expanded into a new distillery. German Sonnenschein released a 10 year old single malt in 2000 but closed in 2001 and now sells only liqueur and wine. Cradle Mountain, aka Small Concern Whisky Distillery, closed around 1998 but their Single and Double Malt (the latter a blended malt where Springbank is included) are still on the market.

The following pages do not claim to be a complete listing of malt distilleries outside Scotland, Ireland and Japan. One of the reasons is that several producers worldwide (especially in India) claim that their bottle contents are single or blended malt whisky but it is often difficult to get this verified. We have therefore chosen not to include them in this book. Another reason for the listing lacking completeness is the small and often temporary distillery projects which turn up now and then but which can hardly be called distilleries even if the end product is single malt whisky.

An example of such a project is St Austell Brewery and The Cornish Cyder Farm which joined forces three years ago and produced 400 litres of malt whisky in a one-off project of which we will see the results in 2011. Another example is the excellent Drumchork Hotel in Aultbea, Scotland which persuaded the authorities to issue a licence despite still sizes considerably below the legal size. The whisky will be called Loch Ewe.

EUROPE

Austria

DISTILLERY: Wolfram Ortner Destillerie
FOUNDED: 1990
OWNER/MANAGER: Wolfram Ortner
www.wob.at

Fruit brandies of all kinds are Wolfram Ortners main produce as well as cigars, coffee and other luxuries. For the last few years he has also been producing malt whisky. New oak of different kinds (Limousin, Alolier, Nevers, Vosges and American Oak) is used for the maturation process. Ortner calls his whisky Nock-Land Whisky after the National Park Nockberge from where the water for distillation is obtained. His first single malt, WOB DÖ MALT Vergin began selling in 2001 and his latest release is the 2000 Guiseppe 48%. A new product line, in which Ortner mixes his whisky with other distillates such as orange/muscatel, is called WOB Marriage.

DISTILLERY: Waldviertler Roggenhof
FOUNDED: 1995.
OWNER/MANAGER: Johann & Monika Haider
www.roggenhof.at

6 000 bottles were produced annually since its inception in 1995 until 2004, but capacity has been enhanced from 2005 and is expected to reach 30 000 bottles annually of both blended and single malt respectively. The whisky matures on Manhartsberger Sommereiche, i. e. new Austrian oak. Two single malts are available: Gersten Malzwhisky J. H. (light malt) and Gersten Malzwhisky J. H. Karamell (dark, roasted malt). Three different rye whiskies are also produced.

DISTILLERY: Reisetbauer
FOUNDED: 1995 (whisky)
OWNER/MANAGER: Julia & Hans Resisetbauer
www.reisetbauer.at

A family-owned distillery near to Linz in northern Austria. Specialised in brandies and schnapps made of fruit but has had single malt whisky in its range for a few years. The first release was in November 2002 and a number of different varieties have appeared since then, most of them as cask strengths. The whisky is matured on casks that previously have contained Chardonnay or Trockenbeerenauslese.

Belgium

DISTILLERY: PUR.E. Distillerie
FOUNDED: 1997
OWNER/MANAGER: Etienne Bouillon
www.belgianwhisky.com

The first distillation from this Belgian distillery is matured in ex bourbon casks from Kentucky since 29 October 2004 and Etienne Bouillon expects to bottle it on 30 October 2007. A blended malt is planned for 2008. Annual production of single malt is expected to reach 90 000 bottles a year. Bouillon plans to sell his production continuously in order for customers to be able to follow the maturation during the three coming years.

England

DISTILLERY: Barley Bridge Distillery
FOUNDED: 2006
OWNER/MANAGER: Lakeland Distillers Ltd
www.lakelandwhisky.com

The first plans for a whisky distillery in the Lake District took shape in 2004 by Andrew Currie, son of Harold Currie who founded Arran Distillery and also worked as Marketing Director at Arran for a few years. It is built within the nineteenth century buildings of a former bobbin mill at Staveley near Kendal. The stills, manufactured by MacMillans, are expected to be installed in Novernber 2006 with first distillation in January 2007. The barley will be sourced from Scotland and the estimated volume will be around 25 000 litres the first year.
(Andrew Currie is also involved in plans for setting up a distillery on Vancouver Island, Canada for which permission to distil was obtained in late August 2006.)

DISTILLERY: St. George´s Distillery
FOUNDED: 2006
OWNER/MANAGER: Norfolk Whisky Company
www.norfolkwhisky.co.uk

This will probably be the first of the two new English distilleries to come on stream. The first distillation will take place in autumn 2006 according to plans. In spring 2007 there will be a shop, tearoom and conference facilities and guided tours should be available. The first bottling is planned for June 2010. The distillery is near Thetford in Norfolk and was started by James and Andrew Nelstrop. They managed to interest Iain Henderson in the project, which was fortunate, Iain being a highly esteemed person in the whisky industry, fomerly of Laphroaig and most recently Edradour. The aim is to produce 100 000 bottles a year.

Finland

DISTILLERY: Teerenpeli
FOUNDED: 2002
OWNER/MANAGER: Anssi Pyysing
www.teerenpeli.com

The first Teerenpeli Single Malt was sold as a three-year old in late 2005, but only in the owners' restaurant in Lahti. The first commercial launch is expected in 2007/2008. Teerenpeli uses locally obtained lightly peated malt and the whisky matures in ex sherry and ex bourbon casks. 7 500 bottles are produced annually.

France

DISTILLERY: Glann ar Mor
FOUNDED: 1999
OWNER/MANAGER: Jean Donnay
www.glannarmor.com

Taol Esa, distilled in 1999 and released in May 2004, is the first whisky from this distillery. Only 99 bottles have been released as a trial.
The distillery was not completed until 2005 with its first distillation on the 12th June the same year. Two versions will be produced initially, an unpeated and a peated (35-40 ppm). Jean Donnay makes his whisky in the old style using wooden wash backs, direct heating of the two stills and condensing the vapours in worm tubs rather than using shell and tube condenser.
Glann ar Mor uses first fill Sauternes barriques and ex-bourbon casks for maturation.
Apart from the Glann ar Mor venture, Jean Donnay has also specialised in blending and double maturation of whisky purchased from Scotland. The product range includes Glen Torness 5 years (blended) and Pot Still 8 years and Islay Connection 10 years as blended malts. There is also the Celtique Connexion range of single malts with a finish in different casks.
The whiskies can be found at
www.celtic-whisky.com

DISTILLERY: Distillerie Warenghem
FOUNDED: 1990
OWNER/MANAGER: Warenghem
www.distillerie-warenghem.com

Leon Warenghem founded the distillery already at the beginning of the 20th century but Armorik, the first malt whisky, was not distilled until 1994 and released in 1999. A blended whisky with 25% share of malt, Whisky Breton W. B. is also produced at Warengham. Armorik is available in several European countries and is also exported to Japan.

Taol Esa from Glann ar Mor

Armorik Single Malt

Jean Donnay celebrates the first distillation at Glann ar Mor

Germany

DISTILLERY: Slyrs Destillerie
FOUNDED: 1928
OWNER/MANAGER: Florian Stetter
www.slyrs.de

Slyrs was founded in 1928 and was mainly producing brandy until 1999 when whisky came into the picture. The malt, smoked with beech, comes from locally grown grain and is matured on casks of new American White Oak from Missouri.
The first single malt was Vintage 1999, which was released in 2002 in 6000 bottles. Next vintage (2003) will appear during 2006 and Florian Stetter counts on releasing 10 000 bottles. A new distillery, exclusively dedicated for whisky production, is expected to open in 2006. The whisky can be bought in Germany, Switzerland and Denmark.

DISTILLERY: Whisky-Destillerie Blaue Maus
FOUNDED: 1980
OWNER/MANAGER: Robert Fleischmann
www.fleischmann-whisky.de

This is the oldest whisky distillery in Bavaria. The first distillate, never released on the market, was made in 1983. After 15 years the first whisky, Glen Mouse 1986, appeared on the market. Fleischmann uses unpeated malt and the whisky matures for around eight years in casks of fresh German oak. All whisky from Blaue Maus are single cask and there are currently five single malts; Blaue Maus, Spinnaker, Krottentaler, Schwarzer Pirat and Grüner Hund. According to Mr. Fleischmann the differences between them is in the malt mixture he uses.

Sweden

DISTILLERY: Mackmyra Svensk Whisky
FOUNDED: 1999
OWNER/MANAGER: Mackmyra Svensk Whisky AB
www.mackmyra.se

Mackmyra received the unofficial title 'The World's most northerly distillery' in 1999, previously held by Highland Park. But it only took a couple of years until the Finnish distilleries in Lahti and Pori made claims to the title.
Mackmyra's trials have led to two recipes; one resulting in fruity and elegant whisky and the other more peaty. The peatiness does not stem from peat, but from juniper wood and bog moss.
In 2002, Mackmyra presented an option to reserve casks - Mackmyra Reserve. As the two versions could be obtained matured in ex sherry, ex bourbon or new Swedish oak casks, six versions are available. But that was not all, one could also choose between 30 or 100 litre casks and maturation in interior northern Sweden or in the archipelago of Stockholm, all in all 36 versions! Another storage, in Häckeberga in Scania, became operational in summer 2006. The first official bottling, named Preludium:01, was released in March 2006 and sold out in a few days. The next release was in August and is the second of six in 2006/07; Preludium:02. The Preludium series uses casks both from the pilot distillery which operated 1999-2002 and from the current distillery which started in 2002.

Mackmyra Preludium:02

Schwarzer Pirat (Blaue Maus)

Slyrs Vintage 1999

DISTILLERY: Gotland Whisky
FOUNDED: Construction commences 2006
OWNER/MANAGER: Gotland Whisky AB
www.gotlandwhisky.se

The first island-based distillery in Sweden is about to be realised on the Baltic island of Gotland. The distillery is built and equipped with Scottish assistance and was initially supposed to be located at the farmstead Robbjens in Klinte village. Robbjens will probably become a museum, café and shop while the distillery will be moved to the decommissioned Roma sugar works. The owners hope to start trial distillations in summer 2007. At least two expressions will be offered, one peated with an Islay character and a more mellow variety.

Switzerland

DISTILLERY: Maison Les Vignettes - Swhisky
FOUNDED: 2000.
OWNER/MANAGER: Alex Delaloye
www.swhisky.ch

The first malt distillation by this distillery in Ardon took place in 2001 and 4 000 bottles are produced annually. There have been four different single malts in the range since the start; Annouim, Gwenwed (matured in Syrah casks), Abred (a peaty variety) and Keugant (cask strength 56%). Another four expressions have recently been added; Challenge, Celtica, Skipper (a peated version) and finally Triad, older than the others and finished in a Vosne Romanée cask. A rye whisky is also on the way and will probably be bottled during 2007. The produce is sold in Switzerland and Japan but will probably become available in other European countries in the near future.

DISTILLERY: Whisky Castle
FOUNDED: 2002
OWNER/MANAGER: Ruedi Käser
www.whisky-castle.com

The first whisky from this distillery has now reached the market. It was released in 2006 under the name Castle Hill. The annual production of the distillery is expected to be 5 000 bottles. The whisky is matured in Hungarian and American oak casks and ex-sherry casks.

DISTILLERY: Spezialitätenbrennerei Zürcher
FOUNDED:
OWNER/MANAGER: Heinz Zürcher
www.

Their first release of Lakeland Single malt consisted of 1 000 bottles in 2003. Another distilling was made following the release which explains why the next batch of Lakeland did not appear until summer 2006. Maturation is in oloroso sherry casks.

DISTILLERY: Brennerei-Zentrum Bauernhof
FOUNDED:
OWNER/MANAGER: Edi Bieri
www.swissky.ch

Apart from the distillery in Talacher, Edi Bieri has a mobile distillery intended for fruit distillates. The whisky, named Swissky, occurs in a number of varieties.

Glen Vignettes Gwenwed

Single malt from Whisky Castle

Lakeland Single Malt

DISTILLERY: Whisky Brenneri Holle
FOUNDED: 1999 (for whisky distillation)
OWNER/MANAGER: The Bader family.
www.swiss-whisky.ch, www.single-malt.ch

Switzerland had a law forbidding the use of staple food such as potatoes and grain for making alcohol since World War I. On 1st July 1999 it was abolished and the spirit streamed through the stills of Holle the very same day making it the first Swiss producer of malt whisky.
The whisky is stored on French oak casks, which have been used for white wine (Chardonnay) or red wine (Pinot Noir). Most bottlings are three years old and contain 42% alcohol. A five year old is also released, with three years in Pinot Noir casks and then two years in Chardonnay casks. The latest release was a five-year anniversary bottling in July 2006. Other expressions include a peated version and a cask strength Chardonnay-matured. Annual production amounts to roughly 30 000 bottles. A single grain based on wheat is also planned.

Wales

DISTILLERY: Gwalia Distillery
FOUNDED: 2000
OWNER/MANAGER: Welsh Whisky Company Ltd
www.welsh-whisky.co.uk

Frongoch distillery closed in the late 19th century but after more than a century Wales can now count itself among the whisky-producing nations once again. Adventurous attempts to establish a whisky distillery in the 1990s ended in court after pressure from the Scottish whisky industry but in 1998 four private individuals started Welsh Whisky Company. Equipment was in place two years later and distilling began on 14th September 2000. A new type of still, developed by David Faraday for Gwalia distillery, differs from the Scottish and Irish procedures in that the whole process from wash to new make takes place in one single still.
The first single malt was called Penderyn and was launched on St. David's Day 1st March 2004. 60 000 bottles were produced the first year and the target for 2005 is 80 000 - 100 000 bottles. Several different expressions have already been launched, among them Oloroso, Softly Peated and Madeira finished. A visitor centre is planned for 2007.
In common with many other newly started whisky distilleries, Gwalia has been financially dependent on other produce until the first whisky becomes available on the market. Brecon Premium Vodka, Brecon Dry Gin and Merlyn Welsh Cream Liqueur can be mentioned among these.

Holle Single Malt Swiss Whisky

Penderyn Single Malt from Gwalia distillery in Wales

NORTH AMERICA

USA

DISTILLERY: Clear Creek Distillery
FOUNDED: 1985
OWNER/MANAGER: Stephen McCarthy
www.clearcreekdistillery.com

Like many other small distilleries, Clear Creek started by distilling eau de vie from fruit, especially pears, and then expanded the product line into whiskey. Clear Creek began making whiskey in 1996 and the first bottles were on the market three years later. There is only one expression, McCarthy's Oregon Single Malt 3 years old, at the moment but Steve McCarthy hope to be able to sell both a single barrel cask strength and an 8 year old in the not too distant future. The whiskey reminds much of Islay and the malt is purchased direct from Islay with a phenol specification of 30-40 ppm. It is matured in ex-sherry butts with a finish in new Oregon White Oak hogsheads.
The distillery recently moved premises but is still located in Portland, Oregon. The whiskey is available in several European countries.

DISTILLERY: Triple Eight Distillery
FOUNDED: 2000
OWNER/MANAGER: Cisco Brewers
www.ciscobrewers.com

This is the first North American distillery situated on an island; Nantucket Island, Massachusetts. No whiskey is on the market yet, but the first distillation in 2000 will be bottled at the beginning of 2007 and named Notch (from 'not Scotch'). They currently have 111 barrels in their warehouse and the plan is to release 4 of these barrels as Notch (7 to 8 years old). Annual production will be c 5 000 bottles and the storage is on ex bourbon casks from Brown Forman (Jim Beam).
The Nantucket facility consists of brewery, winery and distillery. The parent company, Cisco Brewers, produces Whales Tale Pale Ale and they use a similar mash for producing the Notch. Triple Eight also produces vodka and rum that is already on the market. Whiskey production will be moved to a new distillery in 2007.

DISTILLERY: Edgefield Distillery
Troutdale, Oregon
FOUNDED: 1998
OWNER/MANAGER: Mike and Brian McMenamin
www.mcmenamins.com

Brothers Mike and Brian McMenamin started their first pub in Portland, Oregon in 1983. It has now expanded to a chain of more than 40 pubs and hotels in Oregon and Washington. Over 20 of the pubs have adjoining microbreweries (the first opened in 1985).
Their first and so far only distillery opened in 1998 at their huge Edgefield property in Troutdale and their first whiskey, Hogshead Whiskey (46%), was bottled in 2002. Annual production amounts to 2000 bottles and maturation takes place in new, charred American Oak casks as well as in ex Bourbon casks. Edgefield also distils brandy and gin.

Notch casks at Triple Eight

McCarthy's Oregon Single Malt

The still room at Edgefield distillery

DISTILLERY: St. George Distillery
FOUNDED: 1984
OWNER/MANAGER: Jorg Rupf/Lance Winters
www.stgeorgespirits.com

The distillery is situated in a hangar at Alameda Point, the old naval air station in San Fransisco. The main produce is based on eau de vie, from locally grown fruit, and American vodka. Whiskey production was picked up in 1996 and the first single malt appeared on the market in 1999. Some of the malt used has been dried with alder and beech.
Maturation is on bourbon barrels (80%), French oak (15%) or port pipes (5%). St. George Single Malt is sold as a three year old, but distiller Lance Winters emphasises that the majority is actually 6-7 years old.

DISTILLERY: Charbay Winery & Distillery
FOUNDED: 1983
OWNER/MANAGER: Miles and Marko Karakasevic
www.charbay.com

Charbay has a wide range of products; vodka, grappa, pastis, rum, port and since 1999 also malt whiskey. The only bottling so far is Double-Barrel Release One from 2002, cask strength and non-chill filtered. There were only 840 bottles and the price tag of $325 may seem off-putting. Maturation takes place in newly charred American white oak barrels. A speciality of Charbay is the addition of dried hops to the wash before distillation. Another single malt (43%) may be released at the more modest price of $85 but there is no indication of when at the moment.

DISTILLERY: Stranahans Whiskey Distillery
Denver, Colorado
FOUNDED: 2003
OWNER/MANAGER: Jess Graber,
George Stranahan et al.
www.stranahans.com

The first whiskey distillery in Colorado cooperates closely with its neighbour, Flying Dog Brewery. The brewery makes the wash based on four different kinds of barley. It finds its way back to Stranahans via a network of pipes for distillation and maturation on casks of charred American White Oak. The barrels come from World Cooperage of Lebanon, Missouri. The costs are lower than those normal for a microbrewery as Stranahans take advantage of an existing brewery for the first stages of production.
This began in March 2004 and according to Colorado laws the whisky has to be matured for two years (compared to three in Scotland) before it may be sold. The first three barrels were bottled in April 2006 and future releases will probably be a four to ten barrel batch but they may release a single barrel as well. Plans also include experiments with port finishes, probably taking place in autumn 2006. Sales volumes are expected to be stable at 33 000 bottles a year from 2007. Stranahans only used one pot still until spring 2005 when another still (made wash still) was installed while the old became spirit still.

DISTILLERY: St. James Spirits
FOUNDED: 1995
OWNER/MANAGER: Jim Busuttil
www.saintjamesspirits.com

Peregrine Rock is the name of the three year old single malt Jim Busuttil produces in Irwindale, east of Los Angeles. The malt comes from Baird Malts in the UK and is medium peated. Heavy charred new American oak barrels, but also ex bourbon barrels from Jim Beam and Jack Daniels are used.

Canada

DISTILLERY: Glenora Distillery
FOUNDED: 1990
OWNER/MANAGER: Lauchie MacLean
www.glenoradistillery.com

Glenora, situated in Nova Scotia is not a microdistillery - unlike most other North American distilleries. The production volume totals a staggering 250 000 bottles a year. The start-up was difficult as funds dried up a couple of times and production stopped on several occasions. Lauchie MacLean took over in 1994 and the operations became more stable. The first launch of Glen Breton took place in September 2000 and the 2000 boxes were sold out in six weeks. Glenora are in a feud with the Scotch Whisky Association (SWA) who maintain the usage of the letters Glen in the name misleads customers to believe that the whiskey is Scottish and therefore wishes to prohibit the use of 'glen' for non-Scottish whiskies. Lauchie MacLean points out that Glen is an established geographical name in this part of Canada.

AUSTRALIA & NEW ZEALAND

Australia

DISTILLERY: Bakery Hill Distillery
FOUNDED: 1998
OWNER/MANAGER: David Baker
www.bakeryhilldistillery.com.au

David Baker at Bakery Hill Distillery is now in full control of the whole production process. Until recently they have used Mountain Goat Brewery to produce their wash. From August 2006 Bakery Hill has its own brewery and is in control of the whole chain from milling to bottling. The first spirit was produced in 2000 and the first single malt was launched in autumn 2003. Three different versions are available - Classic and Peated (both matured in ex bourbon casks) and Double Wood (ex bourbon and French oak). As Classic and Peated also are available as cask strength bottlings, they can be considered two more varieties. They have also recently relaunched a special bottling of Cask 14, the peated malt that resulted in Jim Murray nominating Bakery Hill the 'Best Small Distillery Whisky of the Year' in his Whisky Bible 2005.
There will be some delay before more bottles appear on the market. David Baker's target is to build up spirit levels without releasing any new malt whiskies over the next two years. All unpeated malt comes from an Australian maltster while the malt for the peated version is imported from the UK.

DISTILLERY: Lark Distillery
FOUNDED: 1992
OWNER/MANAGER: Bill Lark
www.larkdistillery.com.au

Lark Distillery is Tasmanian cooperation in action. The malt is mainly supplied by Cascade Brewery in Hobart, the stills are made by Peter Bailly of Knapp Lewer Contracting in Hobart and the casks are prepared by the coopers at Tasmanian Cask Company. Bill Lark obtained his distillery license in 1992. The original establishment was in Kingston but moved to Hobart in 2001. In common with many other small distilleries, Lark looked for alternative products to secure liquidity while the whisky was maturing. Tasmanian Bush Liqueur, based on Tasmanian Pepperberry, and Apple Schnapps deserves mention as an example of these. The current single malt is 3-4 years and lightly peated. The casks are mainly port barrels, shaved and retoasted and cut down to 100 litres but bourbon and sherry casks are also used. Annual production amounts to 15 000 bottles. One can tour the distillery and there is also a recently opened whisky bar.

DISTILLERY: Hellyers Road Distillery
FOUNDED: 1999
OWNER/MANAGER: Betta Milk Co-op/ Laurie House
www: hellyersroaddistillery.co.au

This distillery was previously known as Whisky Tasmania but in connection with the release of the first bottles the name was changed to Hellyers Road Distillery, after Henry Hellyer one of the first European explorers to set foot in

Maturing casks at Bakery Hill distillery

Bill Lark checking the still

Tasmania.
A visitor centre and a website were set up in 2006 and, most importantly, a number of expressions were released for the first time. There are now three varieties of Hellyers Road Whisky in the range: Original, Slightly Peated and Peated. There is also the premium expression Hellyers Road Distillers Choice as well as Southern Fire, intended for the export market. All these are single malt whiskies. Maturation takes place in ex bourbon casks and there are now approx 2 600 casks in their warehouse.

DISTILLERY: Tasmania Distillery
FOUNDED: 1996
OWNER/MANAGER: Patrick Maguire
www.tasmaniadistillery.com

This Tasmanian distillery started production in 1996 and focuses on single malts. It does not use chill-filtering; instead the spirit is allowed to settle for three months prior to bottling. Ex bourbon casks and French oak port are used for maturation. Around 4 000 bottles a year are produced and the product range consists of Sullivan's Cove 40% and Sullivan's Cove Cask Strength 60%, both six to seven years old. Franklin River Single Malt, a new expression which is a vatting of the two types of casks, was released in 2005.

New Zealand

DISTILLERY: Southern Distilleries
FOUNDED: 2005
OWNER/MANAGER: Peter Wheeler and Malcolm Willmott
www.hokonuiwhiskey.com

New Zealand now has a commercial distillery producing malt whisky after a few years of cessation since Wilson's Willowbank Distillery closed in 1996. The single malt is called The Coaster and is stored on bourbon casks. There is also a blended named The MacKenzie which contains 40% single malt. Both The Coaster and The MacKenzie are un-chillfiltered and there is no artificial colouring. To complete the range there are also the moonshine whisky Hokonui and the recently added whisky liqueur The Southerner and the Irish moonshine Poitin. The latest versions of The Coaster and The MacKenzie are between three and four years old and the total yearly production is expected to be 50 000 litres in the near future.

ASIA

India

DISTILLERY: Amrut Distilleries Ltd.
FOUNDED: 1948
OWNER/MANAGER: Jagdale Group
www.amrutdistilleries.com

Amrut is the first Indian distillery with serious aspirations on establishing itself on the European market. Their first single malt (matured 3-4 years) is now available in the UK, the Netherlands, Sweden, France, Germany and Italy.
The main part of its malt production, started in the mid-eighties, is used for their blended whiskies (MaQintosh for example). The malt is produced in Jaipur and Delhi from grain grown in Punjab and Rajasthan. Distilling takes place at Amrut in Bangalore. The casks are mainly ex Bourbon of American oak. The rather harsh climate during maturation gives an Angel's Share of between 12 and 15%.
Rakshit N. Jagdale, grandson of the founder, consolidated the marketing of Amrut Single Malt in Scotland when he studied at the University of Newcastle upon Tyne. Step one included establishing the brand at as many Indian restaurants as possible in Glasgow, the curry capital of Britain. The target, according to Amrut, is to sell 10 000 cases within four years mainly through the UK's 20 000 Indian restaurants. An Amrut cask strength was released in 2006.

The Coaster, Southern Distilleries

Ankara Turk Viskisi

DISTILLERY: McDowell's
FOUNDED: 1988 (malt whisky)
OWNER/MANAGER: UB Group
www.clubmcdowell.com

McDowell's has been part of the United Breweries Group since the 1950s. Other companies in the group are Herbertsons, Triumph Distillers & Vintners and since 2005 Shaw Wallace. The group, owned by Dr. Vijay Mallya, is number three in the world after Diageo and Pernod Ricard and by the recent acquisition of Shaw Wallace has 50% of the Indian market of IMFL (Indian Made Foreign Liquor). Scottish & Newcastle acquired a share in the brewery division of United Breweries in 2005.

The product range includes McDowell's Single Malt (3-4 years) while the different blends make up the major part with Bagpiper and McDowell No. 1. Dr. Mallya, who is also a member of the Indian parliament, is one of the main propagators of the high Indian excise on imported spirits as long as Indian-produced whisky cannot be sold as whisky in Europe (as it is produced from molasses rather than cereals).

Pakistan

DISTILLERY: Murree Brewery Ltd.
FOUNDED: 1860
OWNER/MANAGER: Minoo Bhandara
www.murreebrewery.com

Murree started as a beer brewery supplying the British Army with beer. The assortment was completed with whisky, gin, rum, vodka and brandy. Three single malts have been available since some time; 3, 8 and 12 years respectively. In 2005 an 18 year old single malt was launched. A number of blended whiskies such as Vat No. 1, Lion and Dew of Himalaya also occur. Company sources mention a supply of half a million litres of whisky in underground storage. The brewery makes their own malt (both floor maltings and Saladin box).

Unlike the beer, sold in Indian restaurants in the UK via an Austrian brewery under the slogan "Have a Murree with your curry", the whisky is not available outside of Pakistan. Catchy slogans seem to be the trademark as "Eat, drink and be Murree" also proves. Murree Brewery's owner is, like the owner of Indian McDowell's, a member of his country's National Assembly.

Turkey

DISTILLERY: Tekel
FOUNDED: 1862 (1923 wine and spirits)
OWNER/MANAGER: Nurol, Limak, Özaltin, Tütsab
www.tekel.gov.tr

Both production and sales of tobacco and alcohol in Turkey have been administered by the national company Tekel, which also has a salt division. A change in legislation in 2001 opened a window for privatization and the wine and spirits division was sold to four companies Nurol, Limak, Özaltin and Tütsab. They formed a holding company 'Mey Industry and Trade' to market and distribute the products but kept the company name Tekel.

The range of beverages is large, mainly consisting of wine but vodka, gin, 'cognac' and whisky are also included. The company has produced a whisky named Ankara Turk Viskisi for many years. It can probably not be called a single malt as it is reported to contain a portion of malted rye mixed with malted barley.

AFRICA

South Africa

DISTILLERY: James Sedgwick Distillery
FOUNDED: 1886 (whisky production 1990)
OWNER/MANAGER: Distell Group Ltd.
www.distell.co.za

James Sedgwick Distillery initially produced brandy but converted to whisky in 1990. The first trials with malt whisky were, however, already commenced in 1985 at Robertson & Buxton Distillery in Stellenbosch. When the latter closed, all production was transferred to James Sedgwick. 6 000 bottles of Three Ships 10 year single malt was released for the first time in autumn 2003. The line of blended whiskies is larger: Three Ships Original, Three Ships 5 years, Three Ships Bourbon Cask Finish, Harrier and Knights all amount to 5 000 000 bottles a year.

The whisky is matured on ex bourbon and ex sherry casks and a small share of own malt production goes into the blends. So far, the Three Ships Single Malt seems to be a one-time shot, but new bottlings may be launched according to Master Distiller Andy Watts.

The Whisky Year That Was

Photo: © Chivas Brothers

A great year for Scotch whisky

2005 was a brilliant year for Scotch whisky, in fact the third best year ever regarding quantity. Exports increased with 3.6% with the largest increases in Asia and South America. Europe, on the other hand, continues to disappoint and shows all signs of a mature market. Sales decreased by 5% which was evident in, above all, Italy, Germany, Greece and Portugal. The last sales increase in Europe took place in 2001.

Regarding consumption of Scotch whisky (blended and malts together), France is still the largest market in the world. France surpassed the US already in 1998 and is today responsible for 14% of the world consumption. But the largest growth markets are in South America and, above all, Asia. Consumption increased by 115% in China from 2004 to 2005, 35% in Venezuela, 26% in India and 17% in South Korea. If one looks at bottled malt whisky separately, the worldwide increase in volume is just above 10%. Sales increased by 9% in Europe where for example, exports to France increased by 23%. This means that 8% of today's total number of sold bottles of Scotch is single malt which is equal to a doubling of sales in ten years. A good example of malt whisky's success is found in the UK where consumption has increased by 300% since 1985, while the corresponding figure for blended whisky is a decrease by 45%. Single malts have also increased in the US by over 300% the last two decades, at the expense of other whisky.

The big players

All main actors on the market could take advantage of the good total sales during the year.

Pernod Ricard's sales increased by 68% up to and including June 2006, but this is explained by the take-over of Allied Domecq in 2005. Organic growth was 4%. Their major brands Chivas, Jameson and Glenlivet, all increased between 10 and 12%.
Asia (except Thailand) and Latin America (Venezuela in particular) did well while Europe, mainly Germany, Italy and, partly, Spain was disappointing.
More than half of the company´s profits now come from Asia and the Americas.

Edrington's sales increased by 3.7% and profits by 6.5% in the year to March 2006. The Famous Grouse portfolio did particularly well with over 36 million bottles sold over the year. Macallan and Highland Park also went exceptionally well. Macallan's Fine Oak range has now sold over 1 million bottles since its launch just two years ago. The increase has taken place in Asia, North America, Eastern Europe and the Nordic countries, while there is a decrease in the rest of Europe.

LVMH´s total sales increased by 11.4% and profits by 15.6%. Of this increase, the Wines & Spirits group make up for 6.9% with Moët & Chandon, Veuve Clicquot, Hennessy and Glenmorangie as the main contributors.

The year ending in June 2006 resulted in sales and profit increases of 9% and 6% respectively for *Diageo*. In common with the other groups, Asia and South America were the main markets responsible for this as well as South Africa where Bell´s is the most sold Scotch whisky. Volumes increased slightly in Europe, except for Spain and Portugal. The brand that excelled most was Johnnie Walker Black Label with an 11% increase and which now has half of the Russian Scotch market.

Whyte & Mackay increased sales by 4% and profits by 28% but these figures are from September 30 2005. The company is in the process of restructuring and the bottom line of the present fiscal year will be affected by these charges. Whyte & Mackay blend and Jura have been relaunched as will Dalmore be in autumn 2006. The group wanted to sell Invergordon Distillery in November 2005 for £175 million, but have now removed it from the sales list due to the general positive trend in the business. On the other hand, the rumours that the Indian company United Breweries Group will take over Whyte & Mackay grew stronger in early autumn 2006.

The big brands

Glenfiddich is since long unrivalled as the number one single malt on the sales list. Their sales are double that of the number two, which proves their total dominance over the market. Competition over the second place is tougher. Previously, *Glenlivet* and *Glen Grant* fought over this, but now a new competitor has appeared; *Macallan*, which has experienced a great expansion in recent years. The Fine Oak range, which was introduced to the market in 2004, contributes strongly to this success. Other single malts with significant increases in recent years are *Jura, Dalwhinnie, Auchentoshan, Glen Moray, Talisker* and *Bruichladdich*.
The top 3 are exactly the same as the last years when it comes to blended Scotch; *Johnnie Walker Red Label, J & B* and *Ballantine's*. There is, however, an interesting struggle among premium blends where *Chivas Regal* are putting great effort into reclaiming the top spot, assumed by *Johnnie Walker Black Label* a few years ago.
The success of *Johnnie Walker Green Label* and *Famous Grouse Vintage* proves that the interest for blended (or vatted) malt has increased. Their sales have in a few years reached the same levels as big-selling single malts such as *Laphroaig* and *Balvenie*.

Changes in ownership

2006 has been comparatively calm after the large restructuring that took place in 2005. That year Pernod Ricard bought Allied Domecq, Jim Beam bought Laphroaig and Ardmore and Diageo bought Bushmills. Despite this, one of the world's largest single malt brands, Glen Grant, was taken over by Campari from Pernod Ricard. Old Smuggler and Braemer were included in the acquisition. This was the last sale Pernod Ricard was forced into for competition reasons since they acquired Allied Domecq. It also marks the first time a Scottish distillery has had an Italian owner. Another whisky-related take-over took place in June when Cragellaichie Hotel was bought by London & Edinburgh Inns. A large number of whisky fans are keeping their fingers crossed that the reputable Quaich Bar will be unaffected by this change of ownership.
It is rumoured that Vijay Mallya from Indian United Breweries Group has made a bid for Whyte & Mackay, although there is no confirmation. That Glendronach has been placed on the sales list by Pernod Ricard is also, so far, hearsay while there is also speculation when it comes to a number of the smaller distilleries taken over by Pernod Ricard from Allied.

Changing of the Guards

Dennis Malcolm returned to Glen Grant from Balmenach where he had been for five years and John Campbell became the first Ileach to manage Laphroaig when he succeeded Robin Shields.
Drew Sinclair retired after 40 years at Dalmore and was succeeded by Andrew Scott.
Springbank's Frank McHardy now has the role of Director of Production for Springbank and Glengyle and new Distillery Manager at Springbank is Stuart Robertson from Cragganmore.
Iain Henderson took many by surprise when he left Edradour to help with establishing a distillery in Norfolk. Willie MacDougall became his successor. MacDougall was intended as Donald Renwick's replacement at Lagavulin but it was eventually Graham Logie who took up that position.
Another Islay manager, Stuart Thomson of Ardbeg, also left his post during autumn 2006.
Finally, Richard Cotton was recently appointed as Distillery Manager at Glenfiddich.

New distilleries come on stream

Two new Scottish distilleries have started production since last year; *Kilchoman* on Islay and *Daftmill* in the Lowlands. No mothballed distilleries have re-opened, but Chivas Brothers' planned sale of *Imperial* for real estate development has been stopped.

Two distilleries are planned in England. One is *Barley Bridge Distillery* in Staveley near Kendal in Cumbria which is to be headed by the previous Marketing Director at Arran Distillery, Andrew Currie. The other is *St. George's Distillery* near Thetford in Norfolk, initiated by Norfolk Whisky Company with James and Andrew Nelstrop as the main driving forces there.

Bottling grapevine

(see pp 240-243 for a detailed listing)

Benromach Organic, the first single malt to be fully certified organic by the Soil Association, was released and the first 15 000 bottles sold out in record time. The Swedish distillery *Mackmyra* experienced the same hectic sales; Their *Preludium:01* was first introduced at Whisky Live in London in March 2006 and was rapidly sold out from selected Swedish and UK shops.

Ardbeg released their oldest whisky ever; 1965 (50 years old). It was priced at £2 000. *Caol Ila* released their first bottling of an unpeated version.

Diageo made their last release in the Rare Malts series in November before burying the concept. The Six Classic Malts are now called Classic Malts Selection and encompasses not just the previous six distilleries but also another seven. This means that the Hidden Malts series has also been abandoned while Special Releases, introduced in 2001, will continue. Two new Distiller's Editions (previously exclusive to Six Classic malts) are also released in 2006; *Clynelish* and *Caol Ila*.

Benriach was one of the most productive distilleries during the year with no less than 16 new releases while *Glenfarclas* delighted their fans with ten new vintages, the oldest from 1952. *Glenrothes*, which has released vintages consistently over the last few years, surprised the market in autumn 2005 first with a 30 year old and then a Select Reserve (no age statement). *Macallan's* contribution to the 'very limited and really expensive' bottlings was a 50 year old in a Lalique crystal decanter, initially priced at £3 500.

An eagerly awaited bottling from Bruichladdich appeared in early autumn when their first Port Charlotte, called PC5, a peated cask strength at 63,5%, was released. Another new cask strength was the Nadurra from *Glenlivet*.

The Scotland/India whisky battle

The whisky battle between India and Scotland continues with increased fervour. The background in short:

The Scotch Whisky Association´s main concern is India's high customs duties of between 200 and 500% on imported whisky. They are also worried about the fake bottlings of Scotch whisky which turn up now and then and originate in India.

India, on the other hand, is upset that their own whisky cannot be called whisky according to SWA's standards as it is based on molasses instead of cereals. When SWA lobbied Indian authorities and explained that the imposed tariffs are against World Trade Organisation rules, the Indian Member of Parliament and owner of the conglomerate United Breweries Group, Dr. Vijay Mallya, accused SWA of being 'extremely hostile'. He also let it be known that if SWA did not let Indian produced whisky enter Europe they would continue to fight for the current duties. At the same time, rumour had it that Dr. Mallya was interested in becoming a member of the Scottish whisky industry by acquiring Invergordon Distillery from Whyte & Mackay.

Hopes of reduced Indian duties disappeared in early March 2006 when the Indian government decided to maintain the current levels and the SWA was extremely disappointed.

The debate intensified a month later when Dr. Mallya claimed that SWA's 'attitudes and policies are unacceptable and imperialist' and that 'India is not a British colony'.

A few days later David Williamson at SWA replied; 'If India continues to apply a duty system for imported spirits that is not in line with its international commitments, we will need to consider our options and may be obliged to consider pressing the EU to take the matter to WTO dispute settlement'.

In August, the European Commission, after an eight month investigation, determined that India´s duty system was 'a blatant violation' of WTO rules and if they did not abolish the system, the EU would bring the matter before the WTO.

Simultaneously rumours had it that Dr. Mallya was about to make a bid for all of Whyte & Mackay rather than just Invergordon.

The bottom line is that both parties want to have access to each others markets but for the time being positions seem to be deadlocked.

Distillery websites shaping up

Many distilleries have made a good job during the year regarding the design improvements of their websites. *Bunnahabhain* has made the best effort and has at last got the website it deserves. The flash journey, adapted to the country the web surfer is in, makes a great beginning to a marvellous website.

www.bunnahabhain.com

There is, however, still not enough news and useful information for the dedicated malt whisky fan on most distilleries' sites. *Bruichladdich* is a brilliant exception with useful and detailed information on bottlings, distillery equipment, history, barley, accommodation on Islay etc. The design may not be the trendiest but the content is outstanding. We just hope more distilleries will follow suit.

www.bruichladdich.com

For those of you wanting to dig deeper into the history of whisky, we have prepared a chronology on the following pages...

1644 The Scottish parliament instates a new law on Excise Duty to be paid for each pint of aqua vitae that is produced.

1698 Berry Bros. is founded.

1756 Arthur Guinness Son & Co. is established.

1774 A law prohibiting wash stills less than 400 gallons and spirit stills less than 100 gallons is passed.

1781 New legislation forbids private distilling.

1784 The Wash Act is introduced to encourage legal distilling in the Highlands.

1788 The Lowland License Act makes it difficult to sell whisky from the Lowlands to England.

1793 William Hill (Hill Thomson & Co.) starts up in Edinburgh.

1805 Seager Evans (producer of gin) is formed.

1814 Matthew Gloag embarks on a career as a whisky merchant in Perth.

1814 The Excise Act of this year states that the smallest size of a Highland still was to be 500 gallons.

1816 The Small Stills Act provides relaxation in the Highlands when the smallest allowed size of a still is changed to 40 gallons in all of Scotland.

1820 John Walker establishes himself as a grocer and wine and spirits merchant in Kilmarnock.

1823 An Excise Act states that a licence is required to suppress illicit distilling.

1826 Robert Stein becomes first to invent a patent still for continuous distilling.

1827 George Ballantine becomes established as a grocer and wine merchant in Edinburgh.

1828 J. & A. Mitchell & Co. (Springbank) is founded.

1830 Aenas Coffey patents an improved version of Robert Steins patent still which is named Coffey still and is installed for the first time in 1834 at Grange Distillery.

1830 William Teacher obtains a liquor licence for a shop in Glasgow.

1831 Justerini & Brooks is formed.

1831 Alexander Stewart & Son is founded.

1841 James Chivas forms a company as a merchant and grocer in Aberdeen.

1842 William Cadenhead Ltd is formed.

1844 Allan & Paynter, predecessor to Whyte & Mackay, is founded.

1846 John Dewar is established as a wholesale wine and spirit merchant in Perth.

1853 Andrew Usher & Co. starts to produce blended whisky.

1854 The volume of whisky produced in patent stills now exceeds the volume produced in traditional pot stills.

1857 Walter and Alfred Gilbey start their career as wine merchants in London.

1857 Joseph Seagram & Sons is founded.

1857 William and Robert Hill join forces with William Thomson and found Hill Thomson & Co.

1858 James and John Chivas found Chivas Brothers.

1860 Whisky now starts to be filled in glass bottles rather than stoneware flagons or jars.

1860 Roberston & Baxter is established.

1863 William Sanderson & Son is formed.

1865 Eight Lowland grain distilleries form Scotch Distillers Association.

1865 The passing of The Blending Act allows for malt and grain whisky being blended.

1869 W. P. Lowrie & Co. is founded.

1870 Greenlees Brothers is established.

1874 The North of Scotland Malt Distillers Association is founded.

1875 William Teacher founds William Teacher & Sons.

1877 Distillers Company Limited (DCL) is founded by six grain distilleries – D. McFarlane & Co. (Port Dundas), John Bald & Co. (Carsebridge), John Haig & Co. (Cameron Bridge), McNab Bros & Co. (Glenochil), Robert Moubray (Cambus) and Stewart & Co (Kirkliston).

1879 S. Campbell & Son is founded.

1882 James Whyte and Charles Mackay take over Allan & Paynter and found Whyte & Mackay.

1885 The North British Distillery Co. is formed.

1886 Distillers Company Limited (DCL) is introduced on the stock exchange.

1886 Alexander Walker brings in his sons to the company and founds John Walker & Sons Ltd.

1886 William Grant and Sons is founded.

1887 Highland Distillers is founded by, among others, W. A. Robertson.

1888 John Alicius Haig founds Haig & Haig Ltd.

1890 Mackie & Co. is established.

1893 McDonald & Muir is founded.

1894 John Haig & Co. becomes a limited company.

1895 Gordon & MacPhail is founded.

1895 Arthur Bell & Sons is founded.

1896 Matthew Gloag & Son establish The Grouse (later renamed Famous Grouse).

1898 The Pattison crash.

1906 Buchanan takes over W. P. Lowrie.

1907 Robertson & Baxter buys Haig & Haig.

1911 W. H. Chaplin & Co. buys Long John.

1912 Distillers Company Limited (DCL) acquires Ainslie & Heilbron Ltd.

1914 Scottish Malt Distillers is founded by the distilleries Clydesdale, Glenkinchie, Rosebank, St. Magdalene and Grange.

1915 Buchanan and Dewars merge into Scotch Whisky Brands.

1915 Immature spirits act requires that whisky must be bonded for two years prior to bottling.

1916 The bonding time is increased to three years.

1917 William Sanderson & Son takes over Carstairs & Robertson.

1917 Distillers Company Limited (DCL) acquires J. & G. Stewart.

1917 The Whisky Association, a predecessor to SWA, is formed.

1919 James Barclay and R. A. McKinlay acquire Ballantines.

1919 Greenless Brothers merge with Alexander & Mcdonald and William Williams & Son (owners of Glendullan) and is named Macdonald Greenless.

1919 Scotch Whisky Brands becomes Buchanan & Dewar.

1919 John Haig & Co. and Andrew Usher & Co. join DCL.

1920 Prohibition is introduced in the United States, based on the Volstead Act of October 1919.

1920 Bulloch & Lade joins DCL.

1921 James Calder & Co. joins DCL.

1922 Barclay & McKinlay buys James & George Stodart.

1922 Roberston & Baxter is acquired by DCL, Walker and Buchanan-Dewar.

1924 Sir Peter Mackie dies and the company changes name to White Horse Distillers.

1924 Peter Dawson and John Haig joins DCL.

1925 The Big Amalgamation – DCL merges with Buchanan-Dewar and Walker.

1925 DCL acquires W. P. Lowrie & Co.

1925 DCL buys Scottish Malt Distillers.

1925 DCL buys Macdonald, Greenless & Williams.

1926 Pot-Still Malt Distillers replaces North of Scotland Malt Distillers Association.

1927 DCL acquires White Horse Distillers.

1928 Distillers Corporation of Canada, headed by Sam Bronfman, buys Joseph E. Seagram & Sons and forms Distillers Corporation-Seagrams Ltd.

1933 The Prohibition ends in the USA.

1934 Arthur Bell & Sons buys P. Mackenzie & Co.

1935 William Sanderson & Son merges with Booth's Distillers.

1935 Seager Evans Ltd acquires W. H. Chaplin & Co.

1935 Seagrams acquires Robert Brown Ltd in Glasgow.

1935 Hiram Walker acquires George Ballantine & Son.

1936 Seager Evans buys W. H. Chaplin and the brand Long John.

1936 Lundy & Morrison buys Chivas Bros.

1937 Hiram Walker (Scotland) is formed.

1937 Sanderson & Booth joins DCL.

1942 The Whisky Association is dissolved but is reincarnated the same year as Scotch Whisky Association (SWA).

1943 Berry Brothers changes name to Berry Brothers & Rudd.

1944 DCL buys A. & A. Crawford.

1949 Lundie & Morrison sells Chivas Bros to Robert Brown & Co. (subsidiary of Seagrams).

1950 Seagrams buys Strathisla and transfers administration to Chivas Brothers.

1950 Seagram buys William Walker & Co.

1950 Douglas Laing & Co. is founded.

1951 Morrison Bowmore Distillers Ltd is founded.

1952 George & G. J. Smith Ltd and J. & J. Grant Glen Grant form The Glenlivet & Glen Grant Distillers Ltd.

1952 Justerini & Brooks merges with Twiss, Browning & Hallowes and form United Wine Traders.

1953 DCL purchases Train & McIntyre.

1956 Inver House is founded.

1956 Seager Evans is acquired by Schenley Industries Inc, which is owned by Glen Alden Corporation.

1958 Watney Mann is formed through merger between Watney, Coombe, Reid & Co. Ltd and Mann, Crossman & Paulin Ltd.

1959 Schenley International acquires Gordon Graham (owners of the brand Black Bottle).

1960 Edrington Holdings is formed.

1960 Whyte & Mackay merges with Mackenzie Brothers and takes over Dalmore Distillery.

1961 Ind Coope, Tetley Walker and Ansells form Ind Coope Tetley Ansell (later to become Allied Breweries).

1962 Seager Evans merges with D. Johnston & Co. and becomes owner of Laphroaig.

1962 United Wine Traders merges with W. A Gilbey and forms United Distillers & Vintners.

1963 Ind Coope Tetley Ansell changes name to Allied Breweries.

1963 John Crabbie & Co. Ltd joins DCL.

1964 Inver House Distillers becomes a subsidiary to Publicker Industries.

1965 Invergordon Distillers is formed.

1969 Rapid American Inc. buys Glen Alden Corporation.

1969 Allied Breweries buys Alexander Stewart & Son.

1969 Seager Evans changes name to Long John International.

1970 Highland Distilleries Co. buys Matthew Gloag & Son Ltd.

1970 Hill Thomson merges with Glenlivet & Glen Grant Distilleries and form The Glenlivet Distilleries.

1970 Amalgamated Distilled Products is founded.

1972 International Distillers & Vintners (IDV) is bought by Watney Mann.

1972 Watney Mann (with International Distillers & Vintners) is bought by Grand Metropolitan.

1973 House of Fraser buys Whyte & Mackay and Tomintoul through Scottish and Universal Investments (SUITS).

1974 Lonhro buys Whyte & Mackay.

1975 Pernod Ricard buys Campbell Distillers.

1975 Schenley sells Long John International to Whitbread & Company.

1976 Allied Brewers takes over William Teacher & Sons.

1978 Seagram buys the Glenlivet Distillers Limited.

1978 Allied Breweries buys J. Lyons for £60 million.

1979 Scottish and Universal Investments (SUITS) becomes a subsidiary to Lonrho.

1981 Allied Breweries changes name to Allied-Lyons in December.

1982 DCL launches the series 'The Ascot Malt Cellar' (Rosebank 8 y, Linkwood 12 y, Talisker 8 y, Lagavulin 12 y and the two vatted Strathconnan and Glenleven). This is the predecessor to 'Six Classic Malts'.

1983 Grand Met buys International Distillers & Vintners (IDV).

1985 Scottish & Newcastle Breweries sells their whisky division to Invergordon Distillers for £18.5 million.

1985 Guinness Group buys Bell's for £356 million.

1986 DCL sells A. & A. Crawford to Whyte & Mackay.

1986 Allied Lyons forms a Spirits & Wine Division named Allied Vintners.

1986 Allied Lyons buys 51% of Hiram Walker Gooderham & Worts.

1986 Argyll offers to acquire DCL for £2,5 billion.

1987 Guinness buys DCL, who merges with Arthur Bell to become United Distillers, for £2,35 billion.

1987 Louis Vuitton and Moët Hennessy merge into LVMH.

1988 Andrew Symington and his brother Brian found Signatory Vintage Scotch Whisky, an independent bottler.

1987 Allied Lyons buys the remaining 49% of Hiram Walker Gooderham & Worts.

1988 Allied Distillers becomes a new subsidiary to Allied Lyons and is made up of Ballantine, Long John International, Stewarts of Dundee and William Teacher.

1988 United Distillers launches 'The Classic Malts'.

1988 Management buy-out of Inver House from Publicker Industries.

1989 Lonhro sells Whyte & Mackay to Brent Walker.

1989 Whitbread's wine & spirits division is acquired by Allied Lyons for £545 million.

1989 Management buys out Invergordon Distillers from Hawker Siddely.

1990 Fortune Brands (then called American Brands) buys Whyte & Mackay from Brent Walker for £165 million.

1990 Guinness and LVMH in 12% cross-shareholding.

1991 Allied Lyons launches 'Caledonian Malts' (Tormore, Miltonduff, Glendronach and Laphroaig). Tormore is later replaced by Scapa.

1991 Allied Lyons buys Long John, including Laphroaig, from Whitbread.

1993 United Distillers sells Benromach to Gordon & MacPhail.

1993 Whyte & Mackay (Fortune Brands) buys Invergordon Distillers (and thus Bruichladdich, Tullibardine, Tamnavulin and Tomintoul) for £382 million.

1994 Allied Lyons acquires Pedro Domecq and changes name to Allied Domecq plc.

1994 Seagrams launches 'The Heritage Selection' (Longmorn, Glen Keith, Strathisla and Benriach).

1995 Allied Domecq plc sells Black Bottle to Highland Distillers for £12,8 million.

1995 Blackadder International is founded by Robin Tucek and John Lamond.

1996 Highland Distilleries buys Macallan-Glenlivet plc.

1996 Whyte & Mackay changes name to JBB (Greater Europe).

1997 Guinness and Grand Metropolitan form Diageo. United Distillers and International Distillers & Vintners (IDV), merge and form United Distillers & Vintners (UDV).

1997 United Distillers sells Balmenach to Inver House.

1997 Fortune Brands transfers administration of Whyte & Mackay to Jim Beam Brands.

1998 Diageo sells Dewars and Bombay to Bacardi for £1 150 million.

1998 Highland Distilleries changes name to Highland Distillers Ltd.

1999 Edrington Group and William Grant & Sons buy Highland Distillers for £601 million. Grant and Edrington form 1887 Company, owned 70% by Edrington and 30% by Grant.

1999 Gordon & MacPhail introduces their 'Rare Old Series'.

2000 Allied Domecq suggests Diageo that they jointly acquire Seagram Spirits & Wine, but Diageo declines.

2001 Pernod Ricard and Diageo buy Seagram Spirits & Wine from Vivendi Universal for £5 710 million (5,7 billion) on 21st December. Pernod takes care of the Chivas Group.

2001 Pacific Spirits, owned by Great Oriole Group, buys Inver House Distillers at a price tag of £56 million.

2001 West LB bank and management buy out the Fortune Brands subsidiary JBB (Greater Europe) for £208 million in October. The new company is called Kyndal.

2001 Chivas Brothers and Campbell Distillers form Chivas Brothers.

2001 Murray McDavid buys Bruichladdich from Whyte & Mackay.

2002 Trinidad-based venture capitalists CL Financial buys Burn Stewart Distillers for £50 million.

2003 Kyndal changes name to Whyte & Mackay.

2003 Robert Tchenguiz owns 35% of Whyte & Mackay while West LB holds 21%.

2004 Glenmorangie plc buys Scotch Malt Whisky Society.

2004 Ian Bankier, formerly Burn Stewart Distillers, buys Whisky Shop retail chain for £1,5 million.

2004 Moët Hennessy (owned by Diageo and LVMH) buys Glenmorangie plc for £300 million.

2005 Pernod Ricard buys Allied Domecq.

2005 Pernod Ricard sells Bushmills to Diageo and Laphroaig and Ardmore to Fortune Brands.

2006 Campari buys Glen Grant.

Whisky Magazine Icons of Whisky 2006

www.whiskymag.com

Distiller of the Year
Glenfarclas

Visitor Centre of the Year
Yamazaki

Retailer of the Year (single outlet)
Berry Bros. & Rudd St James`shop

Retailer of the Year (more than one outlet)
Royal Mile Whiskies

Hotel/Restaurant of the Year
Drumchork Lodge, Aultbea, Scotland

Whisky Bar of the Year
The Pot Still, Glasgow

Innovator of the Year
Compass Box London

Ambassador of Whisky
Christine Logan

Lifetime Achievement Award
Robert Hicks

The Annual Malt Advocate Whisky Awards for 2005

www.maltadvocate.com

Best Buy of the Year
The Dalmore 12 year old

American Whiskey of the Year
Sazerac Rye 18 year old

Import Blend of the Year
Black Bottle 10 year old

Import Malt of the Year
Highland Park 30

Distillery of the Year
Buffalo Trace

Pioneer of the Year
Bernheim Original Straight Wheat Whiskey
Woodford Reserve Master's Collection Four Grain Bourbon
Dr. Jim Swan

Industry Leader of the Year
Brett Pontoni

Lifetime Achievement Award
Michael Jackson

Spirit of the Year
Santa Teresa 1796 Rum

Brewery of the Year
Russian River Brewing Company

The San Francisco World Spirits Competition 2006

www.sfspiritscomp.com

The Best
Best of Show Whisky
Laphroaig 30 year old

Top Blended Scotch
Johnnie Walker Green Label

Top North American Whiskey
Rittenhouse Bottled-in-Bond Rye Whiskey, Kentucky

Double Gold Medal
Balblair 16 year old
Caol Ila 12 year old
Caol Ila 18 year old
Caol Ila 25 year old
Clynelish 14 year old
Cragganmore 12 year old
Cragganmore Distiller´s Edition 1992
Dalwhinnie Distiller´s Edition 1990
Glen Ord 30 year old
Glenfiddich 18 year old Ancient Reserve
Glenmorangie 18 year old
Lagavulin 16 year old
Laphroaig 10 year old
Laphroaig 10 year old Cask Strength
Laphroaig 10 year old Quarter Cask
Laphroaig 15 year old
Old Pulteney 17 year old
Old Pulteney 21 year old
Talisker 18 year old
Talisker 175th Anniversary
The Glenlivet 18 year old

International Spirits Challenge 2006

http://iwc2006.webexone.com

Gold
Aberlour 10 year old
Aberlour 12 year old
Ardbeg Lord Of The Isles
Auchentoshan 12 year old
Balblair 35 year old
Balblair 38 year old
The Balvenie Doublewood 12 year old
The Balvenie Founders Reserve 10 year old
The Balvenie New Wood
The Balvenie Portwood
The Balvenie Portwood 21 year old
The Balvenie Thirty
Bowmore Enigma
Bruichladdich Infinity
Bunnahabhain 25 year old
The Glenlivet 18 year old
Glenmorangie 30 year old Oloroso Cask Finsh
Glenmorangie Burr Oak Reserve
Hakushu 18 year old
Hibiki 21 year old
Hibiki 30 year old
Highland Park 12 year old
Lagavulin Distiller´s Edition
Lagavulin 16 year old
The Macallan Fine Oak 8 year old
Talisker 10 year old
Tamnavulin 33 year old

International Wine and Spirit Competition 2006 Awards

www.iwsc.net

Trophy Winners

Single Malt Scotch Whisky (15 years and under)
Glenkinchie The Distiller's Edition 1991

Single Malt Scotch Whisky (over 15 years)
Talisker 18 year old

Single Malt Scotch Whisky (Special edition)
Glenfiddich Ancient Reserve 18 year old

Worldwide Whisky
The Yamazaki 18 year old

Gold (best in class)

Scotch Whisky Single Malt

Cask Finish

15-16yo	Dalwhinnie Distiller's Edition

Highland

10yo	Morrison's Single Highland Whisky 10 year old
12yo	Old Pulteney 12 year old
14yo	Clynelish 14 year old
15yo	Glenmorangie 15 year old
21yo	Glen Garioch 21 year old
35-38yo	Balblair 38 year old

Highland Cask Finish

12yo	Glenmorangie Port Wood Finish
30yo	Glenmorangie 30 year old Oloroso Cask Finish

Highland Cask Strength

28-36yo	The Stillmans Dram 33 year old Tamnavulin

Islands

Islands	Talisker Distiller's Edition

Islands

10yo	Talisker 10 year old
15-16yo	Highland Park 16 year old
18-21yo	Talisker 18 year old
25-30yo	Highland Park 30 year old

Islands Cask Strength

25yo	Talisker 25 year old

Islay

10yo	Laphroaig 10 year old
12yo	Bowmore Enigma 12 year old
14-17yo	Lagavulin Distiller's Edition 1989

Islay Cask Strength

10-12yo	Laphroaig 10year old Cask Strength

Lowland

10-14yo	Glenkinchie The Distiller's Edition 1991

Speyside

10yo	Aberlour 10 year old
12yo	The Glenlivet 12 year old First Fill
14yo	Glenfiddich 1991 Vintage Reserve
16yo	Aberlour 16 year old Double Cask Matured
17-18yo	Glenfiddich Ancient Reserve 18 year old
20-22yo	The Glenlivet 21 year old
+25yo	The Macallan 25 year old Fine Oak
+30yo	The Balvenie Thirty

Speyside Cask Finish

12-14yo	The Balvenie Rumwood 14 year old

Speyside Cask Strength

13-15yo	The Balvenie Single Barrel 15 year old
28-33yo	Convalmore 28 year old

Malt Maniacs Awards 2005

www.maltmaniacs.com

Non-Plus-Ultra Award
Overall top scoring malt out of all 2005 Awards entries
Laphroaig 31yo 1974 49,7% bottled for La Maison du Whisky

Bang-For-Your-Buck Award
Entry with the best performance/price ratio
Laphroaig 10yo Cask Strength 55,7%

Pressure Cooker Award
Entry with the best performance/age ratio
Isle of Jura 5yo 1999 60,6% bottled for The Whisky Exchange

Internal Combustion Award
Entry with the best performance/ABV ratio
Talisker '175th Anniversary' 45,8%

Daily Dram Award
Best affordable, widely available, all-round single malt
Laphroaig Quarter Cask 48%

Single Starlet Award
Most exciting new release in 2005
Bruichladdich Infinity 55,5%

Top Sherry Cask Award
Best bottling exclusively from sherry cask(s)
Blairfindy 24yo1980 55,9%, Blackadder/Sun Favourite Taiwan

Top Bourbon Cask Award
Best bottling exclusively from bourbon cask(s)
Glengoyne 22yo 1982 'Ronnie' 53,6%

Warped Whisky Award
Best bottling matured or finished in 'special' wood
Edradour 11yo 1994 57,1% Gaja Barolo finish

Gentle Giant Award
Best un-peated, un-sherried and un-finished bottling
Macallan 'Coilltean' 1992 55% Samaroli, new American oak

Highlands Award of Excellence
Best Highlands single malt whisky submitted in 2005
Glengoyne 19yo 1986 'Ewan' 51,5%

Speyside Award of Excellence
Best Speyside single malt whisky submitted in 2005
Benriach 28yo 1976 56,9% Signatory

Islay Award of Excellence
Best Islay single malt whisky submitted in 2005
Laphroaig 13yo 1991 59,1% SMWS

Islands Award of Excellence
Best Islands single malt whisky submitted in 2005
Highland Park 36yo 1967 49,7% bottled for The Whisky Exchange

Lowlands Award of Excellence
Best Lowland whisky submitted in 2005
Carsebridge 25yo 1979 56,4% Duncan Taylor

Aeneas Coffey Award
Best grain whisky submitted in 2005
Invergordon 1964 47,1% Adelphi

Multiple Personality Award
Best blended or vatted whisky submitted in 2005
Ben Nevis 34yo 1970 'Single Blend' 50,3% Adelphi

Dark Horse Award
Ahead of the pack, off the beaten track
Craigduff 32yo 1973 49,4% Signatory

New bottlings

The number of single malt bottlings in a year is enormous, not least thanks to independent bottlers. Many of these bottlings are released in very limited numbers and sometimes in selected markets. Still, the possibilities for a whisky enthusiast to get hold of these new expressions have increased significantly thanks to well-stocked retailers selling on-line and offering worldwide shipping. It is virtually impossible to list all new bottlings during a year, there are simply too many and sometimes it is difficult to find information on them. In this list we have selected more than 450 that were released from late 2005 until autumn 2006. All bottlings (except for certain official ones) are listed with year of distillation, age, finish or special maturation (if applicable), alcohol strength and bottler.

Aberfeldy

	21		40%	OB

Aberlour

1995			60,7%	DT
1995			46%	DT

An Cnoc

1991	15		46%	OB
1975	30		50%	OB

Ardbeg

1974			51,8%	OB
1965				OB
1998		Still Young	56,2%	OB
1975	30			DL
1991	14		50%	DL
1991	15		50%	DL
1995	10		50%	DL
1994	11		46%	CAD
1994	12		46%	CAD
1993	12		59,3%	CAD

Ardmore

1993	12		46%	DL
1992	13		46%	SIG

Arran

	10		46%	OB
	100% Proof		57%	OB
	Cognac			OB
	Lepanto		59,4%	OB
	Cream Sherry		57,5%	OB
	Sauternes		56,2%	OB
1995	10		46%	DL
1995	10		53,6%	CAD

Auchentoshan

	18	Oloroso	55,8%	OB
1995	10		46%	DL
1991	15		59%	DR
1981	25	Red wine	57,2%	MM
1999			43%	DT

Auchroisk

1975	30		50%	DL
1993			43%	GM
1989	16		58,8%	CAD
1989	16		46%	CAD

Aultmore

1989	16		50%	DL
1990	16		60,7%	AD
1990	15		43%	IM

Balblair

1973	32		45%	GM
1966	40		43%	GM
1990	16		58,5%	CAD

Balmenach

1990	15		43%	IM
1989	17		54,6%	CAD

Balvenie

	14	Rum	47,1%	OB
	17	New wood	40%	OB
Vintage 1972			47,3%	OB
1979	27		52,5%	CAD

Banff

1976	29		52%	CAD
1980	25		53,1%	DT
1975	30		43,5%	DT

Ben Nevis

	13	Port	61,6%	OB
1963	40		50%	DL
1996	10		46%	DL
1975	30		64,3%	SIG
1992			57,2%	DR
1996			46%	DT
1998			43%	DT

Benriach

	25		50%	OB
	30		50%	OB
	40		50%	OB
1968	37		52%	OB
1972	33		45%	OB
1975	30			OB
1976	29		56%	OB
1978	28			OB
1980	26		55%	OB
1984	21	Oloroso	55%	OB
1986	19			OB
	15	Pedro Ximinez		OB
	15	Tawny port		OB
	15	Dark rum		OB
	15	Madeira		OB
	12	Port		OB
1992	13	Sherry	43%	IM
1995	10		43%	IM
1994	11	Port	59,7%	SIG
1968	37		47%	DT
1990			57,3%	DR

Benrinnes

1989	17		53,1%	CAD

Benromach

Organic			43%	OB

Bladnoch

1991	14		46%	DL
1990	15		50%	DL
1989	16		54,9%	CAD

Blair Athol

1993	12		46%	DL
1993			43%	GM

OB = Official bottling from the owner, AD = Adelphi Distillery, CAD = Cadenhead, DL = Douglas Laing, DR = Dewar Rattray, DT = Duncan Taylor, GM = Gordon & MacPhail, IM = Ian MacLeod, MM = Murray McDavid, SIG = Signatory

Bowmore

1990	16		53,8%	OB
1968	37		43,4%	OB
1995	10		46%	DL
1996	9		46%	DL
1991	14		46%	CAD
1991	14		56,1%	CAD
1989	17		49,6%	DR
1990			54%	DR
1991	15		57,8%	DR
1995	11	Wh. wine	46%	MM
1982	23		50,7%	SIG
1987			58,4%	DT
1982	23		58%	DT
1969	36		43,1%	DT
1968	37		40,5%	DT
1966	40		43,2%	DT

Brora

	30		55,7%	OB
1983	22		50%	DL
1982	23		50%	DL
1981	23		48%	IM
1981	23		58,2%	SIG

Bruichladdich

125th Anniv. 35yo			40,1%	OB
Waves 7			46%	OB
Links V Hoylake 14yo			46%	OB
3D third edition			46%	OB
PC5 (Port Charlotte)			63,5%	OB
Blacker Still 1986			50,7%	OB
Infinity sec. edition			52,5%	OB
Legacy V 34yo				OB
	12	Sec. ed.	46%	OB
1993	12		55,5%	CAD
1991	14		56%	CAD
1993	13		46%	CAD
1990			54.9%	GM
1966	40		42%	DT
1990			46%	DT

Bunnahabhain

18yo			43%	OB
25yo			43%	OB
14yo Pedro Ximinez			52,6%	OB
1971	35			OB
1989	17		50%	DL
1994	10		46%	IM
1994	10	Rum	46%	IM
1966	40		40,3%	MM
1968	37		42,1%	DT

Caol Ila

1997	8		59,8%	OB
1993		Moscatel	43%	OB
1995	10		46&	DL
1980	25		50%	DL
1994	12		46%	DL
1993	11		46%	CAD
1995	11		60,5%	CAD
1995	11		59,6%	CAD
1991	15		46%	CAD
1991	15		56,3%	CAD
1993	12		59,9%	AD
1992	13		59,1%	AD
1991	14		56%	DR
1996	10		43%	IM
1993	12	rum	46%	IM
1993	12		43%	IM
1990	16		46%	IM
1991	15	Red wine	46%	MM
1979	26		62,8%	SIG

Caperdonich

1966	40	Madeira	46%	MM
1994			40%	GM
1994			58,2%	GM
1995		Marsala	45%	GM
1968	37		40,3%	DT
1972			41,9%	DT
1980			53,1%	DR

Cardhu

1982	22		57,8%	OB

Clynelish

1991		Oloroso	46%	OB
1989	17		50%	DL
1992	13		57,2%	CAD
1993	12		60%	CAD
1993	12		46%	CAD
1992	12		59,9%	AD
1995	10		59,3%	AD
1993	12		43%	IM
1992	13		46%	IM
1990	16	Sauternes	46%	MM

Coleburn

1970	36	Wine	62,4%	SIG

Cragganmore

1988	17		55,5%	OB
1989	16		58,6%	CAD
1989	16		46%	CAD
1993	12		59,3%	DR
1985	21	Syrah	56,5%	MM
1985	20		54,9%	SIG

Craigellachie

1996	10		46%	DL
1970	36	Wh. wine	41,5%	MM
1989			54,7%	DR

Dailuaine

1994	10		43%	IM
1994	12		56,2%	CAD

Dallas Dhu

1979	27	Wh. wine	58,2%	MM
1965	30		48,3%	SIG
1975			51%	DT

Dalmore

1995	10		46%	DL
1989	16		56,7%	CAD
1992	14		62%	CAD

Dalwhinnie

1986	20		56,8%	OB

Deanston

	30			OB
1994	11		46%	DL

Dufftown

Singleton of Dufftown 12yo				OB
1993			43%	GM

Glen Albyn

1979	26		57,3%	DT
1974	31		56,7%	SIG

Glenallachie

1993	12		46%	DL

Glencadam

1985	20			DL
1977	27		50%	DL
1989	17		57,8%	CAD
1985	20		48%	IM
1975			54,4%	DR

Glencraig

1974	31		40,3%	DT

Glendronach

1990	16	Port	46%	MM
1990	16		55,9%	CAD

Glen Elgin

1985	20		50%	DL
1978	27		47,5%	AD
1991	15	Wh. wine	46%	MM

Glenfarclas

Ten new vintages				OB
Quarter Cask				OB
1972	33		43,4%	CAD
1973	33		42,6%	CAD
1988	18		55,2%	CAD

Glenfiddich

1973	33		49,2%	OB

Glen Garioch

	8		40%	OB
1994	11		46%	DL
1991	14		50%	DL
1993	13		57,6%	CAD
1988			55,8%	DT

Glenglassaugh

	19			OB

OB = Official bottling from the owner, AD = Adelphi Distillery, CAD = Cadenhead, DL = Douglas Laing, DR = Dewar Rattray, DT = Duncan Taylor, GM = Gordon & MacPhail, IM = Ian MacLeod, MM = Murray McDavid, SIG = Signatory

1960	44			OB
	22			OB
1978	27		50%	DL
1978	28	Syrah	46,6%	MM
1967	38	Wine	59,3%	SIG
1976			53%	DR

Glengoyne

The Stillmen´s Choice;				
1989	15		55,7%	OB
1986	19		51,5%	OB
1982	22		53,6%	OB
Mashmen´s Choice x 3				OB
Manager´s Choice x 3				OB
1995	11		46%	DL

Glen Grant

1992	12	wine	50%	DL
1996	10		46%	DL
1964	42		51,2%	CAD
1969			52,3%	DT
1974			49,8%	DT
1970	35		41,5%	DT
1970	35		54,1%	DT

Glenisla

1977	28		48,6%	SIG

Glen Keith

1991	14		50%	DL
1973	32		50%	DL

Glenkinchie

1987	18		56,5%	CAD

Glenlivet

Nadurra 16yo			57,2%	OB
1980	25		50%	DL
1985	20		50%	DL
1970	35		58,2%	CAD
1976	30		57,1%	CAD
1991	15		59,9%	AD
1968	36		43,1%	DT
1968	37		41,7%	DT
1970			54,8%	DT

Glenlossie

1995	10		46%	DL
1993	12		46%	DL
1966	40		50%	AD

Glen Moray

1963				OB
1964				OB
1989	Signature		57,6%	OB
1990	16		55.8%	DR

Glen Ord

Singleton of Glen Ord 12yo				OB
1967	39		50%	DL
1983	22		55%	CAD

Glenrothes

Select Reserve			43%	OB
1991	15		43%	OB
1985	20		43%	OB
30yo			50,2%	OB
1994				OB
1990	14		46%	DL
1986	19		50%	DL
1990	15		59,5%	CAD
1990	15		46%	CAD
1994	12	Rum	46%	IM
1993	12	Sherry	43%	IM
1968	38	Red wine	45,5%	MM
1968			57,6%	DT
1969	36		51,8%	DT
1970	35		43,5%	DT

Glen Scotia

1991	14		57,7%	CAD
1992	13		66,8%	AD
1991	14		61,6%	AD

Glen Spey

1977	28		50%	DL
1993	12		50%	DL

Glentauchers

1990	15		50%	DL
1990	14		58,5%	AD

Glenturret

1978	27		50%	DL
1990	15		50%	DL
1987	18		52,1%	CAD
1993	11	Port	43%	IM
1980	26	Rioja	47,3%	MM

Glenury Royal

1972	32		50%	DL

Hazelburn

	8	sec. edition	46%	OB

Highland Park

Ambassador´s C. 1996			58,8%	OB
1995	10		46%	DL
1990	16		50%	DL
1994	12		46%	DL
1992	12		50%	DL
1988	18		58,2%	CAD
1988	18		46%	CAD
1989	16		51,6%	CAD
1981	24		56%	AD
1979	27	Syrah	46,2%	MM
1967	39		40,1%	MM
1966	40		41%	DT
1967	39		43%	DT
1992			46%	DT
1997			43%	DT
1990			56,4%	DR

Imperial

1996	10		46%	DL
1991			43%	GM
1994			46%	DT

Inchgower

1980	26		53,2%	DR

Inverleven

1989	16		50%	DL
1987	18		57,9%	CAD
1977	28		56,5%	DT

Jura

1992	14		56,3%	CAD
1987	17		43%	IM
1987	18		43%	IM

Ladyburn

1973	32		40,2%	DT

Lagavulin

1976	30		52,6%	OB
	12		57,5%	OB

Laphroaig

1994	12			OB
1988	17	rum	50%	DL
1987	18		50%	DL
1988	17		50%	DL
1990	15		46%	CAD
1990	16		53%	CAD
1991	14		56,1%	CAD
1993	12		46%	IM
1999				SIG

Ledaig

1992	14		59,6%	CAD
1973	32		45%	IM

Linkwood

1992	12		46%	DL
1989	16		50%	DL
1989	16		55,8%	CAD
1985	20		60,2%	DR
1995	11	Port	46%	IM
1995	10	Am Oak	43%	IM
1983	23	Madeira	52,1%	MM
	15		43%	GM

Linlithgow

1982	21		61,4%	DT

Littlemill

1989	16		59,7%	CAD
1991	15		46%	MM

Lochside

1990	15		50%	DL
1981	24		59,1%	CAD

OB = Official bottling from the owner, AD = Adelphi Distillery, CAD = Cadenhead, DL = Douglas Laing, DR = Dewar Rattray, DT = Duncan Taylor, GM = Gordon & MacPhail, IM = Ian MacLeod, MM = Murray McDavid, SIG = Signatory

Longmorn

1987	18		50%	DL
1994	11	Sherry	43%	IM
1993	11	Madeira	43%	IM
1990	15	Red wine	46%	MM
1990	16		46%	CAD
1973			48,5%	DT

Longrow

100% Proof 10yo			57%	OB

Macallan

Fine Oak 17yo			43%	OB
Lalique 50yo			46%	OB
Vintage 1975			51%	OB
1977	28		48%	DL
1993	12		46%	DL
1983	21		50%	DL
1980	25		50%	DL
1980	25	rum	50%	DL
1979	25		50%	DL
1990	15		50%	DL
1985	21		50%	DL
1989	17		46%	CAD
1989	16		53,3%	CAD
1976	30		45,3%	AD
1989	17		58,4%	DR
1985	21	Sauternes	53,5%	MM
1969	37		41%	MM
1968	37		51,5%	DT
1986			56,5%	DT
1996			46%	DT

Macduff

1969	36		59,1%	DT
1969	37		54,9%	DT

Mannochmore

1990			46%	GM
1992	14		54,6%	CAD
1992	14		46%	CAD

Millburn

1969	36		50%	DL
1974	31		52,3%	CAD

Miltonduff

1994	11		57%	AD

Mortlach

1994	12		50%	DL
1995	10		46%	DL
1990	15		46%	IM
1968	37		45%	GM
1993			46%	DT

Mosstowie

1975	30		48,1%	DT

North Port

1977	29		51,4%	CAD

Old Rhosdhu

1984	22	Red wine	49,3%	MM

Pittyvaich

1990	15		50%	DL
1979	26		52,3%	DT

Port Ellen

1978	27		54,2%	OB
1978	27		54,8%	DL
1979	26		50%	DL
1983	22		50%	DL
1983	23		50%	DL
1980	25		50%	DL
1982	23		47%	IM
1983	23		45,9%	IM
1983	22		46%	MG
1983	23		46%	MG
1974	30		46%	SIG

Pulteney

1997	8		46%	DL
1990	15		59,5%	CAD
1969			43%	GM
1989			46%	DT

Rosebank

1990	15		50%	DL
1989	16		55,3%	CAD
1989	17		54,2%	CAD
1991	14		53,9%	AD
1990	16		46%	IM
1989	17	Wh. wine	55,3%	MM
1991			61,1%	GM
1990			55,4%	DT

Royal Brackla

1993			56,9%	DT

Royal Lochnagar

1971	34			DL
1993	12		46%	DL
1994	11		46%	DL
1996			59,6%	DR

St Magdalene

1982	23		50%	DL

Scapa

1992	14		60,6%	OB
1993	12		46%	DL
1977			57,9%	DT

Speyburn

	25	Solera	46%	OB
1980	26		61,5%	SIG

Speyside

1994	11		58,9%	CAD

Springbank

	9	Marsala	58%	OB
	11	Madeira		OB
	25		46%	OB
1995	10		50%	DL
1993	12		57,5%	DR
1974	31		57,2%	IM
1969	36		57,3%	IM
1991	14		53,9%	CAD
1991			51,1%	DT

Strathisla

1967	39	Red wine	43,6%	MM
1987	14		54,6%	CAD
1967	38		48,8%	DT

Strathmill

1975			49,3%	DR

Talisker

	25		56,9%	OB
	30		51,9%	OB

Tamdhu

1994	10		46%	DL
1977	29		50%	DL
1991	14		60%	AD
1990	15	Port	43%	IM
1994	12	Rum	43%	IM
1991	15		58,9%	CAD

Tamnavulin

1992	14		58,2%	CAD

Teaninich

1975	31		60,8%	DR
1993	12		58,3%	CAD

Tobermory

1996	10		50%	DL

Tomatin

1973 Vintage				OB
18yo				OB
1962 Vintage				OB
1965	40		45,5%	DL
1989	17		56,4%	CAD
1965	41		45,9%	DT

Tomintoul

Old Ballantruan			50%	OB
1967	38		49,2%	AD
1975			48,5%	DR

Tormore

1993	13		50%	DL

Tullibardine

1966	40	Vintage	49,8%	OB
1966	40	W Cup	48%	OB
1993	13	Sherry	46%	OB
1993	13	Port	46%	OB
Single cask 1987				OB
1972	33		43,1%	DR

OB = Official bottling from the owner, AD = Adelphi Distillery, CAD = Cadenhead, DL = Douglas Laing, DR = Dewar Rattray, DT = Duncan Taylor, GM = Gordon & MacPhail, IM = Ian MacLeod, MM = Murray McDavid, SIG = Signatory

Whisky Shops

We have selected more than 100 of the best places to buy whisky in Europe. Many shops also accept mailorders, either on-line or via email, while other only take mailorders. If you know of a good whisky shop that is not included in the list, please send us an email (info@maltwhiskyyearbook.com) so we can make sure it is included in the next edition of Malt Whisky Yearbook.

AUSTRIA

Potstill
Strozzigasse 37
1080 Wien
Phone: +43 (0)676 695 17 02
www.potstill.org
Austria's premier whisky shop with over 1100 kinds of which c 900 are malts, including some real rarities. Arranges tastings and seminars and ships to several European countries. On-line ordering.

Weinturm Linz
Kaarstrasse 11
4040 Linz
Phone: +43 (0)732 73 10 14
www.weinturm.at
A wine specialist with c 150 whiskies in stock. On-line ordering. Orders shipped mainly to Germany and Austria.

BELGIUM

Whiskycorner
Kraaistraat 18
3530 Houthalen
Phone: +32 (0)89 386233
www.whiskycorner.be
A very large selection of single malts, no less than 1100 different! Also other whiskies, calvados and grappas. The site is in both French and English. Mail ordering, but not on-line. Shipping worldwide.

DENMARK

Juul's Vin & Spiritus
Værnedamsvej 15
18-19 Frederiksberg
Phone: +45 33 31 13 29
www.juuls.dk
A very large range of wines, fortified wines and spirits. Around 500 single malts. Also a good selection of drinking glasses. On-line ordering. Shipping outside Denmark (except for Scandinavian countries).

Cadenheads Whisky & Lifestyle
Vintapperstræde 11
5000 Odense C
Phone: +45 66 139 505
www.whiskyandlifestyle.com
A whisky specialist with a very good range, not least of Cadenhead's bottlings (c 100 different). Also a nice range of champagnes, cognacs and rums. Arranges whisky and beer tastings. On-line ordering. Shipping to a few countries outside Denmark.

Whiskyhouse.dk
Peter Bangs Vej 74
2000 Frederiksberg
Phone: +45 38 878 670
www.whiskyhouse.dk
A large range of spirits and beers including c 400 kinds of whisky. Arranges recurrent tastings. On-line ordering.

ENGLAND

The Whisky Exchange (2 shops)
Unit 35, Waterside Trading Centre
Trumpers Way, Hanwell
London W7 2QD
Phone: +44 (0)208 606 9388

The Whisky Exchange
Vinopolis, 1 Bank End
London SE1 9BU
Phone: +44 (0)207 403 8688
www.thewhiskyexchange.com
This is a great whisky shop established in 1999 and owned by Sukhinder Singh. Started off as a mail order business which was run from a showroom in Hanwell, but since some years back there is also an excellent shop at Vinopolis in downtown London. The assortment is huge with well over 1 000 single malts to choose from. Some very rare single malts which can hardly be found anywhere else are offered much thanks to Singh's great interest for antique whisky. There are also other types of whisky and cognac, calvados, grappa, rum etc. On-line ordering and ships all over the world.

The Vintage House
42 Old Compton Street
London W1D 4LR
Phone: +44 (0)20 7437 5112
www.sohowhisky.com
A huge range of over 1400 kinds of malt whisky. Many are rare or unusual and attract collectors. Supplementing this is also a selection of fine wines. On-line ordering with shipping only within the UK.

Milroys of Soho
3 Greek Street
London W1D 4NX
Phone: +44 (0)20 7437 2385
www.milroys.co.uk
A classic whisky shop in Soho founded by John Milroy in 1964 but now owned by the retail wine merchant Jeroboams Group. A very good range with over 700 malts and a wide selection of whiskies from around the world. Supplementing this are selected fine wines. Tastings are arranged in the tasting cellar in the shop. On-line ordering for shipping within the UK. If contacted directly they can ship to other countries as well.

Whiskys.co.uk
The Square, Stamford Bridge
York YO4 11AG
Phone: +44 (0)1759 371356
www.whiskys.co.uk
Good assortment with more than 600 different whiskies. Also has a nice range of armagnac, rum, calvados etc. On-line ordering, ships outside of the UK.

Royal Mile Whiskies
3 Bloomsbury Street
London WC1B 3QE
Phone: +44 (0)20 7436 4763
www.royalmilewhiskies.com
The London branch of Royal Mile Whiskies. See also Scotland, Royal Mile Whiskies.

The Whisky Shop
(See also Scotland, The Whisky Shop)
Unit 1.09 MetroCentre
Red Mall

Gateshead NE11 9YG
Phone: +44 (0)191 460 3777

11 Coppergate Walk
York YO1 9NT
Phone: +44 (0)1904 640300

510 Brompton Walk
Lakeside Shopping Centre
West Thurrock, Essex
Opening November 2006

7 Turl Street
Oxford
Opening November 2006

3 Swan Lane
Norwich
Opening November 2006

10 Paternoster Square
London City EC1
Opening March 2007
www.whiskyshop.com
The first shop opened in 1992 in Edinburgh and this is now the United Kingdom's largest specialist retailer of whiskies with 10 outlets with another four opening soon.
A large product range with over 700 kinds, including 400 malt whiskies and 140 miniature bottles, as well as accessories and books. The own range 'Glenkeir Treasures' is a special assortment of selected malt whiskies. On-line ordering and shipping all over the world except to the USA.

The Wright Wine and Whisky Company
The Old Smithy, Raikes Road, Skipton
North Yorkshire BD23 1NP
Phone: +44 (0)1756 700886
www.wineandwhisky.co.uk
A very good selection of over 500 different single malts to choose from. There is also a range of bourbons, blends and Irish whiskeys. 900 different wines are likely to impress the visitor. There is a mail service, but not on-line. Deliveries within UK.

The Wee Dram
5 Portland Square, Bakewell
Derbyshire DE45 1HA
Phone: +44 (0)1629 812235
www.weedram.co.uk
Large range of Scotch single malts (c 350) with whiskies from other parts of the world and a good range of whisky books. Run 'The Wee Drammers Whisky Club' with tastings and seminars. On-line ordering.

Mainly Malts
3-4 The Courtyard, Bawtry
Doncaster DN10 6JG
Phone: +44 (0)1302 714 700
www.whisky-malts-shop.com
A good range with c 350 different whiskies of which 260 are single malts. Arranges tastings and seminars. On-line ordering with shipping also outside the UK.

Nickolls & Perks
37 High Street, Stourbridge
West Midlands DY8 1TA
Phone: +44 (0)1384 394518
www.nickollsandperks.co.uk
A company dating back to 1797. Mostly known as wine merchants but also has a good range of whiskies with c 300 different kinds including 200 single malts. On-line ordering with shipping also outside of UK.

Potstill
5 College Court
Gloucester GL1 2NJ
Phone: +44 (0)1452 301223
www.potstill.com
A very nice range of over 700 kinds of whisky. Also sells cigars, wines, ports, rums, beer etc.

La Zouch
2 Kilwardby Street, Ashby de la Zouch
Leicestershire LE65 2FQ
Phone: +44 (0)1530 412536
www.lazouch.co.uk
A combined restaurant and shop with an impressive range of whiskies; 400 kinds including 270 single malts. Also a wide range of wine and other spirit. Arranges tastings.

Whisky On-line
43 Coronation Street, Blackpool
Lancashire FY1 4NY
Phone: +44 (0)1253 620376
www.whisky-online.com
A good selection of whisky and also cognac, rum, port etc. A special feature is that the site is automatically translated into eight languages by Babel-Fish. On-line ordering with shipping all over the world.

Berry Bros. & Rudd
3 St James` Street
London SW1A 1EG
Phone: +44 (0)20 7396 9600
www.bbr.com/whisky
A legendary shop that has been situated in the same place since 1698. One of the world's most reputable wine shops but with an exclusive selection of malt whiskies. There are also shops in Dublin and Hong Kong specialising primarily in fine wines. Mail order for wine only.

The Lincoln Whisky Shop
87 Bailgate
Lincoln LN1 3AR
Phone: +44 (0)1522 537834
www.lincolnwhiskyshop.co.uk
Mainly specialising in whisky with more than 400 different whiskies but also 500 spirits and liqueurs and some 100 wines. Mailorders can be made by phone.

Arkwrights
The Dormers, Highworth
Wiltshire SN6 7PE
Phone: +44 (0)1793 765071
www.whiskyandwines.com
A good range of malt whiskies (c 400 kinds) and well-stocked on miniatures. On-line ordering with shipping all over the world except USA and Canada.

The Wine Shop (2 shops)
22 Russell Street, Leek
Staffordshire ST13 5JF
Phone: +44 (0)1538 382408

56 Lawton Street, Congleton
Cheshire CW12 1RS
Phone: +44 (0)1260 295 415
www.wineandwhisky.com
In addition to wine there is a good range of c 300 whiskies and also calvados, cognacs, rums, continental beer etc. They also stock a range of their own single malt bottlings under the name of 'The Queen of the Moorlands'. Mailorders can be made by telephone or email for UK delivery.

The Covent Garden Whisky Shop
3 Russell Street, Coven Garden
London WC2B 5JD
Phone: +44 (0)20 7379 4640
www.coventgardenwhiskyshop.co.uk
One in a chain of shops owned by independent bottlers Cadenhead. Sells Cadenhead's product range and c 200 other whiskies. Ordering via email or telephone.

FRANCE

La Maison du Whisky (2 shops)
20 rue d´Anjou
75008 Paris
Phone: +33 (0)1 42 65 03 16

47 rue Jean Chatel
97400 Saint-Denis
Phone: +33 (0)2 62 21 31 19
www.whisky.fr
France's largest whisky specialist with over 1000 whiskies in stock. Also a number of own-bottled single malts. Two shops and on-line ordering. Ships to some 20 countries.

GERMANY

Weinquelle Lühmann
Lübeckerstrasse 145
22087 Hamburg
Phone: +49 (0)40-25 63 91
www.weinquelle.com
A very impressive selection of both wines and spirits in this shop. Among over 1000 different whiskies of which 850 are malt whiskies. In addition there are 2500 kinds of wine and other spirits, including an impressive range of rums. General information about whisky on the site, part of which is in English. On-line ordering with shipping also possible outside Germany.

Celtic Whisk(e)y & Versand
Otto Steudel
Bulmannstrasse 26
90459 Nürnberg
Phone: +49 (0)911 450974-30
www.whisky.de/celtic
A very impressive single malt range with well over 1000 different single malts and a good selection from other parts of the world. On-line ordering with shipping also outside Germany.

SCOMA - Scotch Malt Whisky GmbH
Am Bullhamm 17
26441 Jever
Phone: +49 (0)4461 912237
www.scoma.de
Very large range of c 750 Scottish malts and many from other countries. Holds regular seminars and tastings. The excellent, monthly whisky newsletter SCOMA News is produced and can be downloaded as a pdf-file from the website. On-line ordering.

The Whisky-Corner
Reichertsfeld 2
92278 Illschwang
Phone: +49 (0)9666-951213
www.whisky-corner.de
A small shop but large on mail order. A very large assortment of over 1200 whiskies. Also sells blended and American whiskies. The website is very informative with features on, among others, whisky-making, tasting and independent bottlers. On-line ordering.

The Whisky Store
Am Grundwassersee 4
82402 Seeshaupt
Phone: +49 (0)8801-23 17
www.thewhiskystore.com
A very large range comprising c 700 kinds of whisky of which 550 are malts. Also sells whisky liqueurs, books and accessories. The website is a veritable goldmine of information about the whisky business and especially so when it comes to photographs of distilleries. There are 7500 photos of 168 distilleries. On-line ordering and will deliver outside of Germany.

Cadenhead´s Whisky Market
Luxemburger Strasse 257
50939 Köln
Phone: +49 (0)221-2831834
www.cadenhead.de
This first Cadenhead shop outside of the UK was established in 2001. Good range of malt whiskies (c 350 different kinds) with emphasis on Cadenhead's own bottlings. Other products include wine, cognac and rum etc. Arranges recurring tastings and also has an on-line shop.

Cadenhead´s Whisky Market
Ackerstrasse 145
10115 Berlin
Phone: +49 (0)30-30874891
www.cadenhead-berlin.de
Cadenhead's second German shop. Good product range with c 350 different kinds of malt with emphasis on Cadenhead's own bottlings as well as wine, cognac and rum etc. Arranges recurrent tastings.

Getraenkewelt-Weiser
Darmstädter Straße 97
64646 Heppenheim
Phone: +49 (0)6252 93190
www.getraenkewelt-weiser.de
A large assortment spanning over 1000 kinds of whisky. Much distillery information on the website. Arranges tastings and seminars. On-line ordering. Shipping only within Germany.

Whisk(e)y Shop Tara
Rindermarkt 16
80331 München
Phone: +49 (0)89-26 51 18
www.whiskyversand.de
Whisky specialists with a very broad range of, for example, 800 different single malts. On-line ordering.

Mara Malt-Rarities
Roland Puhl & Co. GbR
Cahenslystr. 14
65549 Limburg
Phone: +49 (0)6431-41176
Phone: +49 (0)6432-508690
www.maltwhisky-mara.com
Probably the main experts on rare whisky offering over 1000 kinds. Also arranges tastings. Mail orders by fax or phone. Shipping also outside Germany.

Single Malt Collection
(Whisky Wagner)
Hauptstraße 38
79801 Hohentengen a. H.
Phone: +49 (0)77 42 59 31
www.whisky-wagner.de
A very large range of Scottish single malts (c 600). Newsletter. On-line ordering. Shipping also outside Germany.

Whisky & Cigars
Sophienstrasse 8
10178 Berlin-Mitte
Phone: +49 (0)30 2820376
www.whisky-cigars.de
Over 1000 kinds of whisky and a large selection of cigars from all over the world. Tastings are arranged. No mail order.

Malts and More
Hosegstieg 11
22880 Wedel
Phone: +49 (0)40-23620770
www.maltsandmore.de
Very large assortment with over 500 different single malts from Scotland. Islay whiskies are well represented. Also a small selection of cognac, rum etc. Only on-line orders.

Whiskyworld
Ziegelfeld 6
94481 Grafenau
Phone: +49 (0)8555-406 320
www.whiskyworld.de
A good assortment of c 450 whiskies including more than 200 malts. Also has a good range of wines, other spirits, cigars and books. On-line ordering, shipping to Germany, Austria, Switzerland and Liechtenstein.

House of Whisky
Ackerbeeke 6
31683 Obernkirchen
Phone: +49 (0)5724-399420
www.houseofwhisky.de
Aside from over 500 different malts also sells a large range of other spirits (including over 100 kinds of rum). On-line ordering with shipping also outside Germany.

Whisky-Versandhandel.de
(Dixon & Sondheim GbR)
St-Pöltener-Strasse 71
70469 Stuttgart
Phone: +49 (0)711-8 56 07 50
www.whisky-versandhandel.de
Large selection of c 450 whiskies. Also sells shortbread, biscuits, marmalades and tea and arranges tastings. Only on-line orders.

Whiskyscheune
Maibacher Weg 2
61250 Usingen
Phone: +49 (0)6081-15896
www.whiskyscheune.de
Large selection with c 400 Scottish malts in addition to whiskies from other countries. Only mail order.

Whisky-Doris
Germanenstrasse 38
14612 Falkensee
Phone: +49 (0)3322-219784
www.whisky-doris.de
Large range of over 300 whiskies and also sells own special bottlings. Orders via email. Shipping also outside Germany.

Whiskywizard.de
Christian Jaudt
Grabenstrasse 25
66538 Neunkirchen
Phone: +49 (0)6841-7030844
www.whiskywizard.de
Large assortment of single malt (over 500) and other spirits. Only orders on-line, shipping also outside Germany.

Liquids
Heerstrasse 350
50169 Kerpen-Brüggen
Phone: +49 (0)2237-975491
www.liquids-and-more.de
A good range (over 200 single malts) and a fine assortment of whiskies from other countries. Also books and accessories. On-line ordering.

Whisky Depot
Poppenbüttler Landstrasse 1
22391 Hamburg
Phone: +49 (0)40-602 52 34

www.whiskydepot.com
Large assortment of over 400 whiskies. Arranges monthly tastings. Orders can be made via email.

Whisky Spirits
Wallstraße 23
60594 Frankfurt
Phone: +49 (0)69-96 20 06 43
www.whiskyspirits.de
Large assortment of over 500 whiskies. Tastings with different themes. No on-line mail order but goods can be sent home.

Dudelsack (3 shops)
Treibgasse 6
63739 Aschaffenburg
Phone: +49 (0)6021-219654
www.dudelsack.com
One of three in a chain with the two other outlets in Limburg and Mainz. All shops hold recurring whisky seminars. The whisky wholesaler Whisky Max is included in the chain.

Kirschgarten 4
55116 Mainz
Phone: +49 (0)6131-3297518
www.whisky-selection.de
Large assortment of more than 300 kinds of Scottish single malts. On-line ordering.

Bischofsplatz 1
65549 Limburg
Phone: +49 (0)6431-590388
www.dudelsack-limburg.de

Rolf Kaspar GmbH
Ruhrallee 59
45138 Essen
Phone: +49 (0)201-273418
www.adelphiwhisky.de
Agent for Adelphi Distillery in Germany. Arranges regular whisky seminars and has on-line sales.

Finlays Whisky Shop
Zum Köpperner Tal 42 B
61381 Friedrichsdorf
Phone: +49 (0)6175 - 798656
www.finlayswhiskyshop.de
Whisky specialists with a large range of over 300 whiskies. There is an impressive listing of 639 bottlings of Port Ellen on the website. Only on-line orders.

Der Whiskykeller
Wörther Weg 26
55606 Kirn
Phone: +49 (0)6752-94597
www.whiskykeller.de
Large assortment, sells only via email orders.

Grandwhisky
Saint-Priest Strasse 14 A
63165 Mühlheim
Shop: Bahnhofstrasse 60, Mühlheim
Phone: +49 (0)6108-8240987
www.grandwhisky.de
Has a good selection of Irish whiskeys as well as Scottish. Arranges tastings and has useful information on a number of distilleries on the website. On-line ordering.

Wine, Spirits & Cigars
(Whiskypack Spirituosenhandel)
Schnakenberg 15
31608 Marklohe/Lemke
Phone: +49 (0)5021-888150
www.whiskypack.de
Has a nice selection of cigars in addition to whisky, wines and spirits. On-line ordering.

World Wide Whisky
Eisenacher Strasse 64
10823 Berlin-Schöneberg
Phone: +49 (0)30-7845010
www.world-wide-whisky.de
A shop combined with a pub. Arranges tastings and seminars. Has a large number of rarities. Orders can be made via email.

Casa-Verde
Aehrenweg 14
79258 Hartheim
Phone: +49 (0)7633-10 18 56
www.casa-ver.de
A shop that also aranges tastings through its own whisky club. Orders via email.

Whisky24.net
Osterende 131/133
25813 Husum
Phone: +49 (0)4841 - 71842
www.whisky24.net
A whisky bar and restaurant which also sells whisky through on-line ordering.

Art of Whisky
Dorfstrasse 22 A
21640 Neuenkirchen
Phone: +49 (0)4163/826552
www.artofwhisky.de
Run by a group of whisky enthusiasts. Also has a selection of 'Bottled for Art of Whisky'. There is no shop but orders can be made via email

IRELAND

Celtic Whiskey Shop
27-28 Dawson Street
Dublin 2
Phone: +353 (0)1 675 9744
www.celticwhiskeyshop.com
More than 60 kinds of Irish whiskeys but also a good selection of Scotch. Also sells wines and other spirits. On-line ordering with shipping all over the world.

THE NETHERLANDS

Whiskyslijterij De Koning
Hinthamereinde 41
5211 PM 's Hertogenbosch
Phone: +31 (0)73-6143547
www.whiskykoning.nl
An enormous assortment with more than 1400 kinds of whisky including c 800 single malts. Also whisky-related items like decanters, books etc. Arranges recurring tastings. The site is in Dutch and English. On-line ordering. Shipping all over the world.

Whisky- en Wijnhandel Verhaar
Planetenbaan 2a
3721 LA Bilthoven
Phone: +31 (0)30-228 44 18
www.whiskyshop.nl
A wide selection of wines and spirits with no fewer than 1300 whiskies of which 1000 come from Scotland. Email orders.

Wijnhandel van Zuylen
Loosduinse Hoofdplein 201
2553 CP Loosduinen (Den Haag)
Phone: +31 (0)70-397 1400
www.whiskyvanzuylen.nl
Excellent range of whiskies (c 500) and wines. Email orders with shipping to some ten European countries.

Wijnwinkel-Slijterij
Ton Overmars
Hoofddorpplein 11
1059 CV Amsterdam
Phone: +31 (0)20-615 71 42
www.tonovermars.nl
A very large assortment of wines, spirits and beer which includes more than 400 single malts. Arranges recurring tastings. Orders via email with shipping to ten European countries.

Van Wees - Whiskyworld.nl
Leusderweg 260
3817 KH Amersfoort
Phone: +31 (0)33-461 53 19
www.whiskyworld.nl
A very large range of 1000 whiskies including over 500 single malts. On-line ordering.

Cadenhead
Rozengracht 232
1016 SZ Amsterdam
Phone: +31 (0)20-3306287
www.cadenhead.nl
Specialises in Cadenhead's bottlings (c 200 different) but also a good range of another 300 whiskies. Arranges recurrent tastings. On-line ordering.

Le Cellier Amsterdam
Spuistraat 116
1012 VA Amsterdam
Phone: +31 (0)20-638 65 73
www.lecellier.nl
A wide range of spirits, not least vodkas, wines and fortified wines. 200 single malts.

SCOTLAND

Gordon & MacPhail
58 - 60 South Street, Elgin
Moray IV30 1JY
Phone: +44 (0)1343 545110
www.gordonandmacphail.com
A legendary shop that opened already in 1895 in Elgin. The owners are perhaps the most well-known among independent bottlers. The shop stocks more than 800 bottlings of whisky and more than 600 wines and there is also a delicatessen counter with high-quality grocery products. Tastings can be arranged in the shop and there are shipping services both within the UK and overseas. The shop was refurbished two years ago and now attracts visitors from all over the world.

Loch Fyne Whiskies
Inveraray
Argyll PA32 8UD
Phone: +44 (0)1499 302 219
www.lfw.co.uk
This is a legendary shop in western Scotland with an equally legendary owner, Richard Joynson. Joynson is known as a person with a high degree of integrity who does not mince his words on whisky matters and also has a solid knowledge of whisky. Loch Fyne Whiskies are devoted to selling only whisky and whisky-related items. The range of malt whiskies is large and they have their own house blend, the prize-awarded Loch Fyne, as well as their 'The Loch Fyne Whisky Liqueur'. There is also a range of house malts called 'The Inverarity'. Loch Fyne Whiskies also publish the highly readable 'Scotch Whisky Review' which previously was produced by Joynson but now has authorities such as Charles MacLean and Dave Broom on the staff. Also on-line ordering with worldwide shipping.

Royal Mile Whiskies (2 shops)
379 High Street, The Royal Mile
Edinburgh EH1 1PW
Phone: +44 (0)131 2253383

3 Bloomsbury Street
London WC1B 3QE
Phone: +44 (0)20 7436 4763
www.royalmilewhiskies.com
Royal Mile Whiskies is one of the most well-known whisky retailers in the UK. It was established in Edinburgh in 1991. There is also a shop in London since 2002 and a cigar shop close to the Edinburgh shop. The whisky range is outstanding with many difficult to find elsewhere and they are skilled in finding odd types, such as grain whisky and Japanese whiskies. They have the most comprehensive commercial site regarding information on regions, distilleries, production, tasting etc. Royal Mile Whiskies also arranges 'Whisky Fringe' in Edinburgh, a two-day whisky festival which takes place annually in mid August. On-line ordering with worldwide shipping.

The Whisky Shop
(See also England, The Whisky Shop)
Unit L2-02
Buchanan Galleries
220 Buchanan Street
Glasgow G1 2GF
Phone: +44 (0)141 331 0022

17 Bridge Street
Inverness IV1 1HD
Phone: +44 (0)1463 710525

11 Main Street
Callander FK17 8DU
Phone: +44 (0)1877 331936

93 High Street
Fort William PH33 6DG
Phone: +44 (0)1397 706164

Shop Unit 1
Station Road
Oban PA34 4NU
Phone: +44 (0)1631 564409

28 Victoria Street
Edinburgh EH1 2JW
Phone: +44 (0)131 225 4666

Unit 23
Princes Mall
Edinburgh EH1 1BQ
New store opening September 2006

The Brands are Gathering
Retail Shopping Centre
Aviemore Highland Resort
Aviemore PH22 1PN
www.whiskyshop.com
The first shop opened in 1992 in Edinburgh and this is now the United Kingdom's largest specialist retailer of whiskies with 10 outlets and another four opening soon. A large product range with over 700 kinds, including 400 malt whiskies and 140 miniature bottles, as well as accessories and books. The own range 'Glenkeir Treasures' is a special assortment of selected malt whiskies. On-line ordering and shipping all over the world except to the USA.

Robbie's Drams
3 Sandgate, Ayr
South Ayrshire KA7 1BG
Phone: +44 (0)1292 262 135
www.robbiesdrams.co.uk
A whisky specialist with a large selection. Almost 600 kinds of Scotch malt whisky and another 200 whiskies, including a well-developed assortment of Japanese malts. On-line ordering service.

Luvian's Bottle Shop (2 shops)
93 Bonnygate, Cupar
Fife KY15 4LG
Phone: +44 (0)1334 654 820

66 Market Street, St Andrews
Fife KY16 9NT
Phone: +44 (0)1334 477752
www.luvians.com
Wine and whisky merchant with a very nice selection of more than 600 malt whiskies.

The Maltman
(S. R. & E. Barron (Dyce) Ltd.)
119 Victoria Street, Dyce
Aberdeen AB21 7BJ
Phone: +44 (0)1224 722208
www.maltman.co.uk
Specialises in malt whiskies from Scotland. A good range with almost 400 kinds, including a 'Collector's Corner' with some very rare malts. There is a mail order service, but not on-line. Only shipping within the UK.

Scotch Whisky Heritage Centre
354 Castlehill, Royal Mile
Edinburgh
Phone: +44 (0)131 220 0441
www.whisky-heritage.co.uk
The Scotch Whisky Heritage Centre is of course a must for whisky devotees visiting Edinburgh. This is a unique, interactive visitor centre dedicated to the history of Scotch whisky. You can join a tour and discover all the aspects of whisky making. The Model Distillery and the Whisky Barrel Ride are among the highlights. This five-star visitor attraction, which receives c 250 000 visitors a year, has an excellent whisky shop with almost 300 different whiskies in stock. The shop is open to the general public and not only to those who have taken the whisky tour. Do not miss the award-winning Amber Restaurant with its whisky advisor who advises guests when they wish to choose whisky to go with the food. The ingredients are mainly from Scotland and whisky is sometimes used in the cooking.

Robertson's of Pitlochry
46 Atholl Road, Pitlochry
Perthshire PH16 5BX
Phone : +44 (0)1796 472011
A traditional grocer stocking a good range of whiskies, including some very rare ones. Mail order within UK only.

Single Malts Direct
14 Gordon Street
Huntly AB54 8AN
Phone: +44 (0)845 6066145
www.singlemaltsdirect.com
Very good assortment including an exciting range of own bottlings. Good selection of whisky literature. Emphasis on on-line orders, shipping worldwide.

TB Watson Ltd (2 shops)
Fine Wine and Spirit Merchant
11-17 English Street
Dumfries DG1 2BU
Phone: +44 (0)1387 256601
www.tbwatson.co.uk
www.drambusters.com
Large selection of malt whiskies and wines. Also specialises in personalised labels for special occasions. On-line ordering services.

Spirit of Galloway
191 King Street
Castle Douglas DG7 1DZ
Phone: +44(0)1556 504654
www.drambusters.com
This new branch of TB Watsons displays a selection of 400 malt whiskies, along with a wide choice of other spirits and liqueurs from around the world.

Robert Graham Ltd (2 shops)
194 Rose Street
Edinburgh EH2 4AZ
Phone: +44 (0)131 226 1874

71 St Vincent Street
Glasgow G2 5TF
Phone: +44 (0)141 221 6588
www.whisky-cigars.co.uk
A company with its traditions established already in 1874 specialising in Scotch whisky and cigars. They have a nice assortment of malt whiskies (c 100) and their range of cigars is really impressive – no less than 160 Cuban cigars and 175 non-Cuban. On-line ordering with shipping all over the world in addition to the two shops in Edinburgh and Glasgow.

Cadenhead's Campbeltown Whisky shop (Eaglesome)
Reform Square
Campbeltown
Argyll PA28 6JA
Phone: +44 (0)1586 551710
www.wmcadenhead.com
One in a chain of shops owned by independent bottlers Cadenhead. Sells Cadenhead's products and other whiskies with a good range of, for example, Springbank. On-line ordering.

Cadenheads Whisky Shop
172 Canongate, Royal Mile
Edinburgh EH8 8BN
Phone: +44 (0)131 556 5864
www.wmcadenhead.com
The oldest shop in a chain owned by independent bottlers Cadenhead. Sells Cadenhead's product range and a good selection of other whiskies and spirits. Arranges recurrent tastings. On-line ordering.

Duncan Taylor's "Whiskies of Scotland"
Gordon Street, Huntly
Aberdeenshire,
Phone: +44 (0)1466 794055
www.dtcscotch.com
Duncan Taylor is one of Scotland's largest independent bottlers and has quite recently opened a new shop in Huntly which sells videos, books and DVDs on whisky as well as the whole Duncan Taylor range.

George Strachan Ltd (3 shops)
Station Square, Aboyne
Aberdeenshire AB34 5HX
Phone: +44 (0)13398 86121

Golf Road, Ballater
Aberdeenshire
Phone: +44 (0)13398 55452

Castleton, Braemar
Aberdeenshire
Phone: +44 (0)13398 41215
Traditional grocer with a very nice range of whiskies spanning more than 500 different kinds.

John Scott & Miller
15-19 Bridge Street, Kirkwall
Orkney KW15 1HR
Phone: +44 (0)1856 873146
www.jsmorkney.co.uk
The best whisky shop in the Orkneys. A very large range of whisky from all over the world and, naturally, a special selection from Orkneys' two distilleries Highland Park and Scapa. There is also a range of Havana, Dominican Republic and Dutch cigars.

Drinkon
Allanhill, Grange Road
St Andrews, Fife KY16 8LJ
Phone: +44 (0)1334 477333
www.drinkon.com
A large assortment of wine, whisky, armagnac, cognac and other spirits and liqueurs with c 200 single malts to choose from. On-line orders only and shipping within the UK.

Cairngorm Whisky Centre
Inverdruie
Aviemore PH22 1QH
Phone: +44 (0)1479 810574
Good selection of malt whiskies and especially miniatures. Also exhibits on whisky production.

Weespeydram
74 High Street, Grantown on Spey
Morayshire PH26 3EL
Phone: +44 (0)1479 873043
www.weespeydram.co.uk
Newly opened shop which has specialised in Scotch whisky (c 100 different malts). Small selection of marmalades flavoured by different single malts. On-line ordering with shipping all over the world except USA and Canada.

Scotch Malt Whisky Society
www.smws.com
A society with more than 20 000 members worldwide. They are specialised in own bottlings of single casks and release between 150 and 200 bottlings a year. Orders on-line for members only. Shipping only within UK (see www.smws.com for addresses to national branches of SMWS).

SWITZERLAND

P. Ullrich AG
Schneidergasse 27
4051 Basel
Phone: +41 (0)61 338 90 55
Another two shops in Basel:
Laufenstrasse 16
Unt. Rebgasse 18
www.ullrich.ch
A very large range of wines, spirits, beers, accessories and books. Over 800 kinds of whisky with almost 600 single malt. On-line ordering. Deliveries mainly within Switzerland.

Glen Fahrn
Fahrnstrasse 39
9402 Mörschwil
Phone: +41 (0)71 860 09 87
www.glenfahrn.com
A wide range of spirits, fortified wines and champagnes. A large selection of whisky, with over 600 from Scotland. On-line ordering. Ships within Switzerland and to adjacent countries.

Monnier
Büetigenstrasse 30
2557 Studen
Phone: +41 (0)32 373 43 53
www.whiskytime.ch
A large range of whisky including 600 single malts. Also grappas and champagnes. On-line ordering. Shipping mainly within Switzerland.

Eddie's Whiskies
Dorfgasse 27
8810 Horgen
Phone: +41 (0)43 244 63 00
www.eddies.ch
A whisky specialist with emphasis on single malts (more than 500 different). Arranges tastsings.

Scot & Scotch
Wohllebgasse 7
8001 Zürich
Phone: +41 (0)1 211 90 60
www.scotandscotch.ch
A Whisky specialist with a great selection including c 560 single malts. Mail orders, but no on-line ordering. Current pricelist can be obtained through email.

Angels Share Shop
Unterdorfstrasse 15
5036 Oberentfelden
Phone: +41 (0)62 724 83 74
www.angelsshare.ch
A combined restaurant, lounge and whisky shop. More than 400 different kinds of whisky as well as a good range of cigars. Scores extra points for short information and photos of all distilleries (also non-Scottish ones). On-line ordering.

Vinothek and Malt-Whisky Shop of Chur
Reichsgasse 61
7000 Chur
Telefon: +41 (0)79 437 54 44
www.malt-whisky.ch
A wide range of wines and spirits with c 360 whiskies. Also has a large assortment of miniatures. Arranges tastings.

World Wide Whisky - whisky on the internet

There is a plethora of internet sites dedicated to whisky. Many of these are, naturally, commercial mailorder services and can be found in the section on Whisky Shops on pages 244-249. On the following pages; knowledge, news and discussions about whisky is the most important when we select our own 20 or so favourite sites!

www.maltmadness.com

In our opinion, the ultimate whisky site right now! Starting in 1996 by Johannes van den Heuvel the site was supplemented a few years later by maltmaniacs.com (available at maltmadness.com). Here 24 very knowledgeable whisky lovers dissect, debate, attack and praise the varying phenomena of the whisky world. It is doubtlessly the most comprehensive whisky site there is. Read more in our interview with Johannes on the next spread.

www.thescotchblog.com

The Scotch Blog features on-line news and commentaries about the Scotch whisky industry. The author is New Yorker Kevin Erskine, one of the more outspoken whisky personalities. He has a well-developed business network which explains the valuable depth to the commentaries. He is also the author of the book 'The Instant Expert's Guide to Single Malt Scotch' (now in its second edition).

www.whiskycast.com

There are currently only two whisky-related podcasts on the internet. The first was Radio Whisky, set up by Tony Dirksen in June 1995 . The second and perhaps most reputed, is Mark Gillespie´s WhiskyCast, which was first broadcast in November 2005. There are between five and seven new broadcasts each month featuring whisky news and, above all, interviews with many whisky industry personalities. The series of interviews with Jim Murray are highlights among these. Broadcasts are in mp3-format and can be listened to on a computer or downloaded for later listening.

www.thewhiskystore.de

One of Germany's largest whisky dealers on-line. The site is available in English and German. 'Whisky for Beginners' and 'Whisky for Experts' are well worth reading. The most impressive part of the site is the 7 500 photos of 168 distilleries and there is also a listing of accommodation for those planning to visit distilleries.

www.whisky.de

Editor-in-chief for this German site, and for the newsletter Whisky Flash, is Dr. Clemens Dillman - a whisky enthusiast and author of 'W wie Whisky'. The book can be downloaded or ordered as an audiobook. Membership of the club Whiskymania is free and includes a monthly newsletter with whisky news. There are also other membership levels for paying subscribers where weekly newsletters and magazines can be received. The site has an active whisky discussion forum.

www.whisky-distilleries.info

A fairly new and very well maintained whisky site created by Jean-Marie Putz. It is absolutely packed with information about distilleries as well as history and recent bottlings. There are more general features on whisky making, the art of drinking and a glossary of whisky terms. Jean-Marie has also started a whisky forum and publishes a regular newsletter.

www.whiskyguiden.se

An excellent Swedish site with a sister site in English, thewhiskyguide.com. Thorough descriptions of most Scottish distilleries and many from other parts of the world. Has features on whisky regions, production, history and trips and tips on bars, books and shops with continuously updated whisky news. There is also a beer section, focusing on Swedish breweries, but with links to a large number of breweries worldwide.

www.thewhiskyguide.com

The English-language sister site to whiskygyuiden.se (which see).

www.whiskyfun.com

Serge Valentin, one of the Malt Maniacs, presents twice-monthly new, detailed tasting notes. One can, for example, find notes on 110 Ardbegs, 84 Bowmores och 56 Macallans in his archives. He is also a great lover of Brora and presents not just an excellent history of the distillery but also the probably most complete list of Brora bottlings in existence (all in all 144!). Off the malt topic, this site also has plenty of music reviews of both concerts and CDs.

www.scotch-whisky.org.uk

The official site of SWA (Scotch Whisky Association). It features descriptions of Scottish whisky history, whisky production and a directory of members with addresses and other useful information about most Scottish distilleries. Press releases and publications about the industry are also presented and there is a long Q & A section which covers most of what one would want to know about Scotch whisky.

www.lists.uni-karlsruhe.de/archives/malts-l.html

A whisky mailing list that has been around since 1995. The members are very competent and sometimes there are even postings from whisky industry professionals. The discussions are often detailed and the level of knowledge is high so they are interesting for those wishing to expand their whisky knowledge.

www.buxrud.se/whisky.htm

A great site by the well-known and respected Swedish whisky aficionado Ulf Buxrud. Buxrud, who also is a Keeper of the Quaich, lists much in the whisky world; current distilleries, lost distilleries, malt whisky producers outside of Scotland, all existing bottlings in Diageo's Rare Malt series, whisky literature and, importantly, a very complete compilation of links to hundreds of whisky sites.

www.peatfreak.com

Dutch Jeroen Kloppenburg has created this whisky site with features, tasting notes and hundreds of relevant whisky links. Peatfreak is probably one of the best sites sharing news from the whisky world. Choose between reading them on the site or getting them by email. It is also possible to download a free program that helps sorting and keeping tasting notes. On top of that, he holds competitions and games on the site (try the Mouser!).

www.onlymalts.com

This is Norway's best whisky site but it is only presented in Norwegian. Features on distilleries, whisky production, whisky history etc are penned by the editors or members. There are also travel tips, tasting notes of c 150 different whiskies, links to other whisky sites and a discussion forum.

www.whiskyforum.se

A Swedish whisky forum with a small, but not well-visited, section in English. There are 850 registered enthusiasts in the forum and the debate is rich in both quality and number of daily postings. A tasting calendar is presented and there is an archive of reviews with members' tasting notes of almost 1500 different whiskies.

www.scotchwhisky.net

A site that has compiled all basic information about the Scotch whisky business. There are some excellent features presented, such as whisky production and whisky history. It is also a useful site for finding updated news under the heading 'Whisky News'. Information on ownership and bottlings has, unfortunately, not been updated recently.

www.whisky-pages.com

A very recent (summer 2006) and excellent whisky site. Gavin D. Smith and Tom Cannavan, two well-known authors and writers in the world of whisky and wines, are behind it. The site has features, directories, tasting notes, book reviews, whisky news, glossary and a forum. Tom Cannavan is also responsible for wine-pages.com and beer-pages.com.

www.whiskynyt.dk

A Danish whisky site with emphasis on an active members' forum. Updated news on whisky is also presented. Unusual features are lists of whiskies that are artificially or naturally coloured, whiskies that have been sold under other names than their own and a cross-reference list to SMWS's bottlings.

www.whiskyportal.com

The Dane Dennis Klindrup has created a site with main features being whisky news (in cooperation with peatfreak.com) and a list of all the distilleries in the world one can think of (and a few unheard of). Klindrup does not present much material of his own about the distilleries but keeps a plethora of links which can take the whisky surfer to unexplored websites. There is also an impressive list of current whisky events. Those with an interest in rum will find a special section of over 180 distilleries from 49 countries.

www.whiskymag.com

The official website of the printed 'Whisky Magazine'. The best feature is by far the forum which is very active with over 2000 registered members. The site also includes whisky news, an exhaustive list of whisky links and 600 tasting notes from 'Whisky Magazine'.

www.maltadvocate.com

The official website of the American magazine Malt Advocate. One can find a selection of features from the magazine, a guide to retailers in the US, the editor John Hansell´s personal tasting notes for hundreds of whiskies, a small shop and upcoming tasting events.

www.scotlandwhisky.com

A rather new site by, among others, Scotch Whisky Association, Scotch Whisky Heritage Centre and Visit Scotland. The information about the various distilleries is good, but it only covers those with visitor centres. News and Events and suggestions of Eating and Shopping could be more thorough and updated. Improvements can be expected bearing in mind that the site is very new.

Confessiones of a malt whisky maniac

An interview with whisky enthusiast
and creator of maltmadness.com, Johannes van den Heuvel.

***MWY*: Johannes, how did your interest in whisky start?**

Well, my initial interest probably had something to do with the fact that whisky contains alcohol – a substance that can make you feel good (when taken in moderation, that is!). During the 1980's I actually preferred cognac over whisky, but that was because the only whiskies I knew at the time were relatively cheap blends like Grant's and VAT 69. When I had my first encounter with Lagavulin 16yo in 1991, I discovered that there was an entirely different class of whiskies that I didn't know about.

For the first few years I just assumed I had found a 'better' type of whisky and mostly stuck to a few favourites like Talisker 10yo and Lagavulin 16yo. The real 'madness' started around 1995 when I started trying more and more different single malts. This gave me an appreciation for the amazing variety in character and style within the world of single malts. Single malts are not just highly enjoyable drinks in their own right (well, most of the time); there's an entire world to explore beneath the surface. Even after a decade of heavy dramming and studying, I feel I've only scratched the surface.

***MWY*: Why did you decide to develop the interest in whisky into a website?**

I discovered the internet in 1995. I immediately fell in love with the medium and it soon dawned on me that building websites could be a nice way to make a living. However, at the time I didn't have a clue about how to develop a site. So, I just set up a few 'pilot' websites to get acquainted with the technology and acquire the necessary skills. Over time most of these sites were discontinued, but by the time my focus shifted from the technical side of the web to the 'conceptual' side, Malt Madness had developed a momentum of its own and with the help of the Malt Maniacs I kept developing it further.

***MWY*: Now, almost 10 years after the start, the site is a gold mine of malt whisky information with a Beginner´s Guide, Distillery Data, Tasting notes and the Liquid Log (recently turned into a blog). Is all the work you put into it just altruistic or do you make a lot of money from it?**

Hah! MAKE a lot of money? Until we managed to find a hosting sponsor, maintaining the site actually COST quite some money, so I guess you could call that altruistic ;-) Fortunately, after we found a hosting sponsor the costs for keeping the site running have been fairly minimal. I had to buy all the necessary software and hardware for other 'professional' projects anyway and many maniacs spend quite some of their free time writing for MM. That being said, I have been thinking of ways to generate some modest revenues through the site to make it completely self-sustaining and allow us to invest in some hard- and software that would allow us to lift MM to an entirely new level.

As for the massiveness of Malt Madness; in the real world I have problems with throwing stuff away. I don't just save a lot of my empty whisky bottles, I still have newspapers from the early 1990's that I haven't read yet and boxes of floppy disks with Windows95 software. Yes, I know that's a bit peculiar… And it's the same in the virtual world; very little of the material that was written for MM was ever thrown away. So, the site just kept growing and growing and growing...

MWY: **The contents of the site are initiated to say the least. Is it just for the hard core of malt enthusiasts or do you get response from beginners as well?**

Actually, that's a very good point. I still receive many questions and comments from relative novices but the focus of the content has indeed shifted towards the hard core SM fanatics over the last few years. That's one of the main reasons I'm currently working on a reconstruction of the site(s). One section (Malt Madness) will be focused more on 'beginners' while the Malt Maniacs section will be aimed at the real 'anoraks'.

MWY: **How do you go about obtaining all the latest information on distilleries and bottlings? Do you have a 'hotline' to the distillery owners and do they keep sending you samples they want you to try?**

One of the great things about single malt whisky is that it's a very 'personal' product. Over the years I've gotten to know quite a few people working inside the whisky industry as well as hundreds of other fanatics like me. Most press releases, news stories and rumours end up in my inbox sooner or later. In fact, this free flow of information is one of the reasons I fell in love with the internet in the first place. Thanks to the web, we don't have to depend on 'the media' to spoon-feed us advertorials prepared by ad agencies and marketing departments.
I personally think that, ironically enough, the malt whisky boom of recent years can (at least partly) be attributed to the rise of the internet. I think the possibility to freely share opinions and experiences with like-minded spirits around the world is ultimately more interesting than bagpipes, tartans and haggis.

As for 'hotlines' to distillery personnel and bottlers, they can actually be problematic, especially so when information is shared confidentially. Knowing how they made Loch Dhu taste as disturbing as it does, but not being able to share the story is pure torture! And it's always hard to give a severe score to an underperforming malt if you know the person that made or bottled it.

Still, I do my best to score each whisky as objectively as possible – which could be the reason why I mostly receive 'the cream of the crop' from the industry these days. As pleasant as that is for my palate, it could also give me a much skewed perspective on reality. Fortunately, I also buy bottles myself and I receive samples from fellow malt maniacs and members of our audience as well. This allows me to stay in touch with the day-to-day reality on the shelves of liquorists around the world.

MWY: **After some time Malt Madness was supplemented by the Malt Maniacs. Tell me a little more about that.**

A few years after I launched Malt Madness it dawned on me that the site had a critical flaw; it merely reflected my own, purely personal opinion. I despise the discontinued Loch Dhu 10yo mentioned earlier, but some people actually adore it. (In fact, I still receive at least three messages a month from people desperate to find a bottle.) Consequently, I felt that the website needed to offer room for different perspectives and opinions so that the readers can decide for themselves who's judgement they trust the most.

I started publishing some of my e-mail conversations with on-line whisky friends in 1998 and things sort of evolved from there. The first few 'certified malt maniacs' were Davin de Kergommeaux from Canada, Louis Perlman from the USA and Craig Daniels from Australia. In 2002 we published the first proper issue of our E-zine. The team now has 24 members from more than a dozen different countries all over the world. Our backgrounds are very different, but we are united in our passion for single malt whisky.

MWY: **Rumour has it that the whisky industry listens when the Malt Maniacs talk. If that is true, how does your work influence the distillery owners?**

Wow... now you've made me blush...
If we have any influence, it's probably because we've gradually attracted quite a loyal audience over the years. We still get quite a few visits from relative novices that drop by infrequently or find the site through Google, but we also have a 'core audience' of some 15,000 readers that visit the site at least twice a month.

I imagine that these readers are mostly the real fanatics like us. We don't just want to buy a bottle for Christmas or a birthday, but spend hundreds of euro's, dollars or pounds on single malts (and related paraphenelia) each month. I guess that makes us and our readers an 'interesting' target audience for the industry. Of course, the fact that esteemed whisky writers Charles MacLean, Dave Broom and Martine Nouet are members of the team doesn't hurt either.

Last but not least, since we don't depend on advertising or sales to keep the site running, we can write what we bloody well want. Everybody is free to express their undiluted opinion on whatever topic they'd like. Most of the malt maniacs seem able to excersise that freedom responsibly, and I strive to offer as many different perspectives on an issue as possible. I guess that the result could offer the industry a good indication of the opinions amongst the entire 'anoraks' community.

MWY: **Recently you have started a crusade against fake bottlings. How common is the problem with fakes and how do you intend to fight that battle?**

Well, the 'average' consumer in the 'average' market seems to be relatively safe.
The problem is especially prevalent in certain countries (we've seen recent examples from India and Taiwan) and especially on the 'collectors' market.

We used to fight the battle by publishing complete 'case studies' on-line, specifying how we determined if a certain bottle was genuine or not. However, we soon realised that we were providing the fakers with a perfect 'Guide To What Not To Do When Faking Whisky'. So, these days 'fighting the battle' consists mostly of warning people not to buy their whiskies at auctions or on eBay without solid guarantees.

***MWY*: You started the Malt Maniacs Awards in 2003, rating a load of current bottlings in different categories. Now a couple of years later this yearly event is eagerly awaited by a large proportion of the whisky community. How do you go about choosing the bottlings you put to the test and how is the testing itself carried out?**

Up until recently there has been very little choosing involved, actually.
We simply invited everybody in 'the industry' we knew to submit the bottles they wanted. During the first year we received a selection of contestants that offered a fairly accurate representation of what's available to the average consumer, but in recent years things have become more competitive. Not only are more and more sponsors joining each year, they submit more and more 'high end' bottles as well. That is one of the reasons the MM Awards 2006 has a preliminary round during which the 100 'best' contenders are selected by a jury for review by the complete tasting panel.

The tasting procedure itself is very straightforward. The contents of each (70cl) bottle submitted by a sponsor is divided across 12 50cl sample bottles. Each member of the tasting panel receives 100 'blind' samples by mail and has four to six weeks to come up with tasting notes and scores for all malts. This gives most maniacs the time to sample each submission two or even three times. As soon as all twelve individual scores are submitted, the average score is calculated. The average score determines whether or not a whisky earns a medal. Entries scoring 80-84 points receive a bronze medal, 85-89 means silver and anything scoring 90 points or more receives a gold medal. The winners of various awards are chosen from the medal winners.

***MWY*: Amongst the Malt Maniacs, do you tend to have a joint philosophy regarding certain aspects of malt whisky. I´m thinking of colouring, chill-filtering, wood finishes, cask strength bottlings, independent versus official bottlings etc. If there´s not a consensus amongst you, what is your personal view on these matters?**

If we have one joint philosophy regarding malt whisky (and life in general) it's probably about respect for the opinion of others. I don't think there's any one topic that all 24 malt maniacs agree on. Some see wood finishes as a pure evil that diminishes the traditional values associated with single malt Scotch whisky, while others look at finishing as a perfectly acceptable way to offer customers a wider variety of style and character. It's usually the same with other topics, but our respect for the opinions of others ensures that the discourse always remains civilised.

***MWY*: What are your plans for the future of Malt Madness / Malt Maniacs? How will the sites develop?**

We have big plans for the future, but when I write this we haven't figured out all the technical details yet. So, I guess you'll just have to browse by the website and see for yourself ;-)

***MWY*: Do you have any plans to expand into internet radio shows, podcasts, with interviews etc?**

Not at the moment – but that might be just because I never gave it much thought. One of the things I like about the 'website' medium is the interactivity that allows readers to pick and choose the information they want. I've always considered podcasts to be a more 'linear' medium and wasn't too interested, but now that I think about it it could actually be a cool thing. I should probably get one of the other maniacs to do the talking, though; I imagine my heavy Dutch accent would make podcasts by me fairly unintelligable ;-)

***MWY*: With the word malt in both of your whisky internet projects, one gets the feeling that you consider a malt whisky being superior to a blend or a bourbon. Is that true or do you embrace all kinds of whisky?**

This is another matter where opinions within the maniacs are divided.
That being said, I think the majority of the team indeed has a preference for (most) single malts over (most) blends, bourbons and grain whiskies should they be forced to choose. Fortunately, we don't have to choose most of the time – so, most maniacs do indeed embrace all kinds of whisky. In fact, a few maniacs like Lex Kraaijeveld and me get a perverse pleasure from tasting the most obscure whiskies imaginable.

***MWY*: What, in your opinion, is the single most positive thing happening in the malt whisky business today and the single most negative one?**

Positive: the fact that 'the malt whisky industry' is starting to listen to its customers.
Negative: the decline in the use of sherry casks versus the increase in bourbon casks (but that's purely personal; I'm a sherry freak).

***MWY*: Finally, the tradition invites me to ask for your favourite dram but since you´ve already stated that on your site, I´d rather ask for one distillery that never or rarely has let you down?**

I'd have to say Laphroaig. I'm an Islay freak and I've always been able to rely on Laphroaig to provide me with an affordable peaty fix. Admittedly, there are many magnificent Ardbegs as well, but they're not so affordable anymore these days.

Photo: © SWA

Books & Magazines

Charles MacLean´s Whisky Tales
Charles MacLean
Pages: 288
Publisher: Little Books
ISBN: 1904435637

In 'Whisky Tales', Charles MacLean pours a lifetime's passion and knowledge of Scotch whisky into an extraordinary array of anecdotes about this popular drink and those who have loved it, from Robbie Burns to Dave Allen. This is the perfect weekend reading for all whisky lovers - all sorts of 'drams' from ghost stories, tales of illicit smuggling operations and feuding between the Scottish whisky families, to poems and literary celebrations of 'the world's finest spirit' and Scotland's 'most generous gift to the world'. Wide ranging in its scope, yet served up in easily digestible portions, liberally spiced with quirky and unusual stories and quotations, 'Whisky Tales' delves seams which have been previously ignored and opens up long-closed galleries.

Rare Malts: Facts, Figures and Taste
Ulf Buxrud
Pages: 160
Publisher: Quiller Publishing Ltd
ISBN: 1846890071

A beautiful combination of coffee table book and essential encyclopaedia authored by the Swedish whisky aficionado Ulf Buxrud. He presents all 36 distilleries from Diageo's Rare Malts Selection with history, technical facts, flavour profiles, tasting notes and comments. There is also a chapter on whisky tasting and the full story of how Rare Malts Selection was formed. With Buxrud's devotion to whisky in general and Rare Malts in particular, there is probably nobody else who could be more fitted to write this tribute to some of the world's finest single malts.

The Scottish Whisky Distilleries: For the Whisky Enthusiast
Misako Udo
Pages: 576
Publisher: Black and White Publishing
ISBN: 1845021304 (second edition)

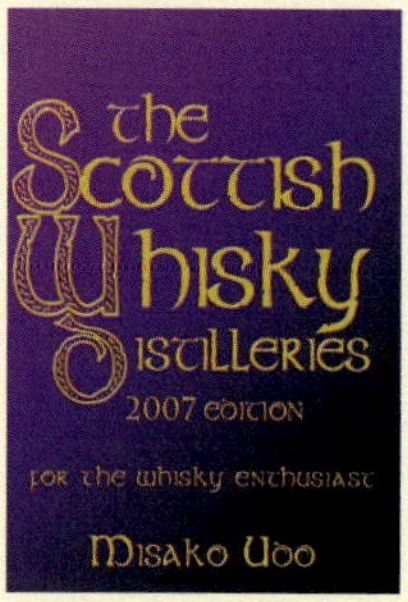

On the one hand, this book is not aimed at the whisky novice. On the other hand it is absolutely essential for the whisky lover. Technical and historical details of every existing and lost distillery in Scotland are presented on almost 600 pages. Misako Udo has made an incredible effort in providing us with this compilation. She presents a wealth of facts that are not described in any other book, achieved by visiting distilleries, interviewing people within the industry and digging deep into archive material. The first edition was presented in 2005 and here is now a second edition expanding the book with almost another 100 pages.

Whisky Bible 2007
Jim Murray
Pages: 336
Publisher: Carlton Books Ltd
ISBN: 1844421473

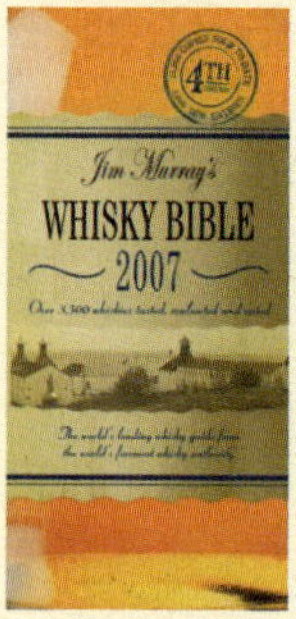

Jim Murray´s Whisky Bible was a roaring success when it was published for the first time in 2003 and is now, in it´s fourth edition, an annual bestseller. It is the first-ever ratings guide to all types of whisky including the more unusual ones from Australia, South America and Asia. Over 3 500 whiskies were tasted, evaluated and rated in the 2007 edition. Jim Murray is an authority on whisky and he writes in an entertaining and precise language unique for the genre.

Whisky

Aeneas MacDonald
Pages: 176
Publisher: Canongate Books Ltd
ISBN: 1841958573

This book was first published in 1930 and in many ways it was the first time a book described Scotch whisky from the drinker's perspective. MacDonald, or George Malcolm Thomson as his real name was, is passionate when he describes why whisky means so much to Scotland and describes when, why and how it should be drunk. Despite being written 75 years ago, MacDonald takes a modern approach to promoting single malt. The well-known author Ian Buxton can be thanked for making this new reprint available.

Instant Expert´s Guide to Single Malt Scotch

Kevin Erskine
Pages: 100
Publisher: Doceon Press
ISBN: 0977199118 (second edition)

The ultimate book for those who wish to learn about whisky but do not know where to start in the apparent jumble of brands and technical terms. Kevin Erskine lends a guiding hand through the world of Scottish single malts. He knows which areas that confuse beginners and is methodical and meticulous in his writing. The book is very educational and refreshingly removed from the snobbism that can be encountered in the world of whisky and whisky drinking. Kevin Erskine is also the editor of thescotchblog.com.

Whisky Classified

David Wishart
Pages: 224
Publisher: Pavilion Books
ISBN: 1862057168

David Wishart tries out a different angle when he presents us with a new flavour profile. He identifies twelve dimensions to the aroma and flavour and the book reviews all the principal malt whiskies that span the flavour spectrum. Wishart has a new and fresh approach, which will be helpful to those having difficulties in assimilating the contemporary style of tasting notes. The book also includes a short description of each distillery and covers the history of whisky-making as well as production methods.

Whisky - The Definitive World Guide

Michael Jackson
Pages: 288
Publisher: Dorling Kindersley Ltd
ISBN: 0751344346

The latest book from Michael Jackson is a combination of a coffee table book and an encyclopedia of whiskies of the world. It treats all varieties from all corners of the earth. It appears up-to-date regarding new distilleries starting up all over the world. Jackson is the main author but there are also contributions from well-known authors such as Dave Broom, Martine Nouet, Jürgen Deibel and Ian Wisniewski. The first 85 pages are devoted to the processes that affect the taste of the final whisky. The following chapters treat e g peat and malting in detail. Pot stills and column stills are presented in a clear way previously unheard of. The influence of wood and maturation is thoroughly covered. This is followed by a section on the whisky countries and the different distilleries. A well-written book crammed with facts! The layout is the best we have seen from a whisky book and it has many beautiful photographs.

Enjoying Malt Whisky

Pär Caldenby
Pages: 208
Publisher: Pär Caldenby
ISBN: 9163181169

Swedish whisky enthusiast Pär Caldenby gives an affectionate amateur's (i. e. a person without commercial interest in / ties to the industry) view on whisky and whisky making. He is anything but an amateur when it comes to understanding the different production stages leading to good whisky. The description of these cover one third of the book and is also the best part. Caldenby is not afraid of questioning and analyzing and gives the reader new insights into the subject. Half of the book is more of a traditional distillery directory with a short history, description of the distilleries´ equipment and a couple of tasting notes. The book is personally written with great affection and devotion to the subject.

The Road To Craigellachie

Hans Offringa
Pages: 190
Publisher: Lipstick Publishing
ISBN: 1904762123

A refreshingly different whisky book without a single tasting note. During a three-day visit to his beloved Craigellachie Hotel in May 2003, Hans Offringa takes us on a journey through time and through Scotland. He tells how his love of whisky began and of all the encounters he has experienced on his journeys in Scotland. The book is written in a humorous style and is a must for anybody contemplating a whisky trip to Scotland.

Still Going Strong: A History of Scotch Whisky Advertising

John Hughes
Pages: 120
Publisher: Tempus Publishing Ltd
ISBN: 0752431749

Johnnie Walker Red Label, Black & White, Bells, J&B, Talisker, Lagavulin - all world famous brands, but what were their origins and what is their history? Whisky, perhaps Scotland's most famous export, has been produced for centuries, but in the nineteenth century, production moved away from small stills to the sort of mass production we see today. With the growth in larger distilleries, there was matching growth in whisky branding and advertising. Scotch, whether malt or blended is now produced by large companies, and the brands are known the world over.

Worts, Worms & Washbacks

John McDougall & Gavin D. Smith
Pages: 208
Publisher: The Angels' Share
ISBN: 1897784651

This is the story of Scotch whisky-making told by an insider, the legendary John McDougall. The book covers the period between 1963 and 1999 during which McDougall worked in distilleries in Speyside, Ayrshire, Islay and Campbeltown before setting up his own business in Kelso. He describes encounters with characters at the different distilleries in a very personal style. The reader gets an insight in the daily work in mashrooms and stillrooms and the changes that the industry has undergone during this 35-year period. Gavin D. Smith, author of many whisky books, has taken down McDougall's experiences.

How to Blend Scotch Whisky

Alfred Barnard
Pages: 36
Publisher: Schobert´s Whisky Watch

When referring to Barnard today one associates to his major tome 'The Whisky Distilleries of the United Kingdom' where he describes, in great detail, the over 150 distilleries he visited on his journeys. A since long forgotten book by the same author has now been published thanks to German whisky author Walter Schobert who discovered it in the Museum of Islay Life and decided to make a reprint in the same craftsmanlike style typical for the time. Barnard takes us through the different stages of creating a blended whisky and there are also contemporary descriptions from the turn of the century of Lagavulin, Laphroaig and Craigellachie. The book is only sold through the Museum of Islay Life to which all profits go.

Whisky: Technology, Production and Marketing

Inge Russell
Pages: 384
Publisher: Academic Press Inc.,U.S.
ISBN: 0126692025

The book explains, in technical terms, the science and technology of producing whisky, combined with stories from industry experts on how to market the product successfully. World experts on Scotch whisky provide detailed insight into whisky production from the processing of raw materials, to the fermentation, distillation, maturation, blending, production of co-products and quality testing. Important information on the methodology used for packaging and marketing whisky in the 21st century is also covered. This is a book for whisky aficionados wishing to take their interest to the next level.

The Malt Whisky Guide
David Stirk
Pages: 256
Publisher: GW Publishing
ISBN: 0953539741

The book covers 140 of the most popular Scottish single malt whiskies. Texts written in a personal style describe each distillery's history and peculiarities followed by tasting notes. Stirk has focused on malts which in most cases are readily available increasing the book's usefulness. High-quality photographic material is provided by Derek Wallace.

The Distilleries of Campbeltown
David Stirk
Pages: 160
Publisher: The Angel´s Share
ISBN: 1903238846

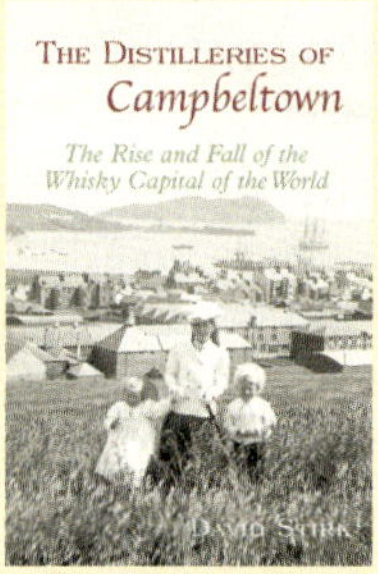

A brand new book about the rise and fall of Campbeltown, once the whisky capital of the world. How did this remote fishing port and royal burgh become the epicentre of Scotland´s greatest export? David Stirk reveals all in this engaging and well illustrated insight into the people who were the movers and shakers behind this huge industry.

Scotch Whisky: A Liquid History
Charles MacLean
Pages: 288
Publisher: Cassell Illustrated
ISBN: 1844034011

One of the most readable whisky books and definitively the most complete covering the colourful history of whisky. MacLean does not merely content himself with describing the history but puts it into a wider context by analysing and explaining the developments.
It is apparent throughout how closely knit Scotch whisky is with the country it stems from and the people who live there. Or, as the author concludes: 'Scotch whisky is far more than merely "liquor in a bottle". It is the very soul of Scotland; truly, the "Spirit of Scotland"'.

Malt Whisky Companion
Michael Jackson
Pages: 448
Publisher: Dorling Kindersley Ltd
ISBN: 1405302348

The Malt Whisky Companion is of course an essential read for any whisky connoisseur. When it was first published it was the first book to describe and rate a large number of single malts from every distillery. This latest edition has seen Jackson sample over 1 000 varieties. Apart from the ratings, each distillery's history and background is treated briefly. The Malt Whisky Companion is a perennial bestseller and most real enthusiasts probably have a copy of each edition on their bookshelves.

Scotland and its Whiskies
Michael Jackson
Pages: 144
Publisher: Duncan Baird Publishers
ISBN: 1844831221

A different book which is a description of a pilgrimage through whisky country. Michael Jackson produces images from his travels through Scotland and succeeds in linking together the whisky with the country and its inhabitants. The magnificent photographs taken by his travelling companion Harry Cory Wright evoke the magic feel and diversity of Scotland´s moors, hills and coasts.

MacLeans´s Miscellany of Whisky
Charles MacLean
Pages: 256
Publisher: Little Books Ltd
ISBN: 1904435238

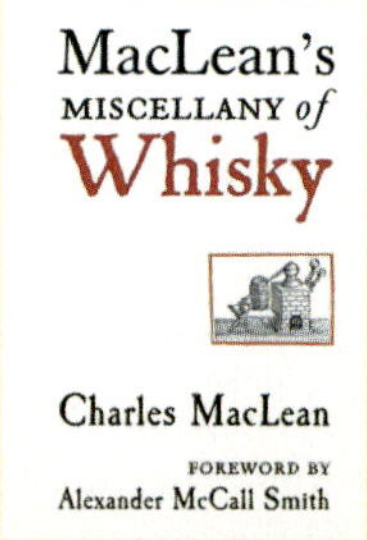

Charles MacLean takes a look at myths and facts from the world of whisky. He presents his thorough knowledge of this wide subject in an entertaining and methodical way. Some questions that are answered are: How has whisky changed over the past hundred years and why? Why have some distilleries closed, while others have flourished? And last but not least - are there really three degrees of drunkenness?

Malt Whisky
Charles MacLean
Pages: 176
Publisher: Mitchell Beazley
ISBN: 1845332407 (revised 2006)

The book is divided into sections with the first covering history from the early distilling in the Middle East to the present time. The next section describes how whisky is made and explains why each malt whisky tastes so different. Thereafter the author describes how to best enjoy malt whisky and the chemical derivation of flavour. A run-through of the different whisky regions does not merely offer whisky, but also culture, nature and history. The final section is a detailed survey of all the malt whisky distilleries operating in Scotland since World War II. The text is, in true MacLean-style, personal and well-informed. Excellent photos by Jason Lowe add extra value.

The Whisky Men
Gavin D Smith
Pages: 288
Publisher: Birlinn Ltd
ISBN: 1841582999

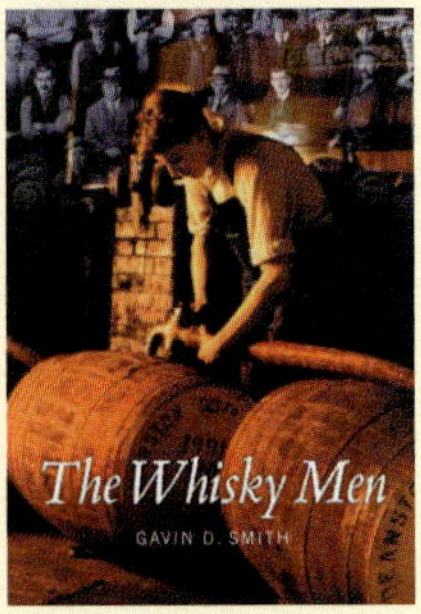

Warehousemen, mashmen, stillmen, coopers, coppersmiths, excisemen, managers, owners and even the occasional illicit distiller give us a unique insight into what the whisky industry has been like to work in during the past half century or so, and how it has changed during that time

Peat Smoke and Spirit
Andrew Jefford
Pages: 416
Publisher: Headline Book Publishing
ISBN: 0747245789

This is the ultimate book on Islay and its whiskies. Islay´s fascinating story is uncovered; from its history and stories of the many shipwrecks which litter its shores, to intimate descriptions of the beautiful wildlife, landscape and topography of the island. The story of seven distilleries and their whisky is interwoven.

Scotch Missed - Scotland´s Lost Distilleries
Brian Townsend
Pages: 208
Publisher: The Angel´s Share
ISBN: 189778497X

This is the definitive book on closed and mothballed distilleries in Scotland and the only one so far. Brian Townsend has compiled information on the many distilleries that haven't survived for one reason or another. A remarkable book with lots of historical black and white photographs.

A to Z of Whisky
Gavin D Smith
Pages: 224
Publisher: Neil Wilson Publishing Ltd
ISBN: 189778466X

The complete A-Z of the world of whisky. Definitions, derivations, sources and meanings of every conceivable whisky-related word are included - from aftershots to wort.

Visiting Distilleries
Duncan and Wendy Graham
Pages: 128
Publisher: The Angel´s Share
ISBN: 1903238641

The first-ever visitor´s guide to whisky distilleries.
The first part of the book deals with the production of whisky and a brief history of distilling in Scotland.
The second and major part is an A-Z of more than 40 distilleries and other related facilities.
These are described comprehensively and are given a 1-7-still rating for overall performance.

Whisky Uisge Beatha - The Water Of Life
Helen Arthur
Pages: 224
Publisher: Firefly Books
ISBN: 1552094251

This is a comprehensive compendium covering the early history of whisky until the present day. Some chapters contain stories untold in other books, for example the sections on well-known whisky families. Another example is 'The Culture of Whisky' where Arthur gives a penetrating account of whisky advertising among other things. Her background as a public relations and advertising consultant for over 20 years gives extra weight.

Scotch - The Whisky Of Scotland In Fact And Story
Sir Robert Bruce Lockhart
Pages: 192
Publisher: Neil Wilson Publishing Ltd
ISBN: 1897784376

A classic work on Scotch and its origins. This book, first published in 1951, was unavailable from 1981 until its re-issue in 1995. This edition was updated and revised by the author´s son Robin. Covering some of the lesser known episodes in the industry´s history and illustrated with anecdotes, this book remains essential for the whisky bookshelf.

Whisk(e)y Treasury
Walter Schobert
Pages: 464
Publisher: The Angel´s Share
ISBN: 1903238013

A milestone in whisky reference books! First published in 1999 as Das Whisky Lexikon this is a truly prodigious reference work covering brands, personalities, blends, distilleries, companies and technical terms.

The Whisky Barons
Allen Andrews
Pages: 128
Publisher: Neil Wilson Publishing Ltd
ISBN: 1897784848

The success of today´s whisky industry is largely due to the commercial drive and foresight of a select group of whisky merchants who took the business by storm in the late 18th and early 19th centuries. This is the story of how Dewar, Buchanan, Walker, Bell and Mackie established their brands and kick-started the industry.

Scotland´s Malt Whisky Distilleries
John Hughes
Pages: 120
Publisher: Tempus Publishing Ltd
ISBN: 0752425927

This is the story of the distilleries that survived during the years and why. The story is one of politics, taxation, social history, location, supply and demand. Illustrated with around 175 colour illustrations of distilleries.

The Island Whisky Trail
Neil Wilson
Pages: 160
Publisher: The Angel´s Share
ISBN: 1903238498

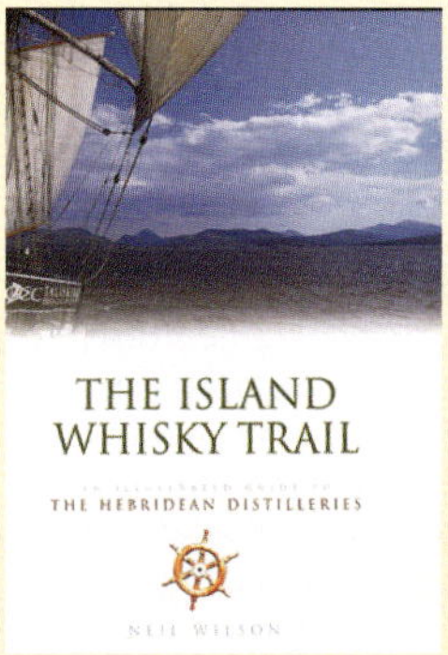

The author has written a guide covering the distilleries of the Hebrides and the west coast of Scotland, based on his numerous trips to the area, the first one in 1984. Also includes maps, travel information and an exciting look at the major role that women played in the history of illicit distilling in the County of Argyll.

Malt Whisky Map of Scotland

Neil Wilson
Pages: 2
Publisher: The Angel´s Share
ISBN: 1903238420

The ultimate whisky map! In full colour the map gives a complete overview of the whisky producing regions of Scotland. Unique distilling notes are incorporated into the map from Jim McEwan along with indexes, website addresses and other essential learning materials.

Handbook of Whisky

Dave Broom
Pages: 160
Publisher: Hamlyn
ISBN: 0600598462

A complete guide to the world's best malts, blends and brands of whisky. The book takes a look at whisky distilleries from the perspective of the people who work there. Also covers the history, distilling process and characteristics of whisky as well as tasting notes for every whisky.

The Whisky Distilleries of the United Kingdom

Alfred Barnard
Pages: 528
Publisher: Birlinn Ltd
ISBN: 1841582662

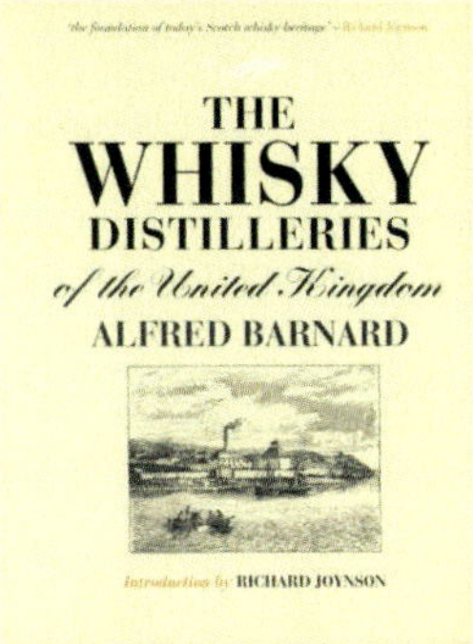

This is the classic whisky book based on Alfred Barnard´s travel in 1885 when he visited over 150 distilleries in Scotland, England and Ireland. The book was first published in 1887 and this is a facsimile edition. Perhaps not the most exciting book in the genre, but definitely an interesting document of an era.

Classic Malt Whisky

Ian Wisniewski
Pages: 192
Publisher: Prion Books Ltd
ISBN: 1853754137

This is a comprehensive book that covers all the aspects of whisky making. The author, Ian Wisniewski, has often shown a particular interest in the scientific angles which is evident in this book. As a counterbalance, the role that malt whisky has played in Scottish culture is also described. An A-Z of brands with brief histories and tasting notes makes it the complete reference book.

The making of Scotch Whisky

John R Hume & Michael S Moss
Pages: 383 pages
Publisher: Canongate Books Ltd
ISBN: 1841950106

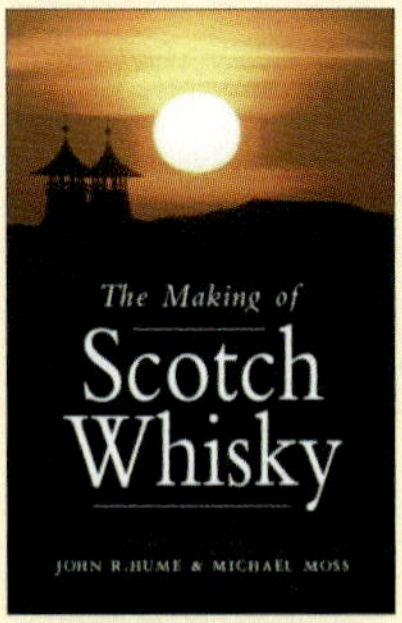

When first published in 1981 it was considered as the bible of the industry and it still remains the standard work. This revised edition takes account of changes in the industry since the book's publication as well as incorporating new research into earlier periods.

A Double Scotch

F Paul Pacult
Pages: 290
Publisher: John Wiley & Sons Inc
ISBN: 0471662712

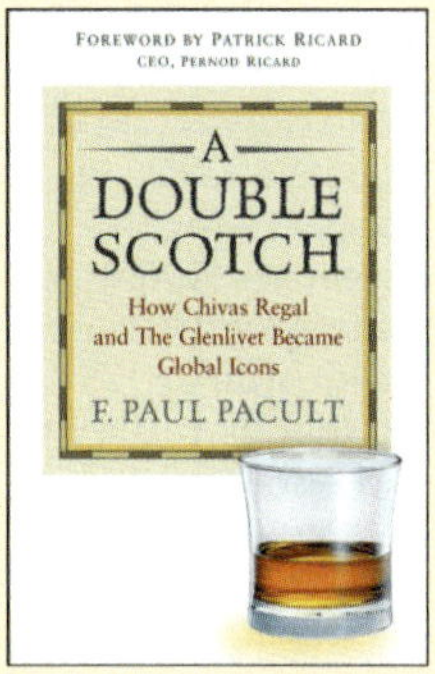

A Double Scotch tells the intertwined success stories of Chivas Regal and The Glenlivet and of the two families who endured numerous hardships to build their brands. This is an inside look at the two brands that made Scotland´s national drink a global phenomenon. A business book, and a fascinating one.

The Scotch Whisky Industry Review

Alan Gray, Charles Stanley Sutherlands
Pages: 268
Publisher: Mediafabrik

The Scotch Whisky Industry Review, produced annually by Alan Gray, is now in its 29th consecutive year and provides a wealth of unique business critical information on the Scotch Whisky Industry.
Copies (£395 in the UK and £420 overseas) can be obtained from Charles Stanley Sutherlands, 2 Multrees Walk, St Andrew Square, Edinburgh EH1 3DQ. (Telephone 0131 550 1200). Alternatively copies can be obtained by Faxing Alan S Gray on +44 (0)131 550 1250 or by Email: alan.gray@charles-stanley.co.uk. Details also on the website www.sutherlands.co.uk/whisky.htm.

Japanese Whisky, Scotch Blend

(The Japanese Whisky King and His Scotch Wife Rita)
Olive Checkland
Pages: 128 pages
Publisher: Scottish Cultural Press
ISBN: 1840170034

The fascinating story about Masataka Taketsuru, founder of Nikka Whisky Co. During his years of study at the University of Glasgow he met his future wife Rita, who later played a significant role in the revival of good relations between Britain and Japan after World War II. A story about East meets West.

Whisky wit and wisdom

Gavin D Smith
Pages: 192 pages
Publisher: The Angels' Share
ISBN: 1897784902

Exploring the lighter and quirkier side of whisky-making, whisky consumption, whisky over-consumption, whisky in literature, whisky and the law and even whisky and death, this book offers stories and anecdotes contributed by whisky industry personalities.

Whisky Magazine

Publisher: Paragraph Publishing
Published 8 times a year.
www.whiskymag.com

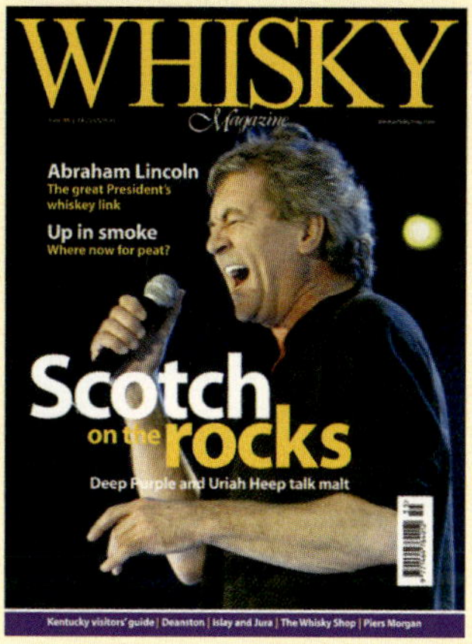

The foremost whisky magazine in the world for several years now. The scope of contents has been broadened to also appeal to readers with a wider whisky interest. Features on, for example, whisky and food, whisky and art and cocktails gives a new outlook on the subject.
The focus is on initiated reporting on all forms of whisky; malt, blended and bourbon. Several of the great whisky writers, such as Michael Jackson and Dave Broom, feature regularly in the magazine. Whisky Magazine also presents the 'Icons of Whisky', the whisky industry's equivalent to the 'Oscar' award. It is awarded annually and categories include 'Distiller of the Year' and 'Innovator of the Year'. Whisky Live festivals are also arranged since a few years over the whole world. The Magazine has an excellent internet site full of whisky-related information and with a readers' discussion forum.

Malt Advocate

Publisher: Malt Advocate, Inc.
Published 4 times a year.
www.maltadvocate.com

An excellent American magazine with focus on whiskies worldwide. John Hansell, the whisky enthusiast and driving force behind the magazine, has engaged some of the world's leading experts, such as Jim Murray and Gary Regan, as writers.
A recurring and popular section is the 'Buyer's Guide' where John Hansell tests and rates new expressions. Malt Advocate also publishes WhiskyNotes, a weekly email subscription service featuring timely whisky news and views which supplements the magazine. Malt Advocate arranges two annual Whisky Fests, with tastings, seminars and master classes, in New York and Chicago.

Scotch Whisky Production

= malt whisky production = malt whisky capacity = grain whisky production = grain whisky capacity

Figures depict production and capacity respectively in million litres of alcohol.
Figures within brackets show capacity utilisation in percentage.

Source: Scotch Whisky Association and The Scotch Whisky Industry Review 2006 (Charles Stanley Sutherlands)

Exports of Scotch Whisky

Top five Scotch Whisky Single Malt brands UK sales %

Brand	2004	2003	2002
Glenfiddich	14,5	15,1	14,9
Glenmorangie	13,9	13,8	13,4
Laphroaig	4,6	4,7	4,3
Glen Moray	3,8	3,6	3,2
The Glenlivet	3,2	3,9	3,0

Top five Scotch Whisky Single Malt brands export sales %

Brand	2004	2003	2002
Glenfiddich	15,1	16,8	18,0
Glen Grant	8,4	9,0	9,6
The Macallan	8,4	6,9	6,2
The Glenlivet	8,2	8,8	8,7
Cardhu	6,6	7,6	8,1

Top five Scotch Whisky Single Malt brands world sales %

Brand	2004	2003	2002
Glenfiddich	15,0	16,5	17,4
The Macallan	7,4	6,2	5,9
The Glenlivet	7,3	7,9	7,6
Glen Grant	6,9	7,4	7,9
Glenmorangie	6,1	6,1	6,0

Source: The Scotch Whisky Industry Review 2006
(Charles Stanley Sutherlands)

Top five Scotch Whisky Blended brands UK sales %

Bell´s	2004	13,9
	2003	14,3
	2002	14,3
Famous Grouse	2004	13,1
	2003	12,1
	2002	11,7
Teacher´s	2004	6,5
	2003	7,3
	2002	7,0
Grant´s	2004	6,0
	2003	5,5
	2002	5,6
Whyte & Mackay	2004	3,7
	2003	3,6
	2002	3,2

Top five Scotch Whisky Blended brands export sales %

J W Red	2004	10,4
	2003	9,5
	2002	10,0
J & B	2004	8,4
	2003	8,3
	2002	8,7
Ballantine´s	2004	7,2
	2003	7,0
	2002	7,1
Dewar´s	2004	5,5
	2003	5,5
	2002	5,7
J W Black	2004	5,3
	2003	4,9
	2002	5,1

Top five Scotch Whisky Blended brands world sales %

J W Red	2004	9,2
	2003	8,4
	2002	8,8
J & B	2004	7,5
	2003	7,4
	2002	7,8
Ballantine´s	2004	6,3
	2003	6,2
	2002	6,3
Grant´s	2004	5,2
	2003	4,7
	2002	5,3
Dewar´s	2004	4,9
	2003	4,9
	2002	5,1

Source: The Scotch Whisky Industry Review 2006 (Charles Stanley Sutherlands)

World consumption of Scotch Whisky

Staples show major markets only. Units in million litres of pure alcohol.
Total world consumption; 307,0 (2005), 308,5 (2000), 288,9 (1996)

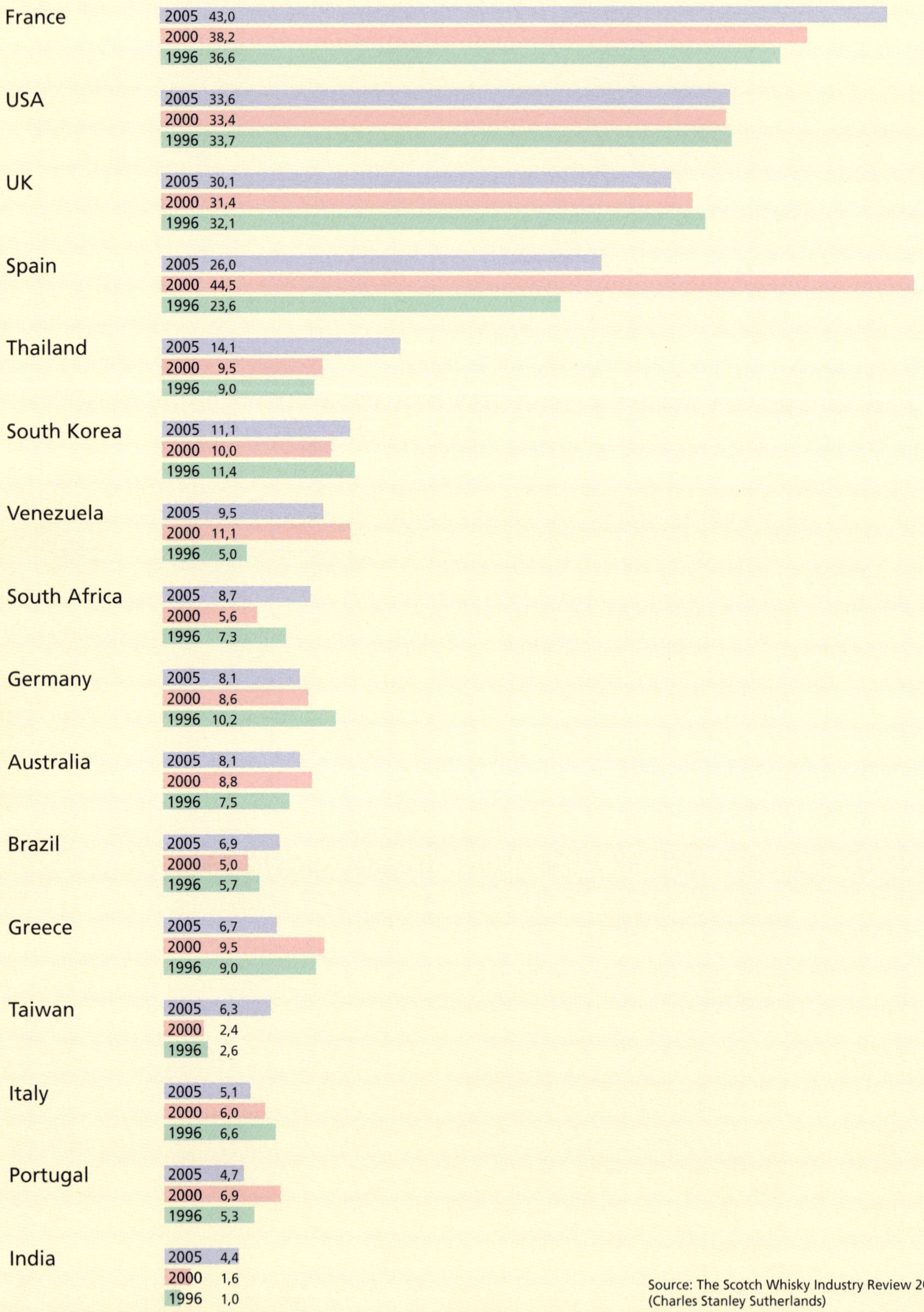

Source: The Scotch Whisky Industry Review 2006
(Charles Stanley Sutherlands)

Distillery Capacity

Litres of pure alcohol, Scottish distilleries only

Glenfiddich	10 000 000
Macallan	6 000 000
Glen Grant	5 900 000
Glenlivet	5 900 000
Balvenie	5 600 000
Glenrothes	5 600 000
Miltonduff	5 500 000
Tomatin	5 000 000
Kininvie	4 400 000
Ardmore	4 200 000
Allt-a-Bhainne	4 000 000
Dufftown	4 000 000
Glenburgie	4 000 000
Glenmorangie	4 000 000
Tamdhu	4 000 000
Glendullan	3 700 000
Caol Ila	3 600 000
Tormore	3 600 000
Aberlour	3 500 000
Glentauchers	3 500 000
Longmorn	3 500 000
Clynelish	3 400 000
Glen Ord	3 400 000
Dailuaine	3 200 000
Dalmore	3 200 000
Tomintoul	3 200 000
Auchroisk	3 100 000
Deanston	3 000 000
Glenfarclas	3 000 000
Benriach	2 800 000
Glenallachie	2 800 000
Mortlach	2 800 000
Craigellachie	2 700 000
Teaninich	2 700 000
Benrinnes	2 600 000
Bunnahabhain	2 500 000
Highland Park	2 500 000
Jura	2 500 000
Loch Lomond	2 500 000
Royal Brackla	2 500 000
Lagavulin	2 400 000
Laphroaig	2 400 000
Macduff	2 400 000
Strathisla	2 400 000
Cardhu	2 300 000
Linkwood	2 300 000
Inchgower	2 200 000
Aberfeldy	2 100 000
Aultmore	2 100 000
Ben Nevis	2 000 000
Blair Athol	2 000 000
Bowmore	2 000 000
Glen Moray	2 000 000
Tullibardine	2 000 000
Talisker	1 900 000
Balmenach	1 800 000
Glen Elgin	1 800 000
Auchentoshan	1 750 000
Glenkinchie	1 700 000
Strathmill	1 700 000
Cragganmore	1 600 000
Fettercairn	1 600 000
Bruichladdich	1 500 000
Glencadam	1 400 000
Glendronach	1 400 000
Glenspey	1 400 000
Balblair	1 330 000
Dalwhinnie	1 300 000
Knockando	1 300 000
Mannochmore	1 300 000
Glengoyne	1 100 000
Glenlossie	1 100 000
Ardbeg	1 000 000
Glen Garioch	1 000 000
Pulteney	1 000 000
Scapa	1 000 000
Speyburn	1 000 000
Tobermory	1 000 000
Knockdhu	900 000
Arran	750 000
Glengyle	750 000
Glen Scotia	750 000
Springbank	750 000
Oban	700 000
Speyside	600 000
Benromach	500 000
Royal Lochnagar	400 000
Glenturret	340 000
Bladnoch	100 000
Edradour	90 000
Kilchoman	90 000

Summary of Malt Distillery Capacity by Category

Category	Litres of alcohol	% of Industry	Average capacity
Speyside (42)	135 700 000	60,5	3 231 000
Islands (6)	9 650 000	4,3	1 608 000
Rest of the Highlands (29)	57 560 000	25,7	1 985 000
Islay (8)	15 490 000	6,9	1 936 000
Lowlands (3)	3 550 000	1,6	1 183 000
Campbeltown (3)	2 250 000	1,0	750 000
Total (91)	**224 200 000**	**100**	**2 464 000**

Summary of Malt Distillery Capacity by Owner

Owner (number of distilleries)	Litres of alcohol	% of Industry
Diageo (27)	59 900 000	26,7
Pernod Ricard (12)	41 100 000	18,3
William Grant (3)	20 000 000	8,9
Edrington Group (5)	18 440 000	8,2
Bacardi (John Dewar & Sons) (5)	11 800 000	5,3
Whyte and Mackay (3)	7 300 000	3,2
Moët Hennessy (Glenmorangie) (3)	7 000 000	3,1
Beam Global (2)	6 600 000	2,9
C L Financial (Burn Stewart) (3)	6 500 000	2,9
Pacific Spirits (Inver House) (5)	6 030 000	2,7
Campari (Glen Grant) (1)	5 900 000	2,6
Tomatin Distillery Co (1)	5 000 000	2,2
Suntory (Morrison Bowmore) (3)	4 750 000	2,1
Angus Dundee (2)	4 600 000	2,0
Loch Lomond Distillers (2)	3 250 000	1,4
J & G Grant (1)	3 000 000	1,3
Benriach Distillery Co (1)	2 800 000	1,2
Nikka (Ben Nevis Distillery) (1)	2 000 000	0,9
Tullibardine Distillery Ltd (1)	2 000 000	0,9
Bruichladdich Distillery Co (1)	1 500 000	0,7
J & A Mitchell (2)	1 500 000	0,7
Ian Macleod Distillers (Glengoyne) (1)	1 100 000	0,5
Isle of Arran Distillers (1)	750 000	less than 0,5
Speyside Distillers Co (1)	600 000	- " -
Gordon & MacPhail (Benromach) (1)	500 000	- " -
Co-ordinated Developm. (Bladnoch) (1)	100 000	- " -
Kilchoman Distillery Co (1)	90 000	- " -
Signatory Vintage (Edradour) (1)	90 000	- " -

Source: The Scotch Whisky Industry Review 2006 (Charles Stanley Sutherlands) with corrections for changes made after publishing.

Shetland
1
2 3
ORKNEY ISLANDS
4 Wick
NORTH HIGHLANDS
5 6
7
8
9
10
11
12
13
14
15
16
Inverness
SKYE
73
Kyle of Lockalsh
SPEYSIDE
17
18 19 20
21
22
23
24
25
Aberdeen
Loch Ness
CENTRAL HIGHLANDS
26
27
28
29
30 31
Fort William
32
EAST HIGHLANDS
33 34 35 36
37
38
Pitlochry
39
Loch Tay
72
WEST HIGHLANDS
Oban
40
MULL
Dundee
41
44
Perth
42
43
St. Andrews
Loch Lomond
45
Stirling
46
50
JURA
47 48
Glasgow
49
53
54
Edinburgh
55
51
52
68 70 67 66 69
71
ISLAY
62
65 63 64
58
ARRAN
59 60 61
Campbeltown
Ayr
THE LOWLANDS
56
Dumfries
Stranraer
57

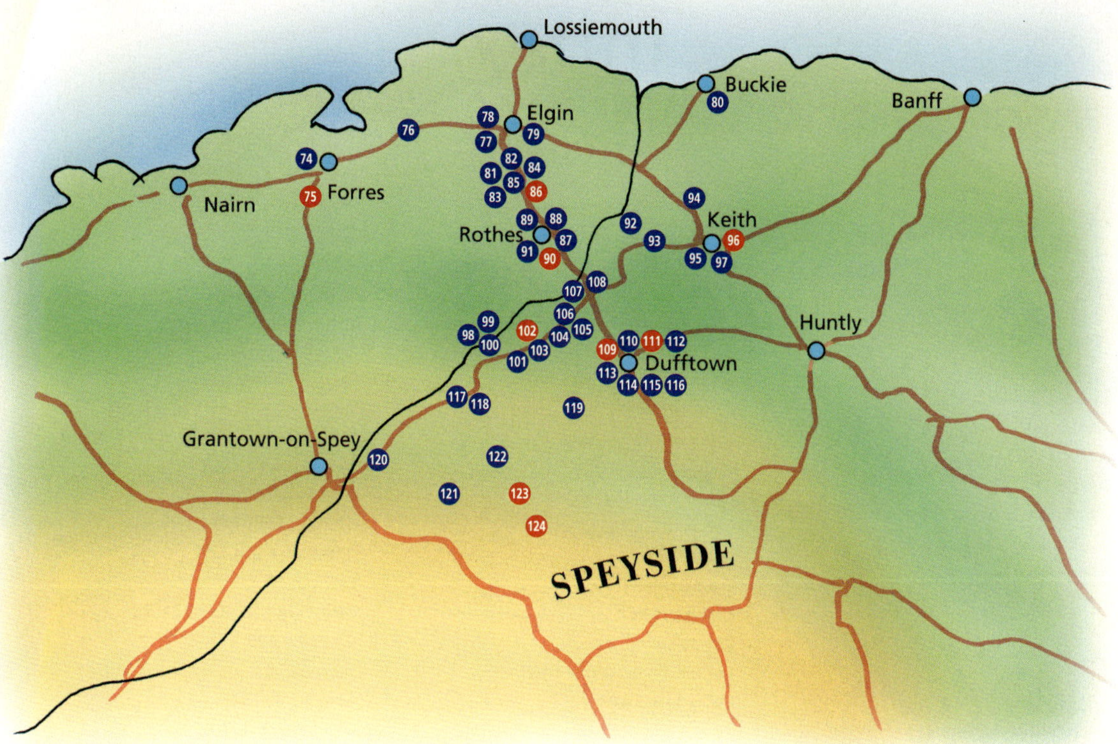

Distilleries in red letters are Speyside — Active — Closed, mothballed, dismantled or demolished — Not yet on stream

39 Aberfeldy
106 Aberlour
119 Allt-a-Bhainne
62 Ardbeg
25 Ardmore
58 Arran
49 Auchentoshan
92 Auchroisk
94 Aultmore
7 Balblair
120 Balmenach
113 Balvenie
19 Banff (d)
30 Ben Nevis
82 Benriach
104 Benrinnes
74 Benromach
9 Ben Wyvis (c)
1 Blackwood
57 Bladnoch
37 Blair Athol
66 Bowmore
124 Braeval (mb)
5 Brora (c)
67 Bruichladdich
70 Bunnahabhain
69 Caol Ila
90 Caperdonich (mb)
99 Cardhu
6 Clynelish
86 Coleburn (dm)
109 Convalmore (dm)
118 Cragganmore
108 Craigellachie
42 Daftmill
103 Dailuaine
75 Dallas Dhu (c)
11 Dalmore
29 Dalwhinnie
45 Deanston
110 Dufftown
38 Edradour
32 Fettercairn
13 Glen Albyn (d)
105 Glenallachie
76 Glenburgie
34 Glencadam
23 Glendronach
116 Glendullan
85 Glen Elgin
35 Glenesk (dm)
101 Glenfarclas
112 Glenfiddich
52 Glen Flagler (d)
24 Glen Garioch
18 Glenglassaugh (mb)
50 Glengoyne
87 Glen Grant
60 Glengyle
96 Glen Keith (mb)
55 Glenkinchie
122 Glenlivet
31 Glenlochy (d)
83 Glenlossie
14 Glen Mhor (d)
8 Glenmorangie
78 Glen Moray
12 Glen Ord
89 Glenrothes
61 Glen Scotia
91 Glenspey
93 Glentauchers
41 Glenturret
22 Glenugie (dm)
28 Glenury Royal (d)
2 Highland Park
102 Imperial (c)
80 Inchgower
47 Inverleven (d)
71 Jura
68 Kilchoman
51 Kinclaith (d)
114 Kininvie
100 Knockando
21 Knockdhu
43 Ladybank
56 Ladyburn (dm)
63 Lagavulin
64 Laphroaig
79 Linkwood
48 Littlemill (d)
46 Loch Lomond
36 Lochside (d)
84 Longmorn
107 Macallan
20 Macduff
81 Mannochmore
15 Millburn (dm)
77 Miltonduff
115 Mortlach
33 North Port (d)
40 Oban
111 Pittyvaich (d)
65 Port Ellen (dm)
4 Pulteney
53 Rosebank (c)
16 Royal Brackla
27 Royal Lochnagar
54 St Magdalene (dm)
3 Scapa
88 Speyburn
26 Speyside
59 Springbank
97 Strathisla
95 Strathmill
73 Talisker
98 Tamdhu
123 Tamnavulin (mb)
10 Teaninich
72 Tobermory
17 Tomatin
121 Tomintoul
117 Tormore
44 Tullibardine

1 Blackwood
2 Highland Park
3 Scapa
4 Pulteney
5 Brora (c)
6 Clynelish
7 Balblair
8 Glenmorangie
9 Ben Wyvis (c)
10 Teaninich
11 Dalmore
12 Glen Ord
13 Glen Albyn (d)
14 Glen Mhor (d)
15 Millburn (dm)
16 Royal Brackla
17 Tomatin
18 Glenglassaugh (mb)
19 Banff (d)
20 Macduff
21 Knockdhu
22 Glenugie (dm)
23 Glendronach
24 Glen Garioch
25 Ardmore
26 Speyside
27 Royal Lochnagar
28 Glenury Royal (d)
29 Dalwhinnie
30 Ben Nevis
31 Glenlochy (d)
32 Fettercairn
33 North Port (d)
34 Glencadam
35 Glenesk (dm)
36 Lochside (d)
37 Blair Athol
38 Edradour
39 Aberfeldy
40 Oban
41 Glenturret
42 Daftmill
43 Ladybank
44 Tullibardine
45 Deanston
46 Loch Lomond
47 Inverleven (d)
48 Littlemill (d)
49 Auchentoshan
50 Glengoyne
51 Kinclaith (d)
52 Glen Flagler (d)
53 Rosebank (c)
54 St Magdalene (dm)
55 Glenkinchie
56 Ladyburn (dm)
57 Bladnoch
58 Arran
59 Springbank
60 Glengyle
61 Glen Scotia
62 Ardbeg
63 Lagavulin
64 Laphroaig
65 Port Ellen (dm)
66 Bowmore
67 Bruichladdich
68 Kilchoman
69 Caol Ila
70 Bunnahabhain
71 Jura
72 Tobermory
73 Talisker
74 Benromach
75 Dallas Dhu (c)
76 Glenburgie
77 Miltonduff
78 Glen Moray
79 Linkwood
80 Inchgower
81 Mannochmore
82 Benriach
83 Glenlossie
84 Longmorn
85 Glen Elgin
86 Coleburn (dm)
87 Glen Grant
88 Speyburn
89 Glenrothes
90 Caperdonich (mb)
91 Glenspey
92 Auchroisk
93 Glentauchers
94 Aultmore
95 Strathmill
96 Glen Keith (mb)
97 Strathisla
98 Tamdhu
99 Cardhu
100 Knockando
101 Glenfarclas
102 Imperial (c)
103 Dailuaine
104 Benrinnes
105 Glenallachie
106 Aberlour
107 Macallan
108 Craigellachie
109 Convalmore (dm)
110 Dufftown
111 Pittyvaich (d)
112 Glenfiddich
113 Balvenie
114 Kininvie
115 Mortlach
116 Glendullan
117 Tormore
118 Cragganmore
119 Allt-a-Bhainne
120 Balmenach
121 Tomintoul
122 Glenlivet
123 Tamnavulin (mb)
124 Braeval (mb)

Index

Bold figures refer to the main entry in the distillery directory.

Index

Bold figures refer to the main entry in the distillery directory.